PROGRAMMING MICROSOFT® VISUAL J++™ 6.0

Stephen R. Davis

Microsoft Press

PUBLISHED BY
Microsoft Press
A Division of Microsoft Corporation
One Microsoft Way
Redmond, Washington 98052-6399

Library of Congress Cataloging-in-Publication Data
Davis, Stephen R., 1956–
    Programming Microsoft Visual J++ 6.0 / Stephen R. Davis.
       p. cm.
    Includes index.
    ISBN 1-57231-701-9
    1. Java (Computer program language)   2. Microsoft Visual J++.
  I. Title.
  QA76.73.J38D39   1998
  005.2'762--dc21   98-31463
                                     CIP

Printed and bound in the United States of America.

1 2 3 4 5 6 7 8 9 QMQM 4 3 2 1 0 9

Distributed in Canada by ITP Nelson, a division of Thomson Canada Limited.

A CIP catalogue record for this book is available from the British Library.

Microsoft Press books are available through booksellers and distributors worldwide. For
further information about international editions, contact your local Microsoft Corporation
office or contact Microsoft Press International directly at fax (425) 936-7329. Visit our Web
site at mspress.microsoft.com.

Acquisitions Editor: Eric Stroo
Project Editor: Alice Turner
Manuscript Editors: Alice Turner, Sally Stickney
Technical Editor: Jean Ross

Preface

As this book goes to press, Microsoft and Sun Microsystems find themselves in litigation over the future development of Microsoft Visual J++. In an interim ruling, the judge in this case has decided that Microsoft must make changes to the Visual J++ 6 programming language. Although Microsoft is contesting this decision, it is complying with the court's ruling in the version of Visual J++ 6 found on this book's CD.

Link to *http://msdn.microsoft.com/visualj/lawsuitruling.asp* to learn more about this litigation and other decisions stemming from this trial.

IMPACT ON VISUAL J++ 6

Most of the changes directed by the court to date have no affect on the text or the code contained within this book. Two changes are significant enough to warrant explanation.

Making Some Visual J++ 6 Extensions to Java Optional

Visual J++ 6 introduces several features that aren't found in Sun Microsystems' version of Java. The court has required that these extensions be disabled by default and be enabled only at the programmer's request.

An option on the Compile tab of the Project Properties dialog box, Disable Microsoft Language Extensions, has been turned on by default. The reader must clear this option to enable the Microsoft extensions in order for many of the programs in this book to compile and execute properly.

In addition, when creating new projects that use the Windows Foundations Classes for Java, such as a Microsoft Windows Application or a COM DLL, the Visual J++ 6 Wizard displays a dialog box warning you that your project requires Microsoft language extensions to operate successfully. You must click the Yes button to enable the extensions. Clicking Yes clears the Disable Microsoft Language Extensions option on the Project Properties dialog box. (After clicking Yes, you'll be warned that your compiled code will run only on Windows operating systems with the Microsoft Virtual Machine for Java installed.)

It is not necessary to enable Microsoft Language Extensions when creating the generic applications and applets described in Part I and at the beginning of Part II.

The Java Native Interface

Version 1.0 of the Java language did not include access to functions written in native assembly language. After Microsoft had already defined a Java interface to native code called the Raw Native Interface (RNI), Sun Microsystems introduced the Java Native Interface (JNI) in Version 1.1 of Java.

Visual J++ 6 adds a greatly improved Java interface to native code called J/Direct. J/Direct provides point and shoot access to the entire Microsoft Win32 API. In addition, J/Direct provides easy access to any code resident in a dynamic-link library (DLL), including DLLs written by the application programmer. As easy as it is to use, J/Direct suffers from two flaws in the opinion of the court: it is Windows-specific and it isn't supported in generic Java.

The new version of Visual J++ 6 includes support for JNI as well as J/Direct.

IMPACT ON YOU, THE READER

The most recent version of Visual J++ 6 can be found as a Trial Edition on this book's companion CD.

Additional information that you will need in order to make effective use of the two changes discussed here, and any future additions to the Visual J++ product as a result of court rulings, can be found in the Reader's Corner at this address:

http://mspress.microsoft.com/prod/books/1269.htm

User help, further code examples, and answers to commonly asked questions can be found in the Reader's Corner as well.

Contents at a Glance

Lest you think that Visual J++ 6 has forgotten about applets, this chapter delves into some of the issues surrounding applets. For example, you learn how to write trusted applets that can access the client's computer from the Internet browser.

Our exploration of applets continues with an examination of applet animation.

Programming Microsoft Visual J++ 6.0 wraps up with a discussion of the WFC Dynamic HTML (DHTML) package. This package provides access to the features of DHTML on both the client and the server without your needing to learn scripting languages. We examine how to use DHTML to display database information. Finally we examine how server-side database access provides unique opportunities for supporting clients "in the field."

If you are migrating to Java from other languages such as Visual C++ or Visual Basic, this quick overview of the Java language is for you.

Table of Contents

Part III Special Topics

Acknowledgments

The appearance of any computer book owes to the hard work of a lot of people besides the person whose name appears on the cover. The readability of this book owes to the constant watchful eye of Alice Turner. Technical accuracy was put to the test by Jean Ross. This book would never have been started without the work of Claudette Moore and Eric Stroo.

The greatest thanks, however, goes to Chris Anderson, who (among other Microsoft employees) patiently helped me through several technical twists and turns despite the considerable demands on his time.

In addition, I want to thank the people at TopherNet Internet service providers for their assistance in setting up and maintaining the help web site at *www.stephendavis.com*.

Thanks to Dr. Maxine Thomas and Dr. Jay Harvey for their support.

Finally, my authoring such a book wouldn't even be conceivable without the constant support of my family, both immediate and extended. Thanks.

Introduction

Microsoft Visual J++ 6 includes an amazing set of new and powerful features. While retaining support for Web development, Visual J++ 6 turns Java into a first-class language for Microsoft Windows applications development.

Programming Microsoft Visual J++ 6.0 contains the complete and simple explanations—together with numerous examples—that you'll need to master each new feature of this powerful and exciting new tool.

Why Did I Write This Book?

Before I first came into contact with Visual J++ 6, I thought I knew something about Visual J++. After all, I had written the manual for Visual J++ 1.0, *Learn Java Now.* It's true that Microsoft had skipped from version 1.1 to 6, but surely that was more of a marketing decision than a technical one. How different could one version of Visual J++ be from the other?

One look at the new Visual J++, with its Microsoft Visual Studio 6 user interface, taught me how wrong I was. At first glance, the new Visual J++ seemed to have more in common with Microsoft Visual C++ and Microsoft Visual Basic than it did with Visual J++. Once I got beyond the initial shock, however, I realized that this was still Java; it just had a new, more powerful user interface and included the new Microsoft Windows Foundation Classes for Java (WFC) class library.

It was clear to me that Visual J++ 6, with its new focus on application development, would become an important environment for developing Windows applications. However, I felt that the typical Java programmer would have a lot to learn before he or she would be in position to fully utilize all that the Visual J++ 6 package has to offer.

Java and Applications: Isn't That a Misprint?

As every Java programmer knows, Java supports two different types of programs: applications and applets. Applications are programs like those generated by other programming languages. Applications are meant to be invoked from the command line or by being double-clicked within a windowing environment like Microsoft Windows. Applets, by comparison, are designed to be run from within a Web page by a browser such as Microsoft Internet Explorer.

Historically, Java applets got all the press. After all, applets can generate those cute features like the scrolling marquees and bouncing balls present in more and more Web pages. Besides, the Web is considered sexy.

Visual J++ 6 changes this "applets-only" way of thinking. Visual J++ 6 turns Java into a first-rate language for developing applications. It adds the powerful new WFC library. An efficient new Forms Designer provides drag-and-drop rapid application development (RAD) access to this library. Additionally, Visual J++ 6 adds such features as direct access to the Win32 API, easy creation of custom toolbox controls and ActiveX controls, and Java access to Dynamic HTML (DHTML).

Aren't there already good languages for Windows applications?

Prior to Visual J++ 6, Windows applications programmers had essentially two language options: Visual Basic or C++ (which comes in various flavors, the most popular flavor being Visual C++). Both of these languages have problems for general Windows application development.

Visual Basic has an extremely powerful user interface. Programmers can create simple Windows-based programs quickly and easily. Grab a few icons off of the toolbar and drop them in the Forms Designer, add some code to handle the input or output, and you are just about done.

The problem with Visual Basic lies in the underlying language. The Basic language doesn't encourage the development of organized, structured programs. Some of the very features that make Basic so adept at writing small programs make Basic difficult to use on larger projects. This has led to the common opinion in public programming circles that for large projects Visual Basic simply "runs out of steam."

Visual C++ lies at the opposite end of the development scale. As the saying goes, "if there's something that Visual C++ can't do, it's just not worth doing." Visual C++ is everything that Visual Basic isn't. It's powerful, it supports large programs, and it's object-oriented.

At the same time, Visual C++ is full of traps and pitfalls—so much so, that there was once a popular book devoted entirely to the topic. Add to this that Visual C++ is difficult to learn. As a teacher of C++, I know firsthand how hard it is for even experienced programmers to master the language. To gain rapid acceptance by the marketplace, C++ leveraged the popularity of its non-object-oriented predecessor, C. As C++ has tried to add new capabilities, its slavish support for C has forced the language into a number of linguistic mazes. It is these traps that make C++ so difficult for the uninitiated.

Finally, until very recently Visual C++ has lacked many of the RAD features of Visual Basic. While Microsoft Foundation Classes (MFC) eases the pain, developing simple Windows applications in Visual C++ is still not nearly as simple as with Visual Basic.

Why Java?

Visual J++ 6 fits comfortably between these two proverbial powerhouses. Visual J++ 6 has all of the RAD features that make Visual Basic so popular. Developing simple Windows applications under Visual J++ 6 is a breeze. Unlike Basic, however, Java is well structured, so it supports the development of larger programs.

At the same time, Java is a much simpler language to learn than Visual C++. Java has not tried to remain compatible with some non-object-oriented predecessor. This has left Java free to adopt a clean syntax without the ditches and potholes into which even experienced C++ programmers can fall.

Why Windows-specific?

The fact that Visual J++ 6 includes WFC to add support for Windows-specific development is surely the most controversial aspect of the language. I like platform-independent solutions as much as the next guy, but when Visual J++ 6 is viewed in the light of its importance as an application development environment, the inclusion of WFC is easier to understand. If Visual J++ 6 is to have a chance as an application development tool, its output has to be able to compete with that of Visual C++ and Visual Basic.

Is it possible to write Windows applications in Java using the platform-independent "Java standard" Abstract Windowing Toolkit (AWT) or using the closely related Java Foundation Classes? Sure. Are they as attractive as other Windows applications? No way. This is not meant as an endorsement of Windows applications over those of Motif or Macintosh or any other windowing environment. Nor is this meant as a slam of AWT. A generic solution like AWT can't compete with WFC when generating Windows applications.

For Whom Was This Book Written?

This book was written with at least three different types of readers in mind.

The Java programmer

First there are the Java programmers. This group includes both users of earlier versions of Visual J++ as well as users of other Java environments. Since this is probably the largest single group of readers, I have dispensed with the usual introductory chapters on Java syntax. From the beginning, *Programming Microsoft Visual J++ 6.0* takes you through the features of Visual J++ until, by the time you reach the end of the book, you'll be in a position to utilize just about every feature that Visual J++ 6 has to offer.

> **NOTE** Visual J++ 6 does introduce a few new wrinkles to the Java language, however. To address this fact, I have added a note—that looks like this note does—to flag language features that are unique to Visual J++ 6 or which might not otherwise be obvious to the reader.

The Visual C++ programmer

A second group of readers are Visual C++ programmers who are curious about this Visual C++ cousin. Maybe Visual C++ has proved a little too complicated or perhaps the lure of Visual Basic's powerful RAD features is too much to resist. This reader is looking for a simpler language with powerful development tools but doesn't want to abandon the C++-like syntax by making the jump to Visual Basic.

Programming Microsoft Visual J++ 6.0 is ideal at helping this reader migrate to Visual J++ 6. The similarity between the Java and C++ syntax means that the examples presented here are understandable to the C++ developer.

> **C++ NOTE** There are a few language features that the C++ reader might not understand right away. In these cases I have included a special note—that looks like this note does—to explain language differences where these differences arise. Readers whose experience is based in C++ will find that these linguistic cheat sheets will ease their conversion to Visual J++.

The Visual Basic programmer

Another large group of readers are Visual Basic programmers who are interested in branching out into a more object-oriented language, but for whom Visual C++—with all its turns and bends—is not the answer. For this group I have included a quick overview of the Java language in the appendix. While it may seem like mastering a programming language in a single section is a lot to ask, Java's straightforward syntax makes it simple to learn. Once you've digested Java syntax and mastered the examples in this book, you, too, will be in a position to utilize the Visual J++ 6 environment.

How Is This Book Organized?

Programming Microsoft Visual J++ 6.0 is divided into three parts.

Part I: Visual J++ Applications

This section describes how to write both platform-independent and Windows-specific console applications in Visual J++ 6. Even in today's world of windowed, colorful applications, there is no faster way to create a calculation-intensive program for personal use than with the console application.

Part II: Windowed Applications

Visual J++ 6 introduces Java to the ranks of easy-to-use but powerful Windows application development languages. *Programming Microsoft Visual J++ 6.0* teaches the reader how to use the new, powerful WFC library of Windows classes. This part demonstrates how to use such built-in tools as the Forms Designer and the Toolbox to develop fast and colorful windowed applications. The final chapter of this part explains how J/Direct gives the Visual J++ 6 programmer access to any user-developed dynamic-link library (DLL) in addition to the entire Win32 API.

Part III: Special Topics

This part explains how to create database applications using the Visual J++ 6 support for ActiveX Data Objects (ADO) 2.0. This makes it easy for Visual J++ programs to access common Microsoft databases such as Visual FoxPro (included in Visual Studio Enterprise Edition), Access, SQL Server, and non-Microsoft databases such as Oracle. There is even support for text-based databases.

This part also demonstrates how to create new Toolbox objects with their own properties and events, and how to convert these toolbox tools into ActiveX components. The remaining chapters in this part explain in detail Visual J++ 6's support for the Web. This discussion includes applet development and WFC support for Dynamic HTML on both the Internet browser and the Web server.

Using the Companion CD

The Sample Files

The CD included with this book contains all the sample programs discussed in the book. All the samples are located in the Samples folder.

Installing the Sample Files

You can view the samples from the CD, or you can install them onto your hard disk and use them to create your own Microsoft Visual J++ applications.

> **NOTE** If you're unable to browse the files in the Samples folder, you might have an older CD driver that doesn't support long file names. If this is the case, to browse the files you must install the sample files on your hard disk by running the setup program.

Installing the sample files requires approximately 3.6 MB of disk space. To install the sample files, insert the CD into your CD-ROM drive and run Setup.exe. If you have trouble running any of the sample files, refer to the Readme.txt file in the root directory of the CD or to the text in the book that describes the sample program.

You can uninstall the files by selecting Add/Remove Programs from the Microsoft Windows Control Panel, selecting Programming VJ++, and clicking the Add/Remove button.

Microsoft Visual J++ 6 Professional Trial Edition

Another folder you'll find on the CD is VJTrial, which contains the files for installing Microsoft Visual J++ 6 Professional Trial Edition. If you don't have Visual J++ 6, you can install this trial version and use it to work with the sample files. You'll find all the information regarding Visual J++ 6 Trial Edition in the Readme files contained in the VJTrial folder. You will also find support information and system requirements in the Readme.txt file in the root directory of the CD.

Support

Every effort has been made to ensure the accuracy of this book and the contents of the companion disc. Microsoft Press provides corrections for books through the World Wide Web at the following address:

http://mspress.microsoft.com/mspress/support/

If you have comments, questions, or ideas regarding this book or the companion disc, please send them to Microsoft Press using either of the following methods:

Postal Mail:

Microsoft Press
Attn: Programming Microsoft Visual J++ 6 Editor
One Microsoft Way
Redmond, WA 98052-6399

E-mail:

MSPINPUT@MICROSOFT.COM

Please note that product support is not offered through the above mail addresses. For support information regarding Microsoft Visual J++, you can call Standard Support at (425) 635-7011 weekdays between 6 a.m. and 6 p.m. Pacific time. You can also search Microsoft's Support Online at *http://support.microsoft.com/support*. Microsoft Visual J++ 6 Professional Trial Edition is not supported.

Part I

Visual J++ Applications

Java isn't normally associated with application development—associated with those cute little applets that jazz up Web pages, sure, but with applications like Microsoft Word or Microsoft Excel, almost never.

You might not know that you have always been able to use Java to create applications. A form can be treated like an applet to create a windowed application. Few programmers do this, however, because the results have not been impressive—at least, not until the advent of Microsoft Visual J++ 6 and its support for the Microsoft Windows Foundation Classes for Java (WFC).

WFC turns Java into a first-class application language. Using WFC, Java programmers can create applications with the same look and feel as applications generated by their Microsoft Visual C++–wielding and Microsoft Visual Basic–wielding brethren while enjoying the ease of Java.

In Part I of this book, you'll see how to build Java console applications. *Console applications* are applications that do not use windows to display information. In appearance they resemble MS-DOS programs.

In the first chapter, I'll demonstrate generic console applications. Chapters 2 and 3 describe WFC-based, Microsoft Windows–specific Java applications.

Chapter 1

Generic Console Applications

This chapter begins with our building a few command line, DOS-like console applications. We'll start with a trivial console application to demonstrate the Microsoft Visual Studio user interface, which Visual J++ 6 shares with the other Visual Studio 6 languages. From there, we'll progress to other console applications that demonstrate additional aspects of the Visual J++ 6 language.

For now, we'll stick with generic, nonwindowed, platform-independent applications. Chapter 2 will begin our ascent of the WFC learning curve.

THE HELLOWORLD1 PROJECT

It seems almost obligatory that the first application in any programming book be the famous "Hello, world" program, so let's begin there.

> NOTE For those of you who are familiar with Java, the "Hello, world" application will already be well known. This application is still a useful exercise for you because we will use it to explore many features of the Visual J++ 6 environment.

WHAT'S A CONSOLE APPLICATION?

The simplest type of application is the console application. Console applications have no windows to deal with; they are designed to be run from the DOS command line. This might be the command line of an MS-DOS window in Windows or of DOS by itself. The output of a console application is simply spit directly back to the same command line.

You can run a console application under Windows by double-clicking the file. This brings up an MS-DOS window within which the console application runs.

> **TIP** Everything I've said here about MS-DOS windows running in Microsoft Windows applies equally well to the UNIX prompt running under Motif.

Although console applications are not very exciting, they're the preferred type of application to use when you're concentrating on performing a function—like calculating pi to the nth digit—and you don't particularly care about attractive output. This type of application is useful for many of the simple utilities you write for your own benefit.

Creating a Console Application Project

In the Microsoft Development Environment (MDE), choose New Project from the File menu. This opens the New Project dialog box. A *project* is a collection of source files, which together build a program.

The New Project dialog box lists two options: Visual J++ Projects and Visual Studio. In the Visual J++ Projects folder, choose the Applications folder and then choose Console Application. Change the project name from Project1 to HelloWorld1. The HelloWorld1 project will be stored in a subfolder with the same name as the project.

The default is for Visual J++ to create the HelloWorld1 folder as a subfolder of \\MyDocuments\VisualStudio. Personally, I think this is a crazy place to put application folders. I create a separate Java folder to store all my applications and applets. (I also have one for Microsoft Visual C++ and one for Visual Basic.) Do as you like, but for this first project I chose Browse in the dialog box and hung my new project subdirectory off the folder c:\user\Visual J++ Programs\Generic Applications. My results are shown in Figure 1-1.

Once you've renamed the project and placed it in the folder of your choice, choose Open. (You can also double-click Console Application.) This causes Visual J++ to build the HelloWorld1 project.

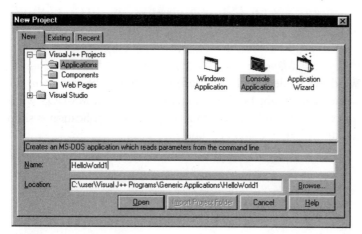

Figure 1-1. *The New Project dialog box showing the application choices, project name, and project folder.*

Project Explorer

To look at the results of our work, open Project Explorer. Project Explorer is to projects what Windows Explorer is to files and Microsoft Internet Explorer is to the Internet: a view into the contents of the project.

The most straightforward way to open Project Explorer is to choose Project Explorer from the View menu. There might also be a button on the toolbar that does the same thing. (I say *might* because you can customize the toolbars to include any buttons that you want. We'll talk about customizing toolbars later in this chapter.)

You can view the files in your HelloWorld1 project by clicking the plus sign next to the project name (just like viewing folders in Windows Explorer). The results are shown in Figure 1-2.

Figure 1-2. *The Project Explorer view of our first project.*

Project Explorer in Visual J++ 6 looks similar to the project view in version 1.1. The major difference is that Project Explorer refers to something called the Hello-World1 solution and lists it as having one project.

What's a solution (other than something mixed in a liquid)?

Visual J++ 6 organizes projects into groups called solutions.

> **C++ NOTE**   A *solution* is a group of projects. Visual C++ 6 and Visual Basic 6 support almost the same functionality but call it a *workspace*.

Grouping projects in this way enables you to perform the same operation on all of the projects at once with a single command. For example, choosing Build on the Build menu rebuilds all projects in the solution.

Even though they are grouped together, projects retain their identity within the solution. For example, projects are deployed independently. Thus, if your solution has a Project1 and a Project2, rebuilding the solution might generate two executable files, Project1.exe and Project2.exe. Projects also have their own properties, so one project might generate an application while another generates an applet.

For now, we will limit ourselves to single-project solutions.

The HelloWorld1 Project Source Code

Within the HelloWorld1 project is a single Java file, Class1.java. Double-click this file in Project Explorer to view the source code file the Console Application Wizard created for us when we opened the new project.

> **NOTE**   All examples for this chapter are located in the Generic Applications subfolder on the book's companion CD.

The following code shows the contents of Class1.java. I've added one line (shown in boldface) to convert the project into the "Hello, world" application.

```
/**
 * This class can take a variable number of parameters on the command
 * line. Program execution begins with the main() method. The class
 * constructor is not invoked unless an object of type 'Class1'
 * created in the main() method.
 */
public class Class1
{
    /**
     * The main entry point for the application.
     *
     * @param args Array of parameters passed to the application
     * via the command line.
     */
    public static void main (String[] args)
    {
        // TODO: Add initialization code here
        System.out.println("Hello, world");
    }
}
```

As you can see, the Console Application Wizard constructs an empty class definition with comments. Notice that the comments are somewhat unusual: they begin with a /** rather than the normal /*. Also notice the appearance of * @param in the middle of the comments.

> **NOTE** The comments preceded by /** are generally called "Javadoc comments" after the Sun Microsystems, Inc. utility Javadoc, which uses these comments to automatically generate class documentation. Visual J++ 6 has extended this concept into a powerful, dynamic feature described later in this chapter in the "Statement Completion" section.

Program execution begins with the *public static* method *main()*.

> **NOTE** The *public* keyword makes the method visible to other classes, and the *static* keyword enables the method to be invoked without an object.

In the line of code I've added, *System* is a global object that retains information about the environment in which the program resides. One of the *System* object's data members is the static member *out* that points to standard output, normally the command line. The *out* data member is of class *PrintStream*. This class has a method *println()*, which prints whatever string is passed to it followed by a newline character.

> **NOTE** Under C++, the syntax for accessing *out* would have been something like *System::out*; however, Java does not use the *::* symbol, preferring instead to stick with the single dot.

To compile HelloWorld1, choose Build from the Build menu. If the program compiles properly, the phrase "Solution update succeeded" appears in the status bar.

To run the program, you have four options:

1. In the Visual J++ user interface, you can choose Start from the Debug menu.

2. In Windows Explorer, you can double-click HelloWorld1.exe.

3. In an MS-DOS window, you can go to the directory containing HelloWorld1.exe and type *HelloWorld1* at the command line.

4. Select Run from the Windows Start menu. Type *HelloWorld1* preceded by the full path to the .EXE file, and choose OK.

Any of these four techniques generate the "Hello, world" output.

> **NOTE**   When running the program using option 1, option 2, or option 4, Windows immediately opens an MS-DOS window in which to run the application. When the program terminates, Windows quickly closes the window. Thus, for a short program like this one, the window might not stay open long enough for you to read the output. There are ways around this problem, several of which we'll visit later on in this chapter. In the meantime, either take my word for it that the output is there or use option 3 to run the program.

The Microsoft Developer Environment 6

Before continuing with more challenging applications, let's use the simple Hello-World1 application as a way to introduce the MDE, the user interface for Visual J++. We've already seen a bit of Project Explorer and the Text editor, but even here there are a few additional features to point out. To look at these features, open the Hello-World1 application in Visual J++.

The Multiple Document Interface and the Single Document Interface

Two fundamentally different modes are available for the MDE. In Multiple Document Interface (MDI) mode, the MDE acts as a single desktop upon which all other windows, such as Project Explorer and the Text editor, reside. In this mode, you can't see Windows applications behind the MDE desktop and MDE windows can't leave the MDE desktop. This is the mode under which previous versions of Visual J++ operated.

In Single Document Interface (SDI) mode, there is no MDE desktop. Rather, the menus, taskbar, and status bar form one window, Project Explorer resides in another window, and each Text editor occupies its own window. In this mode, the MDE windows appear on the Windows desktop in front of whatever applications might be executing in the background.

At first, SDI mode is disconcerting since the different windows seem to have a tenuous connection to each other and to the menu bar. SDI mode is especially confusing if you happen to run Visual J++ twice. When you do that, you really have no idea which windows belong to which MDE. However, once you get used to it, SDI will probably become your preferred style.

You can change from SDI to MDI and back again. To do so, choose Options from the Tools menu, expand the Environment branch and choose General, and select or deselect SDI Environment. You'll have to close and then reopen Visual J++ before the change will take effect.

Docking windows

Another feature of the MDE is docking windows. A window is *docked* when it is firmly attached to another window, generally to its edge. Docking applies only in MDI mode. By default, all windows—except the Text editor—have docking set on.

Docking windows takes some getting used to; learning a few basics will help. First, if you place a dockable window near another dockable window (especially near the menu or toolbars), the MDE automatically snaps them together, issuing an audible snapping sound to confirm the action.

You can try to undock the window by dragging it away; however, the window is likely to simply redock in some other configuration. A better alternative is to double-click the title bar, which automatically undocks the window and keeps it undocked. Now you are free to move the window wherever you like. Double-clicking the title bar again throws the window back to its previous docked position.

If you're like me and don't like docking windows next to each other, you can right-click the title bar to disable the docking feature and leave it undocked. Before you do that, however, I want to show you one other docking mode that I find fits my personality very well.

Sometimes a window will disappear as soon as you disable docking. Usually this is because the window is just barely outside the parent window. Before you give the window up for lost, click the maximize button on the MDE title bar and look for it, usually along the bottom of the screen. If you still can't find it, you can reenable docking for the window you're looking for by choosing the window in the Window menu and then selecting Dockable from the Window menu.

In addition to docking windows next to each other, the MDE supports docking windows on top of each other. It's a little tricky to get the first two windows to dock in this mode; you basically want to drag two similarly sized windows directly on top of each other. Once you do, the top window will reappear within a window with a tab attached. The back window is hidden except for its tab, which appears immediately beside the top window's tab.

To add another window to the tabbed group, follow these steps:

1. Make the window visible by choosing View from the Edit menu and selecting the appropriate option.

2. Use the mouse pointer to grab the window by the title bar.

3. Drag the window to the tab labels.

Step 3 isn't obvious. Your first instinct might be to drag the window on top of the tabbed window group; however, this simply docks the window to the window pair.

My preference is to dock all MDE windows (except for Text editor windows) to the single tabbed window, as shown in Figure 1-3. Notice that I have widened the tabbed window to the point where each tab label is completely visible. As I shrink the window, the MDE truncates the labels more and more until it eventually removes them.

Figure 1-3. *A tabbed window containing most of the MDE development windows.*

The Text editor

The most important window the programmer uses is the Text editor; this window contains the Java source code.

Color coding

View the Class1.java source file in the Text editor and one thing jumps out at you right away. (If you've closed the Text editor, double-click Class1.java in Project Explorer to reopen it.) The Text editor color codes the different statement types, using green for comments, blue for keywords, and black for executable statements.

Indentation settings

As you type, the Text editor can help you to implement a consistent indentation style. Depending on what style settings you have selected, the editor automatically indents statements and aligns open and close braces. To adjust these features, choose Options on the Tools menu and under the Text Editor branch choose Java Format.

Smart editor

The Text editor also checks syntax as you type. As soon as it detects a syntax error, it places a squiggled red line underneath the offending statement, as shown in Figure 1-4. (This is similar to the way Microsoft Word underlines misspelled words.) You can disable syntax error checking by choosing Java Tasks under Text Editor in the Options dialog box.

```
Class1.java [Code]*                                    _ □ ×
      * constructor is not invoked unless an object of t
      * created in the main() method.
      */
     public classs Class1
     {
         /**
          * The main entry point for the application.
          *
```

Figure 1-4. *Smart editor syntax checking.*

Statement Completion

The final feature of the Text editor I'll point out is the automatic object browser, called the Auto List Members feature. As soon as you enter a dot (".") after either a class or an object name, Auto List Members drops down a list of all the possible entries. For example, Figure 1-5 shows the Text editor after you have entered the dot following the word *System*.

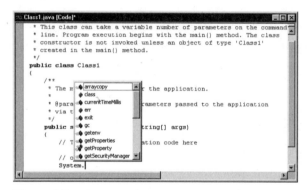

Figure 1-5. *The Text editor's Auto List Members feature.*

Members marked with a brick that has racing stripes (this brick is colored magenta on a color display) represent member methods and functions. Two racing bricks represent a method or function with more than one implementation. Members marked with a brick that doesn't have racing stripes (this brick is colored teal) represent data members.

That process repeats itself upon entering the dot after *System.out.* After you select the *println()* method from the list, the Parameter Information feature displays the method arguments as shown in Figure 1-6. Here you can see that I paged down through a list of the 10 *println()* methods defined for the *PrintStream* class (the class of *out*) until I found the one I wanted, in this case the fourth one in the list. This version of the *println()* method takes a *String* and returns a *void* (that is, nothing). The parameter information continues to display until I type the close parenthesis.

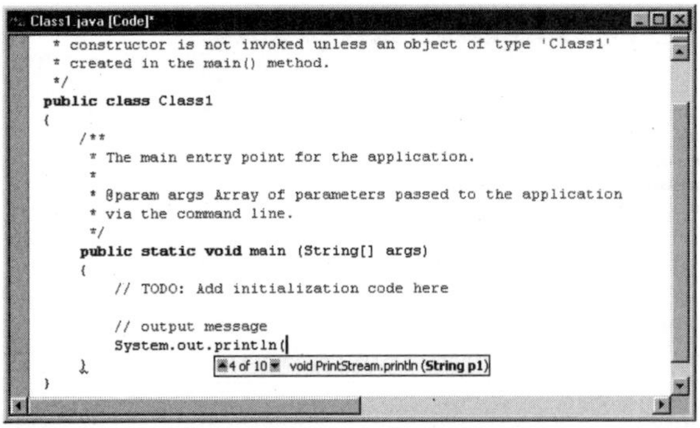

```
Class1.java [Code]*                                          _ □ ×
      * constructor is not invoked unless an object of type 'Class1'
      * created in the main() method.
      */
     public class Class1
     {
         /**
          * The main entry point for the application.
          *
          * @param args Array of parameters passed to the application
          * via the command line.
          */
         public static void main (String[] args)
         {
             // TODO: Add initialization code here

             // output message
             System.out.println (
                     ◄ 4 of 10 ► void PrintStream.println (String p1)
         }
     }
```

Figure 1-6. *Method arguments displayed in the Text editor.*

The Statement Completion feature, which includes the Auto List Members and the Parameter Information features, extends to functions you write. As soon as you save your source file, the Text editor adds any methods you have created to the Auto List Members list. If you include /**-style Javadoc comments in front of your functions, the comments appear along with the method name. In addition, as you begin to enter the arguments to the method in the Text editor, the comments following the Javadoc *@param* appear.

Statement Completion, which includes the Auto List Members and the Parameter Information features, drastically reduces the number of trips you take to the Visual J++ documentation. Java is a small language with a very large class library that is made even larger by the addition of WFC. Being prompted by lists of available data members and methods, along with their arguments, is a great help in programming with Java and WFC.

The Object Browser

Oddly enough, once the Statement Completion list has closed there appears to be no way to make it reappear, short of deleting the dot and retyping it. Another path to the same functionality is the Object Browser.

To use the Object Browser, you choose Other Windows from the View menu and pick Object Browser from the list. When you type *System* in the filter box at the top of the browser window and press Enter, the Object Browser searches through all members of all packages and returns every class that contains a reference to the word *System*. Notice that a number of the entries it finds are not what we're looking for. Nonetheless, the correct *System* class was in the list.

When you select the *System* class under java.lang, its members are displayed in the members pane. Select the object that we're looking for, *out*, and a full description of the object is displayed at the bottom of the Object Browser, as shown in Figure 1-7.

Figure 1-7. *The Object Browser enables you to look for and get detailed class information.*

The Task List

The Task List window is another extension of the Text editor. The MDE searches the comments in Java source files that you are editing for particular keywords. For example, the various wizards put the phrase *TODO:* in places where they think you need to add code to complete your program.

When the environment finds these keywords, it adds them to the Task List. Thus, the Task List is an ongoing list of what is left to be done. Figure 1-8 shows the Task List items for our HelloWorld1 application.

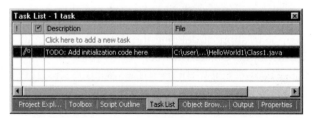

Figure 1-8. *The Task List resulting from the HelloWorld1 application, showing one task left to be done.*

Double-clicking the *TODO* item takes you to the proper line within the Java source code. (Notice that the *TODO* shown in Figure 1-8 was left only because I did not edit it out when I added the *println()* code.)

The Task List contains more than just *TODO* entries. You are free to add your own entries to the list of comment keywords that the environment is searching for.

Compiler errors are added to the Task List as well. In addition, you can display the different types of entries in the Task List independently by right-clicking the Task List window and selecting the type of task you would like to see.

(I don't know if it's just me, but I find the name of the Task List confusing. I keep expecting to see a list of the tasks executing under the operating system rather than the tasks left for me to do.)

Toolbar customization

In Visual J++, you can customize a toolbar and create new toolbars. To customize a toolbar, first make sure that the toolbar you want to edit is visible by choosing Toolbars from the View menu and selecting the toolbars you want to see. (You can also de-select the toolbars you don't want to see.)

To edit a toolbar, choose Toolbars on the View menu and then select Customize. Once the Customize dialog box appears, the toolbars are in edit mode and you can get rid of a tool by simply dragging it off the toolbar. To add a tool to a toolbar, select the Commands tab and find the menu command you want to add. If the command has an icon, drag it from the dialog box to where you want it on the toolbar as shown in Figure 1-9.

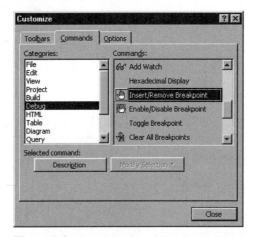

Figure 1-9. *Preparing to add the Insert/Remove Breakpoint tool to the Standard toolbar.*

If the menu command you want to put on a toolbar doesn't have an icon associated with it, you can add it to the toolbar anyway. For example, the Close command on the File menu doesn't have an icon. Dragging this command to the toolbar produces the not-so-pleasing result shown in Figure 1-10. (Notice the word "Close" between the disk-like icons.)

You can assign a tool an icon from a list of standard icons. With the Customize dialog box still open, click the Close tool with the right mouse button. This will display a list of properties that you can set for the icon. Select Change Button Image and a list of standard icons that you can use is displayed. Select the one that appeals to you the most. Figure 1-11 shows my selection.

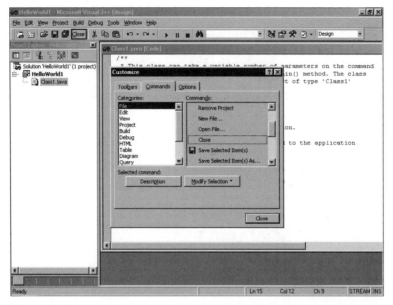

Figure 1-10. *Adding the Close command initially results in the command's name being on the toolbar.*

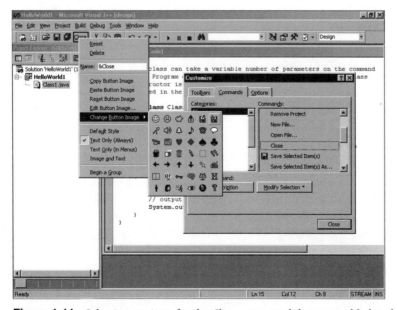

Figure 1-11. *Selecting an icon for the Close command that was added to the Standard toolbar.*

Once you've selected an image, both the command name and the image appear on the toolbar. You might leave it that way for awhile, until you've become accustomed to what the image stands for. Eventually you'll want to reclaim the precious toolbar territory by getting rid of the word. To do so, open the Customize dialog box again, right-click the tool, and select Default Style. This will remove the command label, leaving only the icon.

On a toolbar, groups of tools are separated by vertical chisel lines. To add a chisel line, you right-click the icon that is to the right of where you want the chisel line. From the drop-down menu, select Begin a Group.

Each of the toolbars can be edited independently. However, my preference is to edit one toolbar (generally the Standard toolbar), add all of the tools I find most useful, and leave it visible all the time.

LET'S SIEVE OUT RUMORS OF POOR PERFORMANCE

One concern that many readers may have about using Java as a language for application development is efficiency. Before getting deep in application development, let's address that concern.

To see how good Visual J++ 6 performance is, I decided to use the aged, but still serviceable, Sieve of Eratosthenes benchmark. (Eratosthenes is pronounced era-TOS-the-knees.) First I wrote the sieve program in Java and compiled it under Visual J++ 6. Then I converted the program to C++ and compiled, executed, and timed that version. A comparison of the two programs indicates how Visual J++ 6 stacks up to C++.

This benchmark does a reasonable job of testing program logic, simple arithmetic, and array referencing. It does not test floating point math, the calling of functions, screen input and output (I/O) (which is more a function of the hardware and the operating system than the programming language anyway), or a number of other things.

The Sieve benchmark does do something that some programmers might consider useful: it searches for, finds, and, in this example, counts prime numbers. The Sieve benchmark does these tasks by using a very simple algorithm. First it assumes that every number between 2 and (in this case) one million is prime. It records this assumption by declaring an array of one million Booleans and setting every array element to *true*. (You could set the length to one million minus one because we're starting with 2, but coding is much easier if you just declare the full array and skip the first element.) The Sieve then starts looking through the array. Every time it finds a value of *true*, it knows that it's found a prime, so it counts the prime by incrementing a counter. However, the Sieve recognizes that multiples of a found prime are not prime, so it loops through the array and sets every multiple of the current prime to *false*. Once the program reaches the end of the array, the Sieve benchmark terminates.

The Sieve in Visual J++ 6

The Sieve function code is shown here:

```
/**
 * Sieve - This class calculates prime numbers using the
 *          venerable Sieve of Eratosthenes algorithm.
 *          It is being used to compare Java performance
 *          to that of C++.
 */
public class Class1
{
    // iteration count
    static final int ITR = 10;

    /**
     * The main entry point for the application.
     *
     * @param - this program takes no arguments
     */
    public static void main (String[] args)
    {
        // fetch the current time in milliseconds
        long startTime = System.currentTimeMillis();

        // allocate some variables that we'll need later
        int primeCount = 0;
        boolean[] prime = new boolean[1000000];
        int lng = prime.length;

        // repeat the process multiple times so
        // that it will take long enough to get an
        // accurate measurement
        for (int i = 0; i < ITR; i++)
        {
            // first create an array of Booleans, where
            // each member of the array stands for a number
            for (int j = 0; j < lng; j++)   // NOTE 1
            {
                prime[j] = true;
            }

            // now loop through looking for prime numbers
```

(continued)

```
                // (skip 0 and 1, they don't count)
                primeCount = 0;
                for (int j = 2; j < lng; j++)  // NOTE2
                {
                    if (prime[j])
                    {
                        // found a prime, count it
                        primeCount++;

                        // now set all of the multiples of
                        // the current prime number to false
                        // because they couldn't possibly be
                        // prime
                        for (int k = j; k < lng; k += j) // NOTE 3
                        {
                            prime[k] = false;
                        }
                    }
                }
            }

            // done!
            long stopTime = System.currentTimeMillis();

            // output the number of primes
            System.out.println("Number of primes = "
                                            + primeCount);

            // and the number of iterations
            System.out.println("Number of iterations = " + ITR);

            // now display the time difference
            System.out.println("Time delta = "
                                    + (stopTime - startTime)
                                    + " milliseconds");
        }
    }
```

The program begins, as do all Java applications, at the function *main()*. Then it immediately uses the method *System.currentTimeMillis()* to record the current time (starting from some arbitrary point) in milliseconds. Next it allocates an array of Boolean values called *prime*. This is the array that the program will use to keep track of what is and what isn't prime.

C++ NOTE Java declares a type called *boolean* rather than relying on *int*. In addition, in Java an array must be declared off of the heap and uses a syntax slightly different than that of C++: *boolean[] prime = new boolean[1000000]*. In fact, the *[]* can go either before or after the variable name *prime*.

```
/**
 * Check the argument to see whether it exists. If so, is it
 * okay to overwrite it? If not, it throws an exception.
 *
 * @param outputFileName - the file name to overwrite
 */
private static void okayToCopy(String outputFileName)
    throws IOException
{
    // first check whether the file exists
    File file = new File(outputFileName);
    if (file.exists())
    {
        // it does, so check whether it's okay to overwrite it
        System.out.println("File exists. Overwrite? [Y or N]");
        byte[] answer = new byte[1]; // read in a single byte
        System.in.read(answer);
        if (answer[0] != 'Y' && answer[0] != 'y')
        {
            throw new IOException("Copy failed");
        }
    }
}
}
```

Changing the main class name

Notice that in the previous example I have stopped calling the main class *Class1*. Instead, I renamed the main class to match the project name. To rename the main class, you start in the usual way by using the Console Application Wizard to create the Echo1 project, as we did with the HelloWorld1 project at the beginning of this chapter. As usual, the wizard creates the one and only Java source file and names it Class1. First you rename the file in the Project to Echo1. This necessitates that you change the class name to *Echo1* as well.

> NOTE There can be only one public class per Java source file and its name must *exactly* match that of the Java source file in which it resides. As we will see in Part II, this is necessary so that browsers can find applet classes quickly and easily.

Unfortunately, changing the names isn't enough. If you compile the Echo1 program after changing the project name and class name, the compiler claims that it can no longer find *Class1*. This is because the Console Application Wizard directs the Project file to start debugging with *Class1*. (Visual J++ 1.x used to ask the user for the class name the first time the program was run. This turned out to be a nuisance, so now the Wizard sets the class name.)

To change the class name in the Echo1 project, you right-click the Echo1 project in Project Explorer and choose Echo1 Properties. From there, you select the Launch tab. In the When Project Runs, Load: list box, select the only class available, *Echo1*, and then choose OK. The resulting Properties page is shown in Figure 1-14.

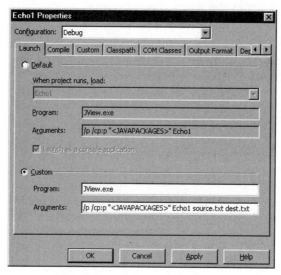

Figure 1-14. *The project Properties window after the launch class has been changed from* Class1 *to* Echo1.

NOTE Even though *Echo1* was the only option available, you must still manually select it and apply it. This option won't be available until you have edited the name to *Echo1* in the Java source file.

The Echo1 source code

Echo1 begins by importing the *java.io* package. This is where the file I/O classes reside.

C++ NOTE Importing a package is the Java equivalent to including a C++ *#include* file at compile time and adding the corresponding library at link time. The package informs Visual J++ of our intent to access classes from the *java.io* package.

Once Echo1 begins execution, it immediately checks to see whether the user has provided two arguments. It does that by checking the length of the *args* argument.

C++ NOTE The *args* argument to *main()* is an array of *String* objects, each one corresponding to an argument to the program.

If the user doesn't know what a console application does, it is common to simply run it without any arguments. In that case, it is important that the program provide the user some help by explaining what arguments it expects and what it does with them.

Before the program begins the actual copy operation, it opens up a *try* block. Most of Java's file operations throw an *IOException* when something goes wrong, so we better be prepared to catch these exceptions.

The first order of business before we can actually copy anything is to open the input file. The program does this by creating a *FileInputStream* object with the input file name. The *FileInputStream* constructor opens the file provided. If the file doesn't exist, it throws an *IOException* explaining as much.

Notice how the program follows this up by wrapping the *FileInputStream* class in a *BufferedInputStream*. Doing this is almost always a good idea. The *FileInputStream* class isn't buffered, which means that every time a read is performed the class must go back to the disk to get the data. The *BufferedInputStream* class adds a buffer to reduce the number of disk reads. Thus, if the program reads a single byte, the *BufferedInputStream* class reads an entire block. (The actual size of the block is dependent on the operating system and the underlying disk, but it's some natural size, usually a multiple of 1024 bytes.) The *BufferedInputStream* class returns a single byte to the caller and retains the remaining data. When the program asks for another byte, the class returns the next byte from the buffer without going back to the disk. Since memory operations are much faster than disk accesses, *BufferedInputStream* can speed up I/O access considerably.

The *false* value passed to the *FileOutputStream()* constructor indicates that the program doesn't want to append a file if the output file already exists. Instead, it wants to truncate any existing output file. Before the program opens the output file, however, it invokes the static method *okayToCopy()* to see whether it's okay to overwrite an existing file. The method *okayToCopy()* accepts the name of the output file. It throws an *IOException* if it isn't okay to overwrite an existing file.

> **NOTE** Unlike C++, a method must use the *throws* keyword to declare any exceptions that it, or any method it calls, might throw.

The *okayToCopy()* method first checks for the presence of the target file by creating a *File* object. You might think that a *File* object is used to perform I/O, but its real use is for testing the properties of a file on the disk. The method *File.exists()* returns *true* if the *File* object is pointing to an existing file.

If the target file does exist, the program asks the user whether it should be overwritten or not. If the user enters anything other than *y* or *Y*, the program throws an *IOException* and thereby saves the target file from extinction. (This exception is handled back at the end of *main().*) Otherwise, the *okayToCopy()* method returns to the caller.

Once the source and target files have been opened, there's nothing left but the *while* loop that performs the read and write operations. The method *Input-Stream.available()* returns a count of the number of bytes available to be read in the input file. The *InputStream.read()* method reads up to the number of *buffer* bytes. The return value is the number of bytes actually read. The call to *OutputStream.write()* writes the number of bytes from *buffer* that are indicated by *bytesRead*, starting at offset 0.

The More Sophisticated Echo2

The Echo2 program presents several enhancements to the Echo1 program. First, the second argument—the destination file—is optional. If it isn't present, output goes to standard output. Further, Echo2 accepts the */C* switch, which if present indicates that the input is a text string that is to be capitalized before being output to the destination stream.

While this may not sound like much, I have also added several techniques to Echo2 that you can use in other applications.

The *Echo2* class

The following code represents the *Echo2* class:

```
/**
 * Echo2 - Copies the first argument to the second.
 *          If output file is not given, output goes to
 *          standard output. If /C switch is present,
 *          attach a filter to convert each word to
 *          uppercase.
 */
import java.io.*;

public class Echo2
{
    // global data
    // input file object
    InputStream in = null;

    // output file object
    OutputStream out = null;

    /**
     * The main entry point for the application.
     *
     * @param arg[0] - the input file (optional)
```

```
 * @param arg[1] - the output file
 */
public static void main (String[] args)
{
    // start parsing arguments
    try
    {
        boolean caps = false;
        String input = null;
        String output= null;

        int nextArg = 0;
        // first look for switches
        if (args[nextArg].equalsIgnoreCase("/C"))
        {
            caps = true;
            nextArg++;
        }

        // save input argument
        input = args[nextArg++];

        // the output file name is optional -
        // an exception here is okay
        try
        {
            output = args[nextArg++];
        }
        catch(Exception e)
        {
        }

        // create an object to do all the work
        new Echo2(caps, input, output).copy();
    }
    catch(IOException e)
    {
        print("Error:" + e.getMessage());
    }
    catch(Exception e)
    {
        print("Enter: echo2 [/C] source [dest]");
        print("to copy <source> to <dest>");
        print("If dest is absent, output is to standard output");
        print("/C -> capitalize each word");
    }
}
```

(continued)

```
/**
 * The Echo2 constructor sets up the files.
 * By providing an object, the program now has a place
 * to store things.
 * @param capitalize - TRUE->capitalize each word on output
 * @param input     - the name of the input file (null->none)
 * @param output    - the name of the output file
 */
Echo2(boolean capitalize, String input, String output)
    throws IOException
{
    // open the two files:
    // first the input file; an error here is fatal
    FileInputStream fin = new FileInputStream(input);
    in = new BufferedInputStream(fin);

    // must be okay - use either standard output or the
    // specified output file as output
    out = System.out;  // the default is standard output
    if (output != null)
    {
        okayToCopy(output);
        out = new FileOutputStream(output, false);
    }

    // if we are to convert to upper case, then...
    if (capitalize)
    {
        out = new CapFilterOutputStream(out);
    }
}


/**
 * Perform the copy operation.
 *
 */
void copy()
    throws IOException
{
    byte[] buffer = new byte[1024];
    while(in.available() > 0)
    {
        int bytesRead = in.read(buffer);
        out.write(buffer, 0, bytesRead);
    }
}
```

```
/**
 * Write input to standard output.
 *
 * @param outputFileName - the file name to overwrite
 */
static void print(String outString)
{
    System.out.println(outString);
}


/**
 * Check the argument to see whether it exists and whether it's
 * okay to overwrite it. If not, it throws an exception.
 *
 * @param outputFileName - the file name to overwrite
 */
private static void okayToCopy(String outputFileName)
    throws IOException
{
    // first check whether the file exists
    File file = new File(outputFileName);
    if (file.exists())
    {
        // it does, so check whether it's okay to overwrite it
        System.out.println("File exists. Overwrite? [Y or N]");
        byte[] answer = new byte[1]; // read in a single byte
        System.in.read(answer);
        if (answer[0] != 'Y' && answer[0] != 'y')
        {
            throw new IOException("Copy failed");
        }
    }
}
}
```

The *main()* function in Echo2 looks quite a bit different from its Echo1 ancestor. This is primarily because Echo2 must be flexible enough to handle a varied number of arguments.

Echo2 first initializes each of the three variables it intends to read from the argument list. The program then defines the index *nextArg* to be used in scanning through the argument list. Echo2 compares the first argument to the *"/C"* string using *String.equalsIgnoreCase()*. If this function call returns *true*, the program knows that the /C switch is present. In this case, the program sets the *caps* flag to *true* and then increments *nextArg* to point to the next argument.

C++
NOTE   The two argument variables, *input* and *output*, are initialized to *null*. *null* isn't numerically equivalent to 0, as it is in C++, but is a unique value.

The program assumes the next argument to be the name of the input file. If either of these first two arguments are not present, *args[]* will be referenced beyond the end of the array, which will cause Java to throw an *ArrayIndexOutOfBoundsException*. This exception will be caught at the bottom of *main()* by the *catch(Exception)* catch phrase.

Next the program attempts to reference the second file name, except this time an *ArrayIndexOutOfBoundsException* does not represent an error because the second file name is optional. Therefore, the program catches the possible exception on the spot. In that event, *output* retains its *null* value.

Once the arguments have been parsed, *main()* creates an object of the class *Echo2* and then immediately passes that object to *Echo2.copy()*.

C++ NOTE Under Java, it is perfectly legal to allocate an object off the heap and then immediately use it as the object of a method call.

Why create an *Echo2* object?

The *main()* method is static and therefore has no object associated with it. This isn't a problem with programs that consist of only a single function, like Echo1. However, in larger object-oriented programs it is more convenient to store information in the data members of a class object. Creating an object in the static member *main()* provides just such a place to store information.

The constructor for the *Echo2* class performs and looks a lot like the file creation logic in Echo1. The primary difference is that Echo2 first assigns *System.out* to the output object *out*. If an output file name is present, the output object is replaced by a *FileOutputStream* opened on that output file. This works because *PrintStream*—the class of *System.out*—and *FileOutputStream* both extend a common base class, *OutputStream*.

Finally, Echo2 creates a *CapFilterOutputStream* object to perform the capitalization function.

NOTE *CapFilterOutputStream* extends the base class *FilterOutputStream*. You can use subclasses of *FilterOutputStream* to perform conversion operations on data being sent out of an output stream.

The *copy()* and *okayToCopy()* methods are basically identical to their Echo1 equivalents.

The *CapFilterOutputStream* class

Now all that's left is to present the *CapFilterOutputStream* class (located in the Echo2 program) that performs the capitalization operation. The source code is as follows:

```
/**
 * CapFilterOutputStream - A filter output stream
 *                         that converts its output to
 *                         uppercase.
 */
```

```
class CapFilterOutputStream extends FilterOutputStream
{
    // the list of characters which cause capitalization
    static String specialChars = " .-\t";

    // the output stream to use for actual output
    OutputStream os = null;

    CapFilterOutputStream(OutputStream os)
    {
        super(os);
        this.os = os;
    }

    /**
     * Write the buffer in capitalized form.
     *
     * @param buffer - buffer to write
     * @param offset - where to start
     * @param length - number of bytes to write
     */
    public void write(byte[] buffer, int offset, int length)
        throws IOException
    {
        // make a string buffer out of the byte array -
        // here we are assuming a text byte array
        // (we use StringBuffer because you can write
        // directly to it)
        String s = new String(buffer, offset, length);
        StringBuffer sb = new StringBuffer(s);

        // convert the StringBuffer into uppercase according
        // to the rules of this class
        toUpper(sb);

        // now convert the string back into an array of bytes,
        // and write it out using the base class' method
        buffer = sb.toString().getBytes();
        os.write(buffer, 0, buffer.length);
    }

    /**
     * Write the buffer in capitalized form.
     *
     * @param buffer - buffer to write
     */
```

(continued)

```
public void write(byte[] buffer)
    throws IOException
{
    write(buffer, 0, buffer.length);
}


/**
 * Capitalize the buffer provided.
 *
 * @param buffer - buffer to write
 * @param offset - where to start
 * @param length - number of bytes to write
 */
static void toUpper(StringBuffer sb)
{
    // loop through the new buffer, capitalizing any
    // alphanumeric that appears after a special
    // character
    boolean cap = true;
    int length = sb.length();
    for (int i = 0; i < length; i++)
    {
        char c = sb.charAt(i);

        // if we're supposed to cap this letter...
        if (cap)
        {
            // and if this is a letter...
            if (Character.isLetter(c));
            {
                // then capitalize and restore it
                c = Character.toUpperCase(c);
                sb.setCharAt(i, c);

                // okay, it's done
                cap = false;
            }
        }
        else
        {
            // (not in cap mode)
            // look for one of the special characters
            cap = (specialChars.indexOf((int)c) != -1);
        }
    }
}
```

The *CapFilterOutputStream* class extends the *FilterOutputStream* class by overriding the *write()* method.

TIP It is something of a Java standard that when you extend a class, the name of the new class should contain the name of the base class in addition to some prefix to indicate what the new class does. In this case, *CapFilterOutputStream* extends *FilterOutputStream* to provide capitalization. That way, a programmer who uses your class knows immediately what your class does and what class it's based on.

NOTE The term *extend*, when used for class inheritance, is the Java equivalent of the colon in C++.

The *CapFilterOutputStream* class starts by defining a string of special characters. The program assumes that these characters divide words. As a result, the program capitalizes the first letter appearing after any one of these characters.

The *CapFilterOutputStream* class overrides the *write(byte[], int, int)* method to implement the capitalization. The *write()* method begins by converting the byte buffer passed to it into a *StringBuffer*. (There are several methods for character manipulation provided by the *StringBuffer* class.) Then it calls *toUpper()* to capitalize the *StringBuffer* and uses the *write()* method of its base class to perform the actual I/O.

The *toUpper()* method loops through the *StringBuffer sb* one character at a time. If the capitalization flag *cap* is set to *true* and the character is a letter, the character is converted to uppercase and restored to the *StringBuffer*. If the flag isn't set, the character is looked up in the set of *specialChars*. If the *indexOf()* method returns a −1, the *c* character isn't one of the special characters. If *indexOf()* returns anything other than −1, the *c* character is one of the special characters.

The output in Figure 1-15 shows the results of running Echo2.

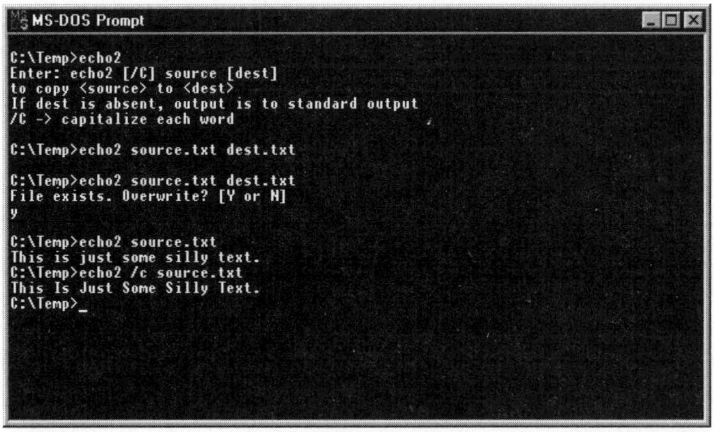

Figure 1-15. *Output from the Echo2 program showing different options.*

Reading Formatted Data

The standard Java *FileInputStream* and *FileOutStream* classes we have used until now are ideal for reading in large blocks of data. Containing nothing more than the simple *read()* and *write()* methods, these classes are extremely limited in their formatting capability. The *DataInputStream* and *DataOutputStream* classes are provided for the purpose of extending formatting options. For example, the following code snippet can be used to read a floating point grade, an integer number of class hours, and a class name from a file named courses.txt.

```
FileInputStream fin = new FileInputStream("courses.txt");
DataInputStream din = new DataInputStream(fin);

float  grade = din.readFloat();
int    hours = din.readInt();
String title = din.readUTF();
```

> **NOTE**   Since Java assigns 16 bits to each character in a string, Java methods do not normally have to worry about 1-, 2-, and 3-byte Unicode characters. The *readUTF()* method reads Unicode Text Format-8 (UTF-8) files that might have been written in another language such as C++ and converts the data into a Java string. Unfortunately, *readUTF()* reads to the end of the file. There is no *DataInputStream* equivalent to the C++ *getLine()* function, which reads until the end of the line.

CONCLUSION

For many purposes, especially for the small "throw-away" programs that you write for yourself, console applications are ideal. Java is a friendly language and Visual J++ 6 is a friendly environment for the development of console applications. In this chapter, you've seen several techniques programmers commonly use in the development of generic console applications.

In the next chapter, you'll see how using WFC makes the job of writing powerful, console-based Microsoft Windows applications even easier.

Chapter 2

Introduction to WFC: The I/O Package

In Chapter 1, we examined the simplest type of application: the command line DOS-like console application. In that chapter, I limited the discussion to language features that are portable to any implementation of Java, irrespective of platform.

In this chapter, I'll use the simple Echo1 console application from Chapter 1 to introduce the Windows Foundation Classes for Java (WFC), a set of classes unique to Microsoft Windows and to Microsoft Visual J++ version 6.

THE WINDOWS FOUNDATION CLASSES

WFC is a large library of Java classes—much too large for us to cover in one chapter. In fact, investigating the classes that make up WFC will consume all of Part II and much of the remainder of this book. In this chapter, we'll discuss one package of classes—the file input/output (I/O) package *com.ms.wfc.io*. From this discussion, you will get a basic knowledge of how WFC works. You will be able to use this information when we investigate windowed applications in Chapter 4.

The Organization of WFC

WFC is organized into a series of packages as follows:

Package	Package description
com.ms.wfc.app	Provides classes that encapsulate Windows application operations such as threads, messaging, and access to the Clipboard and the Windows registry.
com.ms.wfc.core	Used by the Java development tools. Most of these classes are not used directly by the programmer.
com.ms.wfc.data	Provides access to data stored in databases by means of ActiveX Data Objects (ADO).
com.ms.wfc.html	Provides classes for accessing Dynamic HTML. This is the only WFC package that is devoted to applet development.
com.ms.wfc.io	Includes the classes that perform file input/output (I/O). This package is presented in this chapter.
com.ms.wfc.ui	Provides the WFC user interface for Windows applications.
com.ms.wfc.util	A catchall package of unrelated utility classes.

The *com* in the package name indicates that a package isn't intrinsic to Java. The rules of Java require this prefix to avoid name collisions with packages provided by other companies. The *ms* presumably stands for Microsoft. Thus, the full name of the *File* class within the WFC *io* package is *com.ms.wfc.io.File*.

NOTE   Don't panic; the *import* statement makes using the prefix optional, as you will see in the examples later in this chapter.

Why WFC?

Before we talk about how to write WFC-based applications, I think I should answer the question, "Why?" This is really two questions in one: "Why create Windows-specific Java applications?" and "Why use WFC?"

In answer to the first question, once an application has been compiled into an executable, it is automatically specific to the operating system for which it was compiled. Thus, to say that your .EXE file is limited to running under Windows isn't a limitation at all. True, you can deploy Java programs as .class files, but for applications the prospect of forcing the user to supply JVIEW or an equivalent Java application viewer doesn't seem practical. The point is that you can recompile source code that uses the generic Java library functions to run under any operating system. However, using WFC limits your applications to run under only Microsoft Windows. You must decide whether this is a limitation that you can live with.

I should point out that you would be limiting yourself to about 95 percent of all of the desktop machines in the market. In addition, if Microsoft Windows is your only operating system and you're writing an application for your own use, this is no limitation at all.

To offset this restriction of using WFC, you would expect to receive some benefits. Here we arrive at an answer to the second question above. The WFC package provides four distinct advantages to the Windows programmer:

■ WFC classes have more expressive power than does Java alone.

■ Many of the WFC classes look a lot like the classes provided by other windowing languages, such as Microsoft Visual C++. This similarity reduces the learning curve for non-Java Windows programmers. In many cases, the similarity in classes gives WFC the same look and feel as the C++ MFC library.

■ Tying WFC to the Windows operating system makes WFC-based applications more responsive by reducing the code distance between the application code and the underlying operating system. In addition, the number of repaints is significantly reduced. (For reasons unknown to me AWT-based applications repainted more than they needed to, resulting in slower application performance than with the WFC-based applications.)

■ The development tools provided with Visual J++ 6 use WFC to enhance greatly the programmer's application development capability.

Let's examine the first three assertions by looking at the WFC package *ms.com.wfc.io*. I'll spend the remainder of the book demonstrating the development tools.

THE I/O PACKAGE

From the programmer's standpoint, the WFC *ms.com.wfc.io* package consists of two families of classes: the *IByteStream* family and the *IReader/IWriter* family. The *IByteStream* family, which includes the file I/O class *File*, provides the basic read and write operations and is the more fundamental of the two. The *IReader/IWriter* family provides the extra features necessary for the manipulation of ANSI text.

Any Java program you want to perform WFC file I/O should import *com.ms.wfc.io* rather than the conventional *java.io* package. You should not try to import both the *wfc.io* and *java.io* packages in the same program since several classes have the same name in both packages—for example, the class *File*.

The *IByteStream* Family

The most fundamental class IN the *IByteStream* family is the *File* class, which is demonstrated in the following WFCEcho1 application.

> **NOTE**   All the sample applications in this chapter are located in the Windows Applications subfolder on the companion CD.

WFCEcho1

The following program is the WFC equivalent of the Echo1 program presented in Chapter 1. This program relies on the class *File* to handle all of its I/O needs.

```
/**
 * WFCEcho1 - copies the file args[0] to the file args[1]
 *            using the WFC I/O package.
 */
import com.ms.wfc.io.*;

public class WFCEcho1
{
    // standard input and output
    static File in  = File.openStandardInput();
    static File out = File.openStandardOutput();

    /**
     * The main entry point for the application.
     *
     * @param arg[0] - the input file
     * @param arg[1] - the output file
     */
    public static void main(String[] args)
    {
        // make sure that the user understands what
        // to do
        if (args.length != 2)
        {
            print("Enter: wfcEcho1 source dest\n");
            print("to copy <source> to <dest>\n");
            System.exit(-1);
        }

        // catch any problems at the bottom of the
        // program - no matter what the problem, we'll
        // output an error message and terminate
        try
        {
            // if the output file exists, make sure it's okay
            // to overwrite it
            okayToCopy(args[1]);
```

```
        // it's okay, so copy away
        File.copyOver(args[0], args[1]);
    }

    // catch any exception thrown
    catch(Exception e)
    {
        print("Error:" + e.getMessage() + "\n");
    }
}

/**
 * Check the argument to see whether it exists, and then
 * whether it's okay to overwrite it. If not, it throws an
 * exception.
 *
 * @param outputFileName - the file name to overwrite
 */
private static void okayToCopy(String outputFileName)
    throws Exception
{
    // first check whether the file exists
    if (File.exists(outputFileName))
    {
        // it does, so check whether it's okay to overwrite it
        print("File exists. Overwrite? [Y or N]");
        String answer = read();
        if (!answer.equalsIgnoreCase("Y"))
        {
            throw new Exception("Copy failed");
        }
    }
}

/**
 * Print a message to standard output.
 *
 * @param outString - string to output
 */
private static void print(String s)
{
    out.writeStringCharsAnsi(s);
}

/**
 * Read a single character from standard input.
 */
```

(continued)

```
private static String read()
{
    // keep reading until we see a character
    char[] cArray = new char[1];
    do
    {
        cArray[0] = (char)in.readByte();
    } while(!Character.isLetter(cArray[0]));

    // convert the character into a string
    return new String(cArray);
}
}
```

If you ignore for a minute the code to write messages to standard output and to read from standard input, the code to perform the actual echo function is simple. First, the *File* class provides a *File.copyOver(src, dest)* method that copies the *src* file to the *dest* file.

The only logic we have to provide in WFCEcho1 is the *okayToCopy()* method. Just like its predecessor in the Echo1 program in Chapter 1, *okayToCopy()* checks whether the destination file exists, and if it does, checks whether it's okay to write over the destination file. The *File* class makes even this job a little easier. The *File.exists(name)* method returns *true* if a file of *name* exists. Since the *exists()* method is static, it's not necessary to create a *File* object before calling its *exists()* method.

What is *File*, anyway?

When I'm trying to understand a class, I like to see where it fits in the package hierarchy. Figure 2-1 shows the chain of *com.ms.wfc.io* classes of which *File* is a member.

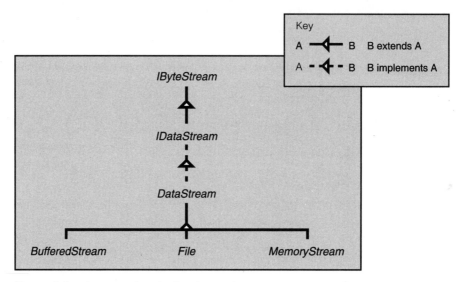

Figure 2-1. *The WFC I/O File class hierarchy.*

You can see that *File* extends a class called *DataStream*. Much like the Java standard *InputDataStream* and *OutputDataStream* classes, the WFC *DataStream* class provides formatting capability. This class provides methods to output *chars*, *ints*, *floats*, *doubles*, and *Strings* as well as *bytes*. You will also notice that *File* has two brethren, the *BufferedStream* and *MemoryStream* classes. *BufferedStream* provides a buffering capability, and *MemoryStream* allows file I/O to a byte array in memory.

NOTE The *DataStream* class, with its formatting capabilities, is much like the C++ *ios* class upon which most of the C++ *iostream* classes are built.

Interface-based packaging

The WFC package is interface-based, as opposed to other Java packages, which tend to be class-based. For example, notice that the *File* class extends the *DataStream* class; *DataStream* implements the *IDataStream* interface; and *IDataStream* in turn extends the interface *IbyteStream*. The methods of other WFC classes will (almost) never require a *File* object, or even a *DataStream* object. Instead, the methods of other classes require an object that implements the *IDataStream* interface or, more often, the *IByteStream* interface. Of course, you are free to pass a *File* object to such a method since the *File* object implements these interfaces. However, you might want to write your own class to implement one of these interfaces without basing your class on *DataStream*. This enables you to avoid the excess baggage of inheritance by implementing just those features required by the interface.

NOTE A class implements an interface using the *implements* keyword. An interface looks like a class prototype declaration except that it does not have any data members. Implementing an interface represents a promise to provide a function in your class for each of the prototype declarations in the interface. See Appendix A for more details.

NOTE Interface names under WFC always begin with a capital I. WFC avoids giving a class a name beginning with I. This makes interface names easy to pick out of a classy crowd.

Standard I/O with the *File* class

Notice how the WFCEcho1 program uses the class *File* to access standard I/O.

NOTE We'll see later in this chapter that the *IReader/IWriter* group of classes is better for accessing standard I/O.

The public static methods *File.openStandardInput()* and *File.openStandardOutput()* return a *File* object that is tied to the program's standard input and output. The *okayToCopy()* method in WFCEcho1 defines two local functions that access these standard *File* objects: *print()*, which performs output, and *read()*, which performs input.

NOTE   Like a file class in other languages such as C++, the single WFC class *File* is capable of both input and output.

The *print()* function is straightforward enough. The method *File.writeString-CharsAnsi()* outputs the *String* class object in ANSI format as required by the system console. The similarly named method *File.writeString()* outputs the string in Java's Unicode 16-bit format.

The *read()* function is slightly more complicated. This function uses the *File.readByte()* method to read individual keystrokes until it sees a letter. Like *File.writeString()*, the *File.readChar()* method reads Java 16-bit Unicode characters that require two 8-bit keystrokes. Therefore, *read()* calls *readByte()* instead of *readChar()*.

The *read()* function calls *readByte()* in a loop to read 8-bit characters (bytes) until it sees a character that is a letter. This loop is sort of a kludge: the *isLetter()* test makes sure that the program isn't confused by some stray carriage return or line feed left in the input buffer from a previous invocation of the program.

The *IReader/IWriter* Group

The *File* class looks downright clumsy when it accesses the keyboard for input. This is because *File* is not designed to handle ANSI input and output. A group of classes that implement the *IReader* and *IWriter* interfaces is much more adept at performing text I/O.

WFCEcho2

In the following WFCEcho2 application, the *okayToCopy()* method is rewritten to use the proper *IReader-based* and *IWriter*-based classes. Only the *okayToCopy()* method is shown here because most of the remainder of the program has not changed. The entire WFCEcho2 application is on the companion CD-ROM.

```
/**
 * Check the argument to see whether it exists, and then
 * whether it's okay to overwrite it. If not, it throws an
 * exception.
 *
 * @param outputFileName - the file name to overwrite
 */
private static void okayToCopy(String outputFileName)
    throws Exception
{
    // first check whether the file exists
    if (File.exists(outputFileName))
    {
        // it does, so check whether it's okay to overwrite it
        Text.out.writeLine("File exists. Overwrite? [Y or N]");
```

```
        String answer = Text.in.readLine();
        if (!answer.equalsIgnoreCase("Y"))
        {
            throw new Exception("Copy failed");
        }
    }
}
```

The first thing you will notice is the absence of the *print()* method. It has been replaced by a direct call to *Text.out.writeLine()*. The class *Text* is a placeholder for the public static members *in, out,* and *err. Text.out* is an object of class *TextWriter* that is tied to standard output. The *TextWriter* class is ready made to handle ANSI character output to the screen and to the printer through the *writeLine()* and *write()* methods. The *writeLine()* method tacks a newline character onto its output, whereas *write()* does not.

The *TextWriter* class, with its superior string-handling methods, is nice. However, the *File* class did okay in outputting ANSI characters; it was in performing ANSI character input that the *File* class fell down. The *TextReader* class is a big improvement over *File* for reading ANSI text strings. In WFCEcho2, I can use the single call to *Text.in.readLine()* to return a *String* object containing the entire line, without resorting to the tricks I had to use in WFCEcho1. The basic logic of the *okayToCopy()* method is identical to its predecessor.

Where do *TextReader* and *TextWriter* fit?

Figure 2-2 shows the hierarchy of the *IReader* and *IWriter* groups. The *IReader* interface defines the methods necessary to perform basic ANSI text output. The abstract class *Reader* implements these methods without knowing what type of object it is reading from. The concrete class *TextReader* extends the *Reader* class to read from a file. An underlying *File* class data member performs the output. Similarly, the class *StringReader* reads ANSI text from a Java *String* class.

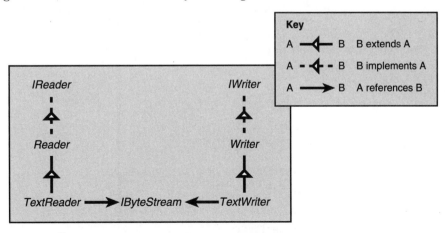

Figure 2-2. *The hierarchy of the* IReader *and* IWriter *groups.*

C++
NOTE The relationship between *TextReader* and *Reader* isn't unlike that of *ifstream* and *ios* in C++, with *File* playing the role of the C++ *filebuffer*. *TextReader* uses *Reader* to perform formatting chores and *File* to perform the actual input.

In a similar vein, the abstract class *Writer* implements the *IWriter* interface. The concrete *TextWriter* class uses the class *File* to extend *Writer*'s formatting capabilities to files. *StringWriter* performs the same trickery on Java strings.

Combining the Two Groups

TextReader and *TextWriter* each provide a simple constructor that takes as input the name of the file to be read or written. These default constructors take care of the chore of creating a *File* object and storing it away locally. When using these constructors, however, you must be willing to live with these default creation and storage options.

Fortunately, you don't have to live with these default constructors. You can construct the *File* object yourself and pass the result to the *TextReader* or *TextWriter* constructor. This combination gives you the control provided by the *File* class with the advanced text handling capabilities of the *TextReader* and *TextWriter* classes.

WFCEcho3

The WFCEcho3 program demonstrates how to combine the *File* class with the *Text-Reader* and *TextWriter* classes. Just to prove that we haven't lost any capability when compared with the standard Java *io* classes, WFCEcho3 performs Echo2's trick of capitalizing each word in the provided text.

```
/**
 * WFCEcho3 - copies the file args[0] to the file args[1]
 *            using the WFC I/O package. This time capitalize
 *            the output (the way we did in Echo2) by extending
 *            the TextWriter class and overriding write(String)
 *            and writeLine(String).
 */
import com.ms.wfc.io.*;

public class WFCEcho3
{
    // class variables
    TextReader  inText;   // used to read the input file
    TextWriter  outText;  // used to write to output file

    /**
     * The main entry point for the application.
     *
     * @param arg[0] - the input file
     * @param arg[1] - the output file
     */
```

```
public static void main(String[] args)
{
    // make sure that the user understands what
    // to do
    if (args.length != 2)
    {
        Text.out.writeLine("Enter: wfcecho3 source dest");
        Text.out.writeLine("to copy <source> to <dest>");
        System.exit(-1);
    }

    // catch any problems at the bottom of the
    // program - no matter what the problem, we'll
    // output an error message and terminate
    try
    {
        // copy the file
        WFCEcho3 wfc = new WFCEcho3(args[0], args[1]);
        wfc.copyOver();
    }

    // catch any exception thrown
    catch(Exception e)
    {
        Text.out.writeLine("Error:" + e.getMessage());
    }
}


/**
 * Open the specified input and output files as Text files.
 *
 * @param in - name of input file
 * @param out - name of output file
 */
public WFCEcho3(String in, String out)
    throws Exception
{
    // first open the input file and convert
    // it into a TextReader
    File inFile = new File(in, FileMode.OPEN,
                           FileAccess.READ);
    inText = new TextReader(inFile);

    // now the output file - prompt before overwriting
    File outFile = null;
```

(continued)

```
        try
        {
            outFile = new File(out,FileMode.CREATE_NEW, FileAccess.WRITE);
        }
        catch(IOException e)
        {
            okayToOverwrite(out);
            outFile = new File(out, FileMode.CREATE, FileAccess.WRITE);
        }
        outText = new CapTextWriter(outFile);
    }

    /**
     * Copy the file one line at a time.
     */
    public void copyOver()
        throws Exception
    {
        // read a line at a time and then
        // write it back out; once we read a
        // null, we've hit end-of-file
        String s;
        while((s = inText.readLine()) != null)
        {
            outText.writeLine(s);
        }
        outText.flush();
    }

    /**
     * Make sure it's okay to overwrite the existing file.
     *
     * @param outputFileName - the file name to overwrite
     */
    private static void okayToOverwrite(String outputFileName)
        throws Exception
    {
        // prompt the user
        Text.out.writeLine("File exists. Overwrite? [Y or N]");
        String answer = Text.in.readLine();
        if (!answer.equalsIgnoreCase("Y"))
        {
            throw new Exception("Copy failed");
        }
    }
}
```

Just as in Echo2, this program creates a class object and then uses that object to perform the copy operation in the following two statements:

```
// copy the file
WFCEcho3 wfc = new WFCEcho3(args[0], args[1]);
wfc.copyOver();
```

The constructor

The *WFCEcho3* class constructor uses the following statement to create a *TextReader* object from a manually created *File* object:

```
File inFile = new File(in, FileMode.OPEN, FileAccess.READ);
inText = new TextReader(inFile);
```

The first argument, *in*, contains the name of the file to open. The second argument, *FileMode.OPEN*, says that we want to open an existing file. If the file doesn't exist, it won't be created and an IOException will be thrown. The class *FileMode* is a placeholder for all of the different mode constants. The third argument, *FileAccess.READ*, says that we are opening the file in *READ* mode (as opposed to in *WRITE* or *READWRITE* mode). Opening a file in *READ* mode allows other applications to read the file at the same time. An optional fourth argument uses the *FileShare* placeholder to specify whether it's okay to share the file with other computers on the LAN. The next line passes the constructed file object to the *TextReader(File)* constructor.

The following lines from WFCEcho3 create a *TextWriter* object from a manually generated *File* object:

```
File outFile = null;
try
{
    outFile = new File(out,FileMode.CREATE_NEW, FileAccess.WRITE);
}
catch(IOException e)
{
    okayToOverwrite(out);
    outFile = new File(out, FileMode.CREATE, FileAccess.WRITE);
}
outText = new CapTextWriter(outFile);
```

This code segment first tries to create a new file in write mode using the *CREATE_NEW* mode. In *CREATE_NEW* mode, the constructor throws an exception if the file can't be created, perhaps because it already exists. The *WFCEcho3()* constructor catches that exception and retries the request using the *CREATE* mode, if *okayToOverwrite()* approves. Unlike *CREATE_NEW*, *CREATE* will delete the output file if it exists.

The *okayToOverwrite()* method is identical to its predecessors.

Copying

WFCEcho3 implements its own *copyOver()* method, which copies the contents of the source file to the destination file. It does this by reading the *TextReader* object one line at a time using the *readLine()* function and writing each line out to the *TextWriter* object using *writeLine()*. The fact that *readLine()* strips the newline character at the end of each line is of no consequence because *writeLine()* compensates by adding a newline character.

The *copyOver()* method continues to read and write until the *String* returned by *readLine()* is a *null*, indicating that the function has hit the end of the file.

Once control has exited the loop, *copyOver()* still has one important task to perform. Before returning, *copyOver()* calls *TextWriter.flush()*. Both *TextReader* and *TextWriter* are buffered, meaning that text is accumulated into conveniently sized blocks to improve program performance. This is particularly important when reading something as small as individual lines from a text file. Calling *flush()* forces any buffered output to disk. If you forget to call *flush()*, you are likely to lose the last few bytes of your output.

Alternatively, you can call *TextWriter.setAutoFlush(true)*. Setting autoflush to *true* forces *TextWriter* to flush its buffer after every call to *writeLine()*. While this will relieve you of the need to call *flush()*, the increased disk activity will most likely greatly reduce your application's performance.

> **NOTE**   Remember to set autoflush to *true* for small output files or for output files that are not accessed often, or to call *flush()* at the end to force all output buffers to disk.

Text.out flushes the buffer by default. Thus, if you are performing large amounts of output to standard output you probably want to set autoflush to *false*.

> **NOTE**   *TextWriter* doesn't support the C++ *iostream* equivalent *tie()*, by which the output file is automatically flushed when the program reads from the "tied" input file.

Capitalization

If you look more closely at the code snippet from the *WFCEcho3* constructor, the output *File* object is used to create a *CapTextWriter* class rather than a *TextWriter* class.

The class *CapTextWriter* extends *TextWriter* by capitalizing any text passed to its *write()* or *writeLine()* method. This class appears in the following code:

```
/**
 * CapTextWrite - a TextWriter that capitalizes
 *                output through write(String) or
 *                writeLine(String).
 */
import com.ms.wfc.io.*;
```

```java
public class CapTextWriter extends TextWriter
{
    String specialChars = " -.;\t\n";

    /**
     * Constructor.
     *
     * @param outFile - File object to use for output
     */
    public CapTextWriter(File outFile)
    {
        super(outFile);
    }

    /**
     * Write a line of text after capitalizing each word.
     *
     * @param s - the string to output
     */
    public void writeLine(String s)
    {
        super.writeLine(toUpper(s));
    }

    /**
     * Write a line of text after capitalizing each word.
     *
     * @param s - the string to output
     */
    public void write(String s)
    {
        super.write(toUpper(s));
    }

    /**
     * Capitalize the buffer provided.
     *
     * @param s - string to capitalize
     */
    String toUpper(String s)
    {
        // first convert the string into a string buffer
        StringBuffer sb = new StringBuffer(s);

        // loop through the new buffer, capitalizing any
        // alphanumeric character that appears after a special
        // character
```

(continued)

```
boolean cap = true;
int length = sb.length();
for (int i = 0; i < length; i++)
{
    char c = sb.charAt(i);

    // if we're supposed to cap this letter...
    if (cap)
    {
        // and if this is a letter...
        if (Character.isLetter(c));
        {
            // then capitalize and restore it
            c = Character.toUpperCase(c);
            sb.setCharAt(i, c);

            // okay, it's done
            cap = false;
        }
    }
    else
    {
        // (not in cap mode)
        // look for one of the special characters
        cap = (specialChars.indexOf((int)c) != -1);
    }
}

// now convert that back into a string for output
return sb.toString();
    }
}
```

Notice that this class is declared *public*. Being declared *public* means this class can be used by any other class that needs capitalization of output. It also means, however, that *CapTextWriter* must reside in its own *CapTextWriter.java* file.

Adding a file to your project

To create a new Java file and make it part of an existing project, activate Project Explorer and right-click the project name. From the context menu, select Add, and from the submenu, choose Add Class. Visual J++ will prompt you for the class name. In this case, providing the name *CapTextWriter* provides you with an empty Java source file and attaches that file to the project.

> **NOTE**   Adding a file to the project ensures that the file is recompiled whenever the project is rebuilt and the file has changed.

If the Java file you want to add to the project already exists, select Add from the context menu. Choose Add Class, select the Existing tab, and select the Java file to add.

Converting text to upper case in *CapTextWriter*

The constructor for the *CapTextWriter* class does nothing more than pass its argument to the base class constructor.

> **NOTE** When used as a function, *super()* invokes the base class constructor. When used in this way, *super()* can be called only from the constructor and it must be the first line of the constructor.

CapTextWriter defines the method *toUpper(String)* to convert the *String* passed to it into an equivalent *String* but with each word capitalized. The *toUpper()* method uses the same logic as the *toUpper()* method in the Echo2 program. It first converts the input *String* into a *StringBuffer* object. *StringBuffer* is more efficient to use when you are modifying the text string often. In addition, the *StringBuffer* class provides the convenient *charAt()* and *setCharAt()* methods.

Just as in Echo2, *toUpper()* loops through each character in the *StringBuffer* object. If the *cap* flag is *true* and the character is a letter, *toUpper()* converts the character to upper case and writes it back into the *StringBuffer* object before setting *cap* to *false*.

If *cap* is false, *toUpper()* uses the *String.indexOf()* method to compare the retrieved character to a string of characters it knows to be word separators. If the index returned by *indexOf()* is −1, the character was not one of the separator characters and *cap* is set to *false* again. If the index is anything other than −1, the character was a word separator and *cap* is set to *true*.

The *CapTextWriter* class calls *toUpper()* on the *String* input. It then overrides the *write()* and *writeLine()* methods by calling *super.write()* and *super.writeLine()* to perform the actual output.

> **NOTE** When used in this way, *super* is a *this* pointer that has been converted to the current class's base class. Thus, if *this* is of class *CapTextWriter*, *super* points to the current object but is of class *TextWriter*. The absence of a *super* pointer in C++ forces the C++ programmer to refer to the base class by name from within the code. This is a source of errors when the base class changes. The Java programmer never has to refer to the base class except in the *extends* statement.

Outputting Different Object Types

The *Writer* class supports the output of various object types. This is demonstrated in the code on the following page.

```
/**
 * WriteTest1 - outputs several types of objects
 *              using the Writer class.
 */
import com.ms.wfc.io.*;

public class WriteTest1
{
    /**
     * The main entry point for the application.
     */
    public static void main (String[] args)
    {
        TextWriter out = Text.out;
        out.setAutoFlush(true);

        out.writeLine("This is a String");
        out.write("This is an int = ");
        out.writeLine(10);

        out.write("This is a double = ");
        out.writeLine(10.10);

        out.write("This is a Student = ");
        out.writeLine(new Student("Jenny", "Davis", 12, 3.5));

        try
        {
            Thread.currentThread().sleep(2000);
        }
        catch(Exception e)
        {
        }
    }
}

class Student
{
    String firstName;
    String lastName;
    int    semesterHours;
    double gradePointAverage;

    Student(String firstName,
            String lastName,
            int    semesterHours,
            double gradePointAverage)
    {
```

```
        this.firstName = firstName;
        this.lastName  = lastName;
        this.semesterHours = semesterHours;
        this.gradePointAverage = gradePointAverage;
    }
}
```

Both *write()* and *writeLine()* are overloaded for each of the intrinsic variable types plus *String* and *Object*. Providing a *writeLine(Object)* allows the *Student* object created in the above example to be passed to *writeLine()*. However, as you can see in Figure 2-3, the output is not what you might expect.

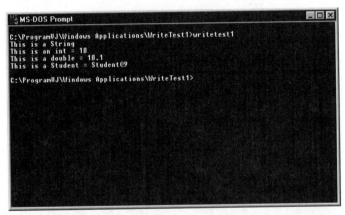

Figure 2-3. *The output from* writeLine(Object) *is disappointing.*

NOTE   The call to *sleep()* delays the program long enough to allow the user to see the output before the program terminates and the MS-DOS window is closed. This delay isn't necessary when you execute the program from the command line.

Extending *writeLine()*

Fortunately, *writeLine(Object)* calls *Object.toString()* to create a string it then passes to *writeLine(String)*. This means that by overriding the *toString()* method you can extend *writeLine()* to output any new class you might define.

The following code snippet from the WriteTest2 example shows *Student* extended by the addition of a *toString()* method. Figure 2-4 shows the output from WriteTest2.

```
class Student
{
    String firstName;
    String lastName;
    int    semesterHours;
    double gradePointAverage;
```

(continued)

```
Student(String firstName,
        String lastName,
        int    semesterHours,
        double gradePointAverage)
{
    this.firstName = firstName;
    this.lastName  = lastName;
    this.semesterHours = semesterHours;
    this.gradePointAverage = gradePointAverage;
}

public String toString()
{
    StringWriter sw = new StringWriter();
    sw.write(lastName + ", " + firstName);
    sw.write(" - "
             + gradePointAverage + "/"
             + semesterHours
             + " [GPA/semesterHours]");
    return new String(sw.getStringBuffer());
}
}
```

Figure 2-4. *The output from* writeLine(Object) *with* Student.toString() *added.*

CONCLUSION

In this chapter, you've seen how you can use the WFC *com.ms.wfc.io* package to enhance your applications; examined the *IByteStream* family of classes, including its most important member *File;* and learned how the constructors of *File* provide the same fine-grain control as file type objects in other Visual languages. In addition, we examined the *IReader/IWriter* family of classes, which are designed to provide easy access to ANSI text input and output.

For simplicity's sake, I've limited the discussion so far to console applications. Windowed applications use the WFC *com.ms.wfc.io* package in exactly the same way.

Chapter 3 will look at the WFC Utility (*com.ms.wfc.util*) package. Once again, we can examine the majority of this package while remaining under the simplifying confines of the console application.

Chapter 3

The WFC
Utilities Package

The WFC utility package *com.ms.wfc.util* consists of a collection of classes that make your console applications easier to write and more trouble-free. In this chapter, I'll present some of the more useful classes contained in the utility package.

We'll begin with the *Debug* class, taking some time to discuss how this class integrates with the Microsoft Visual J++ 6 debugger. From there, we'll go through a series of collection classes, starting with the arrays class. All the code discussed in this chapter is located in the Windows Applications folder on the companion CD.

THE *DEBUG* CLASS

Debugging is one of those topics that books and language developers never seem to give enough attention to. A good debugging environment aids the programmer by providing a more user-friendly environment within which to develop products faster, and aids users by helping to produce a more bug-free product.

Visual J++ 6 supports debugging in three ways: with its first-rate debugger, with its conditional compilation feature, and with its implementation of the WFC *Debug* class.

The Visual J++ 6 Debugger

The Visual J++ 6 debugger provides numerous capabilities. Even if you are familiar with the features of other debuggers, you will find it worthwhile to quickly review the features of the Visual J++ 6 debugger. A thorough explanation of the proper use of a debugger is beyond the scope of this book, but I'll touch on some of the most commonly used features.

Setting breakpoints

The most important capability of any debugger is the ability to set breakpoints. A breakpoint is a flag indicating that program execution is to stop at a particular line of code. You can set breakpoints only on executable statements; that excludes declarations, *import* statements, *package* statements, and comments.

The simplest way to set a breakpoint is to place the cursor on the line that you want to be a breakpoint and then click the Insert Breakpoint button on the Debug toolbar. (Selecting Insert Breakpoint from the Debug menu or pressing the F9 key works just as well.) A solid red circle in the left margin of the Text editor indicates a breakpoint.

You can set more than one breakpoint before executing the program. As soon as execution reaches any breakpoint that you have set, your program is paused and the Microsoft Visual Studio window reappears. A yellow arrow points to the breakpoint where your program is paused.

Stepping through the program

Once your program is paused at a breakpoint, you can continue program execution by clicking the Continue button on the Debug toolbar or by choosing Continue from the Debug menu. Alternatively, you can step through the program. Stepping means the program executes one statement at a time, pausing after each statement.

An issue arises when you are stepping through a program. When the debugger reaches a function call, does it treat the call as a single statement or does it step into the function and pause at each statement in the function? The debugger enables you to choose how to deal with function calls by providing two commands. The Step Over command treats the function call as a single statement, executing every instruction within the function without pausing until control returns to the calling method. (Step Over is something of a misnomer since the debugger doesn't step over anything.) The Step Into command causes the program to step into the function, pass control to the first statement of the function, and pause execution.

For statements that call functions whose source code isn't accessible, Step Over and Step Into are the same. For example, with library functions Step Into doesn't step into the function because it can't. In this case, Step Into acts just like Step Over.

To terminate execution of a program that is paused, either click the End button on the Debug toolbar or choose End from the Debug menu.

NOTE A Microsoft Windows–based program that has been paused by the debugger looks like it has crashed; its window won't refresh even when it gains focus.

Displaying debug information

Being able to pause the program isn't much use if you can't see what your program is doing. Fortunately, the Visual J++ debugger provides several windows to give insight into the program's inner workings. You can open any of these windows by selecting Debug Windows from the View menu and then selecting the appropriate command from the submenu.

To view the values of simple variables while a program is paused, you place the mouse pointer on the variable you are curious about. If the variable is in scope, after a second or two its value appears. However, this method works only for simple variables—variables of an intrinsic type. Besides, going around pointing at each variable can get tiresome if you're debugging a large function.

If you want to see all of the variables defined in your function, open the Locals window. This window displays all variables that are local to the current function along with their current value and type. As you step through your program, values that change are highlighted in red. The Watch window is similar to the Locals window, except the Watch window enables you to select what it displays and it isn't limited to variables local to the current function. Both windows allow you to expand objects to see the values of the objects' data members.

Another useful display window is the Call Stack window. This window displays the name of the current function along with the value of the arguments passed to it. Below that, the Call Stack window displays the function that called the current function and the arguments passed to it. The Call Stack window repeats this process until it reaches the first function. (In the case of a console application, the first function is always *main()*.) Double-clicking any function moves the display to the point where that function was called. A solid green arrow in the left margin points to the call.

Figure 3-1 shows the Visual J++ debugger with the Locals, Watch, and Call Stack windows visible at one time. In the background, you can see the Text editor window with the source code of the class being debugged. Currently, the program is paused on the breakpoint line designated by an arrow.

The lower left corner of the figure shows the Watch window with a Watch set on *this,* which has been partially expanded to display many of the internal data members. In the lower right is the Locals window showing the local variables. The call stack trace is in the upper right in the Call Stack window.

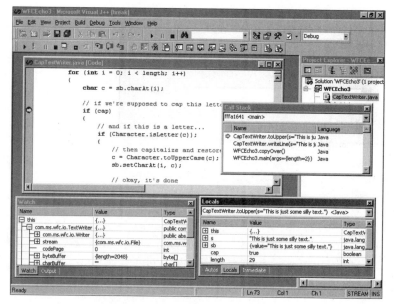

Figure 3-1. *The Visual J++ debugger showing the main debug windows open simultaneously on the program WFCEcho3.*

Setting conditional breakpoints

Often you will want to set a breakpoint that stops the program only when certain conditions are true. For example, if a problem occurs only after the program has processed most of the records in a large data file, you wouldn't want to hit a breakpoint at every record; you would want to pause only on the first record that creates the problem. A conditional breakpoint can make debugging much simpler in instances such as this.

NOTE The program always stops when a regular breakpoint is encountered. The program stops when it encounters a conditional breakpoint only when a series of conditions are true.

To set a conditional breakpoint, first you set a breakpoint in the normal fashion. Then you choose Breakpoints from the Debug menu. Select the breakpoint you want to edit, and then choose Properties; the dialog box shown in Figure 3-2 is displayed. This figure shows that the breakpoint on line 16 won't pause the program until the tenth time the program passes through line 16 of *CapTextWriter.toUpper()* and the value of the variable *cap* is *true*.

NOTE In the Java Breakpoint Properties dialog box, the Condition box can contain any Boolean expression. For conditions too complicated to be easily expressed in a breakpoint condition, you can write your own static Boolean function to invoke from the Condition box.

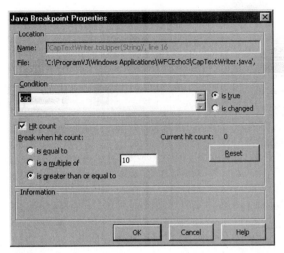

Figure 3-2. *The Java Breakpoint Properties dialog box showing a conditional breakpoint.*

You can see the details of a breakpoint from the Text editor by pointing at the breakpoint symbol on the left with the mouse pointer. After a second or two, a small window pops up displaying the details of the breakpoint.

CONDITIONAL BREAKPOINTS:
HOW DOES VISUAL J++ DO THAT?

A conditional breakpoint isn't exactly what it seems. Program execution pauses every time control reaches a breakpoint whether the breakpoint is conditional or not. If the breakpoint is unconditional, control passes to the Text editor immediately. If the breakpoint is conditional, Visual J++ first evaluates the conditional expression and the hit count. If the conditional expression or the hit count are not satisfied, Visual J++ immediately continues running the program.

The net effect is that if a condition isn't met, the conditional breakpoint slows program execution somewhat. Exactly how much it slows down depends on how often the conditional breakpoint is hit. For example, a conditional breakpoint set in a small loop will probably slow the program down a lot. Using conditional breakpoints is still a lot better than stepping through code by hand, but program execution speed is something to keep in mind.

Setting a break on exception

Another type of breakpoint is designed to alleviate a frustrating situation that can arise when you test your program. Let's say you know that under a given set of inputs your program aborts by throwing an exception. (If your program handles the exception, it might not abort, but the condition causing the exception still might be unexpected.) You know which exception is being thrown and the input that causes it, but you don't know what condition is causing it to be thrown.

The break-on-exception breakpoint handles this situation by pausing program execution immediately when an exception is thrown. The settings you choose when you set the breakpoint determine whether the program pauses if the exception is handled.

To set a break-on-exception breakpoint, choose Java Exceptions from the Debug menu. From the list of exception classes, select the type of exception you want to trap. If you select Break Into The Debugger, the exception you've selected, plus all subclasses of that exception, are marked with a white "X" in a red ball, as shown in Figure 3-3. (Normally the ball is gray.)

When the exception you've selected occurs, the debugger immediately takes control. You can see at which line the exception was thrown, the value of all variables (by means of the Locals and Watch windows), and a trace of how control got to the exception in the first place (by means of the Call Stack window).

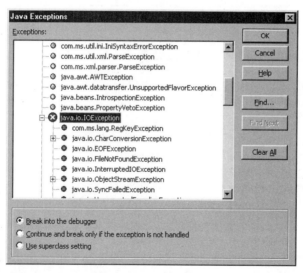

Figure 3-3. *The Java Exceptions dialog box showing a break-on-exception breakpoint for the* IOException *class.*

Conditional Compilation

It is often useful to add code during debugging that should not be included in the final release version. One common reason for adding this extra code is to display data that would be inconvenient to view through the debugger. Visual J++ provides for this need by including the *#if, #endif,* and *#define* conditional directives.

The *#if* directive must be followed by a Boolean expression. If the expression evaluates to *false*, any code appearing between *#if* and *#endif* is excluded from compilation. The *#if* directive is unlike a normal *if* statement in that the expression following *#if* can only be defined as one of the following types:

■ Intrinsic constants.

■ Constants that have been defined using the *#define* directive.

■ Constants that have been defined among the Project Properties in the Conditional Compilation Symbols text box on the Compile tab.

> **NOTE** This feature is called conditional compilation because the compilation of code between *#if* and *#endif* is conditional upon the value of the expression following the *#if*. I should stress that conditional compilation is a compile-time test involving constants defined by means of either a compiler switch or the *#define* expression.

> **C++ NOTE** No Java compiler prior to Visual J++ 6 shares this useful conditional compilation feature with its C++ cousin.

Defining conditional compilation constants in the Project Properties dialog box is the most useful of the three options. For example, the constant *DEBUG* is automatically defined for the Debug configuration, as shown in Figure 3-4.

Defining *DEBUG* as shown in Figure 3-4 is equivalent to using the following statement:

```
#define DEBUG
```

This in turn is equivalent to the following statement:

```
#define DEBUG true
```

Visual J++ assumes that the value of an undefined compile-time constant is *false*.

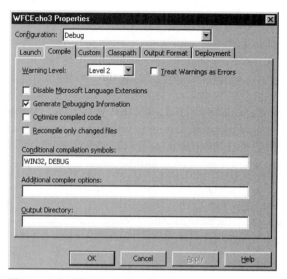

Figure 3-4. *The Compile tab of the Project Properties dialog box enables the programmer to define compile-time constants quickly.*

Since *DEBUG* is defined under the Debug configuration but not under the Release configuration, I can easily add the following boldface code to the *toUpper()* function:

```
/**
 * Capitalize the buffer provided.
 *
 * @param s - string to capitalize
 */
String toUpper(String s)
{
    #if DEBUG
        Text.out.writeLine("Capitalizing:" + s);
    #endif

    // first convert the string into a string buffer
    StringBuffer sb = new StringBuffer(s);

    // and so on...
}
```

The call to *writeLine()* is included in the compiled executable file under the Debug configuration but isn't included under the Release configuration.

Using the *Debug* Class

The classes within the Java libraries, including the classes in the WFC library, are very good about testing for and detecting erroneous conditions. It is uncommon for a Java program to simply crash without an exception being thrown that gives some indication of the problem.

You should follow this example in classes that you write. For example, the *CapTextWriter.toUpper(String)* method from the WFCEcho3 program discussed in Chapter 2 accepts an input *String,* which it then converts to uppercase. Unfortunately, *toUpper()* doesn't test the assumption that it will be passed a valid *String* object; it trusts the program to do the right thing. What if the program passes a *null* instead?

> **NOTE** Unlike in C++, a *null* is the only invalid value that the program could pass.

The following shows the *CapTextWriter* class updated to test for and handle invalid input.

```
/**
 * CapTextWrite - a TextWriter that capitalizes
 *                output through write(String) or
 *                writeLine(String).
 */
import com.ms.wfc.io.*;
import com.ms.wfc.core.*;
import com.ms.wfc.util.Debug;

public class CapTextWriter extends TextWriter
{
    String specialChars = " -.;\t\n";

    /**
     * Constructor.
     *
     * @param outFile - File object to use for output
     */
    public CapTextWriter(File outFile)
    {
        super(outFile);
    }

    /**
     * Write a line of text after capitalizing each word.
     *
     * @param s - the string to output
     */
```

(continued)

65

```java
public void writeLine(String s)
{
    // the following code outputs a message to the debug
    // console if a null value is passed
    Debug.assert(s != null, "Null string passed to writeLine");
    assert(s != null, "Null string passed to writeLine");
    super.writeLine(toUpper(s));
}


/**
 * Write a line of text after capitalizing each word.
 *
 * @param s - the string to output
 */
public void write(String s)
{
    Debug.assert(s != null, "Null string passed to write");
    assert(s != null, "Null string passed to write");
    super.write(toUpper(s));
}


/**
 * If the condition c is false, throw an exception
 * containing the text s.
 *
 * @param c - condition to test
 * @param s - string to output
 */
void assert(boolean c, String s)
    throws WFCInvalidArgumentException
{
    if (!c)
    {
        throw new WFCInvalidArgumentException(s);
    }
}


/**
 * Capitalize the buffer provided.
 *
 * @param s - string to capitalize
 */
String toUpper(String s)
{
    // same as before...
}
}
```

If the Boolean value is *false*, *Debug.assert(boolean, String)* outputs the *String* to the debugger's output window. The locally defined *assert(boolean, String)* throws an exception containing the message string if the Boolean assertion is *false*.

> **NOTE** Notice that *assert()* throws the exception *WFCInvalidArgument-Exception*. This is the exception thrown by *TextWriter.writeLine()*. If a method that overrides another method throws an exception, it must throw the same exception class or a subclass of that exception class.

The DebugTest application tests the updated *CapTextWriter* class while simultaneously demonstrating another *Debug* helper method.

```
/**
 * DebugTest - demonstrate the features of the Debug class.
 */
import com.ms.wfc.io.*;
import com.ms.wfc.util.Debug;

public class DebugTest
{
    /**
     * The main entry point for the application.
     */
    public static void main (String[] args)
    {
        try
        {
            try
            {
                // create a CapTextFile on standard output
                CapTextWriter out =
                    new CapTextWriter(File.openStandardOutput());
                out.setAutoFlush(true);

                // try a legal test message
                out.writeLine("this is a test string");

                // output object information to debug output
                out.writeLine(Debug.getObjectText(out));

                // now try a null message
                String s = null;
                out.writeLine(s);
            }
            catch(Exception e)
            {
```

(continued)

```
                        Debug.printException(e);

                        Text.out.writeLine();
                        Text.out.writeLine("Exception message follows:");
                        Text.out.writeLine(e.getMessage());

                        Text.out.writeLine();
                        Text.out.writeLine("Stack traceback follows:");
                        e.printStackTrace();

                        Thread.sleep(2000);
                    }
                }
            catch(Exception e)
                {
                }
        }
}
```

The program begins by creating a *CapTextWriter* object on standard output. Setting automatic flushing to *true* ensures that any valid output occurs before the program terminates.

Armed with this output object, the program first outputs a valid string. It follows this by outputting debug information to the debugger's output window. This has effect only when the program is running under the debugger; otherwise, *Debug.getObjectText()* returns an empty string.

The program then purposely sets a String variable to *null* and passes this to *writeLine()*.

The exception thrown from *writeLine()* is caught on the line after the call. First, the *catch* phrase outputs exception information to the debug window. Again, this *Debug* function has no effect unless executed under the debugger. Next the exception handler outputs the exception message followed by an exception stack trace.

The output from this program is shown in Figure 3-5.

NOTE   I ran this program by invoking *jview /vst DebugTest.class*. Doing this generates slightly more detailed stack trace output (the */vst* stands for verbose stack trace). This works only if the application was compiled with the debug setting enabled.

Figure 3-5. *The output from the DebugTest program showing the detailed stack traceback.*

CONTAINERS

As their name implies, containers are objects that contain other objects. You are familiar with the most common of all containers, the array. A positive feature of arrays is that they are efficient, both in how they are allocated and in how they are accessed. A negative feature is that arrays are not convenient: they are fixed in size and they are not indexed, so it is difficult to find specific elements within an array.

The WFC *util* package provides a number of other container types. No single container type solves all of the problems of the array—there is no perfect container. However, each container class provides some unique advantage. In addition, the utility package provides a number of utilities that aid in sorting the contents of a container.

NOTE As WFC grows, other forms of containers will likely be added to those currently present.

Arrays

Mechanisms for creating an array and accessing its members are built into the Java language. There is no keyword for sorting an array, however. Fortunately, the *Array-Sorter* class is provided to sort arrays of objects.

Since we will need something to sort, let's begin by defining a *Student* class.

Creating the *Student* class

The following *Student* class is the most rudimentary class I could devise to define a student. This class is stored in the file Student.java.

```
/**
 * A generic Student class.
 */
public class Student
{
    String name = null;
    int    ssNumber = 0;

    /**
     * Create a real student.
     *
     * @param name - the name of the student to create
     * @param ssNumber - the Social Security number
     */
    Student(String name, int ssNumber)
    {
        this.name     = name;
        this.ssNumber = ssNumber;
    }

    /**
     * Retrieve the Social Security number.
     */
    int getSSNumber()
    {
        return ssNumber;
    }

    /**
     * Convert Student into an informative string.
     */
    public String toString()
    {
        String s = name + "(" + ssNumber + ")";
        return s;
    }
}
```

The *Student* class must of course have a *name* member to record the student's name. Since students at our school are registered by Social Security number, the *Student* class needs an *ssNumber* data member as well. The *Student* constructor initializes these two data fields, while the *getSSNumber()* and *toString()* methods allow access to the values stored in the data fields. A host of other fields and associated methods might be required by a real student class, but these will do for the examples in this chapter.

Sorting an array of objects

Sorting arrays of information is a common problem—so common, in fact, that *com.ms.wfc.util* includes an *ArraySorter* class. This class can sort an array of any type of objects as long as you can provide a comparison function. You do this by creating a class that implements the *IComparer* interface. This interface defines only a single method, *int compare(Object o1, Object o2)*. This method returns a value of 1 if *o1* is greater than *o2*, −1 if *o2* is greater than *o1*, and 0 if the two values are equal. Exactly what is meant by the phrase "*o1* is greater than *o2*" is up to you to define.

The following SortStudent program creates an array of *Student* objects and then sorts it using the *ArraySorter* class.

```
import com.ms.wfc.io.*;
import com.ms.wfc.util.*;

/**
 * Sort a Student class using the ArraySorter class.
 */
public class SortStudent
{
    /**
     * The main entry point for the application.
     *
     * @param args Array of parameters passed to the application
     * via the command line.
     */
    public static void main (String[] args)
    {
        // create an array of students
        Student[] array = new Student[]
                {
                    new Student("Shepherd, James", 234567890),
                    new Student("Smith, Harold",  123456789),
                    new Student("Davis, Stephen", 345678901)
                };

        // output the unsorted array
        output("Unsorted array", array);

        // sort the array
        ArraySorter.sort(array, new StudentComparer());

        // now output again
        output("Sorted array", array);
    }
```

(continued)

```
/**
 * Output an array.toString() to standard output.
 *
 * @param msg - message to tack onto output
 * @param array - array to output
 */
static void output(String msg, Object[] array)
{
    Text.out.writeLine(msg);
    for (int i = 0; i < array.length; i++)
    {
        Text.out.writeLine(array[i].toString());
    }
    Text.out.writeLine();
}
}


/**
 * A class to provide the Student comparer method.
 */
class StudentComparer implements IComparer
{
    /**
     * Compares two students by comparing their ssNumbers.
     *
     * @param o1 - first student
     * @param o2 - second student
     * @return 1, 0, or -1 depending on relationship of o1 to o2
     */
    public int compare(Object o1, Object o2)
    {
        Student s1 = (Student)o1;
        Student s2 = (Student)o2;

        if (s1.ssNumber < s2.ssNumber)
        {
            return -1;
        }
        if (s1.ssNumber > s2.ssNumber)
        {
            return 1;
        }
        return 0;
    }
}
```

As always, control begins with the method *main()*. The program begins by creating an array of three *Student* objects.

NOTE The definition of the *array* variable demonstrates a syntax unique to Java. The first line declares an array of class *Student[]*. The calls to *new* within the braces initializes the array to contain three *Student* objects.

NOTE I used the Add Class command on the Project menu to add the Student-.java file to the project. This ensures that there is always an up-to-date copy of *Student.class* in the same directory as the remainder of the project.

Once it is created, the array is output to standard output using the local static *output()* method. The array of *Student* objects is then sorted by invoking the sole method of *ArraySorter*, the public static method *sort()*. The first argument is the array of *Student* objects. The second argument is an object that implements the *IComparer* interface.

The class *StudentComparer* implements the *IComparer* interface by providing a *compare(Object, Object)* function capable of sorting students. The *compare()* function begins by casting the *o1* and *o2* objects into the *Student* objects *s1* and *s2*. This cast is justified because we know that this class is used only on arrays of *Student* objects. Once the two objects *s1* and *s2* have been created, *compare()* returns a –1, 0, or 1 based on a comparison of the objects' Social Security number values.

The *output()* method is then called again to output the sorted array and demonstrate that *ArraySorter* worked as planned.

The output of the *SortStudent* program is shown in Figure 3-6.

Figure 3-6. *The* ArraySorter *class makes it easy to sort arrays of objects, like the* Student *objects shown here.*

NOTE C++ programmers will recognize this definition of an interface with a single method as Java's replacement for function pointers. The Java approach is both more type safe and safer. You'll see Java defining an interface with a single method again in the discussion of event handlers in Part II.

Sorting an array of strings

In the *StudentSort* example, I chose to sort the students by Social Security number. The most common approach to sorting, however, is to put objects in alphabetical order based on their string representation. Accordingly, the WFC *util* package includes the *StringSorter* class. This class serves a number of functions related to sorting strings.

You can use the *StringSorter* class to sort arrays of *String* objects as follows:

```
// create an array
String[] stringArray = {"array1",
                        "array3",
                        "array2"
                       };

// now sort the array
StringSorter.sort(stringArray);
```

The *StringSorter* class can also be used to sort other types of objects. For objects other than *String* objects, *StringSorter.sort()* invokes the *toString()* method to convert the objects to *String* objects and then sorts the objects based on the returned strings.

For example, the following code segment would sort the students in alphabetical order based on their names followed by Social Security number, since this is the value returned by *Student.toString()*.

```
// declare an array of Students
Student[] array = new Student[]
            {
                new Student("Shepherd, James", 234567890),
                new Student("Smith, Harold",   123456789),
                new Student("Davis, Stephen", 345678901)
            };

// now sort them based on value returned by toString()
StringSorter.sort(array);
```

The *StringSorter.sort()* method provides other syntaxes, some of which allow for the inclusion of sort options. The options are defined as *final static* fields within the *StringSorter* class itself. Since these fields are defined as bit fields, multiple options can be combined with an OR (|) operator to increase the amount of control the application program has over the sort.

For example, the following call is identical to the previous example except it sorts the *Student* objects based on the name values without regard to case or any special symbols that might appear in their names.

```
StringSorter.sort(array, StringSorter.IGNORECASE |
                  StringSorter.IGNORESYMBOLS);
```

The *StringSorter* class can handle a large percentage of array sorting problems.

Lists

A list is similar to an array except that a list isn't a fixed size. In many applications, the program doesn't know beforehand how many objects it needs to contain.

There are two flavors of lists. The generic list is contained in *java.util.Vector.* The version specific to WFC is *com.ms.wfc.util.List.* Although the methods of these classes are not identical, they share most of the same features.

A common use for a list might be in a program that reads student names from a file. Such a program doesn't know how many student names are in the file until it has gone through the process of reading them. With a list, the program can read each student name and add it to the list. With an array, the program would have to make two passes through the file: an initial pass to count the number of student names so that the program would know how big to allocate the array, followed by a second pass to actually read the names and assign them to the array.

NOTE   For really large data files, your application should use a database rather than a list.

Sorting lists of students

The following example reads student information from the keyboard and then sorts it. This version uses a list because it doesn't know how many students the user is likely to enter.

```
import com.ms.wfc.io.*;
import com.ms.wfc.util.*;

/**
 * Add a series of Student objects to a list and then output
 * the list.
 */
public class StudentList
{
    /**
     * The main entry point for the application.
     */
    public static void main (String[] args)
    {
        // create an empty list
        List list = new List();

        // enter Student objects until user enters null
        for (;;)
        {
            Text.out.writeLine(
                "Enter student name (blank line to terminate)");
            String name = Text.in.readLine();
```

(continued)

75

```
                    if (name.equals(""))
                    {
                        break;
                    }
                    Text.out.writeLine("Enter Social Security number:");
                    int ssNumber = Integer.parseInt(Text.in.readLine());

                    Student s = new Student(name, ssNumber);
                    list.addItem(s);
                }

            // output the list
            output("Unsorted list", list);

            // now sort the list
            list.sort(new StudentComparer());

            // output the sorted list
            output("Sorted list", list);
        }
        /**
         * Output the contents of a list to standard output.
         *
         * @param label - message to tack onto output
         * @param list - list to output
         */
        static void output(String label, List list)
        {
            Text.out.writeLine();
            Text.out.writeLine(label);
            int length = list.getSize();
            for (int i = 0; i < length; i++)
            {
                Object o = list.getItem(i);
                Text.out.writeLine(o.toString());
            }
        }
    }
}

/**
 * A class to provide the Student comparer method.
 */
class StudentComparer implements IComparer
{
    // same as in StudentSort example...
}
```

The program begins by creating an empty list. It then enters a loop that prompts the user for the student's name. If the user enters an empty line, control exits from the loop. Once the program has read the name, it then prompts for and reads the student's Social Security number, which it converts into an integer. The name and Social Security number are used to create a *Student* object which is appended to the list by calling *list.addItem()*. (Note that the program is not tolerant of illegal input.) Once the list has been created, *main()* continues as in the previous example by displaying the unsorted list, sorting the list, and then displaying the sorted list.

The *List.sort()* method is similar to the *ArraySorter.sort()* method in that it relies on a user-defined *IComparer* object to sort whatever type of object is contained in the list. The *StudentComparer* class used in this example is identical to the version used in the SortStudent example.

One other difference between lists and arrays is in the way that the elements of the list are accessed in the *output()* method. *List.getItem(i)* returns the *i*th member in the list, whereas an array would be accessed directly, as in *Array[i]*.

Figure 3-7 shows the output from a trial run of the StudentList example.

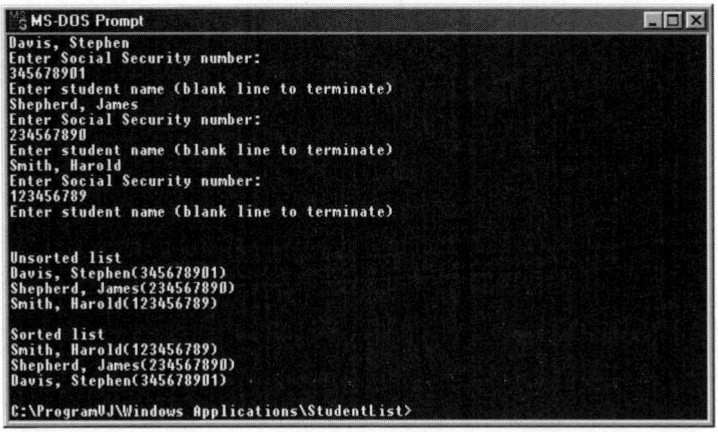

Figure 3-7. *An example run of StudentList showing the sorted output following the unsorted output.*

Using *StringSorter* to sort lists

In the StudentList example, I could have sorted the list by simply changing the *StudentComparer* class as follows:

```
/**
 * The following StudentComparer sorts the students by
 * name while ignoring the case of the letters used.
 */
class StudentComparer implements IComparer
{
    public int compare(Object o1, Object o2)
    {
```

(continued)

```
        return StringSorter.compare(o1.toString(),
                                     o2.toString(),
                                     StringSorter.IGNORECASE);
   }
}
```

This version of *StudentComparer* uses the *StringSorter.compare()* routine to perform a comparison of the string returned by *Student.toString()* while ignoring the case.

Enumerating through a list

In the two student program examples, you might have noticed how it was necessary to modify the *output()* function to match the particular type of container we were using. Wouldn't it be nice if there was a way to access all types of containers irrespective of their internal details? In fact, there is.

The *IEnumerator* interface provides universal access to all types of containers. This interface provides three methods for navigating the contents of a container, as shown in the following table.

Method	*Description*
hasMoreItems()	Returns *true* as long as the enumerator isn't pointing to the last member.
nextItem()	Returns a reference to the object pointed at by the enumerator, and moves the enumerator to the next object in the container.
reset()	Resets the enumerator to the beginning of the container.

The following version of *output()* works for arrays, lists, and other types of containers:

```
static void output(String label, IEnumerator enum)
{
    Text.out.writeLine();
    Text.out.writeLine(label);
    while(enum.hasMoreItems())
    {
        Object o = enum.nextItem();
        Text.out.writeLine(o.toString());
    }
}
```

Rather than accept a reference to the container itself, this version of *output()* accepts an enumerator that has been initialized to point to the container. After outputting the preamble, *output()* iterates through the container using *nextItem()* until *hasMoreItems()* returns *false.*

To invoke this version of *output()*, the array-based *SortStudent* class would use the following:

```
// create an enumerator for the array
output("Sorted list", new ArrayEnumerator(array));
```

The list-based *StudentList* would make the following call:

```
// pass a List enumerator to output
output("Sorted list", list.getItemEnumerator());
```

The actual class of enumerator being passed to *output()* is different in the two cases, but since both implement the *IEnumerator* interface, *output()* doesn't care.

> **NOTE**   Arrays are handled differently than other types of containers, because arrays are an intrinsic part of Java and can't be subclassed. All other container types work like *List* by providing a *getEnumerator()*-type method.

Hash Tables

Neither the array nor the list are convenient for looking up items. In the case of the unsorted student list, if the user wanted to look up a student by Social Security number, the program would be forced to perform a linear search until the Social Security number is found.

The *HashTable* class is particularly convenient and computationally quick for looking up items. The following example program demonstrates the use of the *Hash-Table* class to store *Student* objects and then recall them rapidly:

```
import com.ms.wfc.io.*;
import com.ms.wfc.util.*;

/**
 * Add a series of Student objects to a hashed dictionary.
 */
public class StudentHash
{
    /**
     * The main entry point for the application.
     */
    public static void main (String[] args)
    {
        // create a default-sized hash table
        HashTable table = new HashTable();

        // enter Student objects until user enters null
        for (;;)
        {
```

(continued)

```
            // get the Student object
            Text.out.writeLine(
                "Enter student name (blank line to terminate)");
            String name = Text.in.readLine();
            if (name.equals(""))
            {
                break;
            }
            Text.out.writeLine("Enter Social Security number:");
            int ssNumber = Integer.parseInt(Text.in.readLine());
            Student student = new Student(name, ssNumber);

            // add it to the table using the Social
            // Security number as the key
            Integer key = new Integer(student.getSSNumber());
            table.setValue(key, student);
        }

        // now look up entries in the hash table by Social
        // Security number
        for(;;)
        {
            // get the Social Security number
            Text.out.writeLine("Enter S. S. number to look up entry:");
            String keyString = Text.in.readLine();
            if (keyString.equals(""))
            {
                break;
            }

            // look up the student by number entered
            Integer key = new Integer(keyString);
            Student s = (Student)table.getValue(key);

            // output the student value returned
            if (s == null)
            {
                Text.out.writeLine("Entry not found");
            }
            else
            {
                Text.out.writeLine(s.toString());
            }
        }
    }
}
```

This version reads entries similarly to its list-based predecessor. To add the student entries to the container, this version uses the *HastTable.setValue(Object key, Object value)* method. The *key* argument will be used to look up the *value* argument later. Since we want to look up students by Social Security number, the program uses the *int* returned from *getSSNumber()* as the key; however, since the key must be an object, the program must first convert the *int* into an *Integer*.

Once the student information has been stored in the hash table, the program uses *HastTable.getValue(key)* to look up the student. The Social Security number read from the user entry is converted into an *Integer* object, which is passed to *getValue()*. If *getValue()* returns a *null*, no student was found with that Social Security number.

CONCLUSION

This chapter has demonstrated a portion of WFC's *util* package, an assortment of classes you can put to good use in your console applications. You've seen the *Debug* class and you've seen a few of the container classes including *List, HashTable,* and a series of classes to support arrays.

Part II
Windowed Applications

In Part I, we concentrated on Microsoft Visual J++ console applications. These types of programs are okay for accomplishing simple tasks. Modern programs, however, require the use of colorful windows that use sophisticated controls.

In this section, you'll learn how to create windowed applications. Chapter 4 covers non-platform-specific windowed applications. Because there is only so much you can do using generic techniques, the balance of Part II is devoted to Microsoft Windows–specific graphical user interface (GUI) components.

By the time you've finished Part II, you'll be in a position to write sophisticated and professional Windows-based applications.

Chapter 4

Generic Windowed Applications

Microsoft Visual J++ 6 is extremely adept at creating windowed Microsoft Windows–specific applications. This doesn't mean, however, that Visual J++ 6 can't generate a generic, platform-independent windowed application; it can do this just fine.

To prove this point, we'll write the same windowed program twice. In this chapter, we'll use the Abstract Windowing Toolkit (AWT) to create a generic application that will execute on practically any platform. In Chapter 5, we'll use the Windows Foundation Classes for Java (WFC) tools available in Visual J++ 6 to turn this generic application into a Windows-specific application.

> **NOTE** If you don't care anything about writing platform-independent windowed applications, or if you are already familiar with AWT, you might want to go directly to Chapter 5 for its discussion of Microsoft Windows–specific applications.

WHY SOLVE THE SAME PROBLEM TWICE?

The exercise of solving the same application twice, once using AWT and again using WFC, serves three purposes. First, there can be times when you will need to write a windowed application that is portable across multiple platforms. Java is one of the few modern languages that provides that capability.

Second is the possibility that you might be asked to use your PC as a cross-platform development tool to create an application designed to execute on a different platform than your PC is using. This chapter gives you much of the knowledge you would need to satisfy such a demand. Along the way, we'll examine some of the strengths and weaknesses of AWT.

Third, seeing how an AWT application is constructed will give you a vantage point from which you can view the Windows-specific Rapid Application Development (RAD) tool approach demonstrated in Chapter 5. From looking at the two different approaches, you'll gain an appreciation of the differences and similarities between the AWT and WFC approaches.

NOTE   This chapter doesn't discuss the Java Foundation Classes (JFC) introduced with Java 1.1 from Sun Microsystems, Inc.; however, JFC classes and AWT share most properties. JFC simply adds graphical features to those supported by AWT.

THE PROBLEM

Our goal is to create an application that opens a window looking reasonably like that shown in Figure 4-1.

In this application, the user enters any text in the text box. If the user then enters a file name in the File Name box and chooses Submit, the program saves the contents of the text box to an ANSI 8-bit character file and terminates. If the user chooses Cancel, no file is created and the contents of the text box are abandoned as the program closes. The user also can specify an existing filename as a parameter when starting the program, in which case the program will open with the contents of that file in the text box.

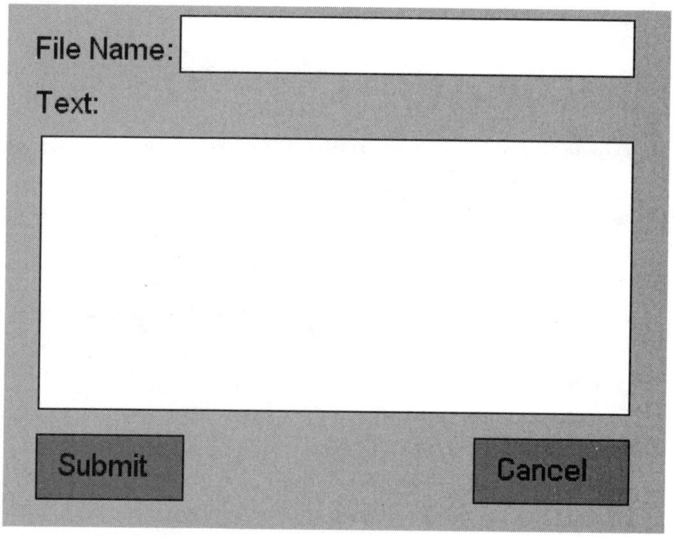

Figure 4-1. *The application window we are trying to create.*

AWT's User Interface Problem

Small deviations in the output between different graphical libraries are to be expected. You can't expect any two libraries to generate identical output. This has been something of a problem for AWT.

Perhaps you remember the religious wars that used to rage over the Apple Macintosh interface. Apple had strictly defined the Macintosh interface in every detail. The size and placement of buttons was prescribed. The placement of menu items was hotly debated. Programs that committed the unforgivable sin of changing the size of a dialog box button or moving a menu item were resoundingly punished in the market place by disappointing sales. Similar, although less intense, wars raged over the user interfaces of other operating systems.

This isn't to say that such standards are bad—quite to the contrary. I admit to some confusion and frustration when a Windows-based application's first two menus are not File and Edit and the last menu isn't Help. Standards enable users to quickly acclimate to different user interfaces.

Roughly speaking, there are three windowed user interface standards in use today: Windows, Motif (for UNIX), and Apple Macintosh. All three are similar, but each has its own unique peculiarities. To name one trivial difference, Windows uses a two-button mouse, while Motif requires a three-button mouse and Macintosh advocates claim that there's no need for more than one. Proponents of each interface claim small interface differences to be enhancements, but for the most part they're just differences.

User interface differences pose a problem for AWT. A platform-independent AWT application is exactly that: platform independent. The AWT application shares traits with all three of the standard interfaces. Due to differences in the Java Virtual Machine (VM) that executes the Java byte codes, an AWT application looks slightly different—slightly more Windows-like—on a Windows machine than on a Motif machine. At the same time, an AWT application doesn't conform completely to any one of the three common interfaces.

An AWT application really presents a fourth interface style, different from each of the three major standards and not widely adopted by any of them. For applets that reside in the Internet browser world, this isn't much of a problem; the World Wide Web presents its own set of user interface standards. However, it is a problem for applications. Unless the AWT interface style becomes widely adopted, it's difficult to see how AWT-based applications can compete with existing user interface standards.

> NOTE   The ability to handle a single file name argument gives a program lim-
> ited drag-and-drop capability. As we will see later in the book, when you drag
> a file to our application under Windows, Windows will automatically run the pro-
> gram and provide the file name as its first argument.

Figure 4-1 on page 86 shows the interface drawn rather simply using a paint program so as not to demonstrate a preference between the AWT or WFC approach.

The exact color of the buttons, text boxes, and window background isn't criti-cal as long as the controls stand out from the background. Although not shown in Figure 4-1, the application should respond appropriately to the window minimize, maximize, and close buttons. For example, clicking the close button in the upper right corner of the window should have the same effect as choosing Cancel.

INTRODUCTION TO THE ABSTRACT WINDOWING TOOLKIT

Let's look at some of the principles behind AWT before looking at an AWT-based solution to our hypothetical programming problem. AWT consists of a set of classes contained within the package *java.awt*. In this section, we'll study the contents of the *java.awt* package.

AWT Components and Containers

Many of the classes that make up AWT represent widgets of one type or another. The purposes of classes like *Button*, *Label*, *Checkbox*, and *Scrollbar* are clear. The hier-archy of these widget classes is shown in Figure 4-2.

The first thing to notice in Figure 4-2 is that the classes making up AWT have a common base class in *Component*. The abstract class *Component* defines a set of methods that all AWT components share. For example, all components share the *resize()* method to resize an object and the *setVisible(boolean)* method to make an object visible or invisible.

The second thing you might notice from Figure 4-2 is that the AWT component classes break down into two groups. The simple component classes are those along the right side of the figure. These classes represent discrete widgets that might ap-pear on the interface.

The second set of classes is the compound components that extend the abstract class *Container*. *Container* classes are classes that can contain components. For example, a *Window* class might contain multiple *Button* objects. Thus, the most important method that *Component* adds is the method *add()*, which enables a pro-gram to add a component to the container. For example, a button can be added to a dialog.

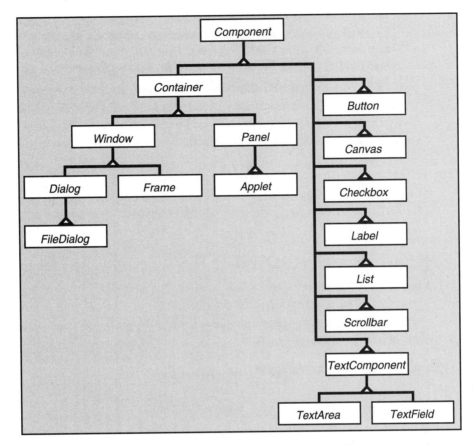

Figure 4-2. *The class hierarchy of the Abstract Windowing Toolkit.*

Several subclasses of *Container* are of particular note. The class *Applet* represents an applet that runs within an Internet browser. We'll return to this class in the discussion of applets in Part III.

Frames, dialogs, and panels

The class *Frame* represents what we as users might call a window. A *frame* is a window with defined edges, a title bar, and minimize, maximize, and close buttons on the far right side of the title bar. By default, the frame can be resized by dragging any side or corner with the mouse. (The resizing capability can be turned off programmatically.)

The class *Dialog* represents a window that is similar in appearance to a panel. The distinguishing feature of a dialog is that it can be modal, meaning that mouse and keyboard input is allowed to the dialog box only as long as the dialog box is visible. A panel represents an area of the screen. The class *Panel* is the simplest concrete implementation of the abstract *Container* class.

NOTE Remember that you can't create an instance of an abstract class because an abstract class has one or more abstract methods. An abstract method is a method that has been declared but not implemented—in other words, a method containing no code. A subclass of an abstract class becomes concrete by implementing all of the abstract methods.

Unlike a frame, a panel has no visible borders and no title bar. Since a panel isn't visible, it doesn't really have any properties of its own. This might lead you to wonder, "What good is a panel anyway?"

NOTE The class *Container* extends the class *Component*, which means that a container is a component. A container can therefore be added to a container like any other component. There is one exception: even though *Frame* extends *Component*, because of its window-sizing buttons a frame can't be added to a container.

The primary use of a panel is to group components located within another container, such as a frame or dialog. This still doesn't completely address the need for a panel, but before I try to fully answer that question let's look at a simple example of a frame without panels: SimpleFrame.

NOTE The complete code samples from this chapter are located in the Generic Applications folder in the sample files on the companion CD.

A simple frame example

```
/**
 * This class demonstrates a simple AWT frame.
 */
import java.awt.*;

public class SimpleFrame extends Frame
{
    /**
     * The main entry point for the application.
     */
    public static void main (String[] args)
    {
        SimpleFrame sf = new SimpleFrame();
        sf.init();
    }

    /**
     * Add a few components to the container and
     * make the frame visible.
     */
    public void init()
    {
```

```
          // add a few components
          add(new Label("Enter name:"));
          add(new TextField(10));
          add(new Button("Submit"));

          // now set the size...
          this.setSize(300, 100);

          // and make the results visible
          setVisible(true);
     }
}
```

Like all the applications we have seen so far in this book, this program was created using the Console Application Wizard. Also, like all Visual J++ applications, this program begins execution with the *public main()* method. The *main()* method performs two steps. First it creates an object of class *SimpleFrame*. It then invokes the *init()* method of *SimpleFrame* to populate the frame with components.

NOTE Using an *init()* method to populate the frame is common because it follows the pattern of an applet, as we'll see in Part III.

The *init()* method adds three components:

- A label bearing the text "Enter name:".

- An edit box into which the user can enter text.

- A button bearing the label "Submit".

Finally, the *SimpleFrame* object sets its size to be 300 units wide and 100 units tall. Since display characteristics are somewhat machine-dependent, a unit has never been exactly defined; however, on most platforms, including the PC, it corresponds to a pixel.

The result of this program is shown in Figure 4-3.

Figure 4-3. *The disappointing results from our first AWT frame.*

Notice that only the Submit button is visible in the resulting frame. Although the output is disappointing, there are a lot of features present for relatively little code. By extending *Frame, SimpleFrame* has a title bar, although it doesn't populate the title bar with a title. In addition, *SimpleFrame* has the three window buttons. The maximize and minimize buttons actually work, but the close button has no effect. This is because the base class *Frame* knows how to handle maximizing and minimizing the window but doesn't know how you want to terminate your program gracefully.

AWT Layout Managers

In the output from the *SimpleFrame* object shown in Figure 4-3 on the preceding page, only the Submit button is visible. Why is this so?

The problem is that as the program added components to the *SimpleFrame*, it didn't tell the *Frame* base class where to put each object. Not knowing any differently, *Frame* put each object in the middle, one on top of the other. Since the button was the last object to be added, it's the only one visible.

"No problem," says the experienced Microsoft Visual C++ or Microsoft Visual Basic programmer. "I'll just add a few calls to the *setPosition()* method to position the components relative to each other in the frame." However, this doesn't work because AWT has no such method. This seems surprising until you consider that the same Java program is intended to work on different types of machines with different screen resolutions and sizes. Java applets must even be able to run under the control of an Internet browser. Therefore, Java can make no assumptions about the size or resolution of the display.

The border layout manager

Rather than use absolute positioning, Java uses a series of layout managers that position the components relative to each other in the container. All of the layout managers use some form of relative positioning. Instead of using pixel positions to set the absolute position of each component in SimpleFrame, you, for example, place one component to the left of another or put a component on the right side of the frame. With some layout managers, you can divide the available horizontal space, vertical space, or both, evenly between the components.

The default layout manager for the *Frame* class is *BorderLayout*. The *Border-Layout* layout manager attaches components relative to the four borders of the frame. For whatever reason, the founders of Java weren't fond of left and right directions; they named the frame borders West, East, North, and South instead. (They could have just as well used Port, Starboard, Bow, and Stern.) Whatever is left over is called Center (there is no compass direction for where you're at).

The changes to the *init()* method to utilize the *BorderLayout* layout manager are shown in the following code.

```
public void init()
{
    // add a few components
    add("West",   new Label("Enter name:"));
    add("Center", new TextField(10));
    add("East",   new Button("Submit"));

    // now set the size...
    this.setSize(300, 100);

    // and make the results visible
    setVisible(true);
}
```

Figure 4-4 shows the results of this version of the *init()* method.

Figure 4-4. *The somewhat improved output obtained by using relative placing of the components within the frame.*

While Figure 4-4 is certainly an improvement over its predecessor, this still isn't really what we might want. For example, the *TextField* object is several rows high even though it can accept only a single line of text. Is there not some way to further improve the appearance of SimpleFrame?

Using panels with the *BorderLayout* layout manager

To improve the appearance of SimpleFrame, you must understand exactly how the *BorderLayout* manager works. It takes the following steps:

1. It allocates space to the components assigned to the North and South sides of the frame. These objects are stretched horizontally to consume all of the available horizontal space from one side of the frame to the other, and are assigned only as much vertical space as they need.

2. It expands the components assigned to the West and East sides of the frame vertically to fill any remaining vertical space left by the North and South objects. These objects are assigned only as much horizontal space as they need.

3. It expands the Center component to fill any remaining space.

    The result looks like the diagram shown in Figure 4-5.

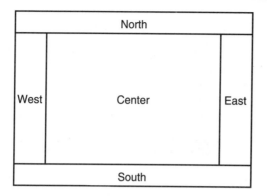

Figure 4-5. *The regions of the* BorderLayout *layout manager.*

One improvement over the last version of the *init()* method would be to bundle the prompt and the input text area into a single line and place this near the top of the frame. We could then put the Submit button at the bottom. Under this scenario, the center would remain empty.

The following version of *init()* does exactly this through the use of the *Panel* class:

```
public void init()
{
    // add a few components
    // use a panel to combine the label and text field
    // along the top of the display
    Panel panel = new Panel();
    panel.setLayout(new BorderLayout());
    panel.add("West",   new Label("Enter name:"));
    panel.add("Center", new TextField());
    add("North", panel);

    // now put the button at the bottom
    add("South", new Button("Submit"));

    // now set the size...
    this.setSize(300, 100);

    // and make the results visible
    setVisible(true);
}
```

Here you can see that the panel is assigned a *BorderLayout* object using the *setLayout()* method. We didn't have to specify the layout for the *Frame* object because the default layout is already *BorderLayout*, but the panel receives a different layout by default. The label and text field are then attached to the *panel* object.

Once the layout manager for the panel has been established, the label is placed on the West side of this invisible panel. All remaining space is allocated to the text field. Once it is completed, the *panel* object is added to the north side of the frame. The border layout manager of the frame will stretch the panel horizontally to fill the available horizontal space. The vertical size of the panel is set by the space needs of the label and the text field. The Submit button is then placed along the South side of the window. The result is shown in Figure 4-6.

Figure 4-6. *The improved output resulting from the use of panels to group components.*

Other layout managers

There are many other Visual J++ layout managers besides the *BorderLayout* layout manager. For example, the simple *FlowLayout* manager allocates space from left to right in a row until it runs out of horizontal space, at which point it moves down to the second row and starts allocating horizontal space again.

A complete discussion of layout managers is beyond the scope of this book. In any case, by means of judicious and clever use of panels you can generally achieve the results you want with the *BorderLayout* manager and perhaps one or two other managers.

AWT Events

By using panels and the *BorderLayout* manager, we have improved the appearance of SimpleFrame, but the program still doesn't do anything. Neither choosing the Submit button nor clicking the frame's close button has any effect. In this section, I will show you how to modify SimpleFrame to actually do something. This new program, SimpleActiveFrame, terminates when you click the close button or displays the contents of the text field on standard output when you choose the Submit button.

```
/**
 * This class demonstrates a simple AWT frame that
 * can respond to a button press. (This application uses
 * the older Java 1.0-style event processing.)
 */
import java.awt.*;

public class SimpleActiveFrame extends Frame
{
```

(continued)

```java
// name field
TextField name;

/**
 * The main entry point for the application.
 */
public static void main (String[] args)
{
    SimpleActiveFrame sf = new SimpleActiveFrame();
    sf.init();
}

/**
 * Add a few components to the container and
 * make the frame visible.
 */
public void init()
{
    // add a few components
    // use a panel to combine the label and text field
    // along the top of the display
    Panel panel = new Panel();
    panel.setLayout(new BorderLayout());
    panel.add("West",   new Label("Enter name:"));
    panel.add("Center", name = new TextField());
    add("North", panel);

    // now put the button at the bottom
    add("South", new Button("Submit"));

    // now set the size...
    this.setSize(300, 100);

    // and make the results visible
    setVisible(true);
}

/**
 * When the Submit button is pressed, the action event
 * will bubble up to the frame. Read the name and
 * display on standard output.
 *
 * @deprecated
 */
public boolean action(Event e, Object o)
{
    // read the text out of the TextField
    String s = name.getText();
```

```
        // display it on standard output
        System.out.println("Name = \'" + s + "\'");

        // returning true indicates that we've handled
        // the event successfully
        return true;
    }


    /**
     * Events are always passed to handleEvent() first.
     * Action events get passed on to action() by default.
     * Other events are either handled or ignored by default.
     * Here, we handle the WINDOW_DESTROY event, which is otherwise
     * ignored.
     *
     * @deprecated
     */
    public boolean handleEvent(Event e)
    {
        // if this is a WINDOW_DESTROY event...
        if (e.id == Event.WINDOW_DESTROY)
        {
            // terminate the program
            System.exit(0);

        }
        return super.handleEvent(e);
    }
}
```

The only difference between the *SimpleActiveFrame* class and its predecessor *SimpleFrame* is the addition of the two methods *action()* and *handleEvent()*. The *action()* method handles the clicking of the Submit button and *handleEvent()* handles the *WINDOW_DESTROY* event, which occurs when the user clicks the window's close button.

What's an event?

An event is an object that is generated when something happens. For example, if the user clicks a button, the VM generates a button click event. When the user presses a key, the VM generates two events: one for the key going down and another for the key going up. Through these events, the VM communicates to the program what is going on in the outside world.

All events extend the class *Event*. This base class contains basic information, like a reference to the object that originated the event and the type id of the event. A reference to the type id is generally useful for window events; *Event* contains a list of possible ids. For mouse events, the *Event* class records the position of the mouse at the time of an event such as the button down or button up event. There is also a time in the *Event* class, but this does not refer to the time of day or the time of year; you can use this time only to compare two events to determine which occurred first or how far apart in time the two events were.

As events occur, the VM creates an *Event* object and passes it to the *Component.handleEvent()* method.

> **C++ NOTE**   Visual J++ applications have a Windows message dispatch loop, just like a Visual C++ program does; however, this loop is hidden from the Visual J++ programmer by the Java event mechanism. Windows messages get turned into *Event* objects which are processed as described here. The Visual J++ programmer does have access to the idle loop processing by means of WFC, as we will see in Chapter 10.

The *Component.handleEvent()* method ignores all events. This method is overridden in superior classes, such as *Frame*, to handle whatever events they can. For example, the *Frame.handleEvent()* method knows how to handle the *WINDOW_MINIMIZE* and *WINDOW_MAXIMIZE* events.

The *Frame.handleEvent()* method does not know how to handle the *WINDOW_DESTROY* event; *SimpleActiveFrame* must override *handleEvent()* to provide such processing. If the id of the *Event* object passed to *SimpleActiveFrame.handleEvent()* is *Event.WINDOW_DESTROY*, then *SimpleActiveFrame.handleEvent()* calls *System.exit()* to terminate the program. For other *Event* ids, *SimpleActiveFrame.handleEvent()* passes the *Event* object to *super.handleEvent()*. This allows the base class to continue to provide whatever default processing it is capable of.

> **CAUTION**   If you override *handleEvent()*, be sure to pass any events you do not handle on to *super.handleEvent()* for processing.

Notice that the return type of *handleEvent()* is *boolean*. A *true* return value indicates that the event has been processed and does not require any further processing. The *SimpleActiveFrame.handleEvent()* method includes a *return true* statement even though control will never return from the *exit()* call. This serves no purpose other than instructional.

What's an action?

There is a certain class of events called action events. An *action event* is an event resulting from some action by the user. For example, a button click is an action event.

Like all events, action events first get passed to the *handleEvent()* method. If they are not processed there, action events then get passed on to the *Component.action()* method. Like the *handleEvent()* method, the *action()* method can be overridden to process the event. For example, in SimpleActiveFrame we could have extended *Button* into a new class, say *SubmitButton*, with its own *action()* method.

This method would automatically get invoked whenever that button was clicked.

It isn't necessary to create a new subclass for every AWT object you create, however. The default processing for *Component.action()* is to pass the event to the *action()* method of the parent component, so you can handle all action events in the frame if you prefer. The *SimpleActiveFrame.action()* method reads the text from the text field using the *getText()* method and passes the text on to *println()* to be output to standard output. This output appears in the DOS window from which the application was started.

> **NOTE** There are reasons why you might not want to handle action events in the frame. Depending on your design, it might be cleaner to put the action event handler in a *SubmitButton* class so that all submit processing is in one place.

The only real difference between the *action()* method and the *handleEvent()* method is that the *action()* method has fewer events to deal with. For example, since SimpleActiveFrame has only one component, the Submit button, we were able to assume that the action event originated from the button component.

Why the warnings?

You might notice that when you compile SimpleActiveFrame several warnings appear in the task list indicating that *handleEvent()* and *action()* have been "deprecated." This means that in one of the base classes these methods have been flagged with the *@deprecated* pragma. (In fact, I have even flagged both methods with the *@deprecated* pragma in this class just to show you how it's done.)

Flagging a method as deprecated indicates that although the method works now, the designers of Visual J++ might remove that method from future versions of the class library. The *action()* and *handleEvent()* methods are deprecated because Java 1.1 introduced a new event-handling approach. I have presented the version 1.0 event-handling approach here because it is so pervasive in the Java community that all Java programmers need to be familiar with it for the foreseeable future.

I will present Java 1.1 event handling in Chapter 5, where we can contrast it with WFC event handling.

THE AWT SOLUTION

Now that you are armed with some knowledge of component layout managers and event handling, let's return to solving the original problem. The AWT-based solution to the problem posed by Figure 4-1 on page 86 is shown in the WindowedApp program beginning on page 100.

```
/**
 * This class implements a windowed application using the
 * Abstract Windowing Toolkit.
 */
import java.awt.*;
import java.io.*;

public class WindowedApp extends Frame
{
    // topEdit - the edit field for the file name
    TextField topEdit     = new TextField();

    // edit - the multiline text area
    TextArea  edit         = new TextArea();

    // we'll need two buttons
    Button    okButton     = new Button("OK");
    Button    cancelButton= new Button("Cancel");

    // panels are invisible containers that you can place in
    // a frame to achieve (more or less) the grouping effect
    // of the text fields and buttons that you desire
    Panel     topPanel    = new Panel(new BorderLayout());
    Panel     centerPanel = new Panel(new BorderLayout());
    Panel     bottomPanel = new Panel(new BorderLayout());
    Panel     bottomLeftPanel  = new Panel(new BorderLayout());
    Panel     bottomRightPanel = new Panel(new BorderLayout());

    /**
     * The main entry point for the application.
     *
     * @param args Array of parameters passed to the application
     * via the command line.
     */
    public static void main (String[] args)
    {
        // create a WindowedApp and then call its init()
        // method; this makes the application solution as much
        // like an applet as possible
        (new WindowedApp(args)).init();
    }

    /**
     * Constructor - if arguments are passed to the program,
     * assume that the first argument is the name of a file
     * to load into the edit window.
     */
    public WindowedApp(String[] args)
```

```
{
    // if there's an argument, this is an input file
    if (args.length == 1)
    {
        try
        {
            // open an input file with the argument provided
            FileReader fr = new FileReader(args[0]);

            // now read the contents of the file and store
            // it into the edit buffer...
            int input;
            String s = new String();
            while ((input = fr.read()) != -1)
            {
                char c = (char)input;
                s = s + c;
            }
            s = convertFrom(s);
            edit.setText(s);

            // and store the name into the file name text line
            topEdit.setText(args[0]);
        }

        // if there's an error, just report it and give up any
        // hope of opening the file
        catch(Exception e)
        {
            System.out.println("Can't open input file");
        }
    }
}

/**
 * Set up the WindowedApp window.
 */
public void init()
{
    // start by resizing the frame and setting its title
    // (leave the frame resizable)
    setSize(300, 150);
    setTitle("AWT Application");

    // first, handle the file name text field -
    // put the label on the left, a small space on the
    // right, and the text field in the middle
```

(continued)

```
            topPanel.add("West", new Label("File Name:"));
            topPanel.add("Center", topEdit);
            topPanel.add("East", new Label(""));

            // create two buttons at the bottom;
            // put each in its own panel with a
            // little space on each side
            bottomLeftPanel.add("West", new Label(""));
            bottomLeftPanel.add("East", new Label(""));
            bottomLeftPanel.add("Center", okButton);

            bottomRightPanel.add("West", new Label(""));
            bottomRightPanel.add("East", new Label(""));
            bottomRightPanel.add("Center", cancelButton);

            // now place the two button panels in the bottom
            // panel - use a grid layout, because this divides
            // the available space up evenly between the two
            // buttons (one row, two columns)
            bottomPanel.setLayout(new GridLayout(1, 2));
            bottomPanel.add("West", bottomLeftPanel);
            bottomPanel.add("East", bottomRightPanel);

            // put the text entry field in the center panel -
            // put the label at the top and let the text area
            // take up the rest of the space
            centerPanel.add("North", new Label("Edit:"));
            centerPanel.add("Center", edit);

            // establish a border layout manager for the frame
            // and then add the three panels
            setLayout(new BorderLayout());
            add("North", topPanel);
            add("South", bottomPanel);
            add("Center", centerPanel);

            // put a little space on either side of the edit area
            add("West", new Label(""));
            add("East", new Label(""));

            // finally, now that we're all ready,
            // show the frame (frames are created hidden)
            setVisible(true);
        }

    /**
     * Process the OK button.
     */
```

```java
void processOK()
{
    // if there's a file name in the text field,
    // write the contents of the edit field to that file
    String sFileName = topEdit.getText();
    if (sFileName != null)
    {
        try
        {
            // read the text field
            String s = edit.getText();
            s = convertTo(s);

            // write the contents of the text field
            // to a file using the file writer
            FileWriter fw = new FileWriter(sFileName);
            fw.write(s);
            fw.close();

            // verify that all went well
            System.out.println("File " + sFileName + " saved");
        }
        catch(Exception e)
        {
            // notify error message
            System.out.println("Output error: " + e.getMessage());
        }
    }

    // exit program
    processCancel();
}


/**
 * Convert output for display on MS-DOS terminal by adding
 * carriage returns after every newline character.
 */
String convertTo(String s)
{
    int offset = 0;
    while ((offset = s.indexOf("\n", offset)) != -1)
    {
        StringBuffer sb = new StringBuffer(s);
        sb.insert(++offset, '\r');
        s = sb.toString();
    }
    return s;
}
```

(continued)

```java
/**
 * Convert input by stripping carriage returns.
 */
String convertFrom(String s)
{
    int offset = 0;
    String cr = "\r";
    while((offset = s.indexOf(cr, offset)) != -1)
    {
        String s1 = s.substring(0, offset);
        String s2 = s.substring(offset + 1, s.length());
        s = s1 + s2;
    }
    return s;
}


/**
 * Process Cancel button by terminating program.
 */
void processCancel()
{
    System.out.println("Program terminating");
    System.exit(0);
}


/**
 * Events are passed to the window to inform it of every
 * action that occurs to the window. We are interested in
 * the following events:
 * WINDOW_DESTROY - occurs when user clicks the x window dressing
 * OK button - save file and exit
 * Cancel button - just exit
 */
public boolean handleEvent(Event e)
{
    // if the event target is a button...
    if (e.target instanceof Button)
    {
        // check for OK button...
        if (e.target == okButton)
        {
            processOK();
            return true; // return true to indicate that
                         // we've handled the event
        }

        // now check for Cancel button
        if (e.target == cancelButton)
```

```
        {
            processCancel();
            return true; // control will never get here
        }
    }

    // if this is a Window destroy event...
    if (e.id == Event.WINDOW_DESTROY)
    {
        // then process it like a Cancel
        processCancel();
        return true;    // control will never reach here
    }

    // OK, we don't know what it is -
    // pass it on to the base class for default processing
    return super.handleEvent(e);
    }
}
```

As always, execution begins with the *main()* method. This method creates a *WindowedApp* object and then uses this object to call *init()*.

C++ NOTE This construct of creating an object by calling *new* and then immediately using the object to invoke a method is a direct application of the C++ philosophy that every expression has a type and a value (even though this construct isn't actually supported in C++).

Again please note that the statements in the *init()* method could have been placed directly in the constructor; however, the type of work done by *init()* must be separated from the constructor in applets, so Java programmers routinely separate it in applications as well.

The class initialization performs the following steps:

1. It invokes the constructor of the super class. In this case, *Frame.Frame()* builds the base frame object.

2. It constructs each of the member objects. This includes *topEdit, edit, okButton, cancelButton*, and a number of *Panel* objects. Each of the panels is created with *BorderLayout* as its layout manager. (The default for a *Panel* object is the *FlowLayout* layout manager.)

3. It executes the code contained in the constructor. In this case, the constructor code checks to see if a file name was provided as an argument to the application. If it was, the constructor opens that file using a *FileReader* object.

4. It reads the contents of the file one character at a time until the end-of-file character is reached. Each character is returned as an *int* and so must be converted into a character before being added to the string *s*.

5. Once input is complete, the constructor stores the accumulated string *s* into the *edit* object using the *setText()* method.

6. It then assigns the file name to the *topEdit* object.

> **NOTE** The file name text area is of type *TextField*, whereas the edit area is of type *TextArea*. A *TextField* type is designed to accommodate a single line of text, whereas the considerably more sophisticated *TextArea* type can handle multiple lines of text.

The *init()* method starts by sizing the frame to some convenient size. It then sets the title of the frame. This title appears on the frame's title bar.

To understand the remainder of *init()*, you'll need to understand the plan of attack. This plan is shown in Figure 4-7. First the overall frame is divided into three panels. The upper panel contains the file name label and the file name edit box. Adding a null label to the right side of the panel keeps the edit box from extending all the way to the right edge of the frame.

On the bottom are the two buttons OK and Cancel. These are each placed in their own panel so that they can be surrounded by null labels, to give a little separation between the buttons and their surroundings. The button panels are attached to a common *bottomPanel* object using a *GridLayout* layout manager. *GridLayout* will divide the available horizontal space equally between the two buttons.

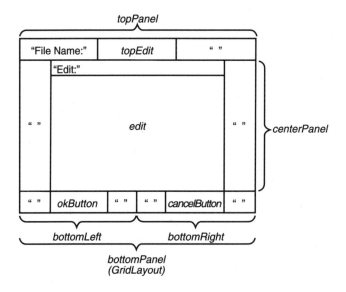

Figure 4-7. *The plan of attack for laying out the components for WindowedApp.*

Finally, the text box is placed in the middle of the center panel with null labels on both sides for separation.

Event handling

All of the event handling in WindowedApp is performed in the *handleEvent()* method, rather than by processing the button input in the *action()* method.

The *target* field of the *Event* passed to *handleEvent()* references the object that first received the event. Thus, if the *target* is an instance of *Button*, this event must have originated from clicking one of the buttons.

C++
NOTE The *instanceof* keyword replaces the dynamic cast mechanism in C++; it returns *true* if the object on the left is an instance of the class on the right. This includes any base classes. Thus, an object that is an instance of *Button* is automatically an instance of *Component*. All objects are instances of *Object*.

If the event target is the *okButton* object, the program calls *processOK()*. If the event target is the *cancelButton* object, the program passes control to *processCancel()*. The program checks for the *WINDOW_DESTROY* event that would originate from clicking the close window button. The program handles the close window button exactly like the *cancelButton* object.

NOTE Calling functions to handle the various events rather than handling them in place is a good idea because it keeps the *handleEvent()* method as simple as possible.

The *processCancel()* method outputs a termination message prior to calling *System.exit()* to terminate the application.

The *processOK()* method begins by getting the file name from the *topEdit* text area. If the file name isn't *null*—that is, if there is a file name—the program creates a *FileWriter* object to handle output. The *FileWriter* constructor throws an exception if anything goes wrong during the opening process. WindowedApp catches this exception, outputs an error message, and continues processing.

Once the *FileWriter* object has been created, the program fetches the contents of the edit area and writes it to the *FileWriter* object.

Converting to and from

The methods *convertTo()* and *convertFrom()* are present to fix an AWT problem with the *FileReader* and *FileWriter* objects. The *FileWriter* object converts the *String* passed to it into a series of ANSI characters by ignoring the upper byte of each character. This would be fine for a UNIX machine; however, for a Windows machine, one further conversion is necessary. The newline character ("\n") must also be converted into a newline-carriage return ("\n\r").

The *convertTo()* method handles this conversion by searching recursively for newline characters using the *String.indexOf()* method. When the *indexOf()* method returns an offset of −1, the function knows that the conversion is complete. Until then, *convertTo()* inserts a carriage return at the offset following the offset that was returned. The next search begins with the character following the carriage return that was just inserted. The *convertTo()* method returns the resulting string.

The *convertFrom()* method takes the opposite tack, using a loop to search for carriage returns. Every time a carriage return is found, *convertFrom()* breaks the string into two strings, the first containing the characters before the carriage return and the second containing the characters after the carriage return. The program then concatenates the two strings. This process is repeated in a loop until the method returns the resulting string with all carriage returns removed.

The Result

The output from the AWT-based WindowedApp is shown in Figures 4-8 through 4-10. To get a feel for the output's dynamic characteristics, I have shown it in various sizes.

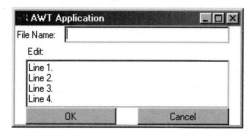

Figure 4-8. *The long awaited output from WindowedApp in its default size.*

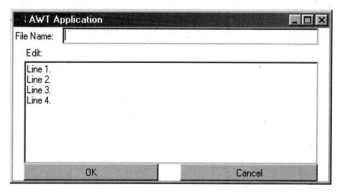

Figure 4-9. *The output from WindowedApp expanded to roughly twice its original size.*

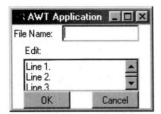

Figure 4-10. *The output from WindowedApp shrunk to about half its size.*

You can see that as the window expands the text box components and buttons expand and reposition to retain their proportionality. This is a direct result of the *BorderLayout* layout manager, which ties the objects to the frame borders. We carefully placed the labels within the layout scheme so that they retain their original size and position irrespective of the size of the window.

If you continue to shrink the window, the text box shrinks proportionally until there is no longer enough room to display all of the text. At this point, the *TextArea* object displays scroll bars to allow access to all of the text, as shown in Figure 4-10.

NOTE While it might be tempting to use the *TextArea* object for displaying large amounts of text, this won't work. The *TextArea* object size is limited in the size of *String* that it can accept. To build an editor capable of handling large files, you will need to perform dynamic file manipulations that are beyond the scope of this book.

DEPLOYMENT TYPES

Strictly speaking, the WindowedApp application isn't platform independent. The source code certainly is, relying as it does on AWT user interface calls. However, the .EXE file that results from compiling this source code under Visual J++ 6 is as firmly tied to Microsoft Windows as any other .EXE file that you might encounter; in fact, in some ways it's more firmly tied.

The reason for this is that the .EXE file generated by Visual J++ 6 does not include the AWT class library. This library is tucked safely away in a Windows subdirectory known only to the VM and Java computer geeks. As a result, our Visual J++ .EXE files will only execute on a Windows machine that has Microsoft Internet Explorer or the Java SDK installed.

Visual J++ 6 supports other deployment options, however. For one thing, compiling WindowedApp.java generates a WindowedApp.class file whether or not it generates an .EXE file. This WindowedApp.class file can be executed on any machine for which you have an application viewer.

The viewer supplied with Visual J++ is named JVIEW. To use JVIEW, you would enter the following on the command line:

```
jview WindowedApp.class myfile.txt
```

Alternatively, you can use the application viewer that comes with the Sun Microsystems Java Development Kit for the PC. You can also execute the same .class file on a UNIX machine using a viewer intended for that environment.

I'll have more to say about deployment in the discussion of applets and the Web later in this book. Meanwhile, it is a good idea to keep in mind exactly what you mean by platform independence in the context of Visual J++ 6 executable files.

CONCLUSION

In this chapter, we've covered the basics of the Abstract Windowing Toolkit (AWT). You've learned how to use Visual J++ 6 together with AWT to build platform-independent windowed applications. In Chapter 5, you'll see how the WFC-based tools available in Visual J++ 6 change the nature of building windowed applications.

Chapter 5

Microsoft Windows Applications

In Chapter 4, we created a windowed application based on the Abstract Windowing Toolkit (AWT). Hopefully that exercise hasn't scared you away from using Microsoft Visual J++ to build an application for the Microsoft Windows operating system. As you'll see in this chapter, the tools built into Visual J++ 6 help you to build powerful, Windows-based applications quickly and easily.

Let's start by rebuilding the AWT-based WindowedApp application from Chapter 4 as a Windows application based on the Windows Foundation Classes for Java (WFC). (All the code discussed in the chapter is in the Windows Applications folder of the sample files on the companion CD.)

DESIGNING WINDOWEDAPP

To create this application, we'll use the Windows Application builder. Close any projects that you might have open in Visual J++ by choosing Close All from the File menu. Now choose New Project from the File menu. Select Applications from the Visual J++ Projects as we did when creating console applications. This time, however, select Windows Application instead of Console Application. (Don't confuse this choice with the Application Wizard option.) For a project name, enter WindowedApp, as shown in Figure 5-1.

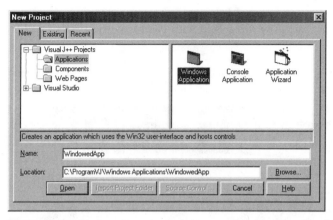

Figure 5-1. *The New Project window immediately prior to building the Microsoft Windows version of WindowedApp.*

Once your display looks like that shown in Figure 5-1, choose Open. This creates a project with a single .java file. Rather than carrying the default name Class1.java, as with console applications, this project has the default source file name Form1.java. (The reason for this name difference will become obvious shortly.) For now let's leave the name as it is; you'll see how to change it later.

Using the Forms Designer

To open the file for editing, double-click Form1.java in the Project Explorer window. A window similar to that shown in Figure 5-2 will appear. This is the Forms Designer. (You can also open the Forms Designer by selecting Form1.java and choosing Designer from the View menu.)

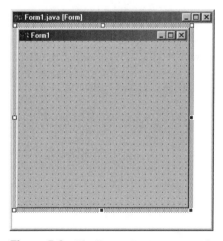

Figure 5-2. *The Forms Designer provides a different view of a Visual J++ application.*

To use the Forms Designer, you'll need two additional windows: the Toolbox and the Properties window. Let's deal with each in turn.

The Toolbox

To open the Toolbox, select Toolbox from the View menu. (There is also a Toolbox button on the standard toolbar that you can use.) The Toolbox (in List View) is shown in Figure 5-3. To view the WFC controls, click the WFC tab. Perhaps you're more clever than I am, but it took me a few minutes to figure out that clicking the arrows next to the tabs scrolls the current list of available tools up and down. You can get a more condensed, albeit cryptic, view of the available tools by right-clicking the mouse within the WFC Controls panel and clicking List View to turn it off. This displays the tool icons without their labels.

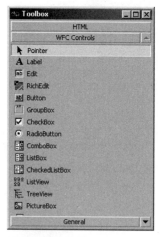

Figure 5-3. *The Toolbox showing some of the available WFC tools.*

We'll first use the Toolbox tools to build the file name input area of our windowed application. (If you've forgotten the application we're trying to build or if you skipped over Chapter 4, refer to Figure 4-1 on page 86.) Click the Label control in the Toolbox. Now click a spot within the Forms Designer. A label is displayed bearing the text "label1", as shown in Figure 5-4.

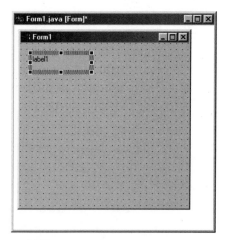

Figure 5-4. *Clicking Label in the Toolbox and then clicking within the Forms Designer creates a* Label *object.*

The Properties window

With the label still selected in the Forms Designer window, enter *File Name*. As soon as you begin to type, the Properties window appears. (If you do like I do and group the various Visual J++ windows in a tabbed window, the Properties window will immediately cover the Toolbox.) The text you type is displayed within the label in the Forms Designer and the *text* property value box in the Properties window. See Figure 5-5.

Figure 5-5. *The Properties window for the* Label *object in Categorized order.*

Shown in Figure 5-5 along with the *text* property are the other properties of a Label control. By default, these properties are arranged alphabetically. In Figure 5-5, they have been grouped by clicking the Categorized button at the top of the Properties window. You can show or hide the properties within a group by clicking the plus or minus sign next to the group title. The values of most properties can be changed by clicking the value box and typing. For example, change the *name* property of the *Label* object by entering *fileNameLabel*.

Let's try changing one of the compound properties such as the *font* property. Click the plus sign to expand the font subproperties. Now select the desired font from the drop-down list under the *name* property, and then select the font size and weight. I left the font name the same, but changed the size and weight to 14-point boldface to make the label stand out a little better than it would using the default font.

Position properties

There are two more points about the Properties window worth noting. First, if you scroll down to near the bottom of the properties list, you'll see a group of properties collectively known as Position. Under Position, you'll see an *anchor* property whose default value is *Top, Left*. The *anchor* property specifies what side of the form the object is attached to, which in turn determines how the label reacts when the form is resized. Below the *anchor* property is the *dock* property. Selecting the arrow in the *dock* property's value box opens a window much like the one in Figure 4-5 on page 94, which describes the *BorderLayout* layout manager. This isn't an accident. The *dock* property places the object within the form using an approach much like a border layout.

Second, at the bottom of the Position property group under the *location* and *size* properties are the x and y coordinates of the *Label* object within the form and the object's width and height, respectively. Unlike AWT, WFC allows the programmer to place objects absolutely.

NOTE The ability to place objects using x and y offsets will be familiar to programmers of Microsoft Visual Basic and Microsoft Visual C++.

Although you can set the location and size of a control from the Properties window, it's generally easier to set location and size properties graphically. To set the location, point at the control, press down the mouse button, and drag the control to position it. To set the size, individually drag the sizing handles on the perimeter of the selected control. Make the Label control as small as you can while still being able to see the label text.

Finishing the WindowedApp Interface

Once you finish editing the properties of the *fileNameLabel* label, you'll need to add an Edit control to contain the file name. Drag an Edit control from the Toolbox and place it beside the *fileNameLabel* object. Drag the right side of the Edit control until it just about meets the right side of the form.

Now right-click the Edit control and select Properties from the shortcut menu. This is another way to select the Properties window. Since we don't want the *Edit* object to contain the default phrase *edit1* as the initial value, delete this text in the object's *text* property. Notice that the text also disappears from the control in the Forms Designer. Set the *anchor* property of the *Edit* object to *Top, Left, Right*. This will ensure that the Edit control resizes horizontally to match the size of the window.

Create another label, and position it below the *fileNameLabel* object. Change this new label's *text* property value to *Text*. Set its font, font size, and font weight to match the font properties of the *fileNameLabel* object.

Add another Edit control immediately below the text label. Before attempting to resize this control object, you must set its *multiline* property to *true*. Only then will you be allowed to resize the control vertically as well as horizontally. Resize this second Edit control so that it takes up most of the remaining room within the form, but leave enough space for two buttons at the bottom. (Don't worry, you can always resize the form after the buttons are in place.) Set this *Edit* object's *anchor* property to *Top, Left, Bottom, Right*. Clear the default value from the *text* property.

Finally, add the two buttons. Drag a Button control to below the second Edit control, and set the *Button* object's *text* property to *Submit*. Set the *anchor* property to *Left, Bottom*. Repeat the process for the Cancel button, except set its *anchor* property to *Bottom, Right*.

When you finish, your Forms Designer window should look as shown in Figure 5-6. Continue to adjust the fields until they look right to you, and then click the Save All toolbar button.

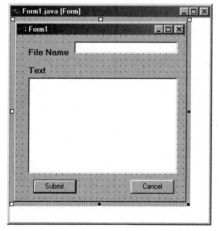

Figure 5-6. *The completed WindowedApp interface, shown in the Forms Designer.*

What Did This Do (and What Did This Not Do)?

To those readers accustomed to earlier versions of Visual C++, the Forms Designer isn't a great surprise. Even Visual J++ 1.0 had some limited form design capability. The main difference between those tools and the Visual J++ 6 Forms Designer lies in the way the Forms Designer works. The output from Visual J++ form design tools went into a file called a Resource file, which had to be compiled by the resource compiler and included in the project. The output from the Forms Designer is instead contained in the Form1.java file.

To see the code you've generated by creating the form for the WindowedApp project, you'll first need to make sure that your design handiwork has been saved to disk. To do so, choose Save All from the File menu (or click the Save All toolbar button). Now choose Code from the View menu, or click the View Code toolbar button on the Project Explorer window.

The first thing you'll notice is that Form1.java already contains a fair amount of code. Much of this code was generated by the Windows Application builder when it first created the file. As you scroll through the code, however, you'll notice that the method *initForm()* is shaded and carries the admonition not to edit it directly. This is the code generated by the Forms Designer as a result of your design work.

To prove that this code was generated by the Forms Designer, you might want to conduct the following experiment. Scroll the Text editor display down until you reach the section of Java code that sets up the multiline *Edit* object. The name of this object is *edit2,* unless you changed it during the design process. In any case, this is the only object that calls the *setMultiline()* method. Within this section of code, find the call to the *edit2.setSize()* method. Now position the Text editor so that the call to *setSize()* is still visible even when the Forms Designer window has the focus. Resize the *edit2* object in the Forms Designer. The source code won't change immediately. However, as soon as you save the form, the size specified in the *setSize()* call in the Text editor changes to match the new size in the Forms Designer.

Building the Application

There is one last property to set: the form's title. To do this, select the form and change its *text* property in the Properties window.

Now you are ready to build the WindowedApp application. Choose Save All from the File menu again, and then build the project. The program should compile into a Windows .EXE file without complaint. Executing WindowedApp.exe generates the output shown in Figure 5-7.

Compare the output of your project with the planned output shown in Figure 4-1 on page 86. If your output doesn't match, you still have some editing to do in the Forms Designer.

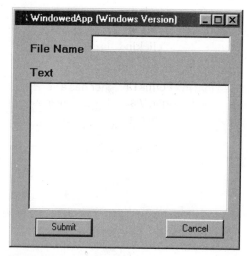

Figure 5-7. *The appearance of our initial WindowedApp application.*

ADDING ACTION TO WINDOWEDAPP

An amazing number of things work in WindowedApp, considering that we have yet to write a single line of code. You can enter a file name into the file name Edit control. You can enter and edit text in the multiline Edit control in the middle of the form. You can minimize and maximize the window. You can even close the window by clicking the window's close button. The only things that don't work are the two buttons we added. Of course, the problem is that neither the Forms Designer nor WFC has any idea what these two buttons are for. We still have to define that.

From the Forms Designer, double-click the Cancel button. This opens the Text editor on the newly added method *button2_click()*. (This method name assumes that *button2*, the second button we added, is the name of your Cancel button.) Visual J++ automatically designates the *button2_click()* method to handle the action event that results from clicking the Cancel button (more on that later in the next section of this chapter).

Edit the *button2_click()* method so that it looks like the following code:

```
/**
 * This method is invoked when the user clicks Cancel.
 */
private void button2_click(Object source, Event e)
{
    dispose();
    Application.exit();
}
```

The *dispose()* method closes all open windows in this application and returns their assets to the heap. The call to *Application.exit()* terminates the application. Rebuild and test the application. Now clicking the Cancel button closes the application.

> **NOTE** If you're getting the idea that the Forms Designer has a very "Microsoft Visual Basic feel" about it, you're exactly right. Visual J++ 6 combines the ease-of-use features of Visual Basic with the C++-like object-oriented Java programming language.

Adding the Submit Action

Of course, the real key to this program's functionality is the Submit button's action handler. Double-click the Submit button to create the *button1_click()* method. The code for the *button1_click()* method is similar to the code for the Submit button of the AWT application in Chapter 4, except for differences between the *java.io* classes and the WFC *TextWriter* class. Add code to your *button1_click()* method so that it looks like this:

```
private void button1_click(Object source, Event e)
{
    // get the name of the output file
    String fileName = edit1.getText();

    // if there is one...
    if (!fileName.equals(""))
    {
        // open the file with a TextWriter
        TextWriter tw = new TextWriter(fileName, false);

        // get the contents of the text edit field
        // and save to the disk (notice that getLines()
        // returns an array of lines, which must be saved
        // in the file individually)
        String[] array = edit2.getLines();
        for (int i = 0; i < array.length; i++)
        {
            tw.writeLine(array[i]);
        }

        // closing the file automatically flushes the
        // file, plus it ensures that the user can save
        // the contents again in the future
        tw.close();
    }
}
```

You'll also need to add an *import* statement at the top of the Form1.java file to import *com.ms.wfc.io.** Importing this package will allow the application to gain access to the *TextWriter* class.

This *button1_click* method starts by fetching the output file name from the *edit1* object using the *getText()* method. If the file name isn't equal to the null string, the program attempts to create a *TextWriter* object out of it. The program then calls *edit2.getLines()*. This method returns an array of *String* objects, each one representing a different line of text in the edit area.

To write the text lines out to disk, the program enters a *for* loop that writes out each line of text as long as *i* is less than the length of the *String* array. Once the loop is complete, the output to the file is flushed by closing the file before exiting.

NOTE   Since WFC is written for the Windows environment, it isn't necessary to convert newline characters to newline/carriage return characters as was the case in Chapter 4. This relieves some of the programming burden.

Setting Default Actions

Now that the buttons actually do something, we can assign them to be the default Accept and Cancel buttons. Visual J++ chooses the Accept button when the user presses the Enter key and the form has focus; it chooses the Cancel button when the user presses the escape key.

NOTE   Generally you want the Accept button to take some positive action and the Cancel button to bail out without changing anything. The Enter key will not activate the Accept button when focus is inside a multiline edit box.

To set the default Accept and Cancel buttons, select the form and then find the *acceptButton* property in the Properties window. Clicking the arrow in the property's value box exposes a drop-down menu containing the names of our two buttons *button1* and *button2* (unless you changed the names during the design process). Select *button1*—the Submit button. Repeat the process for the *cancelButton* property except select *button2*—the Cancel button.

THE COMPLETE WINDOWEDAPP SOLUTION

The complete Windows version of WindowedApp follows.

```
import com.ms.wfc.app.*;
import com.ms.wfc.core.*;
import com.ms.wfc.ui.*;
import com.ms.wfc.html.*;

import com.ms.wfc.io.*;
```

```
/**
 * This class can take a variable number of parameters on the command
 * line. Program execution begins with the main() method. The class
 * constructor is not invoked unless an object of type 'Form1' is
 * created in the main() method.
 */
public class Form1 extends Form
{
    public Form1(String[] args)
    {
        // Required for Visual J++ Form Designer support
        initForm();

        // I added the following call and the
        // next two functions manually
        processArgs(args);
    }

    /**
     * This function processes the input arguments
     * to the program.
     */
    void processArgs(String[] args)
    {
        // if an argument is present...
        if (args.length == 1)
        {
            // open it as a file name
            TextReader tr = new TextReader(args[0]);

            // read a line at a time; add each line
            // to an array of strings
            String s;
            String[] accum = new String[1];
            for (int offset = 0;
                 (s = tr.readLine()) != null;
                 offset++)
            {
                // if the array is not big enough...
                if (offset >= accum.length)
                {
                    // double its size
                    accum = expand(accum);
                }
                accum[offset] = s;
            }
```

(continued)

```
                // now store the lines in the
                // text edit area
                edit2.setLines(accum);

                // and save the name of the file
                edit1.setText(args[0]);
        }
    }

    /**
     * Double the length of the array passed.
     *
     * @param array - the array of Strings to expand
     */
    public static String[] expand(String[] array)
    {
        // allocate an array twice as big
        String[] newArray = new String[2*array.length];

        // null out the array first
        for (int i = 0; i < newArray.length; i++)
        {
            newArray[i] = null;
        }

        // then copy over members from the source array
        for (int i = 0; i < array.length; i++)
        {
            newArray[i] = array[i];
        }
        return newArray;
    }

    /**
     * Form1 overrides dispose so it can clean up the
     * component list.
     */
    public void dispose()
    {
        super.dispose();
        components.dispose();
    }

    /**
     * This method is invoked when the user clicks Cancel.
     */
    private void button2_click(Object source, Event e)
    {
```

```
        dispose();
        Application.exit();
}


/**
 * This method is invoked by the Submit button to
 * save the contents of the text edit window
 * into a file.
 */
private void button1_click(Object source, Event e)
{
    String fileName = edit1.getText();
    if (!fileName.equals(""))
    {
        TextWriter tw = new TextWriter(fileName, false);

        // get the contents of the text edit field
        // and save to the disk
        String[] array = edit2.getLines();
        for (int i = 0; i < array.length; i++)
        {
            tw.writeLine(array[i]);
        }
        tw.close();
    }
}


/**
 * NOTE: The following code is required by the Visual J++ form
 * designer.  It can be modified using the form editor.  Do not
 * modify it using the code editor.
 */
 Container components = new Container();
 Label fileNameLabel = new Label();
 Edit edit1 = new Edit();
 Label label1 = new Label();
 Edit edit2 = new Edit();
 Button button1 = new Button();
 Button button2 = new Button();

 private void initForm()
 {
     fileNameLabel.setFont(
         new Font("MS Sans Serif", 14.0f,
                 FontSize.CHARACTERHEIGHT,
                 FontWeight.BOLD,
                 false, false, false));
```

(continued)

```
fileNameLabel.setLocation(new Point(20, 20));
fileNameLabel.setSize(new Point(80, 20));
fileNameLabel.setTabIndex(0);
fileNameLabel.setTabStop(false);
fileNameLabel.setText("File Name");

edit1.setAnchor(ControlAnchor.TOPLEFTRIGHT);
edit1.setLocation(new Point(100, 10));
edit1.setSize(new Point(180, 20));
edit1.setTabIndex(1);
edit1.setText("");

label1.setFont(
    new Font("MS Sans Serif", 14.0f,
            FontSize.CHARACTERHEIGHT,
            FontWeight.BOLD,
            false, false, false));
label1.setLocation(new Point(20, 50));
label1.setSize(new Point(40, 20));
label1.setTabIndex(2);
label1.setTabStop(false);
label1.setText("Text");

edit2.setAnchor(ControlAnchor.ALL);
edit2.setLocation(new Point(20, 70));
edit2.setSize(new Point(260, 160));
edit2.setTabIndex(3);
edit2.setText("");
edit2.setMultiline(true);

button1.setAnchor(ControlAnchor.BOTTOMLEFT);
button1.setLocation(new Point(30, 240));
button1.setSize(new Point(75, 23));
button1.setTabIndex(4);
button1.setText("Submit");
button1.addOnClick(new EventHandler(this.button1_click));

button2.setAnchor(ControlAnchor.BOTTOMRIGHT);
button2.setLocation(new Point(200, 240));
button2.setSize(new Point(75, 23));
button2.setTabIndex(5);
button2.setText("Cancel");
button2.addOnClick(new EventHandler(this.button2_click));

this.setText("WindowedApp (Windows Version)");
this.setAcceptButton(button1);
this.setAutoScaleBaseSize(new Point(5, 13));
this.setCancelButton(button2);
```

```
        this.setClientSize(new Point(292, 273));

        this.setNewControls(new Control[] {
                            button2,
                            button1,
                            edit2,
                            label1,
                            edit1,
                            fileNameLabel});
    }


/**
 * The main entry point for the application.
 *
 * @param args - Array of parameters passed to the application
 * via the command line.
 */
public static void main(String args[])
{
    Application.run(new Form1(args));
}
}
```

As always in a Visual J++ application, even a Windows application, control begins with *main()*. (The *main()* function is at the bottom of the source file.) This function creates a new instance of our main form class, *Form1*, passing the input arguments as arguments to the constructor. The class *Form1* extends the WFC class *Form*.

> **NOTE** *Form* is the WFC class that most corresponds to the AWT *Frame* class.

The first statement in Form1 is a call to *initForm()*, whose code constructs the form you built with the Forms Designer.

Immediately following is a call to the function *processArgs()*. If an argument is provided to the program when it is first started, *processArgs()* assumes it is a file name and reads the contents of the file into the multiline Edit control. The details of how it does this are discussed below.

> **NOTE** The function *processArgs()* and the helper function immediately following it are the only two functions in this program that I added completely without the help of the Visual J++ 6 Rapid Application Development (RAD) tools. All of the other functions in this program were built either wholly or in part by the Windows Application builder or the Forms Designer.

The *initForm()* Method

On the one hand, as a programmer you might not be interested in the contents of the *initForm()* method at all. After all, you didn't create it and you shouldn't edit it except by means of the Forms Designer. Nevertheless, I think it is important to understand how the code generated by automatic tools like the Forms Designer works. You can learn a lot from the code generated by the experts. In addition, you never know when you might need to do the same coding tasks without the help of the Forms Designer.

Immediately preceding the *initForm()* method are all of the data members that *initForm()* references. Unless you change their names in the Properties window, they carry fairly mundane names like *edit1*, *edit2*, and so forth. (As you saw with the label *fileNameLabel*, you are free to change object names to anything meaningful to you.) Since these objects appear with initializers, they are actually constructed prior to *initForm()* being called.

> **C++ NOTE**   Initializers execute as part of the constructor. They are invoked after the constructor for the base class has been called and before the first statement in the constructor.

You can see that the objects are formatted within *initForm()* in the order you created them in the Forms Designer. In this example, the first object created was the *fileNameLabel* object. The first method called on this object is *setFont()*. This call creates a new font using the parameters provided in the Properties window.

> **NOTE**   It is possible to change the font when using AWT, but the choice of fonts and font properties is very limited.

The *initForm()* method then sets the location of the label and its size. The class *Point* is nothing more than a holder for an x and a y value. The tab order is set by *setTabIndex()*. This is the order in which objects gain focus when the user presses the tab key. Control starts with element 0 and continues to element 1, 2, and so on until wrapping around back to 0 again. Finally, the call to *setText()* sets the actual label itself.

The remaining objects within the form are initialized following the same pattern. Once all of the objects have been initialized, the following statement is used to attach all of the individual objects to the *Form1* object at once:

```
this.setNewControls(new Control[] {
                        button2,
                        button1,
                        edit2,
                        label1,
                        edit1,
                        fileNameLabel});
```

This statement creates an array of *Control* objects and initializes that array to references to the controls—*button2, button1, edit2,* and so on—that we created during the design phase. The resulting array of controls is passed to *setNewControls()*, which attaches each control to *this,* the *Form1* object.

> **NOTE** This "allocate array off the heap and initialize" statement is a Visual J++ extension to C++.

Editing *initForm()*

Now that I've told you that you shouldn't edit *initForm()*, let me tell you that it is possible to do. As long as the Forms Designer is open, the area of code including *initForm()* is darkened and the Visual J++ Text editor won't let you touch it. However, once you close the Forms Designer you are free to change this function any way you want.

If you are careful and stick with the pattern of calls the Forms Designer has established, the changes you make in the Text editor will be picked up the next time you open the Forms Designer. To prove this point, let's close the Forms Designer. Now scroll into the *initForm()* method and change a property. I chose to add the following two lines to the edit2 section:

```
edit2.setAcceptsTab(true);
edit2.setWordWrap(false);
```

The first statement enables tab processing, which by default is disabled, and the second turns off word wrap.

Try changing something that is visible in the Forms Designer. I chose to change the title of *Form1* by editing the call *this.setText()*.

Now reopen the Forms Designer and select the object you edited. You'll notice that your changes are now visible in the Forms Designer. If you made the changes that I did, you'll see that the title of the form has been updated in the Forms Designer and that the *acceptsTab* and *wordWrap* properties of the *edit2* Edit control in the Properties window have changed.

I wouldn't advise adding any extraneous code within *initForm()*, because the Designer won't know what to do with it, but if you prefer to edit object properties in the Text editor rather than use the Properties window, feel free.

The *processArgs()* Method

The second method called by the *Form1* constructor is the *processArgs()* method. As the name implies, this method processes the arguments passed to the program. If an argument isn't provided, the method exits without doing anything.

If there is a single argument, *processArgs()* assumes the argument is the name of a text file to read and passes the name to *TextReader,* which in turn creates a text reader object to read the input file. This it does by calling *readLine()* in a loop that executes until *readLine()* returns a *null,* indicating that there are no more lines of text to read. As each line is read in, it is added to an array of strings. If there is no more room in the array, the locally-defined method *expand()* is called to double the size of the array.

Once the input file has been read into an array of strings, this array is written into the edit box by means of the call *edit2.setLines().* Finally, the name of the file is written into the file name edit field.

The *expand()* function doubles the size of the string array passed it. First, it allocates a new array of strings twice the size of the array passed to it. It then copies the contents of the input array into the new array before returning a reference to the new array.

Event Handlers

If you look closely at the objects being initialized in *initForms(),* you'll see that there is a significant difference between how the two buttons and the rest of the objects are initialized. The two buttons include a call to *addOnClick(),* passing it something called an *EventHandler.* To understand this call, you need to know something about event processing under AWT version 1.0, AWT version 1.1, and WFC.

AWT Version 1.0 event handling

The AWT that accompanied the original release of Java had a simple event-handling scheme. When an action occurred, such as a mouse button click or a keystroke, an object of class *Event* was created. This object was passed to the *handleEvent()* method of the *Component* object that was being pointed at or that had focus at the time of the event.

The programmer had the options of handling the event there or letting the default *Component.handleEvent()* method take care of it. The default method would first try to give someone else a chance by passing the event to whatever *Container* object the component was attached to. Thus, a *Button* object would pass the event to the *Frame* object to which it was attached. This "bubbling up of events" enabled the programmer to handle all events in one central location.

If the event was not handled in any of the *handleEvent()* methods, *Container.handleEvent()* would do one of the following:

■ For certain types of events, such as a window minimize or a window maximize event, it would handle the event.

■ For action events, it would pass the event on to the *Container.action()* method, which by default repeated the process of passing the event to any parent container's *action()* method.

■ For the most common event types—like keystrokes, mouse down events, mouse up events, and so on—*handleEvent()* would call for each event a specially-named method that was designed to handle just that event. For example, the mouse down event would result in the object's *mouseDown()* method being invoked. Again, the default action was to bubble the event up to the parent container for processing.

For example, the following program uses the *action()* method of the parent frame to detect a button being clicked:

```java
import java.awt.*;
public class Class1 extends Frame
{
    Button okButton;
    Button cancelButton;

    public void init()
    {
        add(okButton = new Button("OK"));
        add(cancelButton = new Button("Cancel"));
        setVisible(true);
    }

    /**
        * Gets called whenever an object within the frame
        * is "activated."
     */
    public boolean action(Event e, Object o)
    {
        // check to see which object was activated
        if (e.target == okButton)
        {
            // handle the OK button here...
            return true; // indicates we've handled event
        }
        if (e.target == cancelButton)
        {
            // handle the Cancel button here...
            return true;
        }

        // return false to indicate we haven't handled
        // the event
        return false;
    }
}
```

The *action()* method in the frame class receives action events that occur within the frame. The method must then test which object received the action event. In this case, we are interested only in the two buttons, since these are the only objects we added to the frame.

The problem with this approach is that it isn't very neat. The single *action()* method can get pretty complicated if there are a lot of components in the frame. Worse yet, it disperses the button logic across the application. Pretty soon the single *action()* method contains logic for menu items, along with check boxes, radio buttons, and other object types all mixed together.

A more modular means of handling the action event within the button object is as follows:

```java
import java.awt.*;

public class Class1 extends Frame
{
    public void init()
    {
        // TODO: Add initialization code here
        add(new OKButton());
        add(new CancelButton());
        setVisible(true);
    }
}


class OKButton extends Button
{
    OKButton()
    {
        super("OK");
    }

    public boolean action(Event e, Object o)
    {
        // handle the OK button here
        return true; // indicates we've handled event
    }
}

class CancelButton extends Button
{
    CancelButton()
    {
        super("Cancel");
    }
```

```
    public boolean action(Event e, Object o)
    {
        // handle the Cancel button here
        return true; // indicates we've handled event
    }
}
```

Here the action event handler has been moved to the component by creating a separate subclass for each button, with each subclass having its own *action()* method. This approach is modular in that it keeps each button's event handling code together with the rest of the button's logic and separate from the event handling code of other components. Thus, *CancelButton.action()* contains the code to handle the Cancel button and nothing more. The primary drawback with this approach is that it ends up creating a lot of subclasses.

> **NOTE** This event-handling approach that uses the *handleEvent()* and *action()* methods is still supported in Visual J++ 6. In fact, this is the method we used for event processing in Chapter 4. However, both *handleEvent()* and *action()* are marked as deprecated, which means that although the method is still present it might be removed in future versions of the language.

AWT 1.1 event delegation

Seeing the benefits of modular event processing, the authors of Java version 1.1 formalized this concept somewhat in a mechanism known as *event delegation*.

Event delegation uses an event-processing model based on special interfaces known as *listeners*. For example, the action event can be handled by any class that implements the *ActionListener* interface. To implement the *ActionListener* interface, a class has only to provide the function *actionPerformed()*. Other listener interfaces are provided for other classes of events, each with its own version of the *actionPerformed()* method to be implemented.

Event delegation gives the programmer increased flexibility. The listener for a given component can be in a separate class. In some cases, multiple components can share the same listener. More often, the listener is an inner class within the component itself, as shown in the following example.

```
import java.awt.*;
import java.awt.event.*;

public class Class1 extends Frame
{
    public static void main(String[] args)
    {
        (new Class1()).init();
    }
```

(continued)

```java
    public void init()
    {
        add("West", new OKButton());
        add("East", new CancelButton());
        setVisible(true);
    }
}

class OKButton extends Button
{
    class OKActionListener implements ActionListener
    {
        public void actionPerformed(ActionEvent ae)
        {
            // handle the OK button action here
        }
    }

    OKButton()
    {
        super("OK");

        // add an object to the list of listeners for
        // an action on this object
        addActionListener(new OKActionListener());
    }
}

class CancelButton extends Button
{
    class CancelActionListener implements ActionListener
    {
        public void actionPerformed(ActionEvent ae)
        {
            // handle the Cancel button action here
        }
    }

    CancelButton()
    {
        super("Cancel");
        addActionListener(new CancelActionListener());
    }

}
```

Here you can see that the OK and Cancel buttons each define their own inner classes to implement the *ActionListener* interface. The call to *addActionListener()* tells AWT to invoke the class's listener when an action occurs on that button. Inner classes were a new feature with version 1.1 of the Java standard, added specifically to support event delegation.

> **NOTE** A listener doesn't have to be an inner class. Using an inner class keeps all of the component logic together.

Listeners are even more modular than their predecessor. The action processing code can be both bundled up within the button class and at the same time segregated into an inner class.

The problems with *handleEvent()* and event delegation

Both of the event-handling mechanisms we've been discussing have problems. The *handleEvent()* mechanism, although simple, suffers from numerous deficiencies. First, there is the problem of function complexity that I already mentioned. Second, the event linkage is completely static. That is to say, the decision where a particular event will be processed is made at compile time and can't be changed while the program executes.

Event delegation solves both of these problems. First, it encourages the programmer to handle the event in the object closest to where the event occurred. Second, the action listeners can be added and removed during program execution using the *addOnXXX()* and *removeOnXXX()* methods, where *XXX* is the name of the event. Third, multiple action listeners can be added to the same event, resulting in a sort of multicast capability.

There are several problems with event delegation, however. First, event delegation results in the creation of multiple, often trivially small classes to handle events for the different objects. A large form with a large number of objects requires more code to define listeners than to actually do the work. This situation is somewhat relieved by the addition of inner classes, but not completely. To use event delegation, the Forms Designer would need to create and keep track of numerous small listener classes.

Second, to use event delegation, tools must have access to the source code. This isn't a problem for programmer tools such as the Forms Designer; however, more and more users are looking for fourth-generation and fifth-generation tools that enable dynamic linking of objects by the user.

Delegates

In response to some of the problems with the conventional and event delegation models for event handling, Visual J++ 6 has introduced a new event-handling mechanism that Microsoft calls *delegates*.

What is a delegate?

A delegate is a class that can be used to reference an object/method combination. It is easier to explain a delegate by example than with words. The following code, from the DelegateDemo application on the companion CD, declares a delegate called *FunctionDelegate*, assigns a method to the delegate, and finally, invokes that method through the delegate.

```
import com.ms.wfc.io.*;

// declare a delegate for a function that accepts two
// ints and returns an int (this actually creates
// a subclass of the class Delegate)
delegate int FunctionDelegate(int a, int b);

public class Class1
{
    // declare an object of type FunctionDelegate
    FunctionDelegate f;

    public static void main (String[] args)
    {
        (new Class1()).test();
    }

    /**
     * This function compares its two arguments, outputs
     * an indication of which is greater, and then returns
     * the greater of the two values. (No consideration is
     * made for equal values.)
     * This function is only intended as a test of
     * FunctionDelegate.
     */
    int targetFunction(int a, int b)
    {
        Text.out.writeLine("A is " +
                        ((a > b) ? "greater" : "less") +
                        " than B");
        return (a > b) ? a : b;
    }

    Class1()
    {
        // create a new object of class FunctionDelegate
        // with the function targetFunction() and the
        // current object
        f = new FunctionDelegate(this.targetFunction);
    }
```

```
/**
 * This function simply tests FunctionDelegate.
 */
void test()
{
    int a = 10;
    int b = 20;

    Text.out.writeLine("A = "
                        + a
                        + ", B = "
                        + b);
    Text.out.writeLine("Invoking delegate");
    int result = f.invoke(a, b);
    Text.out.writeLine("Delegate returned "
                        + result);
    }
}
```

This example defines a delegate named *FunctionDelegate*, which extends the class *Delegate*. *Class1* includes a data member *f* of class *FunctionDelegate*. The constructor for *Class1* creates a new *FunctionDelegate* object with the object/method combination of *this.targetFunction()*.

Let's stop for just a minute and analyze what has happened so far. The keyword *delegate* is unique to Visual J++ 6; it isn't a part of the standard Java language and isn't ever likely to be given Sun Microsystem's pronouncements on the subject. (If you care about my opinion, see the sidebar at the end of this section.)

The following assignment creates an object of class *FunctionDelegate* and initializes it with the object/method combination of *this* and *targetFunction*.

```
f = new FunctionDelegate(this.targetFunction)
```

The *this* object is of class *Object* and the object *targetFunction* is of class *Method*. (The class *Method* was introduced to the Java language by Sun Microsystems as part of the language reflection package [java.lang.reflect].)

Notice that the prototype of *targetFunction()* matches the declaration of *FunctionDelegate* exactly. In other words, *FunctionDelegate* was declared to accept methods that take two integers as arguments and return an integer. That's exactly what was passed when the object *f* was created.

CAUTION The delegate declaration must exactly match the type of the method passed to the delegate class constructor. (Note, however, that the type of the target object isn't specified.)

Having created a delegate object *f*, we can invoke the object/method pair pointed at by *f* using the method *invoke()*. This is exactly what the function *test()* does. First, *test()* defines a couple of integers, *a* and *b*. It then invokes the object and method referenced by *f* and passes them the arguments *a* and *b*. The output of this simple test program is shown in Figure 5-8.

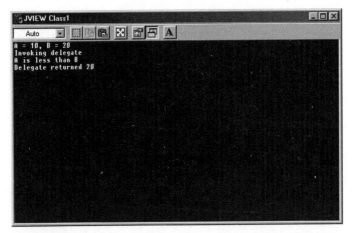

Figure 5-8. *The output of the DelegateDemo program, which declares and then invokes a delegate.*

WHAT ABOUT THE *DELEGATE* KEYWORD?

Personally, I am a little ambivalent about the introduction of the *delegate* keyword. I've never been a big supporter of religious wars of language purity; but still, it's not good to add new keywords to a language, especially a language designed to be portable like Java. It's actually worse than you might think. The implementation of delegates requires additions to the Java Virtual Machine (VM). Thus, code generated using the delegate keyword won't execute on another vendor's VM.

On the other hand, Sun Microsystems isn't above such shenanigans. After all, Sun introduced the inner class feature primarily to make their newly introduced event delegation less objectionable. Further, the Visual J++ delegate feature does make it easier to write event handlers. Gone is the need to construct an entire class just so you can tie a single function to an event. And of course, there's always the argument that you don't have to use delegates. But WFC uses delegates, so as soon as you adopt WFC you are in Windows territory anyway.

In effect, Microsoft has introduced to the Java language a type-safe, object-oriented way of defining C++ callback functions. Recent C++ converts to Java will love this feature—and Java purists will hate it. I would love to see the delegates feature become part of standard Java, but until it does I remain ambivalent.

Delegates and WFC event handling

WFC uses delegates as a means of registering event handlers. For example, WFC includes a delegate class *MouseEventHandler*. The *Control* class prewires the mouse events, such as mouse down, mouse up, and mouse move, to invoke any registered *MouseEventHandler* objects. An application program registers a *MouseEventHandler* by calling *addOnXxx()*, where *Xxx* represents the type of event. (For every *addOnXxx()*, there is a corresponding *RemoveOnXxx()* that removes the handler delegate.)

Returning to our *WindowedApp* example, let's look at this statement:

```
button1.addOnClick(new EventHandler(this.button1_click));
```

This line of code creates an *EventHandler* delegate object with the current object (*this*) and the method *button1_click()* and registers the delegate object (perhaps as one of several) to handle the *onClick* event emanating from *button1*.

How is a delegate different from a C callback function?

Visual C++ programmers will immediately recognize delegates as the Java equivalent of a callback function in C. Some operating systems use this callback mechanism to enable a program to register a function to handle a particular event. (The XWindows/ Motif system makes significant use of callback functions.)

> **NOTE** In C one could make the following declaration: *void addOnClick(int (*)(int, int));*. This declares a method *addOnClick()* that takes as its argument the address of a function. That function takes two integers and returns an integer. (Presumably this would be the function to handle the *onClick* event.)

Both callbacks and delegates are an efficient means for handling such events; however, delegates are superior to C callback functions in several ways. First, delegates are type safe. Theoretically, C callback functions are also type safe, but because you can recast a pointer in C, in practice programmers always seem to pass invalid program addresses. Java doesn't allow recasting. The method passed to the delegate's constructor must match the delegate's declaration. In addition, the *Delegate* class checks to make sure that what it's being passed is actually a method.

Second, callback functions are not inherently object-oriented. For example, Motif makes no provisions for the object half of the object/method pair in its callback mechanism. This is a constant nuisance to the C++ programmer. Delegates are built to store both the object and the method.

Finally, delegates are secure. A less-trusted piece of code can't use a delegate to gain access to more-trusted code. (Trusted and untrusted code types will be discussed in the section on applet security in Chapter 14. All application code is trusted.)

Multithreading

There is still one more aspect of the WindowedApp application that remains unexplained: the last function in the file but the very first to execute, *main()*. The *main()* function contains a single statement:

```
Application.run(new Form1(args));
```

The constructor for *Form1* creates the form as edited by the Forms Designer. The resulting *Form* object is passed to *Application.run()*. This function enters the Windows message dispatch loop, which fields Windows messages and dispatches them by means of the event-handling mechanism described earlier. Control remains in this message dispatch loop until the *Form* calls *Application.exit()* to terminate the program.

If you are a seasoned Windows programmer, this last paragraph will make perfect sense to you. If it does not, don't panic. I will present a complete discussion of *Application* and multithreading in Chapter 10.

CONCLUSION

In this chapter you've built your first Microsoft Windows application using Visual J++. You used the Windows Application builder to construct a framework. You followed that with the Forms Designer to build the user interface elements. If you followed along with the construction of the same application in Chapter 4, you'll probably be as impressed as I am at how much easier it is to build the WindowedApp interface using the Forms Designer. Finally, you added the few lines of WFC-based Java code necessary to complete the application.

In the next few chapters, you'll see the other WFC controls in action.

Chapter 6

Simple Input Controls

Chapter 5 demonstrated the ease with which you can use the Microsoft Visual J++ Windows Application builder and Forms Designer to build Microsoft Windows–based applications. In this chapter, we'll continue by investigating the simple input controls available in the Windows Foundation Classes for Java (WFC) Toolbox. The code for all the samples in this chapter is located in the Windows Applications subfolder on the companion CD.

BUTTONS

The simplest input controls of all are buttons. There are three types of buttons: the simple button, the radio button, and the check box. The following ButtonDemo applications demonstrate all three button types.

Reading Button Values

The ButtonDemo1 program, whose code is shown later in this chapter, outputs a single test string in one of three different fonts. In addition, the test string can be formatted as bold or italic. These settings are controlled using buttons of different types.

Since the choice of font is mutually exclusive, I chose to set the font using a set of three radio buttons. The bold and italic properties are independent, so I chose to use a separate check box for each of these options. A Submit button at the bottom causes the button settings to take effect. An edit box across the top of the window displays a test string in the selected font type and format.

NOTE   Use check boxes to set properties that are both binary ("on" or "off") and independent of each other. Use radio buttons to set properties that are mutually exclusive. Use a regular push button to take some action.

The Forms Designer work

To begin, create the button demonstration application using the Windows Application builder. (Choose New Project from the File menu. The default project type is Windows Application.) Give this first version of the program the name ButtonDemo1. Open the Project Explorer window and double-click on Form1.java to bring up the Forms Designer. From this point, start dragging objects from the Toolbox to the Forms Designer. Figure 6-1 shows the Forms Designer and the Properties window for one of the buttons during the later stages of developing the ButtonDemo1 application.

The check boxes are straightforward to create. Select the CheckBox tool in the Toolbox, and place it in the Forms Designer. Once you've placed the check box, just start typing the label; the Forms Designer will automatically update the check box's *text* property in the Properties window. I also chose to change the name by editing the *name* property in the Properties window. It's a good idea to use names that are a combination of the button label and the button type. Thus, *checkBox1* becomes *boldCheckBox* and *checkBox2* becomes *italicsCheckBox*.

For the radio buttons, you will first need to build a group box. A group box groups radio buttons both visually and logically. The group box groups radio buttons visually by placing a small box around them. It groups the radio buttons logically in that the radio buttons contained within a group box are mutually exclusive: choosing one radio button causes all other radio buttons in the same group box to not be chosen.

Select the GroupBox control in the Toolbox and drag it to the Forms Designer. Now resize the group box to be large enough to hold three radio buttons and their labels.

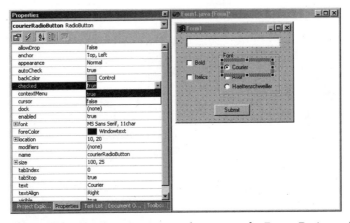

Figure 6-1. *The ButtonDemo1 application in the Forms Designer during the final stages of construction.*

NOTE When initially placing objects in the Forms Designer, don't worry too much about their exact dimensions. You can always resize things once you get all the objects in place on the form. In addition, there are two ways to place any control in a form: you can either drag the control from the Toolbox and drop it on the form, or you can click the control and then click within the form. There is no difference.

Once the group box is in place, you can begin adding radio button controls. For this application, you will need three radio buttons, each titled with the name of a font. Making sure that the radio boxes are properly aligned is easy when you have the Snap To Grid feature of the Forms Designer enabled. You will also need to set one of the radio buttons to be initially chosen—by default, radio buttons are not chosen.

NOTE Users are accustomed to seeing one (and only one) radio button in a set selected at all times. Starting the application with none selected is confusing.

I selected the first radio button, the Courier button, to be initially chosen by setting the *checked* property to *true* in the Properties window, as shown in Figure 6-1.

An Edit control across the top and a Submit button near the bottom finishes the design of the ButtonDemo1 application's form.

The code

After adding functionality, the code for the ButtonDemo1 application is as follows:

```
import com.ms.wfc.app.*;
import com.ms.wfc.core.*;
import com.ms.wfc.ui.*;
import com.ms.wfc.html.*;

/**
 * This class demonstrates the different button types.
 */
public class Form1 extends Form
{
    public Form1()
    {
        // Required for Visual J++ Form Designer support
        initForm();

        // at startup act like the Submit button has been
        // pushed; this will create the initial font and
        // update the outputEdit field with the test message
        submitButton_click(null, null);
    }
```

(continued)

```
/**
 * Form1 overrides dispose so it can clean up the
 * component list.
 */
public void dispose()
{
    super.dispose();
    components.dispose();
}


/**
 * Handle the Submit button by reading the button settings,
 * creating a font to match, and then updating the
 * text in the outputEdit object with that font.
 */
private void submitButton_click(Object source, Event e)
{
    // create a font based on the button settings
    // first; read the check boxes
    boolean bold = boldCheckBox.getChecked();
    boolean italics = italicsCheckBox.getChecked();

    // convert the weight check box into an integer
    // by choosing the appropriate weight from the list
    // of possibilities
    int weight = bold ? FontWeight.BOLD : FontWeight.NORMAL;

    // now find which radio button is selected; get a
    // list of all the radio buttons attached to the
    // Font group box, and loop through to see which one is
    // checked
    String fontName = null;
    Control[] control = fontGroupBox.getControls();
    for (int i = 0; i < control.length; i++)
    {
        // if this radio button is checked...
        RadioButton rb = (RadioButton)control[i];
        if (rb.getChecked())
        {
            // then use the name on the button as
            // the font name
            fontName = rb.getText();
        }
    }

    // create a font with the data
    Font font = new Font(fontName, 14, FontSize.POINTS,
                        weight, italics, false, false);
```

```
        // now update the outputEdit field with the font
        outputEdit.setText("This is a test string.");
        outputEdit.setFont(font);
}


/**
 * NOTE: The following code is required by the Visual J++ form
 * designer.  It can be modified using the form editor.  Do not
 * modify it using the code editor.
 */
Container components = new Container();
Edit outputEdit = new Edit();
CheckBox boldCheckBox = new CheckBox();
CheckBox italicsCheckBox = new CheckBox();
GroupBox fontGroupBox = new GroupBox();
RadioButton courierRadioButton = new RadioButton();
RadioButton arialRadioButton = new RadioButton();
RadioButton haettenschweillerRadioButton = new RadioButton();
Button submitButton = new Button();

private void initForm()
{
    this.setText("Button Demo");
    this.setAutoScaleBaseSize(new Point(5, 13));
    this.setClientSize(new Point(245, 184));

    outputEdit.setLocation(new Point(20, 10));
    outputEdit.setSize(new Point(200, 20));
    outputEdit.setTabIndex(0);
    outputEdit.setText("");
    outputEdit.setReadOnly(true);

    boldCheckBox.setLocation(new Point(20, 50));
    boldCheckBox.setSize(new Point(50, 25));
    boldCheckBox.setTabIndex(1);
    boldCheckBox.setText("Bold");

    italicsCheckBox.setLocation(new Point(20, 80));
    italicsCheckBox.setSize(new Point(50, 25));
    italicsCheckBox.setTabIndex(2);
    italicsCheckBox.setText("Italics");

    fontGroupBox.setLocation(new Point(90, 40));
    fontGroupBox.setSize(new Point(130, 90));
    fontGroupBox.setTabIndex(3);
    fontGroupBox.setTabStop(false);
    fontGroupBox.setText("Font");
```

(continued)

```
            courierRadioButton.setLocation(new Point(10, 20));
            courierRadioButton.setSize(new Point(100, 25));
            courierRadioButton.setTabIndex(0);
            courierRadioButton.setTabStop(true);
            courierRadioButton.setText("Courier");
            courierRadioButton.setChecked(true);

            arialRadioButton.setLocation(new Point(10, 40));
            arialRadioButton.setSize(new Point(100, 25));
            arialRadioButton.setTabIndex(1);
            arialRadioButton.setText("Arial");

            haettenschweillerRadioButton.setLocation(new Point(10, 60));
            haettenschweillerRadioButton.setSize(new Point(110, 25));
            haettenschweillerRadioButton.setTabIndex(2);
            haettenschweillerRadioButton.setText("Haettenschweiller");

            submitButton.setLocation(new Point(80, 150));
            submitButton.setSize(new Point(75, 23));
            submitButton.setTabIndex(4);
            submitButton.setText("Submit");
            submitButton.addOnClick(
                        new EventHandler(this.submitButton_click));

            this.setNewControls(new Control[] {
                            submitButton,
                            fontGroupBox,
                            italicsCheckBox,
                            boldCheckBox,
                            outputEdit});
            fontGroupBox.setNewControls(new Control[] {
                            haettenschweillerRadioButton,
                            arialRadioButton,
                            courierRadioButton});
        }


        /**
         * The main entry point for the application.
         *
         * @param args Array of parameters passed to the application
         * via the command line.
         */
        public static void main(String args[])
        {
            Application.run(new Form1());
        }
    }
```

As always, the *initForm()* method is created automatically by the Forms Designer. In one way, this *initForm()* method is different from the versions we have seen so far: it contains a hierarchy of objects. Instead of adding the radio buttons to the form, this *initForm()* adds them to the *fontGroupBox* object. The *fontGroupBox* object is then added to the form.

Grouping the radio buttons in the *fontGroupBox* container is what makes the radio buttons mutually exclusive. This also enables us to read the radio button values out of the container, as you will see later.

Double-clicking the Submit button in the Forms Designer created and registered the *submitButton_click()* method, and then I manually added the functionality for the button to the method. This method first reads the two check boxes *boldCheckBox* and *italicsCheckBox*. The Boolean *bold* value is then turned into an integer font *weight* value by using the enumerated class *FontWeight*.

To determine which font radio button is selected, *submitButton_click()* loops through the radio buttons contained in the *fontGroupBox* container. It does this by first calling the *fontGroupBox.getControls()* function. This function returns an array containing references to the objects contained within the *fontGroupBox* object. Since we didn't add anything but radio buttons to the group box, all of these *Control* objects are of type *RadioButton*. As soon as the loop finds a button whose *getChecked()* method returns *true*, the function reads the name of the button by calling *getText()*. The name of the button is the name of the font we want to be applied.

Armed with this information, *submitButton_click()* creates a *Font* object. It then applies the font and font format to the text in the *outputEdit* Edit control. An example of output from this program is shown in Figure 6-2.

Figure 6-2. *Output from ButtonDemo1 showing a particularly attractive font selection.*

Handling Button Updates Automatically

In many applications, you would like the button settings to take effect immediately rather than after the user clicks on a submit button of some type. The ButtonDemo2 application beginning on the following page updates the ButtonDemo1 functionality so that clicking any of the check boxes or radio buttons causes the displayed text to be updated immediately. Accordingly, the Submit button has been removed. Note that the *initForm()* function isn't included in the following code but is present in the code contained on the companion CD.

```
import com.ms.wfc.app.*;
import com.ms.wfc.core.*;
import com.ms.wfc.ui.*;
import com.ms.wfc.html.*;

/**
 * This class demonstrates the different button types.
 */
public class Form1 extends Form
{
    // maintain the state of the object
    boolean italics;
    boolean bold;
    String  fontName = "Courier";

    public Form1()
    {
        // Required for Visual J++ Form Designer support
        initForm();

        // update the output to display the initial state
        updateState();
    }

    /**
     * Form1 overrides dispose so it can clean up the
     * component list.
     */
    public void dispose()
    {
        super.dispose();
        components.dispose();
    }

    /**
     * Update the output edit field to reflect the current
     * state.
     */
    private void updateState()
    {
        // convert the weight into an integer
        // by choosing the appropriate weight
        // from the list of possibilities
        int weight = bold ? FontWeight.BOLD : FontWeight.NORMAL;
```

```
        // create a font from the current state
        Font font = new Font(fontName, 14, FontSize.POINTS,
                             weight, italics, false, false);

        // now update the outputEdit field with the font
        outputEdit.setText("This is a test string.");
        outputEdit.setFont(font);
}

private void boldCheckBox_click(Object source, Event e)
{
    CheckBox cb = (CheckBox)source;
    bold = cb.getChecked();
    updateState();
}

private void italicsCheckBox_click(Object source, Event e)
{
    CheckBox cb = (CheckBox)source;
    italics = cb.getChecked();
    updateState();
}

private void radioButton_checkedChanged(Object source, Event e)
{
    RadioButton rb = (RadioButton)source;
    if (rb.getChecked())
    {
        fontName = rb.getText();
    }
    updateState();
}

/**
 * NOTE: The following code is required by the Visual J++ form
 * designer.  It can be modified using the form editor.  Do not
 * modify it using the code editor.
 */
Container components = new Container();
Edit outputEdit = new Edit();
CheckBox boldCheckBox = new CheckBox();
CheckBox italicsCheckBox = new CheckBox();
GroupBox fontGroupBox = new GroupBox();
RadioButton courierRadioButton = new RadioButton();
RadioButton arialRadioButton = new RadioButton();
RadioButton haettenschweillerRadioButton = new RadioButton();
```

(continued)

```
private void initForm()
{
    // ...created by Forms Designer...
}

/**
 * The main entry point for the application.
 * ...
 */
public static void main(String args[])
{
    Application.run(new Form1());
}
}
```

This version contains several data members that represent the state of the object. The variable *italics* is *true* when the font is to be italicized. Similarly, the variables *bold* and *fontName* represent further font state information.

The event handler that previously handled the Submit button is now somewhat simplified because it no longer reads the button settings directly. In addition, I renamed the handler to *updateState()*. The *updateState()* method updates the output edit text to reflect the current state of the form object as stored in its data members.

The event handlers such as *boldCheckBox_click()* and *italicsCheckBox_click()* are called when the user selects or clears the check box. These methods update the state of the object by updating the appropriate data member and then invoking *updateState()* to reflect the new state information in the output text.

Using the active properties page of the Properties window

The same approach of using one method per button could have been applied to the radio buttons as well; however, a large number of radio buttons can result in a lot of very small event handler functions. As a demonstration of another approach, I included in ButtonDemo2 the function *radioButton_checkedChanged()* to handle a change in state of any of the radio buttons. To use a common function to handle multiple buttons, you can't use the simpler double-click method to establish the event handler. Double-clicking a button causes the Forms Designer to create a unique handler for that button.

To establish an existing function as an event handler or to establish an event handler for an object other than the object's default event, you must use the active properties page of the Properties window. Open the Properties window, and click the object to make the properties of the object visible. Now click the Events button (with the lightning bolt symbol) at the top of the Properties window. This switches the Properties window display to show the events this object receives. These are the active properties of the object, as opposed to the passive data properties of the object we have been viewing up until now.

For the previous example, I chose to attach my *radioButton_checkedChanged()* method to the *checkedChanged* event of each of the radio buttons. This event occurs whenever the selection state of the button changes—that is to say, when a button goes from checked to unchecked or the other way around. To attach the method to the event, click the *checkedChanged* event property and click on the arrow in the property setting box. This displays all of the methods in Form1.java that have the proper prototype to handle the *checkedChanged* event—that is, all methods that return a *void* and take an *Object* and an *Event* as arguments. I selected my *radioButton_checkedChanged()* method from the drop-down list, as shown in Figure 6-3. This list also includes the event handlers for the bold and italics buttons, since their prototypes also match the requirements for the *checkedChanged* event. If you have yet to write the method you want to attach to the button, you can alternatively type what will be the function name into the property setting box.

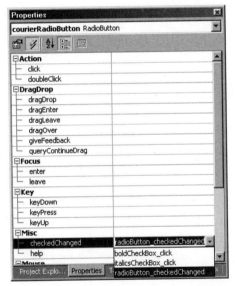

Figure 6-3. *The Properties window showing the active properties of the object—the events that object receives.*

The *radioButton_checkedChanged()* method is only slightly more complicated than its check box equivalents. The *checkedChanged* event occurs when the radio button is being checked either on or off. This would be important if we were saving the state of the radio buttons as a set of Boolean variables. However, since we are only saving the name of the currently checked radio button we want to ignore the event triggered on the radio button as it goes from on to off; hence the *rb.getChecked()* test at the beginning of the *radioButton_checkedChanged()* method.

The output from ButtonDemo2 appears identical to its predecessor except for the absence of the Submit button.

The state approach to handling events

The state event-handling approach used by ButtonDemo2 is common: record the states of the buttons and menu selections within data members of the object and then use a single *updateState()* method to output that state information. This approach has the following advantages:

- It divides the input code (the event handlers) from the output code (the *updateState()* method), which makes code easier to understand and maintain.

- It results in a smaller program since it avoids duplication of the output code in each of the handlers.

- It leaves the state of the object recorded so that other functions can refer to this information easily without having to read the buttons and menu options by name.

LIST BOXES

Another type of simple input control is the list box. The Toolbox offers three types of list boxes: the combo box, the list box, and the checked list box. The examples in this section demonstrate the combo box and list box controls.

The ComboBox Control

The combo box control is the simplest of the list box control types. The class *ComboBox* displays a single-line, read-only box with an arrow on the right. When the user clicks the arrow, the combo box drops down a list of objects the user can pick from. When the user chooses from the list, it disappears and the selected object is displayed in the combo box output window.

The combo box list can be static or calculated. The values for a static list are known at the time that you write the code. You can use the Properties window to specify the items in a static list. The values for a calculated list are determined at run time by the application.

Displaying a static list of strings

The simplest combo box is one that contains a static list of *String* objects. The following example application, ComboBox1, demonstrates a *ComboBox* object containing the months of the year. When the user selects one of the months, the application displays the selection in the combo box and in a separate edit box immediately above the combo box. The output from the resulting application is shown in Figure 6-4.

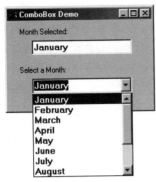

Figure 6-4. *The ComboBox1 demo showing the months of the year displayed in a combo box list.*

The Forms Designer work to create ComboBox1 is straightforward. First drag an Edit control to the Forms Designer and set its *readOnly* property to *true*. Next drag a ComboBox control from the Toolbox to the Forms Designer and change its *name* property to *inputComboBox*. I set both objects' font properties to 14-point bold to make the display stand out better. Adding a couple of labels almost completes the Forms Designer work.

The final task in the Forms Designer is to add the months of the year to the combo box list. To do this, select the *items* property of the ComboBox control in the Properties window. Clicking the ellipsis button in the property setting box for this property opens the String List Editor. Enter the months of the year as shown in Figure 6-5.

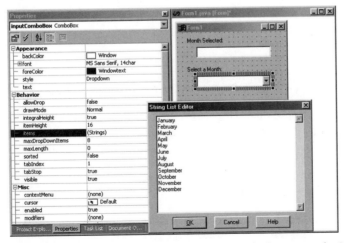

Figure 6-5. *Entering static strings into the combo box using the String List Editor.*

Now all that is left to do for the ComboBox1 application is to add an event handler to copy the month selected in the combo box to the output edit box. Double clicking the ComboBox control in the Forms Designer creates the method *inputComboBox_selectedIndexChanged()*. Add the functionality to this event handler as shown in the following code listing of ComboBox1:

```java
import com.ms.wfc.app.*;
import com.ms.wfc.core.*;
import com.ms.wfc.ui.*;
import com.ms.wfc.html.*;

/**
 * This class displays a static combo box.
 */
public class Form1 extends Form
{
    public Form1()
    {
        // Required for Visual J++ Form Designer support
        initForm();
    }

    /**
     * Form1 overrides dispose so it can clean up the
     * component list.
     */
    public void dispose()
    {
        super.dispose();
        components.dispose();
    }

    /**
     * This method is invoked when the user selects a month
     * from the combo box.
     */
    private void inputComboBox_selectedIndexChanged(Object source,
                                                    Event e)
    {
        // get the index of the selected object
        int index = inputComboBox.getSelectedIndex();

        // get a list of the objects contained in the combo box
        Object[] list = inputComboBox.getItems();

        // pick the one that was selected, and convert it into a string
        String s = list[index].toString();
```

```
        // display the resulting string in the output edit window
        outputEdit.setText(s);
}

/**
 * NOTE: The following code is required by the Visual J++ form
 * designer.  It can be modified using the form editor.  Do not
 * modify it using the code editor.
 */
Container components = new Container();
Edit outputEdit = new Edit();
ComboBox inputComboBox = new ComboBox();
Label label1 = new Label();
Label label2 = new Label();

private void initForm()
{
    this.setText("ComboBox Demo");
    this.setAutoScaleBaseSize(new Point(5, 13));
    this.setClientSize(new Point(232, 139));

    outputEdit.setFont(new Font("MS Sans Serif", 14.0f,
                        FontSize.CHARACTERHEIGHT,
                        FontWeight.BOLD,
                        false, false, false));
    outputEdit.setLocation(new Point(40, 30));
    outputEdit.setSize(new Point(160, 23));
    outputEdit.setTabIndex(0);
    outputEdit.setText("");
    outputEdit.setReadOnly(true);

    inputComboBox.setFont(new Font("MS Sans Serif", 14.0f,
                        FontSize.CHARACTERHEIGHT,
                        FontWeight.BOLD,
                        false, false, false));
    inputComboBox.setLocation(new Point(40, 90));
    inputComboBox.setSize(new Point(160, 24));
    inputComboBox.setTabIndex(1);
    inputComboBox.setText("");
    inputComboBox.setItems(new Object[] {
                        "January",
                        "February",
                        "March",
                        "April",
                        "May",
                        "June",
                        "July",
                        "August",
```

(continued)

```
                              "September",
                              "October",
                              "November",
                              "December"});
        inputComboBox.addOnSelectedIndexChanged(
            new EventHandler(this.inputComboBox_selectedIndexChanged));

        label1.setLocation(new Point(20, 10));
        label1.setSize(new Point(90, 20));
        label1.setTabIndex(2);
        label1.setTabStop(false);
        label1.setText("Month Selected:");

        label2.setLocation(new Point(20, 70));
        label2.setSize(new Point(100, 20));
        label2.setTabIndex(3);
        label2.setTabStop(false);
        label2.setText("Select a Month:");

        this.setNewControls(new Control[] {
                            label2,
                            label1,
                            inputComboBox,
                            outputEdit});
    }


    /**
     * The main entry point for the application.
     *
     * @param args Array of parameters passed to the application
     * via the command line.
     */
    public static void main(String args[])
    {
        Application.run(new Form1());
    }
}
```

The *inputComboBox_selectedIndexChanged()* method is invoked whenever the user selects a new item from the combo box. The index to which the event refers is the index of the currently selected object. The first list item bears the index 0, the next index 1, and so forth.

The *inputComboBox_selectedIndexChanged()* method starts by querying the combo box as to what index the user just chose.

NOTE   At the moment the *selectedIndexChanged()* method is invoked, WFC has updated the index to reflect the newly selected value but has not updated the text. Calling *inputComboBox.getSelectedText()* or *getText()* at this point returns the text associated with the previous index value.

The *inputComboBox_selectedIndexChanged()* method then queries the combo box for a list of the objects it contains. The member of this list at the index position returned from *getSelectedIndex()* is the object the user has just chosen. ComboBox1 converts the selected *Object* into a *String* by calling the method *toString()*. Finally, the resulting string is copied into the *outputEdit* Edit control by calling the *setText()* method.

Why does WFC update the index but not the text?

It might seem curious that at the point the *inputComboBox_selectedIndexChanged()* method is called the index has been updated but the text has not. WFC does this to allow the *inputComboBox_selectedIndexChanged()* method to perform error checking before the user is possibly presented with incorrect output. For example, suppose that in the current program state, the month of February is not allowed because the user has already set the day to 30 or 31.

The following addition to the *inputComboBox_selectedIndexChanged()* method makes it impossible for the user to select February:

```
// if February is selected...
if (index == 1)
{
    // substitute January instead
    index = 0;
    inputComboBox.setIndex(index);
}
```

The call to *setIndex()* resets the index within the combo box. With this addition, whenever the user selects the month of February (index == 1) the function resets the selection to January (index == 0) instead. Once the *inputComboBox_selectedIndexChanged()* method is completed, the combo box displays the new text based on the resulting value of the index. In this case, the month of January is displayed.

If WFC updated the text before calling *inputComboBox_selectedIndexChanged()*, the user would see an annoying flicker as February is displayed and then quickly replaced by January. By waiting to update the display until after the *inputComboBox_selectedIndexChanged()* method has completed, WFC is sure of the text that the program wants to display.

Populating the combo box with different object types

Just because strings are the most common combo box occupants doesn't mean that *String* is the only class you can store in a combo box. In fact, you can add any type of object that you want to a combo box as long as the type you select provides a *toString()* method that returns something the user will recognize. The presence of the *toString()* method is important because the value it returns gets displayed in the combo box list.

For example, the ComboBox2 example application beginning on the following page displays a combo box listing different tree types. When the user selects a

tree type, the application displays the relative wood density and growth rate for
that tree type in the output edit box previously used to display the selected month.
The output from this application is shown in Figure 6-6.

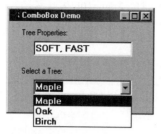

Figure 6-6. *The ComboBox2 application demonstrates that the objects added to a
combo box list are not limited to strings.*

The program listing for ComboBox2 is shown here (with the automatically
generated *initForm()* method and *dispose()* method removed from the listing for
brevity's sake).

```java
import com.ms.wfc.app.*;
import com.ms.wfc.core.*;
import com.ms.wfc.ui.*;
import com.ms.wfc.html.*;

import java.lang.reflect.*;

/**
 * This class displays a static combo box containing TreeType
 * objects. This class also demonstrates the use of the Java
 * reflection features in displaying the name of the enumerated
 * types.
 */
public class Form1 extends Form
{
    public Form1()
    {
        // Required for Visual J++ Form Designer support
        initForm();

        // populate the list with a few different types of trees
        Object[] list = new Object[]
        {
        new TreeType("Maple", TreeHardness.SOFT, TreeGrowthRate.FAST),
        new TreeType("Oak",   TreeHardness.HARD, TreeGrowthRate.SLOW),
        new TreeType("Birch", TreeHardness.SOFT, TreeGrowthRate.MEDIUM)
        };
        inputComboBox.setItems(list);
    }

    ⋮
```

```
/**
 * This method is invoked when the user selects a month
 * from the combo box.
 */
private void inputComboBox_selectedIndexChanged(Object source,
                                                          Event e)
{
    // get the index of the selected object
    int index = inputComboBox.getSelectedIndex();

    // get a list of the items contained in the combo box
    Object[] list = inputComboBox.getItems();

    // index the object selected, and convert it into a string
    // String s = list[index].toString();
    TreeType t = (TreeType)list[index];
    String s   = t.properties();


    // output the string in the output edit object
    outputEdit.setText(s);
}

/**
 * NOTE: The following code is required by the Visual J++ form
 * designer.  It can be modified using the form editor.  Do not
 * modify it using the code editor.
 */
Container components = new Container();
Edit outputEdit = new Edit();
ComboBox inputComboBox = new ComboBox();
Label label1 = new Label();
Label label2 = new Label();

private void initForm()
{
    // ...created by the Forms Designer...
}

/**
 * The main entry point for the application.
 * ...
 */
public static void main(String args[])
{
```

(continued)

```
            Application.run(new Form1());
        }
    }


/**
 * This class describes the relevant properties of a type of tree.
 */
class TreeType
{
    String name;
    int    hardness;
    int    growthRate;

    TreeType(String name, int hardness, int growthRate)
    {
        this.name       = name;
        this.hardness   = hardness;
        this.growthRate = growthRate;
    }

    public String toString()
    {
        return name;
    }

    public String properties()
    {
        Class c;
        Field f;

        // convert the hardness into a string:
        // use the reflection classes Class and Field
        c = TreeHardness.class;    // get the class object
        f = c.getDeclaredFields()[hardness]; // get a list
                                // of the constants
        String hl = f.toString(); // convert that into a string
        hl = hl.substring(hl.indexOf(".") + 1); // keep just the name

        // repeat the process for the growth rate
        c = TreeGrowthRate.class;
        f = c.getDeclaredFields()[growthRate];
        String gr = f.toString();
        gr = gr.substring(gr.indexOf(".") + 1);

        return hl + ", " + gr;
    }

}
```

```
class TreeHardness extends Enum
{
    public static final int SOFT   = 0;
    public static final int MEDIUM = 1;
    public static final int HARD   = 2;

    public static boolean valid(int value)
    {
        return (value >= SOFT) && (value <= HARD);
    }
}

class TreeGrowthRate extends Enum
{
    public static final int SLOW   = 0;
    public static final int MEDIUM = 1;
    public static final int FAST   = 2;

    public static boolean valid(int value)
    {
        return (value >= SLOW) && (value <= FAST);
    }
}
```

Once the form has been initialized by the *initForm()* method, the *Form1* constructor adds three *TreeType* objects to the combo box list. You must program this code manually because it isn't possible to add user-defined types to a combo box using the Properties window.

The *TreeType* class contains nothing more than a tree type name, a wood hardness value, and a growth-rate value. The *toString()* method for *TreeType* returns the tree name.

The *properties()* method displays the hardness and growth rate as a string, but it does so in a very interesting way: *properties()* uses Java's reflection classes.

NOTE The *java.lang.reflection* package allows a method to ask questions about another class.

First *properties()* fetches the *Class* object that describes *TreeHardness*. It then asks the class for a list of all its declared fields. The *getDeclaredFields()* method returns an array of *Field* objects.

NOTE *Fields* is another word for *data members*. *Declared fields* are fields that are declared in the class. This does not include any fields inherited from a base class.

The enumerated class *TreeHardness* has only the members *SOFT, MEDIUM,* and *HARD,* so *getDeclaredFields()* returns an array containing three *Field* objects, one for each data member. (See the sidebar "What's an Enumeration Class?" for an explanation of enumerated classes.) Because we specified an index, *[hardness]*, in our call to *getDeclaredFields()*, the method returns the field corresponding to the current hardness setting rather than returning the entire array.

WHAT'S AN ENUMERATION CLASS?

You might be wondering why I bothered to create a *TreeHardness* and a *TreeGrowthRate* class just to hold a few *public static final int* definitions. There are several points about the *TreeHardness* and *TreeGrowthRate* classes worth noting.

1. Each class extends *Enum*.

2. Each class contains a list of *public static final int* constants.

3. Each class contains the static method *boolean valid(int)*. This method returns *true* if the integer passed it represents one of the valid values for that property. A class that fulfills these requirements is known as an enumeration type.

NOTE There is no *enum* keyword in Java as there is in C++.

Defining your constants within enumeration types has several advantages. First, as you are defining the *TreeType* class, the Statement Completion feature will help you out. As soon as you type *new TreeType(*, Statement Completion gives you a list of arguments. The name of the argument should indicate the name of the class to use in describing it. Thus, the second argument to the *TreeType* constructor is called *hardness,* which prompts me to use the *TreeHardness* class. Once I have typed *TreeHardness.*, Statement Completion drops down a list of possible values including *SOFT, MEDIUM,* and *HARD* (along with some methods and properties inherited from the base class).

NOTE It's a standard Java coding convention to use all capital letters in the names of members of type *public static final int*.

NOTE The *public static final int* data member takes the place of a *const* data member in C++.

The ComboBox2 example application uses the same reflection mechanism to display the available fields that the smart editor uses. Later we'll see that when we define our own controls the Toolbox has access to the enumerated properties of the object using this same reflection mechanism.

The call to *f.toString()* returns the name of the field as a string—*SOFT, MEDIUM,* or *HARD*. Unfortunately for us, the name that *f.toString()* returns includes the name of the class. I added a call to *substring()* on the next line to strip off the class name by removing everything prior to the "." that normally separates the class name from the member's name.

The *properties()* method repeats the process for the growth rate before tacking the two property values together and returning the result as a string.

The *inputComboBox_selectedIndexChanged()* method that handles the combo box selection is the same here as in the earlier ComboBox1 example, except that it calls the *TreeType.properties()* method rather than the *toString()* method. (With the *toString()* call left in place, the program would still work, but only the name of the tree type and not its properties would appear in the output window)

Populating the combo box list dynamically

At the time you're writing a program, it isn't always possible to know what is to go into a combo box. Sometimes a combo box list must be calculated when the program runs. For example, the following ComboBox3 code populates a combo box with the names of the files in the current directory.

```
import com.ms.wfc.app.*;
import com.ms.wfc.core.*;
import com.ms.wfc.ui.*;
import com.ms.wfc.html.*;

import com.ms.wfc.io.*;

/**
 * This class displays a combo box whose contents are
 * calculated at run time from the list of files in the
 * current directory.
 */
public class Form1 extends Form
{
    public Form1()
    {
        // Required for Visual J++ Form Designer support
        initForm();

        // populate the combo box with a list of all file names
        // in the current directory
        inputComboBox.setItems(File.getFiles("*.*"));
    }


    // ...rest of the program is same as ComboBox1...
```

The *public static* method *File.getFiles()* returns a list of all of the files and directories that match the filter passed to it. The *File.getFiles()* method returns this list as an array of *String* objects containing the names of the files. This array is ideal, since this is exactly what we need to pass to the *setItems()* method. Setting the *sorted* property of the *ComboBox* object to *true* in the Properties window ensures that the files' names appear in alphabetical order in the combo box list. The output of executing this program in the test directory is shown in Figure 6-7.

Figure 6-7. *The contents of the combo box must often be calculated at run time, as in this file list.*

The ListBox Control

As powerful as it is, the combo box has one serious limitation: only one member from the drop-down list can be selected at a time. The ListBox control doesn't suffer from this limitation. Visually the list box is rather different from the combo box. A list box has no drop-down list; its list remains visible at all times. Fortunately, you can set the size of the list box in the Forms Designer. If there are more objects in the list box than can be displayed at one time, the list box automatically displays a vertical scroll bar. In addition, the list box has no output window where the currently selected item is displayed; instead, selected items are displayed in inverse video.

The ListBox control has three modes of operation: One (also known as Single Select) mode, Multi Simple mode, and Multi Extended mode. In Single Select mode, only one item can be selected at a time. In Multi Simple mode, the user clicks on an item to select it. Clicking the same item again deselects it. The user can select any number of items but must select each item individually.

Multi Extended mode is the same mode used in Windows Explorer and most other programs that use a list box. With this type of list box the user can select large blocks of items. Clicking one item and then clicking a second while holding down the Shift key automatically selects the two items and all of the items in between. In addition, the user can select or deselect individual items by holding down the Control key. (In effect, as long as the user presses the Control key, the list box operates in Multi Simple mode.)

From the programmer's point of view, the list box is very similar to the check box. In Single Select mode, the list box works the same as the combo box: calling *getSelectedIndex()* from within the event handler returns the index of the selected item.

Usually it's preferable to operate list boxes in Multi Simple or Multi Extended mode. In either of these modes, the event handler must be prepared to read a list of selected items, as shown in the following code.

```
private void selectListBox_selectedIndexChanged(Object source, Event e)
{
    Object[] list = selectListBox.getSelectedItems();

    // ...operate on the list...
}
```

Using this approach might mean entering a *for* loop to iterate through the items in the list.

Multiselect list boxes

The following example, ListBoxDemo, is a file deletion utility that uses the ListBox control to allow the user to select the files to delete. (ListBoxDemo does not actually delete the files selected.) After creating a Windows-based project in the normal way, I used the Forms Designer to create the display shown in Figure 6-8.

Figure 6-8. *The ListBoxDemo program demonstrating how the list box can enable the selection of multiple items.*

The source code for the ListBoxDemo application is as follows. (I left out sections of code, such as those created by the Forms Designer, for brevity).

```
import com.ms.wfc.app.*;
import com.ms.wfc.core.*;
import com.ms.wfc.ui.*;
import com.ms.wfc.html.*;

import com.ms.wfc.io.*;
```

(continued)

```
/**
 * This ListBoxDemo uses a list box to select files to
 * "delete." (Uncomment the call to File.delete() if
 * you want the application to actually delete anything.)
 */
public class Form1 extends Form
{
    String currentPath = ".";

    public Form1()
    {
        // Required for Visual J++ Form Designer support
        initForm();

        updateSelectListBox("*.*");
    }

    ⋮

    private void filterEdit_textChanged(Object source,
                                        Event e)
    {
        String s = filterEdit.getText();
        currentPath = File.getDirectory(s);
        updateSelectListBox(s);
    }

    private void updateSelectListBox(String filter)
    {
        // get a list of the files; ignore any errors
        // that might arise if the directory doesn't exist
        Object[] list = new Object[0];
        try
        {
            list = File.getFiles(filter);
        }
        catch(Exception e)
        {
        }

        // update the select list box with the file names
        selectListBox.setItems(list);

        // update the select list box
        selectListBox_selectedIndexChanged(null, null);
    }
```

```
private void selectListBox_selectedIndexChanged(
                                    Object source,
                                    Event e)
{
    Object[] list = selectListBox.getSelectedItems();

    String[] fileArray = new String[list.length];
    for (int i = 0; i < list.length; i++)
    {
        // if the files selected are not in the
        // default directory, convert the filename
        // into the full path
        String filePath =   currentPath
                            + "\\"
                            + (String)list[i];
        // if the file is a directory...
        if (File.isDirectory(filePath))
        {
            // put an asterisk on the front
            filePath = "*" + filePath;
        }
        else
        {
            filePath = " " + filePath;
        }

        fileArray[i] = filePath;
    }

    outputEdit.setLines(fileArray);
}

private void deleteButton_click(Object source, Event e)
{
    String[] list = outputEdit.getLines();

    for(int i = 0; i < list.length; i++)
    {
        // the following function deletes the file
        // without putting it into the Recycle Bin
        // File.delete(list[i]);
    }

    filterEdit_textChanged(null, null);
}
```

(continued)

```
/**
 * NOTE: The following code is required by the Visual J++ form
 * designer.  It can be modified using the form editor.  Do not
 * modify it using the code editor.
 */
Container components = new Container();
Edit outputEdit = new Edit();
ListBox selectListBox = new ListBox();
Button deleteButton = new Button();
Edit filterEdit = new Edit();
Label label1 = new Label();
Label label2 = new Label();
Label label3 = new Label();

private void initForm()
{
    // ...built automatically by Forms Designer...
}


/**
 * The main entry point for the application.
 * ...
 */
public static void main(String args[])
{
    Application.run(new Form1());
}
}
```

Once *initForm()* has created the form with the associated ListBox control, the *Form1()* constructor calls the *updateSelectListBox()* method to populate the list box with a list of file names. Passing the filter *.* instructs *updateSelectListBox()* to select all files in the current directory. The *updateSelectListBox()* method gets a list of the files that pass the current filter by calling *File.getFiles()*. By catching any exception thrown, *updateSelectListBox()* ignores any errors that *getFiles()* might detect. (For example, *getFiles()* throws an exception if the directory specified doesn't exist.) The resulting list, which might be empty, is passed to the *selectListBox* object for display.

As the user selects items from the file selection list box, WFC automatically invokes *selectListBox_selectedIndexChanged()*. This function gets a list of the selected items by calling *getSelectedItems()*. Knowing that these are the names of files, *selectListBox_selectedIndexChanged()* iterates through the list adding the full path to each file. In addition, if a file is a directory the function adds an asterisk to the front of the file name. The resulting list of file names is displayed in the *outputEdit* object by calling *setLines()*.

The *deleteButton_click()* method is invoked when the user chooses the Delete button. This function gets a list of the files to be deleted from the *outputEdit* object by calling *getLines()*. It then loops through this list "deleting" each file.

NOTE Since deleting files is too dangerous in a simple demo for a book, I've commented out the call to *File.delete()*. If you would like this utility to actually delete the selected files, uncomment the call to *File.delete()* and recompile the program. However, be advised that *File.delete()* deletes each file or directory immediately and does not move the file to the Recycle Bin.

THE RICHEDIT CONTROL

The final control I want to discuss under the topic of simple controls is the RichEdit control. This control is classified as a simple control because it's simple for the programmer to use—but there is nothing simple about the way the RichEdit control operates. The RichEdit control is an editor object that can read and write Rich Text Format (RTF) strings.

RTF is a nonproprietary format supported by most word processors including Microsoft Word. RTF isn't limited to the Windows world; most UNIX editors can read and write RTF files as well. While you can't express every formatting feature in the world in RTF—for example, you can't save revision history in RTF format—as the name implies, RTF is rich in its expressiveness.

Building an RTF File Editor

The following RTFEditor program builds a fairly powerful RTF editor using an edit box for a file filter, a list box in Single Select mode, a rich edit box, and two button controls. The arrangement of objects within the form is shown in Figure 6-9.

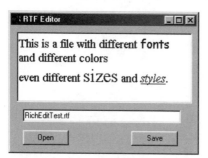

Figure 6-9. *The RichEdit control has no trouble reading an .RTF file generated in Microsoft Word, although it can't display text in different colors.*

The Forms Designer work

To build RTFEditor, drag the RichEdit control from the Toolbox to the Forms Designer and resize it until it takes up most of the available space in the form. Then rename it to *richEdit* and anchor it against all four sides of the form. Anchoring the control in this way ensures that the rich edit box will change size proportionately as the user resizes the form. Next set the control's *wordWrap* property to *false* and its *scrollBars* property to *Both*. This will cause scroll bars to appear whenever the text is too large to fit within the visible window.

Now add an Edit control below the RichEdit control. This Edit control's purpose is to enable the user to enter a file name to open or to save to. Finish the application's interface by adding an Open button and a Save button along the bottom of the form. Anchor these buttons and the file name Edit control to the bottom, left, and right borders of the form.

The code

The code resulting from the form design work and the code I added are shown here.

```java
import com.ms.wfc.app.*;
import com.ms.wfc.core.*;
import com.ms.wfc.ui.*;
import com.ms.wfc.html.*;

/**
 * This class demonstrates the RichEdit control.
 */
public class Form1 extends Form
{
    public Form1()
    {
        // Required for Visual J++ Form Designer support
        initForm();
    }

        ⋮

    private void openButton_click(Object source, Event e)
    {
        // get the file name from the edit box
        String fileName = fileNameEdit.getText();

        // now read the file into the RichEdit control
        loadRichEdit(fileName);
    }

    private void closeButton_click(Object source, Event e)
    {
        String fileName = fileNameEdit.getText();
        try
        {
            richEdit.saveFile(fileName);
        }
        catch(Exception ex)
        {
```

```
                fileNameEdit.setText(ex.getMessage());
        }
}


/**
 * Given a file name, open the file into the
 * RichEdit control.
 */
private void loadRichEdit(String fileName)
{
    // open the specified file
    try
    {
        richEdit.loadFile(fileName);
    }

    // first catch invalid file type
    catch(WFCInvalidArgumentException e)
    {
        richEdit.setText("Invalid (non-RTF) file");
    }

    // handle all others the same way
    catch(Exception e)
    {
        richEdit.setText(e.getMessage());
    }
}


/**
 * NOTE: The following code is required by the Visual J++ form
 * designer.  It can be modified using the form editor.  Do not
 * modify it using the code editor.
 */
Container components = new Container();
Edit fileNameEdit = new Edit();
Button openButton = new Button();
Button saveButton = new Button();
RichEdit richEdit = new RichEdit();

private void initForm()
{
    // ...generated by the Forms Designer...
}


/**
 * The main entry point for the application.
```

(continued)

```
 *  ...
 */
public static void main(String args[])
{
    Application.run(new Form1());
}
}
```

The *openButton_click()* method, which is invoked when the user selects Open, begins by reading the file name from the *fileNameEdit* object. It then passes this name to *loadRichEdit()* for processing.

The *loadRichEdit()* method uses the convenient *RichEdit.loadFile()* method to read the file into the RichEdit control. This method can throw one of two exceptions depending on the problem it detects. If *loadFile()* can find and open the file, but then determines that the file isn't in RTF format, it throws the exception *WFCInvalidArgumentException*. In this case, the *loadRichEdit()* method outputs a specific error message. If *loadFile()* can't open and read the file, it throws an I/O exception. In this case, *loadRichEdit()* relies on the error message in the exception.

The *closeButton_click()* method uses the RichEdit control's *saveFile()* method to save the contents of the RichEdit control to disk.

To test the RTFEditor program, I created a file in Microsoft Word containing several features. I then saved the file in RTF format and opened the file with RTFEditor. The result is shown in Figure 6-9 on page 167. As you can see, RTFEditor has no trouble with the different fonts, font sizes, and font weights. However, in Word the second line is highlighted in green, but RTFEditor isn't capable of displaying lines in different colors (although it can display text in different colors).

Adding Drag-and-Drop Capability

An important feature of any text editor is the ability to support drag-and-drop actions. By this I mean two capabilities that are quite distinct. One is the ability to drag a text file and drop it onto the text editor program's executable file (or its icon) to begin program execution and immediately load the file. Let's call this capability *initial drag-and-drop*. A second capability meant by drag-and-drop is to drag a file to the running text editor program and drop it there to load the file in that program. Let's call this *in-progress drag-and-drop*.

Implementing initial drag-and-drop

Windows handles initial drag-and-drop just as if the user had executed the program from the DOS command prompt. For example, if the user drags file A.rtf and drops it on application B.EXE, Windows executes B and passes it the name A.rtf as a single argument just as if the user had entered the following DOS command:

```
B A.rtf
```

If you have been reading the chapters in order, you will remember that even our console applications in Part I had the ability to read arguments to the program using the *args* array. Thus, you already know how to implement initial drag-and-drop.

Implementing in-progress drag-and-drop

Initial drag-and-drop was easy to handle because the program was not already running. A program is already underway during in-progress drag-and-drop. The only way to get the attention of a running program is through events.

When the user begins dragging a file, Windows pastes the name of the file onto the Clipboard. This data stays on the Clipboard the entire time the mouse is dragging the file.

When the mouse moves onto our RTFEditor, Windows generates messages that Visual J++ 6 converts to three different event types: *dragEnter*, *dragOver*, and *dragDrop*. Any control that implements drag-and-drop must handle these three events.

The *dragEnter* event is generated as the mouse pointer enters the region occupied by the control. The *dragOver* event occurs repeatedly as the mouse moves within the control. Finally, the *dragDrop* event occurs when the user releases the object. (There is also a *dragExit* event, which occurs if the mouse leaves the control without dropping the object, but we won't be using that event.)

The problem

Let's add the ability to process a file dropped on the RTFEditor form. This includes both initial drag-and-drop and in-progress drag-and-drop.

Part of the problem is already solved for us. The RichEdit control appears only after the RTFEditor program has started; therefore, it has no need for initial drag-and-drop capability. However, we will have to add the initial drag-and-drop capability to the RTFEditor program itself. In addition, the RichEdit control handles in-progress drag-and-drop already, but the form that contains this control has no in-progress drag-and-drop capability of its own. We will need to add this capability to the form.

The Properties window

Before we can begin adding drag-and-drop event handlers, we must inform WFC that we intend to allow drag-and-drop on the form. Select the form in the Forms Designer. In the Properties window, set the *allowDrop* property to *true*. The RichEdit control always allows drops.

Switch to the active properties in the Properties window, and select the form again. Now double-click *dragEnter* to create the *Form1_dragEnter()* method; double-click *dragOver* to create the *Form1_dragOver()* method; and double-click *dragDrop* to create the *Form1_dragDrop()* method.

Code changes to support drag-and-drop

The following example shows the code for the RTFEditor application.

```
import com.ms.wfc.app.*;
import com.ms.wfc.core.*;
import com.ms.wfc.ui.*;
import com.ms.wfc.html.*;

import com.ms.wfc.io.*;

/**
 * This class demonstrates the RichEdit control with
 * drag-and-drop capability.
 */
public class Form1 extends Form
{
    public Form1(String[] args)
    {
        // Required for Visual J++ Form Designer support
        initForm();

        // if there is a file name present...
        if (args.length == 1)
        {
            // load it (This probably means that the user
            // has dropped the file name onto the program's
            // name in Windows Explorer or on top of the program's
            // icon in a window. I call this initial drag-and-
            // drop capability.)
            loadRichEdit(args[0]);
        }
    }

    :

    /**
     * Open the file contained in the fileNameEdit text field.
     */
    private void openButton_click(Object source, Event e)
    {
        // get the file name from the edit box
        String fileName = fileNameEdit.getText();

        // now read the file into the RichEdit control
        loadRichEdit(fileName);
    }
```

```
/**
 * Close the file specified in the fileNameEdit text field.
 */
private void closeButton_click(Object source, Event e)
{
    String fileName = fileNameEdit.getText();
    try
    {
        richEdit.saveFile(fileName);
    }
    catch(Exception ex)
    {
        fileNameEdit.setText(ex.getMessage());
    }
}

/**
 * Given a file name, open the file into the
 * RichEdit control.
 */
private void loadRichEdit(String fileName)
{
    // make sure the Edit control displays
    // the file name
    fileNameEdit.setText(fileName);

    // open the specified file
    try
    {
        richEdit.loadFile(fileName);
    }

    // first catch invalid file type
    catch(WFCInvalidArgumentException e)
    {
        richEdit.setText("Invalid (non-RTF) file");
    }

    // handle all others the same way
    catch(Exception e)
    {
        richEdit.setText(e.getMessage());
    }
}
```

(continued)

```
// --------handle the in-progress drag-and-drop--------------
/**
 * Record the drag-and-drop state. If dragEffect is NONE,
 * a FileName was not found on the Clipboard, meaning that
 * there's nothing to copy.
 */
private int dragEffect;

/**
 * When the user drags the mouse into the form, check to
 * see whether there is a file name on the Clipboard. If not,
 * set the dragEffect to NONE. This precludes a drop
 * operation. If there is, set the effect to COPY (since
 * we want to copy the file name from the Clipboard).
 * If there is more than one file name, just take the
 * first one.
 */
private void Form1_dragEnter(Object source, DragEvent e)
{
    // for now, assume that there is no file name on
    // the Clipboard
    e.effect = DragDropEffect.NONE;

    // if there is a FileName data type in the Clipboard...
    IDataObject ido = e.data;
    if (ido.getDataPresent("FileName"))
    {
        // get the file name
        // (there may be more than one)...
        Object o = ido.getData(DataFormats.CF_HDROP);

        // as an array of file names
        String[] fileNames = (String[])o;

        // just take the first file name
        // (if there's more than one, ignore the rest)
        String fileName = fileNames[0];

        // now store that name in the fileNameEdit object
        // (we will need that name when the drop occurs)
        fileNameEdit.setText(fileName);

        // tell the drag operation that this succeeded
        e.effect = DragDropEffect.COPY;
    }

    // save the dragEffect (whether it's successful
    // or not)
    dragEffect = e.effect;
}
```

```
/**
 * Keep setting the dragEffect as long as the mouse is
 * hovering over the form during a drag operation.
 */
private void Form1_dragOver(Object source, DragEvent e)
{
    e.effect = dragEffect;
}



/**
 * When the user drops an RTF file onto the Form,
 * act like the user clicked the Open button. (The
 * file name should have been put in the fileNameEdit
 * text edit field already by the dragEnter event.)
 */
private void Form1_dragDrop(Object source, DragEvent e)
{
    // if the dragEffect is COPY...
    if (dragEffect == DragDropEffect.COPY)
    {
        // proceed with drop operation
        openButton_click(null, null);
    }
}

/**
 * NOTE: The following code is required by the Visual J++ form
 * designer.  It can be modified using the form editor.  Do not
 * modify it using the code editor.
 */
Container components = new Container();
Edit fileNameEdit = new Edit();
Button openButton = new Button();
Button saveButton = new Button();
RichEdit richEdit = new RichEdit();

private void initForm()
{
    //...generated by the Forms Designer...
}

/**
 * The main entry point for the application.
 *
 * @param args - the name of the file to open (optional)
 */
```

(continued)

```
public static void main(String args[])
{
    Application.run(new Form1(args));
}
}
```

The *loadRichEdit()*, *openButton_click()*, and *closeButton_click()* methods are unchanged from previous versions of RTFEditor. The *Form1()* constructor has been updated to handle the arguments passed to *main()*. If there is one argument present, the constructor assumes it is the name of a file and calls *loadRichEdit()* to load the file into the RichEdit control. This is all that is required to handle initial drag-and-drop.

The methods below the *//---handle in-process drag-and-drop---* comment are new to this version of RTFEditor.

The first addition is the data member *dragEffect*. Its meaning will become clear shortly.

Next comes the *Form1_dragEnter()* method, which is invoked as the dragged mouse pointer enters *Form1*. This method has two arguments: the source object and a *DragEvent* object. The *Form1_dragEnter()* method begins by setting the *effect* member of *DragEvent* to *DragDropEffect.NONE*. (This happens to be the default value of *effect*, but it doesn't hurt to include this statement for demonstration purposes.) Setting *effect* to *NONE* tells Visual J++ 6 to not allow the drop event. In addition, this sets the mouse pointer to that funny-looking circle with a slash through the middle, like a European "don't enter" sign (assuming that Windows is using the default pointer set).

The *Form1_dragEnter()* method continues by examining the *data* member of *DragEvent*. The *data* member implements the *IDataObject* interface, which means that it supports a number of methods all related to retrieving and storing data to and from the Clipboard.

NOTE   The *IDataObject* interface is also used to represent objects being pasted from the Clipboard, as we'll see in Chapter 7.

Since the Clipboard can contain almost any type of object, *Form1_dragEnter()* can't assume that something on the Clipboard is the name of a file. The call to *ido.getDataPresent("FileName")* returns *true* if an object of type *FileName* is present on the Clipboard. If *true* is returned, *Form1_dragEnter()* reads the object off the Clipboard by calling *ido.getData()*.

There are two ways to invoke *getData()*. The call *getData("FileName")* is the older, now deprecated way to read a file name from the Clipboard. This method returns the name of the file in the older DOS-compatible 8.3 naming format. Calling *getData(DataFormats.CF_HDROP)* returns the file name in the newer Win32 format. (*DataFormats* is an enumerated class containing a number of different format indicators.)

The object returned by *getData()* is an array of *String* objects. Each *String* in the array contains the name of a file. The *getData()* method returns an array because the user can select a number of files and drop them all at the same time. Since RTFEditor can only open a single file, *Form1_dragEnter()* selects the first file name and ignores the rest. This file name is then stored in the *fileNameEdit* object for two reasons. The first reason is to display the name of the file the user is about to drop. The second reason is that this is the file that RTFEditor will open in the event the drop is performed.

The *Form1_dragEnter()* method then updates the *effect* field in *DragEvent* to *DragDropEffect.COPY*. This has two important effects. First, it changes the mouse pointer to a plus sign to indicate that a drop on this object is allowed (again, assuming the default mouse pointers). Second, updating the *effect* field to *COPY* allows the *Form1_dragDrop()* method to drop the file onto the form.

Finally, the drag effect is saved in the local *dragEffect* data member. Thus, if *Form1_dragEnter()* found a *"FileName"* object on the Clipboard, *dragEffect* is set to *COPY*; if not, *dragEffect* is set to *NONE*.

The *Form1_dragOver()* method simply updates the *effect* data member of the *DragEvent* to the value stored by *Form1_dragEnter()*. This ensures that the mouse pointer continues to appear as the copy symbol.

Now that the *Form1_dragEnter()* method has done all the dirty work of retrieving the name of the file to open from the Clipboard, all *Form1_dragDrop()* has to do is invoke the *openButton_click()* method, exactly as if the user had clicked the Open button. (The test for *dragEffect* equal to *COPY* is not really necessary, since if *effect* were set to *NONE* the drop wouldn't be allowed anyway, but it doesn't hurt anything to be specific.) The *openButton_click()* method loads the file named in the *fileNameEdit* object into the RichEdit control.

The result

Figure 6-10 shows the user dragging the file RichEditTest1 .rtf onto the RTFEditor form. The small arrow with a plus sign in the lower-right corner of the form indicates that

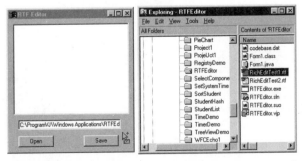

Figure 6-10. *Dragging an .RTF file onto the RTFEditor form changes the cursor to the copy-style plus sign and updates the edit box with the name of the file.*

RTFEditor is prepared to accept a drop at that location. The edit box at the bottom of the RTFEditor form contains the name of the file about to be dropped. (Both the cursor and the edit box were set by the *Form1_dropEnter()* method.)

Figure 6-11 shows the result of dropping the RichEditTest1.rtf file onto the RTFEditor form. Notice that the file is now opened in the RichEdit window and the name and path are displayed in the edit box, ready to be used by the Save button once the user has completed editing the file.

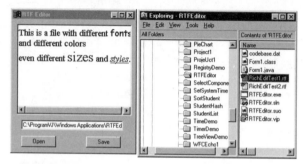

Figure 6-11. *Dropping the .RTF file onto the RTFEditor form opens the file in the RichEdit window.*

Extending drag-and-drop

The drag-and-drop capability shown here involves the dragging of a file onto the RTFEditor form. The *Form1_dragEnter()* method reflected this fact in that what it checked for was an object of type *"FileName"*. As I have already mentioned, Windows supports drag-and-drop of different types of objects other than file names. For example, the user might cut a section of RTF text from one application and drop it onto our RTFEditor.

Extending the file drag-and-drop code shown here to other types of objects is a matter of checking for a different type of object on the Clipboard and recognizing the format of the object returned. Chapter 7 demonstrates the passing of data other than straight text through the Clipboard in the context of the cut-and-paste operation.

CONCLUSION

In this chapter, you've seen examples using all of the simple input control types: buttons, combo boxes, list boxes, edit boxes, and rich edit boxes. The final example of the RTFEditor program might have seemed a bit clumsy without the typical menu options such as File and Edit. The next chapter will solve that problem by introducing menu items to our text editor.

Chapter 7

Menus and Dialog Boxes

The RTFEditor application in Chapter 6 demonstrated how to graft a couple of buttons and an edit box onto a rich edit control to build a fairly functional Rich Text Format (RTF) text editor. However, RTFEditor was limited in what it could do because it was missing two fundamental weapons in the user interface arsenal: menus and dialog boxes. In this chapter, we'll start over and build an editor with the standard menu across the top, a toolbar just underneath the menu, and dialog boxes that are displayed on demand. We'll even add a context-sensitive menu to the editor. (Of course, this editor application won't have all the features that you would expect from a commercial editor. As an exercise, you can add features to the editor later if you want.) All the examples in this chapter are located in the Windows Applications folder on the companion CD.

THE FILE MENU

The left-most menu for any editor is the File menu. Since this menu is as good a place to start as any, we'll build our initial Editor1 application around the File menu. Once we've mastered the File menu, adding further menu items will be a breeze.

The Forms Designer Work

As always, create the Editor1 project using the Windows Application builder. In Project Explorer, double-click Form1.java to open the Forms Designer. The majority of the work on Editor1 can be completed from within the Forms Designer.

Building the menus

To create the Editor1 application, begin by dragging a MainMenu control from the Toolbox to the Forms Designer. Unlike most controls, it doesn't really matter where you drop the MainMenu control—the menu will always appear along the top of the form. As soon as you drop the MainMenu control, a small box appears with the prompt "Type Here".

Start by typing *&File*. The ampersand tells the Forms Designer that the access key for this menu option is F—that is, the user can enter Alt+F rather than click the File menu. Instead of displaying the ampersand, the Forms Designer under- scores the F.

As soon as you begin typing in the first Type Here box, two more Type Here boxes open up: one below for the first submenu item and one to the right for the next menu item. The Edit menu will go to the right of the File menu, but for the Editor1 application let's stick with the File menu. Add the File menu items for New, Open..., Save, Save As..., and Exit. Figure 7-1 shows the Editor1 menu items being edited.

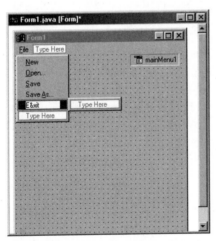

Figure 7-1. *The Forms Designer showing the menu editor for creating menu items.*

Once the File menu is complete, return to the Properties window to give each submenu item a name related to the menu item's function, such as *openFileMI* for the Open menu item on the File menu. At the same time, edit the *shortcut* property to define shortcut keys for the two most common file commands: Ctrl+S for Save and

Ctrl+X for Exit. Figure 7-2 shows the Ctrl+S key combination being assigned to the Save command.

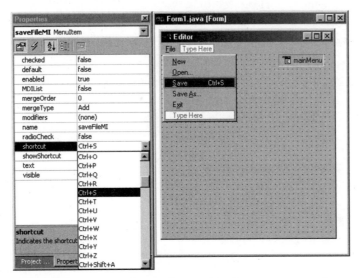

Figure 7-2. *Setting a shortcut key enables the user to access the menu item from the keyboard with two keystrokes.*

Building the dialog boxes

Thinking ahead, it is clear that the Open menu item on the File menu will need to open a dialog box from which the user can select the file to open. Fortunately, the Toolbox includes an OpenFileDialog control that creates just such a dialog box.

To add an Open file dialog box to the application, simply drag an OpenFileDialog control to the form. Like the MainMenu control, it doesn't matter where you put the object. This is because the dialog box is opened as a separate window. I named my OpenFileDialog control *openFD*. In addition, I set the default extension to *.rtf*; if the user enters a file name without an extension, the Open file dialog box will assign this extension. Finally I set the *filter* property to **.rtf*, as shown in Figure 7-3. This sets the initial file filter to search for the RTF files that the editor specializes in. The Open file dialog box is created hidden. I will eventually have to add the code to unhide the Open file dialog box when it is needed.

Repeat this process for adding the dialog box to display when the user chooses Save As (or Save, if the file has never been saved). This time you'll use the SaveFileDialog control. You can use the same property settings as for the OpenFileDialog control, except the name of this object is *saveFD*.

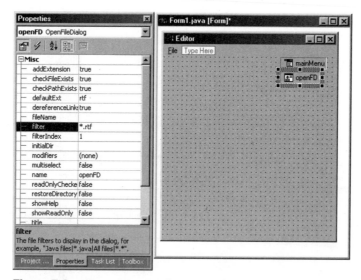

Figure 7-3. *When setting up the OpenFileDialog control, remember to set the filter and the default extension to match the functionality of the application.*

Finishing the design

Only a few final touches remain to the design of the form. First there is the addition of the all-important RichEdit control. Add this control as shown in Chapter 6 and anchor it to all four walls of the form so that it will resize with the form.

Second, add a StatusBar control along the bottom of the form. We'll use this status bar to display the name and path of the file being edited, along with an indication of when the file has changed and therefore should be saved before exiting the application. It is possible to write text directly to the *StatusBar* object, but the output has a flat appearance. To get the 3-D effect of modern applications, it's better to add a *StatusBarPanel* object to the StatusBar control and write to that object. Select the *panels* property of the StatusBar control, and then click the ellipses button in the property setting box. This opens the Panel Editor dialog box, which enables the programmer to add panels. Add a single panel, and then close the dialog box. Set the StatusBar's *showPanels* property to *true*.

Then change the name of the status bar panel to *outputPanel* to reflect its function. I cleared out the default text within the panel; this will be filled in with the name of the file being edited. Setting the panel's *autoSize* property to *Spring* enables the panel to take up all available space within the status bar. Finally, setting the *borderStyle* to *Sunken* (the default) gives the toolbar the desired 3-D effect. Figure 7-4 shows the properties for the status bar panel as we've edited them.

Figure 7-4. *To give the status bar a 3-D effect, first add a panel and then set its* autoSize *property to* Spring *and its* borderStyle *property to* Sunken.

The Code for Editor1

Even though the Forms Designer has done most of the work in building Editor1, there's still a sizable amount of code to be written. To keep Form1.java as simple as possible, I decided to create a separate class to maintain the rich edit and status bar controls. Let's examine this helper class before we get into the *Form1* class.

> **NOTE** Don't be afraid to divide your project into separate classes as long as each new class has a clear purpose. Two small classes are easier to maintain than one large class.

The *RichEditController* class

The primary job of the *RichEditController* class is to provide the *load()* and *save()* methods to load data from disk into the rich edit control and save the contents of the rich edit control back to disk. Along the way, *RichEditController* also keeps the status bar updated with the name of the file currently being edited and an indicator of whether the rich edit control is dirty or not. A rich edit control is *dirty* when its contents have been updated by the user since the last time the contents were saved to disk. Finally, *RichEditController* ensures that the edits are not inadvertently lost if the user forgets to save.

To create a new source file, choose New File from the Microsoft Visual J++ File menu and then select Java File from the Visual J++ folder. This creates a .java file with a default name and adds the file to the project.

You should rename the file to match the name of the class it is to hold. This is a requirement if the class is *public*. You do this by choosing Save As from the File menu and supplying a new name for the file. I named my .java file and class *RichEditController*. The code listing for this module is as follows:

```
/**
 * This class provides the file load
 * and store operations we want for the
 * rich edit control.
 */
import com.ms.wfc.ui.*;
import com.ms.wfc.core.*;
import com.ms.wfc.io.*;
import com.ms.wfc.app.*;

public class RichEditController
{
    // form to which this controller is attached
    Form form;
    EventHandler saveHandler;

    // the rich edit control
    RichEdit re;

    // status bar panels
    StatusBarPanel fileNamePanel;

    // file name
    String    fileName = "";

    /**
     * Create a controller to handle rich edit I/O.
     *
     * @param form - Parent Form
     * @param saveHandler - the File|Save event handler
     * @param re - RichEdit control
     * @param fileNamePanel - file name goes here
     */
    RichEditController(Form            form,
                       EventHandler    saveHandler,
                       RichEdit        re,
                       StatusBarPanel fileNamePanel)
    {
        this.form = form;
        this.saveHandler = saveHandler;
        this.re = re;
        this.fileNamePanel = fileNamePanel;
```

```
    // add event handlers:
    // record whenever text changes
    re.addOnTextChanged(
            new EventHandler(this.re_OnTextChanged));

    // intercept exit - if text changes, give user
    // the chance to save the text
    Application.addOnApplicationExit(
            new EventHandler(this.saveOnChange));
}


/**
 * Note that the rich edit control has changed.
 */
void re_OnTextChanged(Object o, Event e)
{
    if (!textChanged)
    {
        updateStatusBar(true);
    }
}


/**
 * Give the user a chance to save changes.
 */
void saveOnChange(Object s, Event e)
{
    // if the rich edit control hasn't changed...
    if (!textChanged)
    {
        // no worries
        return;
    }

    // otherwise, pop up a message box
    int yn = MessageBox.show("Save file?",
                            "Text changed",
                            MessageBox.ICONWARNING |
                            MessageBox.OKCANCEL);

    // if the user selected OK...
    if (yn == DialogResult.OK)
    {
        // act like she selected File|Save
        saveHandler.invoke(form, e);
    }
}
```

(continued)

```
/**
 * Set the name of the file.
 */
void setFileName(String fileName)
{
    this.fileName = fileName;
    updateStatusBar(false);
}

/**
 * Get the name of the current file.
 */
String getFileName()
{
    return fileName;
}

/**
 * Update the status bar with the name of the file
 * plus an indication of whether the file has changed
 * or not. Update the textChanged flag as well.
 *
 * @param textChanged - the new textChanged value
 */
boolean textChanged = false;
void updateStatusBar(boolean textChanged)
{
    if (this.textChanged != textChanged)
    {
        this.textChanged = textChanged;

        fileNamePanel.setText(fileName
                + (textChanged ? " changed" : ""));
    }
}

/**
 * Open the default file name into the
 * rich edit control.
 */
void load()
{
    // first make sure it's okay to trash current contents
    saveOnChange(null, null);

    // open the specified file
    try
    {
```

```
                re.loadFile(fileName);
                updateStatusBar(false);
            }

            // first catch invalid file type
            catch(WFCInvalidArgumentException e)
            {
                re.setText("Invalid (non-RTF) file");
            }

            // handle all others the same way
            catch(Exception e)
            {
                re.setText(e.getMessage());
            }
        }

    /**
     * Save the contents of the current rich edit control to
     * the current file.
     */
    void save()
    {
        re.saveFile(fileName);
        updateStatusBar(false);
    }
}
```

The *RichEditController* class maintains a number of data members:

- *form* refers to the parent *Form1* object.

- *saveHandler* refers to the *EventHandler* for the Save menu item on the File menu.

- *re* refers to the *RichEdit* object that the current class is to keep track of.

- *fileNamePanel* contains a reference to the panel where the name of the file currently being edited is stored.

- *fileName* contains the name of the file being edited.

- *textChanged* is set to *true* whenever the *RichEdit* object is dirty.

The *RichEditController* class constructor accepts a reference to the form, event handler, rich edit control, and file name status bar panel that the object is to control. After saving these locally the *RichEditController()* constructor establishes two event handlers.

The first event handler *re_OnTextChanged()* is invoked whenever the contents of the *RichEdit* object change. This method simply records the fact that the *RichEdit* object is dirty by setting *textChanged* to *true*. The *updateStatusBar()* method updates the status bar panel to inform the user that the file is now dirty. (If the *textChanged* flag is already set, the function returns without doing anything.)

The *RichEditController* constructor finishes by establishing *saveOnChange()* as the *OnApplicationExit* event handler, meaning that WFC calls *saveOnChange()* before terminating the application. The purpose of *saveOnChange()* is to make sure that the user does not lose any edited data by exiting without saving. To do this, *saveOnChange()* first checks the *textChanged* flag. If its value is *false*, the *RichEdit* object isn't dirty and the function returns without taking any action. If the flag's value is *true*, the function pops up a message box.

NOTE   The message box is also known in some circles as an alert.

Unlike other control types, you do not create a *MessageBox* object yourself. Instead, you invoke the static method *MessageBox.show()* to create and immediately show the message box. The first two arguments to *show()* are the message and the title. The title appears in the title bar of the message box.

The last argument to the *show()* method is the style. This argument is a combination of the icon and the button styles (combined using the OR operator). The different icon styles display different graphical symbols in the message box; the *ICONWARNING* style displays a yield sign. The button styles each display a different set of buttons; the *OKCANCEL* button style creates an OK button and a Cancel button in the message box.

Since message boxes are always modal, the call to *show()* does not return until the user has selected one of the buttons on the message box. The *show()* method returns the value *OK* if the user selects OK.

If *show()* returns *OK*, *saveOnChange()* calls *saveHandler.invoke()*. This invokes the *EventHandler* passed to the class constructor as the Save menu item handler. Calling *invoke()* this way simulates the event actually occurring, exactly as if the user had clicked the Save menu item.

The *getFileName()* and *setFileName()* methods return the current file name and update the current file name, respectively. The *setFileName()* method also updates the status bar to reflect the new name.

The *updateStatusBar()* method uses the *textChanged* flag. Whenever the value of this flag changes, *updateStatusBar()* updates the name of the current default file on the status bar. If the *RichEdit* object is dirty, *updateStatusBar()* tacks the string " changed" onto the end of the file name before writing it to the *fileNamePanel* object.

The *load()* and *save()* methods are similar to like-named methods in the rich edit control example in Chapter 6.

The *Form1* class

Armed with the *RichEditController* class, the code for *Form1* is almost anticlimactic:

```
import com.ms.wfc.app.*;
import com.ms.wfc.core.*;
import com.ms.wfc.ui.*;
import com.ms.wfc.html.*;

import com.ms.wfc.io.*;

/**
 * This class represents the File section of our
 * RTF editor.
 */
public class Form1 extends Form
{
    // rec controls the RichEdit object and the status bar
    RichEditController rec;

    public Form1(String[] args)
    {
        // Required for Visual J++ Form Designer support
        initForm();

        // build a controller for the rich edit control; this
        // will handle all of the I/O duties
        rec = new RichEditController(this,
                new EventHandler(this.saveFileMI_click),
                richEdit, outputPanel);

        // if there is a file name present...
        String defaultDirectory;
        if (args.length == 1)
        {
            // ...then load it...
            rec.setFileName(args[0]);
            rec.load();

            // and record the file's directory;
            defaultDirectory = File.getDirectory(args[0]);
        }

        // otherwise, start in the current directory
        else
        {
            defaultDirectory = File.getCurrentDirectory();
        }
```

(continued)

189

```
        // now set the default directory as the initial
        // directory for both the open and save dialog boxes
        openFD.setInitialDir(defaultDirectory);
        saveFD.setInitialDir(defaultDirectory);
    }

    /**
     * Form1 overrides dispose so it can clean up the
     * component list.
     */
    public void dispose()
    {
        super.dispose();
        components.dispose();
    }

    private void newFileMI_click(Object source, Event e)
    {
        // make sure it's okay to trash current contents
        rec.saveOnChange(null, null);

        // wipe out the contents of the rich edit
        richEdit.setText("");

        // wipe out the old file name
        rec.setFileName("");
    }

    private void openFileMI_click(Object source, Event e)
    {
        // make sure it's okay to trash current contents
        rec.saveOnChange(null, null);

        // open the Open dialog; if user selects OK...
        if (openFD.showDialog() == DialogResult.OK)
        {
            // open the file
            rec.setFileName(openFD.getFileName());
            rec.load();
        }
    }

    private void saveFileMI_click(Object source, Event e)
    {
        // if there is no current file...
        if (rec.getFileName().equals(""))
        {
```

```
                // treat this as a Save As
                saveAsFileMI_click(source, e);
                return;
        }

        // save contents into current file name
        rec.save();
}

private void saveAsFileMI_click(Object source, Event e)
{
        if (saveFD.showDialog() == DialogResult.OK)
        {
                rec.setFileName(saveFD.getFileName());
                rec.save();
        }
}

private void exitFileMI_click(Object source, Event e)
{
        Application.exit();
}


/**
 * NOTE: The following code is required by the Visual J++ form
 * designer.  It can be modified using the form editor. Do not
 * modify it using the code editor.
 */
Container components = new Container();
MainMenu mainMenu = new MainMenu();
MenuItem fileMI = new MenuItem();
MenuItem newFileMI = new MenuItem();
MenuItem openFileMI = new MenuItem();
MenuItem saveFileMI = new MenuItem();
MenuItem saveAsFileMI = new MenuItem();
MenuItem exitFileMI = new MenuItem();
OpenFileDialog openFD = new OpenFileDialog();
SaveFileDialog saveFD = new SaveFileDialog();
RichEdit richEdit = new RichEdit();
StatusBar statusBar = new StatusBar();
StatusBarPanel outputPanel = new StatusBarPanel();

private void initForm()
{
        // ...created by the Forms Designer...
}
```

(continued)

```
/**
 * The main entry point for the application.
 */
public static void main(String args[])
{
    Application.run(new Form1(args));
}
}
```

I added the variable *args* containing the program arguments to the constructor for *Form1* so that if a file name is passed as the first argument to the program, *Form1()* can load the file immediately. This addition is primarily to support initial drag-and-drop capability as explained in Chapter 6.

Upon startup, the *Form1()* constructor invokes *initForm()* to allow the Forms Designer–generated code to create the form. Upon return from *initForm()*, *Form1()* creates the *RichEditController* object described earlier. The *EventHandler* object passed to *RichEditController* points to the method *saveFileMI_click()*.

Once the *RichEditController* object has been created, it can be used to load the file name contained in *args[0]*, if one is present. If there is a file name contained in *args[0]*, the string variable *defaultDirectory* is set to the path to that file; otherwise, *defaultDirectory* is set to the current directory. This *defaultDirectory* value is then used as the initial directory for both the Open file dialog box, *openFD*, and the Save As file dialog box, *saveFD*. (If we don't set the directory, the Windows default directory will be used in both dialog boxes, which I find inconvenient.)

The next five methods (following the *dispose()* method) are each attached to their respective File menu items. For example, double-clicking the New menu item in the Forms Designer created the method *newFileMI_click()*. We added code to this method so that it first calls *saveOnChange()* to make sure that the user isn't mistakenly wiping out any new text that might already be in the rich edit control. If the *RichEdit* object is empty, this call has no effect. The *newFileMI_click()* method then clears out the text within the *RichEdit* object and clears out the current file name.

The *openFileMI_click()* method, which is invoked from the Open menu item, first calls *saveOnChange()* and then opens the Open file dialog box *openFD*. Calling *showDialog()* makes the *openFD* dialog box visible. Since this dialog box is modal, control does not return from *showDialog()* until the user chooses the OK or Cancel button. If *openFD.showDialog()* returns the value *OK*, then *openFileMI_click()* sets the current file name and then loads that file into the *RichEdit* object.

The *saveFileMI_click()* method first checks to see if there is a current file name. If there is, *saveFileMI_click()* invokes *rec.save()* to save the contents of the *RichEdit* object to the file. If there is no current file, *saveFileMI_click()* calls *saveAsFileMI_click()*. Thus, when there is no file name, clicking Save is identical to choosing Save As.

The *saveAsFileMI_click()* method opens the *saveFD* Save As file dialog box. The Save As file dialog box is very similar to the Open file dialog box *openFD*. If the dialog box object returns an *OK* indication, *saveAsFileMI_click()* retrieves from *saveFD* the file name chosen by the user and stores it as the default current file name before calling *rec.save()*.

The *exitFileMI_click()* method simply calls *Application.exit()* to terminate the program. (Remember that before the application exits, *RichEditController.saveOnChange()* will be invoked if the *RichEdit* object is dirty, to allow the user to save any modifications.)

How well does it work?

Figure 7-5 shows Editor1 with the File menu open. From the status bar, you can see the path to the file currently being edited and that the contents of the rich edit window are dirty.

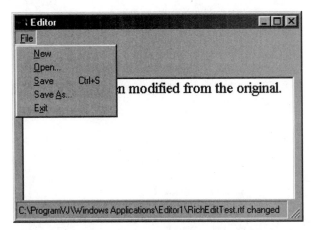

Figure 7-5. *The Editor1 application with a complete set of File menu items.*

Figure 7-6 shows the warning message that appears when you try to open a new file without saving the modified file.

If you click the OK button, Editor1 saves the file and then opens the Open file dialog box as shown in Figure 7-7. (If the file is new and has never been saved, clicking OK will first open the Save As dialog box, allowing you to specify a name and location to save the new file to before opening the Open dialog box.)

What is needed now to turn this initial version into a more full featured editor are a couple of additions, such as an Edit menu, a toolbar, and a context menu.

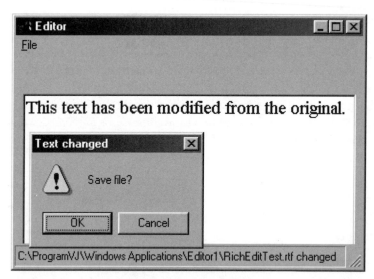

Figure 7-6. *The Text Changed message box warns the user that the edited contents of the rich edit window are potentially about to be lost.*

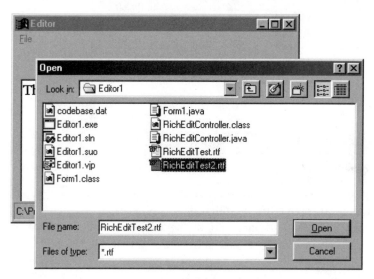

Figure 7-7. *Editor1 uses the standard Open dialog box to allow you to select a file to open.*

WHY PASS AN *EVENTHANDLER* OBJECT?

You may wonder why I bothered passing an *EventHandler* object to the constructor for the *RichEditController* class. *Form1* created an *EventHandler* object from *saveFileMI_click()* and then passed it to the *RichEditController()* constructor. The *EventHandler* object was used in only one place and that was to call *saveFileMI_click()* to save the current file before loading a new one. Why not just call *saveFileMI_click()* directly?

> **C++**
> **NOTE** Using the *EventHandler* class in this way is very much like registering a callback function in C or C++.

A service class, such as *RichEditController*, should make as few assumptions about other user classes as possible. However, *RichEditController* must make assumptions about library classes such as those that make up WFC. For example, when I wrote *RichEditController* I knew that the method *StatusBarPanel.setText()* exists and I knew what its arguments are.

Because *Form1* isn't part of the Java class libraries, you shouldn't assume that any *Form1* object passed will have a *saveFileMI_click()* method or that the method's purpose is to process a Save command. It is much better for the author of *RichEditController* to ask the outside world for a method that performs the Save function.

In effect, that's exactly what the constructor of *RichEditController* is doing. It is saying, "I need a reference to your *Form* object and a reference to your Save handler." Its presence in the constructor's argument list alerts you that such a routine is required. This approach makes no assumptions about what Save routine might be called.

THE EDIT MENU

With the File menu completed, the next major menu item is the Edit menu. In the Editor2 application, I created this menu with the three common commands: Cut, Copy, and Paste. Just for good measure, I added one further menu item, Format, which has the single submenu Font.

The Forms Designer Work

To add the Edit menu, in the Forms Designer click in the Type Here box next to the File menu. From there, add the Cut, Copy, and Paste menu items below the Edit menu. In the Properties window, change the *name* property of these menu items to *cutEditMI, copyEditMI,* and *pasteEditMI* to match the naming convention we used with the File menu items. While changing the names, you can also set the *shortcut* property for these properties to the standard Ctrl+X, Ctrl+C, and Ctrl+V, respectively.

You can add the Format menu with the Font menu item in a similar fashion; however, the Font menu item requires the addition of a FontDialog control. Drag a FontDialog control from the Toolbox and place it next to the OpenFileDialog and SaveFileDialog controls. Rename the FontDialog control to *fontDialog*. Also add a status bar panel named *fontPanel* to the right of the existing panel to provide a place to display the current font selection.

The Code for Editor2

The extra code to handle the edit and font menu items turns out to be a little trickier than you might think. (I have removed the File and RichEditControl sections from the following listing to save space, since they are the same as in the previous example.)

```
import com.ms.wfc.app.*;
import com.ms.wfc.core.*;
import com.ms.wfc.ui.*;
import com.ms.wfc.html.*;

import com.ms.wfc.io.*;

/**
 * This class represents a more complete RTF editor.
 */
public class Form1 extends Form
{
    // ...the File menu section is identical to Editor1...

    private void cutEditMI_click(Object source, Event e)
    {
        // perform a copy
        copyEditMI_click(source, e);

        // now delete the selection by
        // replacing the selected RTF with nothing
        richEdit.setSelRTF("");
    }

    private void copyEditMI_click(Object source, Event e)
    {
        // get the selected text
        String rtf = richEdit.getSelRTF();

        // now put this in the Clipboard
        Clipboard.setDataObject(rtf, true);
    }
```

```
private void pasteEditMI_click(Object source, Event e)
{
    // get an object off the Clipboard that represents
    // its contents
    IDataObject dobj = Clipboard.getDataObject();

    // first check for RTF
    if (dobj.getDataPresent("Rich Text Format"))
    {
        // the getDataPresent() method can return true
        // even when the content is not RTF; if it's not
        // RTF, just catch the illegal format event and
        // keep going
        try
        {
            // get the RTF data as a string, and paste
            // it into the rich edit control
            String s = (String)dobj.getData("Rich Text Format");

            // the string that gets extracted from
            // the Clipboard is null terminated - trim()
            // sets the length to match the text up to
            // the null
            s = trim(s);

            // the resulting text is pasted into the rich edit box
            richEdit.setSelRTF(s);
            return;
        }
        catch(Exception ex)
        {
        }
    }

    // we can handle plain text (although it screws up
    // the format of the RTF data)
    if (dobj.getDataPresent("Text"))
    {
        // first get the text off of the Clipboard and
        // trim it to the terminating null
        String insert = (String)dobj.getData("Text");
        insert = trim(insert);

        // the resulting text is pasted into the rich edit box
        richEdit.setSelText(insert);
        return;
    }
}
```

(continued)

```java
/**
 * Trim a String off at the first null.
 */
static String trim(String s)
{
    for (int i = 0; i < s.length(); i++)
    {
        if (s.charAt(i) == '\0')
        {
            s = s.substring(0, i);
            break;
        }
    }
    return s;
}


private void fontFormatMI_click(Object source, Event e)
{
    // display the font dialog box; if user selects OK...
    if (fontDialog.showDialog() == DialogResult.OK)
    {
        // get the font selected
        Font f = fontDialog.getFont();

        // set the selected area to that font
        richEdit.setSelFont(f);

        // store the name of the font on the status bar
        fontPanel.setText(f.getName());
    }
}


private void richEdit_selChange(Object source, Event e)
{
    // every time the cursor position moves, get
    // the current font and store it in the status bar
    try
    {
        Font f = richEdit.getSelFont();
        fontPanel.setText(f.getName()
                             + ":"
                             + f.getSize());
    }
    catch(Exception ex)
    {
        fontPanel.setText("<mixed>");
    }
}
```

```
/**
 * NOTE: The following code is required by the Visual J++ form
 * designer.  It can be modified using the form editor.  Do not
 * modify it using the code editor.
 */
Container components = new Container();
MainMenu mainMenu = new MainMenu();
MenuItem fileMI = new MenuItem();
MenuItem newFileMI = new MenuItem();
MenuItem openFileMI = new MenuItem();
MenuItem saveFileMI = new MenuItem();
MenuItem saveAsFileMI = new MenuItem();
MenuItem exitFileMI = new MenuItem();
OpenFileDialog openFD = new OpenFileDialog();
SaveFileDialog saveFD = new SaveFileDialog();
RichEdit richEdit = new RichEdit();
StatusBar statusBar = new StatusBar();
StatusBarPanel outputPanel = new StatusBarPanel();
MenuItem menuItem1 = new MenuItem();
MenuItem copyEditMI = new MenuItem();
MenuItem cutEditMI = new MenuItem();
MenuItem pasteEditMI = new MenuItem();
MenuItem menuItem5 = new MenuItem();
MenuItem fontFormatMI = new MenuItem();
FontDialog fontDialog = new FontDialog();
StatusBarPanel fontPanel = new StatusBarPanel();

private void initForm()
{
    // ...created by the Forms Designer...
}


/**
 * The main entry point for the application.
 */
public static void main(String args[])
{
    Application.run(new Form1(args));
}
}
```

The new code starts out simple enough. I created the Copy handler by double-clicking the Copy menu item in the Forms Designer and then adding the necessary code. The new *copyEditMI_click()* method first calls *richEdit.getSelRTF()*, which returns the currently selected text in RTF format. If no text is selected, this call returns an empty string. The second call, to *Clipboard.setDataObject()*, pastes this text to the Clipboard. The method's second argument, *true*, tells the method to copy the text rather than to simply retain a reference to it. This makes the Clipboard data persistent even if the Editor2 application exits.

The *cutEditMI_click()* handler is even easier. First it performs a copy action by calling *copyEditMI_click()*. Then it uses *setSelRTF()* to delete the selected text by replacing the selected text with an empty string.

The *pasteEditMI_click()* method begins by calling *Clipboard.getDataObject()*. Like the data object contained within the in-progress drag-and-drop *DragEvent*, the *Clipboard* object represents the contents of the Clipboard. The Editor2 application is prepared to accept two types of Clipboard contents: RTF or ANSI text.

Since RTF is preferred, *pasteEditMI_click()* checks for the presence of RTF text by calling *getDataPresent("Rich Text Format")* first. This call is supposed to return *true* if RTF text is present on the Clipboard; however, it returns *true* when any text is on the Clipboard, whether it's in RTF format or not.

The call *getData("Rich Text Format")* returns the RTF text as a Java string. The string returned by *getData()* is actually a *null* terminated string. A *null* terminated string makes a lot of sense in a language like C++, but the *null* has no particular significance to Java. The length of the *String* object is the size of the buffer and extends beyond the *null*. The method *RichEdit.setSelRTF()* seems to be able to handle this problem without any ill effects, but to be safe I wrote the function *trim()* to set the length of the *String* object to include the text up to but not including the terminating *null*.

Once the string has been trimmed, it is pasted into the *RichEdit* object using the *setSelRTF()* call. If the string returned from the Clipboard isn't actually RTF data, *setSelRTF()* throws an exception. Since this data might be plain text, *pasteEditMI_click()* catches the exception and continues on without complaint. If *setSelRTF()* runs successfully, the function returns with no further processing.

As a second step, the *pasteEditMI_click()* method checks the Clipboard for the presence of *"Text"*, that is, raw ANSI data. If this data is present, it is read from the Clipboard by calling *getData("Text")* and stored into the variable *insert*. (This allows the user to cut text out of a text editor such as Notepad and paste the text into our RTFEditor.) Once the *insert* variable has been trimmed, we paste it into the *RichEdit* object by calling the method *RichEdit.setSelText()*.

The method *fontFormatMI_click()* handles the Font menu item by opening the *FontDialog* object. If the user exits the dialog box by choosing the OK button, *fontFormatMI_click()* reads the selected font from the dialog box by calling *getFont()*. The currently selected area within the rich edit control is set to this font by calling *setSelFont()*. The name of the font is then stored into the status bar panel *fontPanel*.

The current Editor2 has one final addition to Editor1: it sets *richEdit_selChange()* to handle selection changes in the *RichEdit* object. A *selChange* event occurs whenever the user selects a new section of code or whenever the user moves the insertion point. The method *richEdit_selChange()* first calls *getSelFont()* to find out the font of the current selection. If there is no selection, this call returns the font of the text to the immediate right of the insertion point. Finally, *richEdit_selChange()* displays the name and size of the font in the *fontPanel* object.

If the current selection contains more than one font, the call to *getSelFont()* throws an exception. This exception is captured by *richEdit_selChange()*, which then displays the string "*<mixed>*" in the *fontPanel* object to let the user know that more than one font is currently selected.

ADDING EXTRAS

Our editor is almost complete—only two additions remain. The first addition is a toolbar to provide quick access to the menu item commands. The second addition is the context menu, the type of menu that pops up when the user clicks the right mouse button. This kind of menu is called a context menu because you can assign a different menu to different controls in the form. The Forms Designer can handle both of these additions almost completely.

The Toolbar

There are several steps involved in creating a toolbar. Let's take each of these in turn.

Creating toolbar images

The first step in creating a toolbar is to create a set of images to be displayed on the toolbar buttons. There are several ways to go about this. One approach is to draw your own bitmap image using a paint program. Another approach is to use one of the built-in images that comes with Visual J++. To have these available, you specify that you want to install BITMAPS during Visual J++ installation.

If the bitmap you want is not present in the Visual J++ 6 image library, you can copy one from your favorite application. Simply open the application that has the button image you want to use. Now press the Print Screen key to copy the current screen to the Clipboard. Run the Paint application that comes with Microsoft Windows. Now paste the image into Paint by choosing Paste from the Edit menu. Enlarge the image, and then place a selection box around the button image as shown in Figure 7-8.

Copy the button image to its own file by selecting Copy To from the Edit menu. In the Copy To dialog box, select the name and location for the image file and choose Save. (You could Copy and then Paste the image into a new file, but Copy To ensures the size of the image will be the size of your selection, with no extra white space around the edges and no need for resizing.) When you save the image, select a name indicative of its contents. I used the same naming convention for buttons that I used for the menu items. Thus, I named the image I cut out for the New toolbar button newFile.bmp.

Figure 7-8. *Button images can be copied easily by enlarging the image first.*

You'll repeat this process for each toolbar button you plan to create. For Editor2, I created images for New, Open, Save, Cut, Copy, Paste, and Font toolbar buttons.

Whether you create your own images or use one of those offered by the Visual J++ bitmap library, you'll need to copy the images to an *images* subdirectory of the Editor2 project folder.

Creating a toolbar

Creating the *ToolBar* object is simply a matter of dragging a ToolBar control from the Toolbox to the form. Position the ToolBar control immediately under the menu bar. You might need to resize the RichEdit control to leave room for the toolbar.

Associating the images with the toolbar

Before you can use the images you've just created in your form design, you must create an *ImageList* object and associate this *ImageList* object with the toolbar. Select the ImageList control from the Toolbox, and drop it onto the form. Much like the file dialog boxes and the main menu, it doesn't much matter where on the form you place the ImageList control. The Forms Designer assigns the default name of *imageList1,* which is good enough for me.

Now select the Properties window and click the ImageList control to edit its properties. Double-click the *images* property to open the Image Editor. From here, you can add each of the bitmapped images you created to the ImageList by using the Add button. Figure 7-9 shows the Image Editor after I had added each of the seven images to the ImageList control.

Figure 7-9. *Use the Image Editor to add .BMP files to the ImageList control.*

To add the ImageList control to the toolbar, click the *imageList* toolbar property. Click the arrow in the property value box to drop down a menu listing the only ImageList control in the application, *imageList1*, as a possible candidate. Select *imageList1*.

Creating the toolbar buttons

You are now ready to create the toolbar buttons. Double-click the *buttons* property of the ToolBar in the Properties window to reveal the ToolBarButton Editor. Use the *Add* button to add buttons to your toolbar. I added seven buttons.

Once the buttons have been added, you can change their properties using the Properties window. At a minimum, you will want to change their labels by editing the *text* property. I also renamed the buttons to indicate their function. For example, I applied the name *openFileTBB* for the Open toolbar button. You can also edit the *toolTipText* property from here. (The ToolTip is the string that appears when you point at the button with the mouse pointer.)

You will also need to update the *imageIndex* property to select the appropriate image from the image list. For example, I assigned image 0 to the *fileNewTBB* button.

The completed toolbar's Properties window is shown in Figure 7-10.

Figure 7-10. *Each toolbar button must be edited to have the proper label, name, ToolTip, and image.*

Fixing property problems

A bug in early releases of Visual J++ kept the programmer from setting the *imageIndex* property from the Properties window. These types of problems are not always fatal. For example, to avoid this problem I simply set the *imageIndex* property manually by adding the following code to the constructor:

```
public Form1(String[] args)
{
    // ...same as before...

    // set the image index for each toolbar button
    newFileTBB.setImageIndex(0);
    openFileTBB.setImageIndex(1);
    saveFileTBB.setImageIndex(2);
    copyEditTBB.setImageIndex(3);
    cutEditTBB.setImageIndex(4);
    pasteEditTBB.setImageIndex(5);
    fontFormatTBB.setImageIndex(6);
}
```

Similar problems can be fixed in the constructor if the *initForm()* code generated by the Properties window doesn't appear to be correct.

Associating an action to each button

Unfortunately, toolbar buttons have no active properties in the Properties window, but the toolbar does. So you must create a *toolBar1_buttonClick()* function (double-click the toolbar to create the function skeleton) to handle each of the buttons, as follows:

```
private void toolBar1_buttonClick(Object source,
                                  ToolbarButtonClickEvent e)
{
    // handle each button in turn
    if (e.button == newFileTBB)
    {
        newFileMI_click(source, e);
    }
    if (e.button == openFileTBB)
    {
        openFileMI_click(source, e);
    }
    if (e.button == saveFileTBB)
    {
        saveFileMI_click(source, e);
    }
    if (e.button == copyEditTBB)
    {
        copyEditMI_click(source, e);
    }
    if (e.button == cutEditTBB)
    {
        cutEditMI_click(source, e);
    }
    if (e.button == pasteEditTBB)
    {
        pasteEditMI_click(source, e);
    }
    if (e.button == fontFormatTBB)
    {
        fontFormatMI_click(source, e);
    }
}
```

The *ToolbarButtonClickEvent* parameter contains a reference to the toolbar button that was just clicked. By comparing the reference to the buttons by name, the program can determine which button was selected. Once *toolBar1_buttonClick()* has determined which button was selected, it simply calls the associated menu item click method to perform the actual function.

The Context Menu

To add a context menu to the Editor2 application, first select the ContextMenu control from the Toolbox and drag it to the RichEdit control in the Forms Designer. Double-click the *ContextMenu* object in the Forms Designer to begin adding menu items. The context menu editor works the same as the main menu editor. Figure 7-11 shows the context menu with my menu choices added.

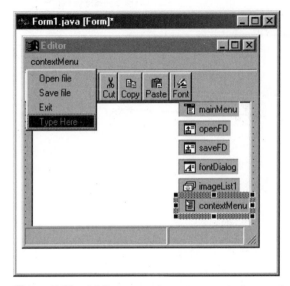

Figure 7-11. *Adding menu items to a context menu is similar to adding items to a regular menu.*

Before the context menu can become functional event handlers must be associated with each menu item. Fortunately, the context menu items are the same as those we created to service the main menu. With the Properties window visible, click the Open File context menu item. From the active properties, edit the *click* property. From the available event handlers, select *openFileMI_click()*. This process is shown in Figure 7-12. Repeat this process for each context menu item.

Finally, edit the *contextMenu* property of the form to associate the context menu with the application. Save the file, and rebuild the project to complete the process.

> **NOTE** Apparently the rich edit control and the toolbar control use the right mouse click for their own purposes and do not propagate it up to the form. In the resulting Editor2 application, clicking the right mouse button pops up the context menu everywhere except the rich edit control and the toolbar control.

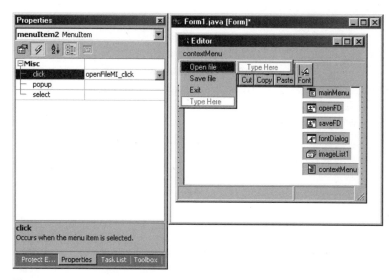

Figure 7-12. *Edit the* click *property to associate an action with each context menu item.*

CONCLUSION: THE FINAL EDITOR

The Editor2 application generated in this chapter is far from a commercial-grade application. Nevertheless, as you can see in Figure 7-13, the application displays many of the features you would want in your own editor applications. Editor2 is capable of editing RTF files, which support editing features such as multiple fonts. Editor2 has a main menu bar with shortcut keys for the most common editing functions. A

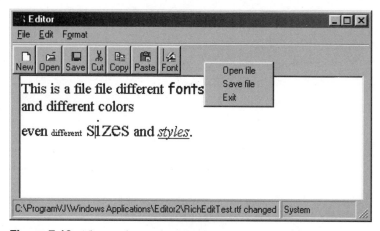

Figure 7-13. *The resulting editor application with menus, toolbar buttons, and context menu (context menu displayed).*

toolbar is present for several of the menu item commands and a context menu can be displayed as well.

Not visible in Figure 7-13 on the previous page is the ability of the editor to handle drag-and-drop operations. Editor2 can also handle cutting and pasting both RTF and plain text, both within the application and between Editor2 and other applications.

By now you should be getting comfortable with the Properties window and the Toolbox. Only a few more Toolbox controls need special mention and we'll tackle these in the next chapter.

Chapter 8

The ListView Control and TreeView Control

In this chapter, we'll take a look at the ListView and TreeView controls. We'll begin by creating a stand-alone application for each. Then I will combine the two into a relatively full-featured FileMgr file manager application.

THE LISTVIEW CONTROL

The ListView control is for viewing lists of objects, much like viewing objects in a simple ListBox control. Unlike the ListBox control, however, a list view is capable of displaying the items it contains as icons or in a multicolumn list that contains the item's associated data.

If you want to know what a list view looks like, open Microsoft Windows Explorer. The control that Windows Explorer uses to display the file names and optional detailed information is a ListView control.

The following ListViewDemo application mimics much of the functionality of Windows Explorer. ListViewDemo populates a ListView control with the names of the files in a directory; the directory is specified in the argument list to the program when the program is started. If no arguments are provided, the program lists names of files in the current directory. Subdirectories are listed before files and both are listed in independent alphabetic order. ListViewDemo supports different viewing modes, including several icon-based modes and a fully detailed report mode that includes the size and modification date of the files. Before starting to work on ListViewDemo, you might want to look ahead to Figures 8-4 and 8-5 to get an idea of what the application looks like in action. All the sample programs in this chapter are in the Windows Applications subfolder on the companion CD.

NOTE   The *ListView* class can be used to display other objects besides files; however, it seems to be almost uniquely suitable for that type of display.

The Forms Designer Work

Figure 8-1 shows the Forms Designer with the application that we are trying to build. ListViewDemo consists of a large ListView control in the middle of the form. Along the bottom are four buttons that are used to switch the list view display from one mode to another. The ImageList controls are used to assign images to the different file types.

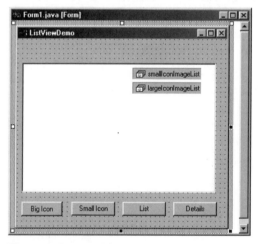

Figure 8-1. *The ListViewDemo application contains only a few controls.*

Begin by creating the Windows application ListViewDemo using the Windows Application builder. Open the form in the Forms Designer. Now position a ListView control in the middle of the form, leaving enough room along the bottom of the form for four buttons.

The ImageList control

Before adjusting the properties of the ListView control, add two ImageList controls to the form. Use the Properties window to name the first ImageList *smallIconImageList* and the second *largeIconImageList*. Add four images to the *smallIconImageList* object as shown in Figure 8-2. (See Chapter 7 for details on how to use the Image Editor to add images to the image lists.) Create whatever images you like; however, the first image needs to be reminiscent of a disk, since this image will be used to flag directories. Choose the other three images to represent HTML files, executable files, and miscellaneous ("don't know") files. Each of these images should be the size of the icon, 16-by-16 pixels.

The *largeIconImageList* object contains the same type of images as *smallIconImageList* except that you will need to increase the *x* and *y imageSize* properties to 32. You must do this before adding the images in the Image Editor.

Figure 8-2. *The icon image lists for ListViewDemo should have an image for directories, HTML files, executables, and miscellaneous files.*

Editing the ListView properties

You are now ready to edit the properties of the ListView control using the Properties window. First change the name of the control to *listView*. Next anchor the ListView control to all four walls (this will ensure that the list view automatically resizes itself if the form in which it resides is resized). Set the *smallImageList* and *stateImageList* properties to point to the *smallIconImageList* object. Set the *largeImageList* property to reference the *largeIconImageList* object.

In addition, you will need to create three columns. Click the ellipses button on the value box for the *columns* property to access the ColumnHeader Editor. Add three objects, and then return to the Properties window to edit the *text* property of the column headers to be File Name, Size, and Last Modified. These headers will appear when the list view is switched to Detailed report mode.

Now make sure that the *sorting* property is set to *None*. This is critical since we will be sorting the displayed list manually. (We have to do this manually because the directories are sorted before the files.) Set the *gridLines* property to *true* if you would like spreadsheet-style gridlines when the list view is in detailed report mode. Set *fullRowSelect* to *true*. In addition, leave the *multiSelect* property set to *true*.

Set the *activation* property to *Twoclick*—*Oneclick* is also acceptable, if you prefer—and set the *headerStyle* property to *Nonclickable* for reasons I will explain shortly. Set the *View* property to *List* to make list view the default view. Set the *autoArrange* property to *true*. Once you have finished, the Properties window should look like that shown in Figure 8-3.

Figure 8-3. *The data properties of the edited ListView demonstrating some of the proper settings for the ListViewDemo application.*

Completing the forms designer work

Add four buttons equally spaced along the bottom of the application. Label them Big Icon, Small Icon, List, and Details, corresponding to the four display modes of the list view. Anchor the left two buttons to the left and bottom of the form and the right two buttons to the right and bottom of the form. Double-click each button to create the *clickEvent()* method for each.

The Code

The source code for ListViewDemo consists of two .java files: the automatically created Form1.java file and a manually created ImageEnum.java class file (select Add Class from the Project menu). The second file is smaller, so let's start there.

The *ImageEnum* class

It is the job of the *ImageEnum* class to define a *final static int* index for each image in the two icon image lists. The source code for this class is as follows:

```
import com.ms.wfc.core.Enum;
import com.ms.wfc.io.*;

/**
 * Controls the indices of the smallIconImageList and
 * largeIconImageList objects.
 */
public class ImageEnum extends Enum
{
    public final static int DATA       = 0;
    public final static int HTML       = 1;
    public final static int EXECUTABLE = 2;
    public final static int DONTKNOW   = 3;

    /**
     * Return true if value is a valid index.
     */
    public static boolean valid(int value)
    {
        return (value >= DATA) && (value <= DONTKNOW);
    }


    /**
     * Given a file name, return the index of the
     * associated image base.
     */
    public static int getImageIndex(String fileName)
    {
        // if any problems arise, just return DONTKNOW
        try
        {
            // if this is a directory...
            if (File.isDirectory(fileName))
            {
                // then always return DATA
                return DATA;
            }

            // otherwise, base the image on the file extension
            String ext = File.getExtension(fileName);

            if (ext.equalsIgnoreCase(".EXE") ||
                ext.equalsIgnoreCase(".BAT"))
```

(continued)

```
        {
            return EXECUTABLE;
        }

        if (ext.equalsIgnoreCase(".HTM") ||
            ext.equalsIgnoreCase(".HTML")||
            ext.equalsIgnoreCase(".ASP"))
        {
            return HTML;
        }
    }
    catch(Exception e)
    {
    }

    // either we didn't find a recognizable extension,
    // or a problem cropped up; either way, DONTKNOW
    return DONTKNOW;
  }
}
```

First you can see the four *final static int* members as mentioned. Each must match the index of the corresponding image. If you added more image types than I did, you will need to add the corresponding data members here. Extending the class *Enum* and overriding the *valid()* method complete the role of this class as an enumeration class.

One further method, *getImageIndex(),* has been added. This method takes as its argument the name of a file and returns one of the class's four constant data members. If the file name refers to a directory, the method returns the constant *DATA*. If the file name extension is .EXE or .BAT, the class returns *EXECUTABLE*. If the file name extension is .HTM, .HTML, or .ASP, the function returns *HTML*. If the file name extension is none of these or if any type of exception is thrown, the function returns *DONTKNOW*, indicating that it was not able to type the file.

The main application code

The source code for Form1.java represents the vast majority of the source code for ListViewDemo.

```
import com.ms.wfc.app.*;
import com.ms.wfc.core.*;
import com.ms.wfc.ui.*;
import com.ms.wfc.html.*;

import com.ms.wfc.io.*;
import com.ms.wfc.util.*;
```

```
/**
 * Demonstrate the ListView class by adding a listing of the current
 * directory, subdirectories first, into the ListView object.
 */
public class Form1 extends Form
{
    // the currently listed directory
    String directory = File.getCurrentDirectory();

    public Form1(String[] args)
    {
        // Required for Visual J++ Form Designer support
        initForm();

        // store the contents of the directory passed
        // to the list view; if no directory passed, use
        // the current directory as the default
        if (args.length == 1)
        {
            directory = args[0];
        }
        createListView();
    }

        ⋮

    /**
     * Fill the list view with the name, size, and date
     * of the files in the specified or current directory.
     */
    void createListView()
    {
        // first, clear out the list view
        listView.setItems(new ListItem[0]);

        // let's add the directories...
        addFilesToListView(listView, true);

        // then add the files
        addFilesToListView(listView, false);
    }

    /**
     * Add files to a list view.
     *
     * @param listView - the list view target
     * @param isDirectory - true->load directories, false->load files
     */
```

(continued)

```
void addFilesToListView(ListView listView,
                        boolean isDirectory)
{
    // create a list of file names using the FileEnumerator
    // class; this class let's you enumerate through all
    // the files that pass a given filter
    List list = new List();
    int index = 0;

    String filter = File.combine(directory, "*.*");
    FileEnumerator fe = new FileEnumerator(filter);
    while(fe.hasMoreFiles())
    {
        // check if this is a directory...
        String fileName = fe.getName();
        String fullPath = File.combine(directory, fileName);
        if (File.isDirectory(fullPath) == isDirectory)
        {
            // whatever it is, it matches what we're looking
            // for; now add the "extra" information
            String[] subItems = new String[2];
            subItems[0] = Long.toString(fe.getSize());
            Time dateTime = fe.getLastWriteTime();
            subItems[1] = dateTime.toString();

            // create an item for the ListView out of this data
            // (convert the file extension into an image index)
            ListItem item =
                new ListItem(fileName,
                             ImageEnum.getImageIndex(fullPath),
                             subItems);

            // add the item to the list
            list.addItem(item);
        }

        // move over to the next file
        fe.getNextFile();
    }

    // now sort the list
    list.sort(new FileNameComparer());

    // and add the sorted list to the list view
    IEnumerator itemEnumerator = list.getItemEnumerator();
    while (itemEnumerator.hasMoreItems())
```

```
        {
            ListItem li = (ListItem)itemEnumerator.nextItem();
            listView.addItem(li);
        }
}


/**
 * Implement the IComparer interface to support List.sort().
 */
class FileNameComparer implements IComparer
{
    /**
     * Compare o1 to o2; return -1, 0, or 1.
     */
    public int compare(Object o1, Object o2)
    {
        ListItem l1 = (ListItem)o1;
        ListItem l2 = (ListItem)o2;

        String f1 = l1.getText();
        String f2 = l2.getText();

        return StringSorter.compare(f1, f2,
            StringSorter.STRINGSORT | StringSorter.IGNORECASE);
    }
}

private void button1_click(Object source, Event e)
{
    listView.setView(ViewEnum.LARGEICON);
}


private void button2_click(Object source, Event e)
{
    listView.setView(ViewEnum.SMALLICON);
}


private void button3_click(Object source, Event e)
{
    listView.setView(ViewEnum.LIST);
}


private void button4_click(Object source, Event e)
{
    listView.setView(ViewEnum.REPORT);
}
```

(continued)

```
/**
 * Handle item activation events.
 */
private void dbl_click(Object source, Event e)
{
    // get the first ListItem selected (in single select mode,
    // there will only ever be one)
    ListItem li = listView.getSelectedItems()[0];
    String dirName = li.getText();

    // if this item is the "."...
    if (dirName.equals("."))
    {
        // then ignore it (there's no change)
        return;
    }

    // if this is the ".."...
    if (dirName.equals(".."))
    {
        // then remove the last directory in the path
        // including the "\\"
        int offset = directory.lastIndexOf("\\");
        directory = directory.substring(0, offset);

        // if there's nothing left...
        if (directory.lastIndexOf("\\") == -1)
        {
            // change the directory to the root
            directory += "\\";
        }
    }

    // otherwise (this isn't "..")
    else
    {
        // make sure this is a directory
        dirName = File.combine(directory, dirName);
        if (!File.isDirectory(dirName))
        {
            return;
        }

        // it is - save it as the new directory
        directory = dirName;

    }
```

```
        // recreate the list view using this new directory
        createListView();
    }

    /**
     * NOTE: The following code is required by the Visual J++ form
     * designer.  It can be modified using the form editor.  Do not
     * modify it using the code editor.
     */
    Container components = new Container();
    ListView listView = new ListView();
    ColumnHeader columnHeader1 = new ColumnHeader();
    ColumnHeader columnHeader2 = new ColumnHeader();
    ColumnHeader columnHeader3 = new ColumnHeader();
    ImageList smallIconImageList = new ImageList();
    Button button1 = new Button();
    Button button2 = new Button();
    Button button3 = new Button();
    ImageList largeIconImageList = new ImageList();
    Button button4 = new Button();

    private void initForm()
    {
        // ...created by Forms Designer...
    }

    /**
     * The main entry point for the application.
     *
     * @param args Array of parameters passed to the application
     * via the command line.
     */
    public static void main(String args[])
    {
        Application.run(new Form1(args));
    }
}
```

FileViewDemo defines one data member, *directory*, which refers to the full path of the directory being listed. The constructor for *Form1* initializes *directory* to the current directory, but if the user provides an argument when FileViewDemo is started, this argument is copied into *directory* instead. Once *directory* has been initialized, the *Form1()* constructor calls *createListView()* to populate the list view with the contents of that directory.

The *createListView()* method

Two of the methods provided by the class *ListView* are *addItem()* and *setItems()*. The *addItem()* method adds a new item to those already present and *setItems()* replaces the current list of items with a new list of items. Both of these methods accept an object of class *ListItem*. Thus, a *ListItem* object describes a row in a list view.

The *createListView()* method begins with clearing out the list view by calling *setItems()* and passing it a zero-length array of *ListItem* objects. Then *createListView()* begins adding files to the now empty list view by calling the *addFilesToListView()* method twice, once for the subdirectory values contained in the *directory* variable and once for the file name values in *directory*.

> **NOTE** Iterating through the directory once for subdirectories and a second time for files might not be the most efficient algorithm, but it decreases the code complexity.

The *addFilesToListView()* method contains three distinct sections. In the first section, *addFilesToListView()* creates a *List* object and adds *ListItem* objects to it using the *FileEnumerator* class.

The *FileEnumerator* class provides a convenient means of iterating through a list of files. The constructor for *FileEnumerator* takes as its argument a file filter. For example, the file filter "C:\temp*.txt" would find all of the .txt files in the \temp directory. The program navigates *FileEnumerator* using three methods: *getName()* returns the name of the file to which the *FileEnumerator* is currently pointing, *getNextFile()* moves the pointer to the next file, and *hasMoreFiles()* returns *true* as long as there are more files in the enumerator.

Before *addFilesToListView()* processes a file name from the enumerator, it must first check to see if the file name refers to a directory or a file. If the return from *File.isDirectory()* is the value the calling method specified in the *isDirectory* parameter *(true* for directories and *false* for files), *addFilesToListView()* retrieves some extra information about the file that, together with the file name, is converted into a *ListItem* object.

The constructor for a *ListItem* object takes three arguments. The first argument is the name of the file. The second argument is the index of the image to display for this file. This index refers to the icon image list associated with the list view, and it is returned from *ImageEnum.getImageIndex()* as described earlier. The final argument to the constructor is an array of *String* objects. In our case, this array refers to the second and third columns in report view mode—the file size and the time of last modification (the "extra" information). Both of these pieces of information come from the *FileEnumerator* class. The constructed *ListItem* object is then added to the *list* object of class *List*.

In the second portion of *addFilesToListView()*, the method sorts the *list* object containing the individual list items. It does this by calling the *List.sort()* method. The only argument to *List.sort()* is an object of a class that implements the *IComparer* interface. The class *FileNameComparer* implements this interface by implementing the method *compare()*, which compares two items of a list and returns a –1, 0, or 1 depending on the relationship between the two list items.

Since we're using the file names to determine the sort order, my implementation of *compare()* first calls *ListItem.getText()* to pull the file names from the two list items that are being compared. Then *compare()* calls *StringSorter.compare()* to perform the actual comparison. This *public static* method is similar to the method *String.compareTo()* except that it allows for the *IGNORECASE* option. In addition, the *STRINGSORT* option causes the *compare()* method to ignore nonalphanumeric characters when performing its comparison.

> **NOTE**   If you're already familiar with Java, you probably already know about the *String.compareTo()* method. If you don't know how this method works, refer to the MSDN Library Visual Studio.

Once the *list* object has been sorted, *addFilesToListView()* iterates through the list using an item enumerator. The item enumerator works with the *List* class in the same way that the *FileEnumerator* class worked on the files in a directory. The call to *list.getItemEnumerator()* returns the list enumerator. The call to *nextItem()* returns the current item and moves the pointer to the next item. The method *hasMoreItems()* returns *false* when there are no more objects left in the list. As each object is removed from the list, it is added to the *listView* object by means of a call to *addItem()*.

The event handlers

The first four event handlers in ListViewDemo are the *button_click()* methods for the four buttons on the form. Each of these simply sets the viewing mode of the *listView* object by calling the *setView()* method and passing it one of the four *ViewEnum* constants.

I created the method *dbl_click()* in the Forms Designer by typing this name into the value box for the *itemActivate* property, which is listed among the active properties of the ListView control. This event is triggered when the user chooses one of the objects in the list. (Whether this requires a single click or a double click depends on the *activation* property of the ListView control that we set in the Properties window earlier.)

The *dbl_click()* method begins by loading the first item in the list the user selected. (More than one item can be chosen if the list view is in multiselect mode, but only the first item in the list is ever loaded.) The method *ListItem.getText()* returns the file name for the selected list item. There are two special cases to be considered. If the user chooses the current directory ".", the application does nothing. If the user selects "..", the application strips off the last directory name in the path and assigns the result to the data member directory. With any other choice, the application tacks the selected file name onto the current directory. If the result is a directory, this result is assigned to the directory variable.

Finally, the method calls *createListView()* to repopulate the list view with the contents of the files contained in directory.

The Result

The result of executing the ListViewDemo application on the current directory is shown in Figures 8-4 and 8-5. Figure 8-4 shows ListViewDemo in list mode and Figure 8-5 shows the same directory in Details report mode.

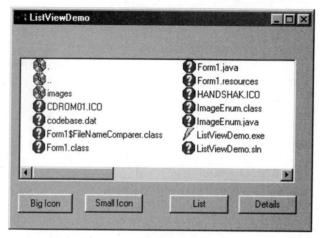

Figure 8-4. *The current directory in list mode showing the images subdirectory, the ListViewDemo executable file, and a series of ListViewDemo support files.*

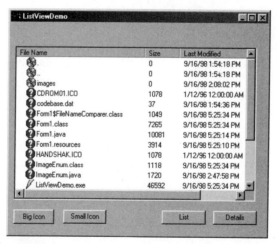

Figure 8-5. *Details report mode shows a lot more information about each file, but doesn't display as many files in the same amount of space.*

Although impossible to demonstrate in a figure, ListViewDemo allows the user to navigate up in the directory structure by double-clicking the ".." entry and down in the directory structure by double-clicking a subdirectory.

THE TREEVIEW CONTROL

Like the ListView control, TreeView is another control that you are already familiar with. Open Windows Explorer; the list of directories in the left pane is a tree view. Another example is the Properties window for the Microsoft Visual J++ Forms Designer.

The ListView control is ideal for displaying large amounts of data along with descriptive information. However, it can't display the hierarchical nature of some information, and this is where the TreeView control comes in. The ability to display hierarchical information makes a tree view the preferred means of displaying directory information.

The following TreeViewDemo program creates a *TreeView* object to display the hierarchy of a given directory. The program populates the tree view with each file in the directory. Subdirectory branches are populated with the subdirectory's contents.

The Forms Designer Work

There isn't much design work to this particular demo. Create a new Windows application in the conventional way, and name this project TreeViewDemo. In the Forms Designer, add a TreeView control from the Toolbox to the form *Form1*. You will need to rename the new control to *treeView*, but most of the other properties in the Properties window are already set correctly.

Add a single-line edit control along the bottom of the form. Change its name to *edit*. Resize the form so that it is considerably taller than it is wide, and then resize the TreeView and Edit controls so that they fill most of the form. Anchor the TreeView control to all four sides of the form. Anchor the Edit control to the left, right, and bottom sides, but not to the top. This will ensure that the Edit control continues to hug the bottom edge if the user resizes the form.

Figure 8-6 shows the resulting form in the Forms Designer window and the properties for the TreeView control.

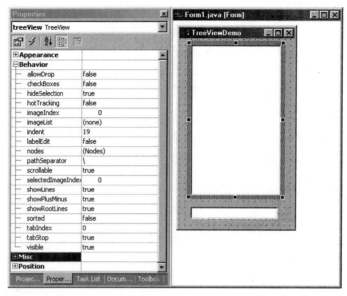

Figure 8-6. *The Forms Designer work for the TreeViewDemo application is fairly simple.*

The Code

Writing the code for the TreeViewDemo application is considerably more complicated than creating the form. The problem lies in the fact that each node that represents a subdirectory of the current directory must be able to be expanded. Any subdirectories within that subdirectory must also be expandable, and so on until the application has built a maze of branches with each branch reaching down into the farthest subdirectory.

Before I show the source code, let me present a programming technique called recursion that helps simplify this problem.

Recursion

Consider for a moment the following problem of calculating the factorial of a number. The factorial of N is equal to N * factorial (N–1). The factorial of 0 is 1. Knowing this, I could write a *factorial()* function as follows. (I'm not saying this is the best way to implement a factorial; it is merely one way.)

```
public static int factorial(int N)
{
    // handle the known case
    if (N == 0)
    {
        return 1;
    }
```

```
        // call yourself to calculate the factorial
        return N * factorial(N - 1);
}
```

At first glance, it would appear that by calling itself this function generates an infinite loop, but consider for a second how this function works. Suppose a program calls *factorial(5)*. Since 5 is not equal to 0, the function would calculate 5 * *factorial(4)*, and *factorial(4)* would then call *factorial(3)*. This process would be repeated until eventually *factorial(1)* calculated *1 * factorial(0)*. At this point, *factorial(0)* would return a 1, which would allow the *factorial(1)* calculation to continue and return a 1 to allow the *factorial(2)* calculation to proceed, and so forth. This approach of having a function call itself is called *recursion*.

Applying recursion to TreeViewDemo

Although the problem of expanding the base node of the tree is very different from calculating a factorial, it is similar in one respect. Once a node for a new subdirectory has been added, the entire process of creating a list of entries representing the contents of that subdirectory must be duplicated. After the new node has been added for the subdirectory, the problem from that point onward is *exactly* the same as the problem of adding the first directory. That being the case, the easiest approach to solving this problem is for the function to call itself recursively.

Let's see how recursion works to create a tree view. The source code for TreeViewDemo appears as follows:

```
import com.ms.wfc.app.*;
import com.ms.wfc.core.*;
import com.ms.wfc.ui.*;
import com.ms.wfc.html.*;


import com.ms.wfc.io.*;
import com.ms.wfc.util.*;

/**
 * Demonstrate the TreeView class by adding a node for each file in
 * the specified directory. Expand subdirectories to include their
 * files as well.
 */
public class Form1 extends Form
{
    public Form1(String[] args)
    {
        // Required for Visual J++ Form Designer support
        initForm();

        // expand the specified node
        String initialPath = File.getCurrentDirectory();
```

(continued)

```
        if (args.length == 1)
        {
            initialPath = args[0];
        }
        treeView.addNode(expandTreeNode("", initialPath));
    }


    /**
     * Expand the directory dirName within path.
     */
    TreeNode expandTreeNode(String path, String dirName)
    {
        // create a node with that directory name
        TreeNode node = new TreeNode(dirName);

        // combine the path with the directory name
        path = File.combine(path, dirName);

        // now create two lists containing the contents of the
        // directory pointed to by path
        List dirList = new List();
        List fileList= new List();
        createSortedLists(path, dirList, fileList);

        // add the directories...
        addDirsToNode(path, node, dirList);

        // then add the files
        addFilesToNode(node, fileList);

        return node;
    }


    /**
     * Add a list of directories to the node pointed to by path.
     */
    void addDirsToNode(String path, TreeNode node, List list)
    {
        // iterate through the list of directories
        IEnumerator itemEnumerator = list.getItemEnumerator();
        while (itemEnumerator.hasMoreItems())
        {
            // get the directory name from the list item
            String dirName = (String)itemEnumerator.nextItem();

            // now add a new node with that name; expand the
            // node to include the contents of the directory as well
            node.addNode(expandTreeNode(path, dirName));
        }
    }
```

```
/**
 * Add the list of file names to the specified node.
 */
void addFilesToNode(TreeNode node, List list)
{
    // iterate through the list
    IEnumerator itemEnumerator = list.getItemEnumerator();
    while (itemEnumerator.hasMoreItems())
    {
        // add each file name to the node
        String fileName = (String)itemEnumerator.nextItem();
        node.addNode(new TreeNode(fileName));
    }
}


/**
 * Put each of the elements of path into either the dirList
 * or the fileList and then sort both.
 */
void createSortedLists(String   path,
                       List      dirList,
                       List      fileList)
{
    // create a FileEnumerator in order to iterate through the
    // current path
    FileEnumerator fe =
            new FileEnumerator(File.combine(path, "*.*"));
    for(;fe.hasMoreFiles(); fe.getNextFile())
    {
        String fileName = fe.getName();

        // ignore the "." and ".." directories
        if (fileName.equals(".") ||
            fileName.equals(".."))
        {
            continue;
        }

        // if this is a directory...
        if (File.isDirectory(File.combine(path, fileName)))
        {
            // then add it to the directory list;...
            dirList.addItem(fileName);
        }
        else
        {
            // otherwise, add it to the file list
            fileList.addItem(fileName);
```

(continued)

```
            }
        }

    // now sort the lists
    dirList.sort(new FileNameComparer());
    fileList.sort(new FileNameComparer());
}

/**
 * Implement the IComparer interface to support List.sort().
 */
class FileNameComparer implements IComparer
{
    /**
     * Compare o1 to o2; return -1, 0, or 1.
     */
    public int compare(Object o1, Object o2)
    {
        String f1 = (String)o1;
        String f2 = (String)o2;

        return StringSorter.compare(f1, f2,
            StringSorter.STRINGSORT | StringSorter.IGNORECASE);
    }
}

    ⋮


/**
 * Invoked when a node in the TreeView is selected.
 */
private void treeView_afterSelect(Object source, TreeViewEvent e)
{
    TreeNode node = treeView.getSelectedNode();
    String fileName = node.getText();
    edit.setText(fileName);
}

/**
 * NOTE: The following code is required by the Visual J++ form
 * designer.  It can be modified using the form editor.  Do not
 * modify it using the code editor.
 */
Container components = new Container();
TreeView treeView = new TreeView();
Edit edit = new Edit();

private void initForm()
{
```

```
       // ...generated by Forms Designer...
    }

    /**
     * The main entry point for the application.
     *
     * @param args Array of parameters passed to the application
     * via the command line.
     */
    public static void main(String args[])
    {
        Application.run(new Form1(args));
    }
}
```

As always, *main()* creates an object of class *Form1*. This time I added the *args* argument to the *Form1* constructor to give the user the option of viewing a directory other than the current directory. After the standard call to *initForm()*, *Form1()* creates a string variable *initialPath* setting it equal to the argument passed to the program, if there is one, or the current directory. *Form1()* then creates a directory node at that directory by calling *expandTreeNode()* and attaches the node to the *treeView* object.

The *expandTreeNode()* method creates an object of class *TreeNode* to represent the current directory. Much like the *ListView* object, you do not attach normal components like a *String* object directly to a *TreeView* object. You must first wrap the *String* in a tree node, and then you attach the tree node to the tree view. Unlike the list view, however, you can also attach a tree node to another tree node. This capability gives the tree view its hierarchical affect.

Once the tree node for the current directory has been created, the *expand-TreeNode()* method calls *createSortedLists()* to create two lists, one of all the subdirectories in the current directory and the other containing the names of all the files.

The *createSortedLists()* method is similar to the *addFilesToListView()* method in the previous example in that it iterates through the contents of the specified directory. Every file it finds (other than the two directories "." and "..", which it ignores) are placed into one of two *List* objects. If the file represents a directory, it is placed in the *dirList* object. If it is not a directory, the name is placed in the *fileList* object. Both lists are then sorted. This approach of maintaining two lists makes *create-SortedLists()* slightly more complicated than its *addFilesToListView()* predecessor. However, it avoids the need to iterate through the directory twice, once for the subdirectories and again for the non-subdirectories.

Once *expandTreeNode()* has captured the contents of the current directory in the two lists and sorted them, it adds the contents of the directory list to the current node by calling the *addDirsToNode()* method and adds the contents of the file list by calling *addFilesToNode()*. Since the latter is the easier of the two, let's consider it first.

The *addFilesToNode()* method starts by creating an *itemEnumerator* interface for the file list. It uses *itemEnumerator* to iterate through the list until *hasMoreItems()* returns false. The call to *nextItem()* returns the current file name string and moves the iterator to the next member in the list. A *TreeNode* object is built to contain the file name returned from *nextItem()*, and then the *TreeNode* object is added to the parent node by calling *addNode()*.

The *addDirsToNode()* method begins in much the same way, by creating and using an *itemEnumerator* interface to iterate through the list of subdirectory names. Rather than simply create a *TreeNode* object to add to the parent node, however, this method calls the *expandTreeNode()* method to add a new directory node, passing it the name of the subdirectory and the path to the current parent node.

As you know already, *expandTreeNode()* continues the process by generating a list of all of the files in that subdirectory. Each of the subdirectories of that subdirectory is then passed to *expandTreeNode()* in turn. In this way, the program uses *expandTreeNode()* to recursively burrow deeper and deeper into the hierarchy of subdirectories until it eventually reaches the end: the subdirectories that contain only files and no further subdirectories.

I added one event handler function to TreeViewDemo. The *afterSelect* event occurs after the user has selected a tree node. To select a tree node, the user clicks the plus sign in front of the node name. In this case, the *treeView_afterSelect()* method retrieves the currently selected node and displays the file name associated with this node in the edit window at the bottom of the form.

Figure 8-7 shows the results of executing TreeViewDemo on my \TEMP directory. As you can see, the directories are listed first. Those nodes that have subnodes

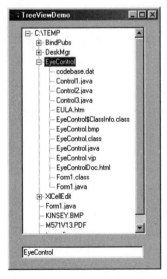

Figure 8-7. *The results of executing the TreeViewDemo on my \TEMP directory.*

are listed with small plus signs. Clicking a plus sign causes the node to expand and show the subnodes within.

PUTTING IT ALL TOGETHER WITH FILEMGR

Both the ListViewDemo and TreeViewDemo applications were intended as simple demos of the ListView and TreeView controls. Even so, the ListViewDemo program uses the list view to effectively give the user access to the contents of a directory, and the TreeViewDemo program demonstrates how the tree view control gives the user a good overview of their directory structure. If we combine these two programs, we can generate a powerful disk copy utility. In fact, this utility would closely resemble Windows Explorer, which comes with 32-bit versions of Windows.

We'll create such a utility, called FileMgr, as an example of an almost-real-world application. FileMgr will have a TreeView control on the left and a ListView control on the right. The tree view will be used to display the directory hierarchy. As the user selects a directory in the tree view, the display of the list view on the right will immediately update to display the files in that directory. The user will be able to select any number of files from the list view and drag them over to the tree view. Dropping the selected files on one of the nodes will cause the FileMgr application to copy the files to the directory at the specified node. Once the files are copied, the user will be given the option of deleting the source files. An edit window across the bottom of the FileMgr window will be used to display the copy and delete commands as they are carried out.

The Forms Designer Work

Begin by copying a TreeView control to the left side and a ListView control to the right side of the form created by the Windows Application builder. Place an Edit control along the bottom. Expand the TreeView and ListView controls so that they take up most of the available space in the form, leaving a comfortable margin between all three controls. The TreeView control doesn't need as much room horizontally as the ListView control. Therefore, I assigned about one third of the horizontal space to the TreeView control and two thirds to the ListView control. You might want to peek ahead to Figure 8-8 on page 233 to see what these controls look like in the Forms Designer.

Anchor the TreeView control to the top, bottom, and left of the form window. Anchor the ListView control to the top, bottom, and right of the form. Anchoring these two controls to both the top and bottom will let the Windows Foundation Classes for Java (WFC) take care of resizing the controls vertically as the form is resized; however, we will resize them horizontally to maintain the 1/3 to 2/3 ratio. Finally, anchor the Edit control to the left, right, and bottom of the form.

Setting the TreeView control properties

First, rename the *TreeView* object to *treeView*. Since the white background of the TreeView control looks a bit garish compared to the gray background of the form, set the TreeView control's background color to *Control* (gray). Since we plan to implement in-process drag-and-drop, set the control's *allowDrop* flag to *true*.

I didn't worry about using images in the TreeViewDemo demo application; however, in this more realistic application we will need to adorn our TreeView control with images.

You can assign two different images to a TreeView control. One image is used for the currently selected node and the other for all other nodes. Normally, a small image of a partially opened folder is used for the selected node and an image of a closed folder is used for the rest. To find such an image, I searched my hard disk for all .ico (icon) files. The two files named OPENFOLD.ICO and CLSDFOLD.ICO appeared to be exactly what I wanted. I created a subdirectory of the project directory named images and copied these two files into that directory. If you can't find suitable images either lying about on your hard disk or somewhere on the Internet, you can create them in Microsoft Paint or some other graphics program. Make the images 16-by-16 pixels in size. Of course, you can always use the images included with this application on the companion CD-ROM.

Drag an ImageList control from the Toolbox, and drop it somewhere on the Forms Designer. Add the two folder images to the ImageList using the Image Editor.

Returning to the TreeView control, set its *imageList* property to *imageList* (the name of the image list you just created); set its *imageIndex* property to be the index of the closed folder image in the image list; and set its *selectedImageIndex* property to be the index of the open folder image.

Setting the ListView control properties

First rename the ListView control to *listView*. Again set the background color to *Control* to match the background of the TreeView control and the form. Set the control's *view* property to *Report*; this will ensure that the file details appear next to the file name. Add three column headers, and set their text to *File Name*, *File Size*, and *Last Modified*. Leave the column properties as they are except for the File Size column. Since this column will be used to display numbers, set its *textAlign* property to *Right* rather than the default *Left*.

Set the *fullRowSelect* property of the ListView to *true*. That way, when the user selects any one of the properties the entire row will be selected. I set the *gridLines* property to *true* because I prefer to see the gray gridlines; however, you can set this property as you please.

Since I personally think that icons don't add that much to the file list, I did not bother to define an image list for the ListView control.

Setting the Edit control properties

Rename the Edit control to *edit*. Clear its *text* property setting so that it is blank. Since this Edit control is used only to receive output, set the *readOnly* property to *true*. Finally, I set the background color to *Control* to match the other two controls and the form.

The resulting form in the Forms Designer is shown in Figure 8-8.

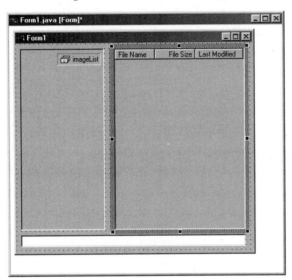

Figure 8-8. *The FileMgr application in the Forms Designer.*

The Code

The code for FileMgr appears in all its glory as follows:

```
import com.ms.wfc.app.*;
import com.ms.wfc.core.*;
import com.ms.wfc.ui.*;
import com.ms.wfc.html.*;


import com.ms.wfc.io.*;
import com.ms.wfc.util.*;

/**
 * This class can take a variable number of parameters on the command
 * line. Program execution begins with the main() method. The class
 * constructor is not invoked unless an object of type 'Form1' is
 * created in the main() method.
 */
public class Form1 extends Form
{
    String directory;
```

(continued)

```
public Form1(String[] args)
{
    // Required for Visual J++ Form Designer support
    initForm();

    // start either from the current directory
    // or from the path specified in the argument list
    directory = File.getCurrentDirectory();
    if (args.length == 1)
    {
        directory = args[0];
    }

    // now populate the treeView with the directory
    // tree starting at the current directory
    treeView.addNode(expandTreeNode("", directory));

    // populate the list with the files in the
    // current directory
    createList();
}

/**
 * Create the fileView list.
 */
private static final ListItem[] clear = new ListItem[0];
void createList()
{
    // first clear out the list view contents by passing
    // it a zero length array of list items
    listView.setItems(clear);

    // reset background color after clearing the list
    listView.setBackColor(Color.CONTROL);
    // now create a list of just the files (no directories)
    List fileList = createSortedList(directory, false);

    // now add them to the list view
    addFilesToListView(fileList);
}

/**
 * Expand the directory dirName within path.
 */
TreeNode expandTreeNode(String path, String dirName)
{
    // create a node with that directory name
    TreeNode node = new MyTreeNode(dirName, path);
```

```
        // combine the path with the directory name
        path = File.combine(path, dirName);

        // create the directory list
        List dirList = createSortedList(path, true);

        // add the directories (don't add the files)
        addDirsToNode(path, node, dirList);
        return node;
    }


/**
 * Add a list of directories to the node pointed to by path.
 */
void addDirsToNode(String path, TreeNode node, List list)
{
    // iterate through the list of directories
    IEnumerator itemEnumerator = list.getItemEnumerator();
    while (itemEnumerator.hasMoreItems())
    {
        // get the directory name from the list item
        ListItem li = (ListItem)itemEnumerator.nextItem();
        String dirName = li.getText();

        // now add a new node with that name; expand the
        // node to include the contents of the directory
        // as well
        node.addNode(expandTreeNode(path, dirName));
    }
}


/**
 * Add the list of ListItem objects to listView.
 */
void addFilesToListView(List list)
{
    // iterate through the list
    IEnumerator itemEnumerator = list.getItemEnumerator();
    while (itemEnumerator.hasMoreItems())
    {
        // add each file name to the node
        ListItem li = (ListItem)itemEnumerator.nextItem();
        listView.addItem(li);
    }
}
```

(continued)

```
/**
 * Create a list of ListItems containing either the
 * names of the directories or the files contained in
 * the directory specified by path.
 */
static final String[] nullStringArray = new String[]{null, null};
List createSortedList(String path, boolean wantDirectory)
{
    List list = new List();

    // create a FileEnumerator in order to iterate
    // through the current path
    FileEnumerator fe =
            new FileEnumerator(File.combine(path, "*.*"));
    for(;fe.hasMoreFiles(); fe.getNextFile())
    {
        String fileName = fe.getName();

        // ignore the "." and ".." directories
        if (fileName.equals(".") ||
            fileName.equals(".."))
        {
            continue;
        }

        // ignore those things that we don't want
        if (File.isDirectory(File.combine(path, fileName))
            == wantDirectory)
        {
            // add the entry to the list (we only need
            // the file size and time of last modification
            // for the files, not the directories)
            String[] info = nullStringArray;
            if (wantDirectory == false)
            {
                // this is a file, get the extra information
                info = new String[2];
                info[0] = Long.toString(fe.getSize());
                Time t  = fe.getLastWriteTime();
                info[1] = t.toString();
            }
            list.addItem(new ListItem(fileName, -1, info));
        }
    }

    // now sort the list
    list.sort(new FileNameComparer());

    return list;
}
```

```
/**
 * Implement the IComparer interface to support List.sort().
 */
class FileNameComparer implements IComparer
{
    /**
     * Compare o1 to o2; return -1, 0, or 1.
     */
    public int compare(Object o1, Object o2)
    {
        String f1 = ((ListItem)o1).getText();
        String f2 = ((ListItem)o2).getText();

        return StringSorter.compare(f1, f2,
            StringSorter.STRINGSORT | StringSorter.IGNORECASE);
    }
}

    ⋮

/**
 * As the form resizes, allocate 1/3 of the horizontal
 * space to the treeView and 2/3 to the listView.
 */
private void Form1_resize(Object source, Event e)
{
    // get the size of the form (don't let it get smaller
    // than some minimum)
    Point formSize = getSize();
    if (formSize.x < 100)
    {
        formSize.x = 100;
    }

    // divide the width 1/3 vs. 2/3
    int treeWidth = (formSize.x - 30) / 3;
    int listWidth = treeWidth * 2;

    // set the treeWidth
    Point treeSize = treeView.getSize();
    treeSize.x = treeWidth;
    treeView.setSize(treeSize);

    // now position and size the listView
    // (positioning is necessary because the listView
    // is right justified in the form)
    Point listSize = listView.getSize();
```

(continued)

```
        listSize.x = listWidth;
        listView.setSize(listSize);

        Point listLoc = listView.getLocation();
        listLoc.x = treeWidth + 20;
        listView.setLocation(listLoc);
    }


    /**
     * As the selected tree element changes, update the
     * right side of the display.
     */
    private void treeView_afterSelect(Object source, TreeViewEvent e)
    {
        MyTreeNode tn = (MyTreeNode)treeView.getSelectedNode();
        directory = tn.getFullPath();
        createList();
    }


    /**
     * Begin the drag operation by copying the selected files
     * onto the Clipboard using the "FileName" descriptor.
     */
    TreeNode previousNode = null;
    private void listView_itemDrag(Object source, ItemDragEvent e)
    {
        // save the currently selected node so that we can return
        // there after the drag-and-drop operation is done
        previousNode = treeView.getSelectedNode();

        // now get the selected files and store them into a
        // MemoryStream (the way Windows Explorer does it)
        ListItem[] selected = listView.getSelectedItems();
        MemoryStream ms = new MemoryStream();
        for (int i = 0; i < selected.length; i++)
        {
            String fileName = selected[i].getText();
            fileName = File.combine(directory, fileName) + ";";
            byte[] buffer = fileName.getBytes();
            ms.writeBytes(buffer);
        }

        // store the MemoryStream onto the Clipboard with the
        // type name "FileMgr"
        DataObject dobj = new DataObject("FileMgr", ms);

        // now perform the drag-and-drop operation
        doDragDrop(dobj, DragDropEffect.COPY);
```

```
        // clear out the previousNode field
        previousNode = null;
}


/**
 * Process the drop operation by reading the FileName
 * entries out and copying them to the selected directory.
 */
private void treeView_dragDrop(Object source, DragEvent e)
{
    // read the filenames out of the DragEvent
    IDataObject data = e.data;
    MemoryStream ms = (MemoryStream)data.getData("FileMgr");
    byte[] buffer = ms.toByteArray();
    String files = new String(buffer);

    // loop through the files passed
    int start = 0;
    int end;
    String targetDirectory = directory;
    while ((end = files.indexOf(";", start)) != -1)
    {
        // get the next file
        String file = files.substring(start, end);

        // create the destination file name by extracting
        // the file name from the source path and prepending
        // the target directory name
        String dest = File.combine(targetDirectory,
                                    File.getName(file));

        // now perform the copy - alert if it fails
        try
        {
            String s = file + "->" + dest;
            edit.setText("copying " + s);
            File.copy(file, dest);
            edit.setText("copied " + s);

        }
        catch (Exception ex)
        {
            MessageBox.show("Copy failed", "Error",
                        MessageBox.ICONERROR |
                        MessageBox.OK);
        }
```

(continued)

```
                    // return the display to the source node
                    if (previousNode != null)
                    {
                        treeView.setSelectedNode(previousNode);
                    }

                    if (MessageBox.show("Delete " + file + "?",
                                        "Confirmation",
                                        MessageBox.ICONQUESTION |
                                        MessageBox.YESNO)
                        == DialogResult.YES)
                    {
                        try
                        {
                            // File.delete(file);
                            edit.setText("deleted " + file);
                        }
                        catch (Exception ex)
                        {
                            MessageBox.show("Delete failed", "Error",
                                            MessageBox.ICONERROR |
                                            MessageBox.OK);
                        }

                        // refresh source directory list
                        createList();
                    }

                    // start looking again after the previous ";"
                    start = end + 1;
                }
        }

        /**
         * As the mouse drags over a tree node, make the tree node active
         * so the user can see its contents.
         */
        private static Point point = new Point();
        private void treeView_dragOver(Object source, DragEvent e)
        {
            // get the location of the mouse pointer on the screen
            point.x = e.x;
            point.y = e.y;

            // now convert this into the location within the
            // treeView object
            point = treeView.pointToClient(point);
```

```
        // find the node at that location...
        TreeNode node = treeView.getNodeAt(point);
        if (node != null)
        {
            // and make it active
            treeView.setSelectedNode(node);
        }
}


/**
 * Delete the files selected in the listView.
 */
private void listView_keyDown(Object source, KeyEvent e)
{
    if (e.getKeyCode() == Key.DELETE)
    {
        // delete all of the files currently selected
        // in the listView
        ListItem[] list = listView.getSelectedItems();
        for (int i = 0; i < list.length; i++)
        {
            String fileName = list[i].getText();
            fileName = File.combine(directory, fileName);
            edit.setText("deleting " + fileName);
            // File.delete(fileName);
            edit.setText("deleted " + fileName);
        }

        // refresh the listView
        createList();
    }
}


/**
 * NOTE: The following code is required by the Visual J++ form
 * designer.  It can be modified using the form editor.  Do not
 * modify it using the code editor.
 */
Container components = new Container();
TreeView treeView = new TreeView();
ListView listView = new ListView();
ColumnHeader columnHeader1 = new ColumnHeader();
ColumnHeader columnHeader2 = new ColumnHeader();
ColumnHeader columnHeader3 = new ColumnHeader();
Edit edit = new Edit();
ImageList imageList = new ImageList();
```

(continued)

```
        private void initForm()
        {
            // ...generated by the Forms Designer...
        }

        /**
         * The main entry point for the application.
         *
         * @param args Array of parameters passed to the application
         * via the command line.
         */
        public static void main(String args[])
        {
            Application.run(new Form1(args));
        }
    }

class MyTreeNode extends TreeNode
{
    String path;

    MyTreeNode(String name, String path)
    {
        super(name);
        this.path = File.combine(path, name);
    }

    String getPath()
    {
        return path;
    }
}
```

As you might have expected, the first part of FileMgr looks like a combination of the code for ListViewDemo and TreeViewDemo. The *Form1()* constructor starts by calling *initForm()*. It then initializes the *directory* string variable, which contains a reference to the current directory, returned from *File.getCurrentDirectory()*, or the argument passed to the program if there is one. (As always, supporting the single argument is primarily to support someone dragging a directory onto the program. I don't really expect anyone to type in a directory path when executing the program from the command line of an MS-DOS box.) The *Form1()* constructor then populates the tree view by calling *addNode()* and passing it the base directory, and populates the list view by calling *createList()*.

These first few functions work more or less the same as their cousins shown earlier in this chapter. I did convert *createSortedList()* back to creating a single list of either the directories or the files in a directory and not both. This is because the tree view needs the directories and the list view needs the files, but neither needs both. Generating a list of both directories and files seemed to slow down the population of the tree view unnecessarily.

Notice also that *createSortedList()* creates a list of *ListItem* objects since this is what the list view requires. In the case of the tree view, *addFilesToNode()* doesn't use the *ListItem* objects other than to call *ListItem.getText()* to retrieve the file name of each list item.

Resizing the two views dynamically

Starting with *Form1_resize()*, we run into all new code. The anchoring mechanism built into WFC is great at handling the resizing of objects within a form as the user resizes the form, but it can't handle all circumstances under which objects need to be resized. In particular, I wanted the tree view to always occupy the left third of the form and the list view to occupy the right two-thirds. To maintain this ratio, I had to write my own function. Notice that I am only concerned with the horizontal sizing; WFC can handle the vertical resizing of the two views just fine.

Using the Properties window of the Forms Designer, I attached *Form1_resize()* to the resize event of *Form1*. This event occurs repeatedly as the form is resized. *Form1_resize()* begins by asking the form exactly how large it is. The function then makes sure that the horizontal size of the function is not less than 100. This sets the minimum width of the application to 100 pixels—anything less than that and you really can't see either the tree view elements or the list view elements.

Once the minimum has been established, *Form1_resize()* calculates the width of the tree view and of the list view, assigning the results to the variables *treeWidth* and *listWidth*. The widths are calculated by taking one-third and two-thirds of the form width minus 30. The function subtracts 30 from the form width because it knows that there is a 10-pixel-wide border on both the left and right side of the form, plus it intends to put a similar 10-pixel border between the two lists.

Setting the width of the *treeView* object is merely a matter of asking the *treeView* object how big it is now, and then replacing the current width with the calculated width.

Setting the width of the *listView* object is a little more complicated, because in addition to setting its width, *Form1_resize()* must position the *listView* object 10 pixels to the right of the right border of the *treeView* object. The extra 10 pixels are to maintain a 10-pixel border between the two views.

Updating the file list dynamically

I created the *treeView_afterSelect()* method to handle the *afterSelect* event of the *treeView* object. This event occurs when the user selects a new node in the tree view hierarchy. The "after" in the event name comes into play because this method is invoked after WFC has updated the display to reflect the selection.

The *treeView_afterSelect()* method asks the *treeView* which node is selected by calling *getSelectedNode()*. You'll notice that I've coded *treeView_afterSelect()* to convert the *TreeNode* object returned from *getSelectedNode()* into something called *MyTreeNode* before using it.

What is *MyTreeNode*?

Just as the *ListView* class is normally populated by *ListItem* objects, so the *TreeView* class is populated by objects of class *TreeNode*. It is the text associated with the *TreeNode* that is displayed in the tree view. The problem is that the *TreeNode* object contains only the name of the directory. When the user selects a *TreeNode*, however, we need the entire path to that directory in order to know how to display the contents of that directory in the list view on the right.

One solution to this problem would be to store the entire path in the *TreeNode* object before we attach it to the *TreeView* object. This is not satisfactory, however, because doing so would cause the *TreeView* object to display this path information on every node. Such information would be annoying because it would be redundant. The path to a particular directory is made obvious by the tree view display itself.

A better solution is to create our own class that extends *TreeNode* by storing the path information that we need. The class *MyTreeNode,* defined at the bottom of the Form1.java file, adds a data member *path* and a method *getPath()* that returns the path information to the base *TreeNode* class. In every other respect, *MyTreeNode* is a *TreeNode*, so it has the ability to be attached to a *TreeView*.

This class creation is an important trick to remember.

> **TIP**   It is perfectly legal to extend a WFC class to add your own data members or methods and then use that class in place of the base class.

As the tree nodes are being constructed, *Form1.expandTreeNode()* adds *MyTreeNode* objects containing both the directory name and the path to that directory to the tree view. Thus, when the user selects a node he or she is actually selecting an object of class *MyTreeNode*. (Remember that because *MyTreeNode* extends the class *TreeNode*, an object of class *MyTreeNode* is also of class *TreeNode*.) The method *treeView_afterSelect()* calls the method *getSelectedNode()* which returns a *TreeNode* class; however, since the objects returned are the same *MyTreeNode* objects we added earlier, *treeView_afterSelect()* can convert the node back into a *MyTreeNode*. In this way, *treeView_afterSelect()* can retrieve the path information stored in the object previously. It can use the path information to create the list view file display.

Handling drag-and-drop

The next three methods in FileMgr—*listView_itemDrag()*, *treeView_dragDrop()*, and *treeView_dragOver()*—support the dragging of files from the list view to a directory in the tree view. (FileMgr does not support the dragging of directories.)

I used the Properties window to attach *listView_itemDrag()* to the *itemDrag* event of the ListView control. This event occurs when the user selects one or more files in the list view and then begins moving the mouse with the left mouse button held down, thereby initiating the drag operation. You saw how to implement a drop method in Chapter 6 with the RTFEditor application by calling *getData()* with the data object passed in the *DragEvent* object to return an array of *String* objects. The *listView_itemDrag()* method in effect reverses that process. First, *listView_itemDrag()* fetches a list of the items currently selected in the list view by calling *getSelectedItems()*. It then creates a *MemoryStream* object to which it writes the full path name of each file followed by a semicolon to act as a file name terminator.

C++ **NOTE**   Remember, the *MemoryStream* class in Visual J++ is equivalent to the *strstream* class in C++; they are both memory buffers that act like files.

Once all the file names have been written to the buffer, a *DataObject* object of type FileMgr is created to contain the *MemoryStream* object. The *DataObject* is then passed to the function *doDragDrop()*, which initiates the drag operation.

It is the method *doDragDrop()* that changes the cursor to indicate to the user that a drag-and-drop operation is in process. Control does not return from the *doDrag-Drop()* call until the user has released the left mouse button.

Similarly, I used the Properties window to assign the *treeView_dragDrop()* method to handle the *dragDrop* event of the tree view. This event occurs when the user lets go of the left mouse button to "drop" the dragged files. The *treeView_drag-Drop()* method is similar to the *dragDrop()* method in Chapter 6. The *treeView-_dragDrop()* method first gets the *DataObject* object out of the *DragEvent* event passed to it. It then gets the FileMgr memory stream from which it begins reading file names under the assumption that the file names are terminated with a semicolon. Each file is then copied to the currently selected directory using the *File.copy()* method. Once the file has been successfully copied, *treeView_dragDrop()* displays a message box giving the user the option of deleting the source file. Whether the file is deleted or not, the source directory is redisplayed in the list view to show the user any changes.

NOTE   The delete operation has been commented out so you don't inadvertently delete important files. If you would like to enable this feature, uncomment the call to *File.delete()*.

The final key function to the drag-and-drop operation is the *treeView_dragOver()* method. I used the Properties window to assign this method to handle the *dragOver* event of the TreeView control. The *dragOver* event occurs repeatedly as the user moves the mouse within the tree view during a drag operation. Contained within the *DragEvent* passed to *treeView_dragOver()* are the screen coordinates of the mouse as it moves. For our purposes, we would like the program to use these coordinates to highlight which tree node the mouse is pointing at. That way, the user has positive feedback as to which node she is about to drop the file(s) on.

The mouse coordinates contained in the *DragEvent* object are relative to the upper-left corner of the screen. Before *treeView_dragOver()* can use them, it must call *treeView.pointToClient()* to transform the screen-relative mouse coordinates to coordinates relative to the tree view. (This transformation involves subtracting the coordinates of the upper left-hand corner of the frame within the screen and then subtracting the location of the tree view within the frame.) The *treeView_dragOver()* method then calls *getNodeAt()*, passing the transformed mouse coordinates, to find out which tree node the user is pointing at with the mouse. If the user is not pointing at a tree node, *getNodeAt()* returns a *null*. If *getNodeAt()* returns a *null*, *treeView_dragOver()* returns without taking any action. However, if *getNodeAt()* does return a tree node, *treeView_dragOver()* makes this the selected node by calling *setSelectedNode()*. This method will highlight the node, change its image from the closed folder to the open folder, and update the ListView control to display the files in the directory corresponding to that node.

Handling the Delete key

To complete the FileMgr capabilities, I added one further feature. If the user presses the Delete key with the mouse pointer in the list view, FileMgr will delete any files selected. I did this both because I felt that the application needed such a function and to demonstrate the handling of key events.

To implement this functionality, use the Properties window to define the *listView_keyDown()* method to handle the event that occurs when the user presses a key. Since this method is attached to the ListView control, this event will only be passed to the list view if the mouse pointer is somewhere within the list view's display area.

The *KeyEvent* object passed to *listView_keyDown()* includes several data fields of interest, including the *keyData* field, which contains the ANSI equivalent of the key that was pressed. For example, *keyData* contains an "a" when the A key is pressed. However, the *keyDown* event also occurs for keys that have no ANSI equivalent, such as the Shift key or the Control key. The Delete key falls into this category.

For these keys, the programmer must rely on the key code. The key code is a unique number assigned to each key on the PC keyboard. (Actually, it's semi-unique, if that's a word, since if your keyboard has two Delete keys, as most do, then both will have the same key code.) Rather than memorize these key codes, programmers should used the enumeration class *Key* which contains constants representing a complete list of all of the key codes, including those for ANSI character keys like the A key.

The member *Key.DELETE* refers to the key code for the Delete key. Our implementation of the *listView_keyDown()* method ignores any key besides the Delete key.

Once the Delete key is detected, the function iterates through the selected files in the list view and deletes them using the *File.delete()* function.

> **NOTE** Once again, this function has been commented out to avoid acciden-
> tal deletion of critical files. If you want to enable this feature, uncomment the call
> to *File.delete()*.

The completed program

Figure 8-9 shows the complete program displaying my \temp directory. You can see the file structure displayed on the left. Most of the folders are displayed with the closed folder icon; however, the currently selected folder, EyeControl, is displayed with the open folder icon. The display on the right shows the contents of that folder. The edit box at the bottom of the applications shows that I have just copied the Form1.java file from \temp\EyeControl to \temp.

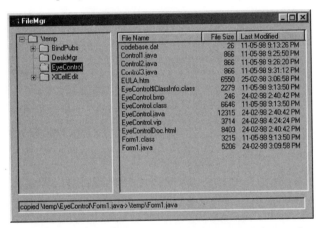

Figure 8-9. *The completed FileMgr program displaying the contents of my \temp directory.*

Why use the *IEnumerator* interface?

Back in *addDirsToNode()* and *addFilesToListView()* you might have noticed the use of the *IEnumerator* interface, whereas in programs in previous chapters (such as ComboBox1 in Chapter 6) I simply called *list.getItems()* to return an array of the objects contained within the list and then manipulated that list. The use of *IEnum-erator* in the examples in this chapter has been primarily for educational purposes, but it has certain advantages.

The fact that the *List.getItems()* call returns an array of objects leads one to believe that a *List* is implemented as an array. This might be, but is not necessarily the case. Suppose I created a list class that maintained its contents in a linked list or a push down stack or any number of other possible data structures. It might be a slow process to create an array of references to these objects. Thus, while the *getItems()*

function returns a data structure that is convenient for the programmer to use (an array), it might not be convenient for the list class to generate.

The *IEnumerator* interface is completely generic. It makes few assumptions about the underlying data structure of the list. Whether an array, a linked list, or a push down stack, the programmer of the list class should be able to generate an efficient enumeration class which implements the three methods required by *IEnumerator*:

- *hasMoreItems()*—determines whether the program has reached the end of the list.

- *nextItem()*—retrieves the current object and moves to the next object.

- *reset()*—starts over from the beginning of the list.

Thus, while using *IEnumerator* might not be quite as convenient for the application programmer, it allows the library programmer the flexibility to implement the underlying list in the most efficient means possible.

CONCLUSION

In this chapter, you've seen both list view and tree view demonstration applications. In addition, you've seen the two combined into a reasonably powerful, "real world" application, FileMgr.

In fact, by now you've seen demonstration applications of many of the widgets that make up WFC. However, for some applications these premade widgets just won't do. In those cases, you need the capability to draw to the display yourself. The next chapter demonstrates how to draw on the display freehand.

Chapter 9

The *Graphics* Class

The Windows Foundation Classes for Java (WFC) library contains enough different types of components to solve most of the problems you will encounter in creating applications. You will occasionally, however, create a program in which you need to draw directly into a window. In these cases, you must rely on the *Graphics* class and the closely related *PaintEvent* class, both contained in the *ms.com.wfc.ui* package. This chapter is devoted to the explanation of those two classes.

This chapter begins by creating a couple of freehand, "Etch-a-Sketch"-like drawing programs. From there, we will move on to examine some of the special considerations that come into play when drawing, rather than writing, text to the screen. The *Graphics* class includes a set of simple drawing objects in its tool set. Too many different drawing objects exist in this class for me to create example programs for each, but I can demonstrate the use of one of these as an example for the rest.

The chapter ends by discussing one of the most difficult problems that arises while using the *Graphics* object: combining freehand painting that uses *Graphics* objects together with WFC controls in the same form. Again, I can't demonstrate every combination, but I will present the solution to one common but sticky problem. The final version of all the sample code in this chapter is in the Windows Applications subfolder on the companion CD.

> **NOTE** The *Graphics* class described in this chapter is part of WFC. The *Graphics* class that is part of the Abstract Windowing Toolkit (AWT) is similar, but not identical.

FREEHAND DRAWING ON THE SCREEN

Occasionally you will be called upon to write an application that enables the user to draw figures freehand. This type of application provides the simplest introduction to the use of the *Graphics* class.

Connecting the Dots

The simplest of all the freehand drawing applications is one we'll call ConnectTheDots. In this application, the user is free to click the mouse anywhere within the form. With every click of the left mouse button, the ConnectTheDots application draws a line between the current position of the mouse pointer and the position of the mouse pointer at every previous mouse click. Clicking the right mouse button clears the screen to allow the user to start over. Even a simple application such as this allows the user to generate some interesting patterns.

The Forms Designer work

Since this application doesn't make use of any Toolbox components, there's almost no Forms Designer work to be done. Create the Windows application as you would any other Microsoft Visual J++ 6 Windows application, and give it the name Connect-TheDots. Change the form's *text* property to *Connect the Dots: Click mouse*. Then switch the Properties window over to the active properties to add a *mouseDown* event handler and a *paint* event handler.

> **NOTE**   The *paint* event is only defined for the *Form* class. You can't use the *paint* event to draw into any other WFC controls.

The code

The code for ConnectTheDots is shown here:

```
import com.ms.wfc.app.*;
import com.ms.wfc.core.*;
import com.ms.wfc.ui.*;
import com.ms.wfc.html.*;

import com.ms.wfc.util.*;

public class Form1 extends Form
{
    public Form1()
    {
        // Required for Visual J++ Form Designer support
        initForm();
    }

    ⋮
```

```
/**
 * If the left mouse button is pressed, add the point
 * to the draw list. If the right button is pressed,
 * clear the list.
 */
List points = new List();
private void Form1_mouseDown(Object source, MouseEvent e)
{
    if ((e.button & MouseButton.LEFT) != 0)
    {
        Point mouseLoc = new Point(e.x, e.y);
        points.addItem(mouseLoc);
    }
    if ((e.button & MouseButton.RIGHT) != 0)
    {
        points.setSize(0);
    }

    invalidate();
}


/**
 * Handle repaints of the form by drawing lines
 * between each of the mouse points in the draw list.
 */
private void Form1_paint(Object source, PaintEvent e)
{
    // first draw the kaleidoscope
    Graphics g = e.graphics;
    int length = points.getSize();
    for (int i = 0; i < length; i++)
    {
        for (int j = 0; j < i; j++)
        {
            Point p1 = (Point)points.getItem(i);
            Point p2 = (Point)points.getItem(j);

            g.drawLine(p1, p2);
        }
    }
}


/**
 * NOTE: The following code is required by the Visual J++ form
 * designer.  It can be modified using the form editor.  Do not
 * modify it using the code editor.
 */
```

(continued)

```
Container components = new Container();

private void initForm()
{
    // ...created by the Forms Designer...
}

/**
 * The main entry point for the application.
 * ...
 */
public static void main(String args[])
{
    Application.run(new Form1());
}
}
```

Other than the *initForm()* method, which simply sets the title for the form and assigns the two event handlers, the program consists almost entirely of the two event handlers, *Form1_mouseDown()* and *Form1_paint()*.

The *mouseDown* event handler code

The program invokes the method *Form1_mouseDown()* when the user clicks either mouse button while the mouse pointer is anywhere in the form. The method receives a *MouseEvent* that contains the location of the mouse within the form at the time the mouse button was pressed, and that contains a *button* variable indicating which mouse button was pressed. This variable *button* consists of an OR combination of the fields *LEFT, MIDDLE,* and *RIGHT* of the enumeration class *MouseButton.* Thus, if the *MouseButton.LEFT* bit is set in *e.button,* the left mouse button was clicked. (More accurately, if the *MouseButton.LEFT* button bit is set, the left mouse button was clicked or was being held down at the same time that some other mouse button was clicked. The distinction isn't important for most applications.)

If *Form1_mouseDown()* determines that the left mouse button was clicked, the method creates a *Point* object to store the mouse location and adds the object to a list of mouse locations called *points.* If it was the right mouse button that was pressed, *Form1_mouseDown()* clears out the list of mouse locations by setting the size of *points* to 0. This gives the user a way to start over. Either way, *Form1_mouseDown()* finishes by calling the method *invalidate()* to display the results.

What's *invalidate()*?

Calling the *invalidate()* method tells WFC that the *Form* object's display is now invalid and must be repainted. WFC asks the object to repaint itself by generating a paint event, which is handled in this program by *Form1_paint().* The paint event is WFC's way of asking the application to re-create the window.

NOTE Even beginning Microsoft Visual C++ programmers will recognize the *invalidate()* method immediately. The only difference between the way Visual J++ 6 and other Microsoft Visual Studio languages handle the invalidation is that under Visual J++, the paint request is processed by means of an event to the form. Experienced Microsoft Windows programmers will probably want to skip over the following explanation of the paint event code.

There are a lot of other ways besides mouse clicks that the display might become invalid. When the window of some other application obscures the window of your application, for example, Windows loses the information contained in the obscured portion. If that portion of the window later becomes visible, the window is invalid and your application needs to redraw it. Or, the user might have minimized the form and now requests that it be displayed. Even simply resizing the form to make it larger results in a display that is at least partially invalid and needs to be re-created by the application.

ISN'T THE INVALIDATE-PAINT MECHANISM OVERLY COMPLICATED?

This mechanism of generating a paint event whenever the window needs refreshing seems overly-complicated. Isn't there some other approach to refreshing the display? In fact, there is.

The problem we have to deal with is that when an application's window is obscured on the screen, Windows loses some information. To avoid this, rather than write to the real screen, our application could write to a virtual screen that is maintained by the operating system. In this virtual world, each window would be maintained individually on its own virtual screen. In this virtual world, the application's window would never be overwritten by some other window because it would always be separate.

The operating system would have to combine these virtual screens onto the single, real screen that the user sees. If a window were minimized, it would be the job of the operating system to figure out which pieces of which virtual windows would be needed to properly update the real screen.

Microsoft Windows doesn't use the virtual screen approach, however. Why?

There are several problems with the virtual screen proposal. The first issue is that it requires large amounts of memory. Each virtual screen must be maintained in RAM that, for speed reasons, can't be swapped to disk. Modern, high-resolution, multicolor screen displays can each consume 2 MB of memory

(continued)

ISN'T THE INVALIDATE-PAINT MECHANISM OVERLY COMPLICATED? *continued*

or more. Today, when memory is cheap, this isn't much of a problem; but Windows was designed in an era when memory was more expensive. (Many people don't remember that the earliest versions of Windows were designed so that, together with the applications, a total of 640 KB of memory was used.) Even today, it seems wasteful to consume 16 MB or more of nonswappable RAM just to maintain windows that aren't even visible.

A second problem is performance. This copying of potentially large amounts of memory could result in slow display performance. Consider, for example, the most common case of an application writing to a completely visible window. Using the virtual screen scenario, Windows would have to write every pixel twice: first when the application wrote to the virtual screen, and again when the operating system copied the window from there to the real screen. With the approach that Windows uses, a window need only be written once to the real screen.

Finally, there is the issue of scheduling. Windows gives the paint event the lowest event priority (other than the idle event, which we'll discuss in the next chapter). If the application receives any other event notification, that event will occur before the paint event. This type of scheduling avoids needless repaints, which would be much harder to avoid using the virtual screen method.

For example, maximizing the size of Microsoft Internet Explorer not only displays images or parts of images that might not previously have been visible on the display, it also causes the browser to reformat text to fully utilize the additional display area. Windows doesn't repaint the browser window until all updates caused by the resizing have been processed. Using the virtual screen method, it would be very difficult to avoid updating the real screen from the virtual screen multiple times and thereby wasting CPU cycles.

The paint event code

The *Form1_paint()* method is fairly simple. The first thing that all *paint()* methods must do is retrieve the *Graphics* object from the *PaintEvent* object. This done, *Form1_paint()* looks at the list of mouse down locations saved in the *points* variable. If this list is empty, which it will be when the program is first displayed, the method does nothing.

> **NOTE** One of the most common mistakes programmers make in writing paint event methods is this: they forget that the operating system sends a paint event to the application as soon as the *Form1* constructor finishes, which is long before the user generates the first input event.

If the *points* variable's list isn't empty, the *Form1_paint()* method iterates through each point in the list, using the *Graphics.drawLine()* method to draw a line between each pair of points in the list. Figure 9-1 shows the ConnectTheDots program display after the user selected four points in a somewhat square pattern. Figure 9-2 shows just one of the interesting combinations the user can create with a small number of points.

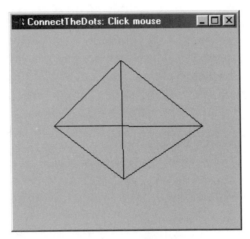

Figure 9-1. *The ConnectTheDots display with four points.*

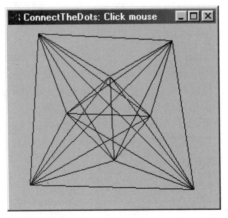

Figure 9-2. *The ConnectTheDots program generating an interesting display with as few as eight points.*

What's a *Graphics* object?

The *Graphics* object is the Visual J++ interface between the application and the display hardware. The *Graphics* object defines numerous draw methods, which the application uses to draw on the screen.

C++ NOTE   The Visual J++ *Graphics* object corresponds to the Microsoft Foundation Classes (MFC) *HDC* class, which is known as the device context.

It's the responsibility of the *Graphics* object to handle differences between different types of hardware. Thus, your application doesn't need to worry about the screen resolution or the number of colors that a particular system can support. If a video card contains special hardware to increase display performance, the *Graphics* object also handles this hardware.

In addition, it's the job of the *Graphics* object to know where your application's window is being displayed on the screen. All coordinates that you supply in your application are relative to the upper-left corner of the window. The *Graphics* object also makes sure that the application doesn't draw outside of its window. The *Graphics* object maintains the integrity of the window's display.

NOTE   Most, if not all, of the graphics display chores are not actually performed by the *Graphics* object. Instead, most of these chores are actually handled by Windows or one of its device drivers, but this detail is unimportant. To Visual J++ programmers, the *Graphics* object is the only interface to the Windows device context and the display API.

The FreeDraw Application

The ConnectTheDots application can generate interesting displays with a relatively small amount of code, but it doesn't represent a very useful application. The following FreeDraw application, which allows the user to generate freehand drawings, is much more useful.

FreeDraw allows the user to draw varied patterns with the mouse. Each pattern (which I'll refer to as a *squiggle*) begins with the user dragging the mouse pointer with the left mouse button pressed and terminates with the user releasing the mouse button. Once the squiggle has been generated, the user can modify its color and width by means of menu commands. When the user starts a new squiggle, he or she can't change previous squiggles. Right-clicking the mouse erases all stored squiggles, effectively erasing the slate.

The Forms Designer work

To create FreeDraw, begin by creating a standard Visual J++ Windows application. Set the *text* property of the form to *FreeDraw*, to match the application name.

Add a main menu to the form. Add two main menu items; label the first *Color* and the second *Width*. Add to the Color menu item several submenu items labeled with the names of some of the fields of the *Color* class, for example *BLACK*, *AQUA*, and *GREEN*. Create submenu items under the Width menu with labels indicating various line widths in pixels: *1, 2, 4*, and *8*.

The *Squiggle* class code

As is often the case, the code for the main program is made easier by creating a helper class. The *Squiggle* class describes a squiggle on the screen. The Squiggle.java file contains the following code:

```java
import com.ms.wfc.ui.*;
import com.ms.wfc.util.*;

public class Squiggle
{
    // two fundamental drawing properties
    Color color;
    int   width;

    // a pen containing the selected properties
    Pen    pen;

    // the points in this squiggle
    List  points = new List();

    /**
     * Create a black squiggle with no points.
     */
    public Squiggle()
    {
        // set the initial color and width
        color = Color.BLACK;
        width = 1;

        // convert the properties into a pen
        calcPen();

        // make sure the list is empty
        points.setSize(0);
    }

    /**
     * Set the color of the squiggle.
     */
    public void setColor(Color color)
    {
        this.color = color;
        calcPen();
    }

    /**
     * Set the width of the squiggle.
     */
```

(continued)

```
        public void setWidth(int width)
        {
            this.width = width;
            calcPen();
        }

        /**
         * Add a point to the squiggle.
         */
        public void addPoint(int x, int y)
        {
            points.addItem(new Point(x, y));
        }

        /**
         * Create a solid pen with the specified width and color.
         */
        private void calcPen()
        {
            pen = new Pen(color, PenStyle.SOLID, width);
        }

        /**
         * Return the current Pen for this squiggle.
         */
        public Pen getPen()
        {
            return pen;
        }

        /**
         * Return the number of points in this squiggle.
         */
        int getSize()
        {
            return points.getSize();
        }

        /**
         * Return a point in this squiggle list.
         */
        Point getPoint(int index)
        {
            return (Point)points.getItem(index);
        }
    }
```

A squiggle consists of a list of points representing mouse pointer locations and a *Pen* object to use in drawing between these points. The list is maintained in an object of type *List* called *points*. The *Pen* object is named *pen*. For our purposes, *Pen* has only the properties of color and width. (There are other properties that you can set for a *Pen* object.) The *color* variable stores the *color* property setting, and the *width* variable stores the *width* property setting.

The constructor for *Squiggle* creates a black *pen* object one pixel wide and an empty list. The next methods, *setColor()* and *setWidth()*, allow the application to change the pen object's properties. Both of these methods call the private method *calcPen()* to reflect the new color and width in a newly created *pen*. The method *addPoint(x, y)* creates a *Point* object from the x and y coordinates that are passed to the method as parameters. The method then adds this *Point* object to the list of points.

The *Squiggle* class provides query functions, such as *getPen()* to return the current *pen* object, *getSize()* to return the size of the list, and *getPoint(i)* to return the *Point* object at index *i* in the *points* list.

The FreeDraw code

The remaining FreeDraw code is retained in the Form1.java source file:

```
import com.ms.wfc.app.*;
import com.ms.wfc.core.*;
import com.ms.wfc.ui.*;
import com.ms.wfc.html.*;

import com.ms.wfc.util.*;
import java.lang.reflect.*;

public class Form1 extends Form
{
    public Form1()
    {
        // Required for Visual J++ Form Designer support
        initForm();
    }

    /**
     * Handle the mouse down event by creating a current list.
     */
    List oldLists = new List();
    Squiggle currentList = null;
    private void Form1_mouseDown(Object source, MouseEvent e)
    {
        // if left mouse button...
        if ((e.button & MouseButton.LEFT) != 0)
```

(continued)

```
        {
            // create a new squiggle list;
            // if there is an old one, add it to the
            // list of lists
            if (currentList != null)
            {
                oldLists.addItem(currentList);
            }
            currentList = new Squiggle();
        }

        // if right mouse button...
        if ((e.button & MouseButton.RIGHT) != 0)
        {
            // start over
            currentList = null;
            oldLists.setSize(0);
            invalidate();
        }
    }

    /**
     * Handle the mouse move event by adding the current
     * mouse pointer location to the current squiggle.
     */
    private void Form1_mouseMove(Object source, MouseEvent e)
    {
        // if right mouse button is not down, ignore it
        if ((e.button & MouseButton.LEFT) == 0)
        {
            return;
        }

        // now record the current mouse pointer position
        currentList.addPoint(e.x, e.y);

        // and repaint the screen
        invalidate();
    }

    /**
     * Handle the repaint event.
     */
    private void Form1_paint(Object source, PaintEvent e)
    {
        // paint the current squiggle
        Graphics g = e.graphics;
        if (currentList != null)
```

```
    {
        drawList(g, currentList);
    }

    // now paint the previous squiggles as well
    IEnumerator ie = oldLists.getItemEnumerator();
    while(ie.hasMoreItems())
    {
        Squiggle list = (Squiggle)ie.nextItem();
        drawList(g, list);
    }
}


/**
 * Draw squiggle by connecting the dots.
 */
static void drawList(Graphics g, Squiggle list)
{
    g.setPen(list.getPen());
    int length = list.getSize() - 1;
    for(int i = 0; i < length; i++)
    {
        g.drawLine(list.getPoint(i), list.getPoint(i + 1));
    }
}

private void colorItem_click(Object source, Event e)
{
    try
    {
        // read the menu item's label...
        MenuItem mi = (MenuItem)source;
        String s = mi.getText();

        // convert that to one of the fields in Color...
        Class c = Color.class;
        Field f = c.getField(s);
        Color color = (Color)f.get(null);

        // and set the current squiggle's color
        currentList.setColor(color);
        invalidate();
    }
    catch(Exception ex)
    {
    }
}
```

(continued)

```
private void widthItem_click(Object source, Event e)
{
    // read the menu item's label...
    MenuItem mi = (MenuItem)source;
    String s = mi.getText();

    // convert that to a number...
    int width = Integer.parseInt(s);

    // and set the width
    currentList.setWidth(width);
    invalidate();
}

/**
 * NOTE: The following code is required by the Visual J++ form
 * designer.  It can be modified using the form editor.  Do not
 * modify it using the code editor.
 */
Container components = new Container();
MainMenu mainMenu1 = new MainMenu();
MenuItem menuItem12 = new MenuItem();
MenuItem menuItem11 = new MenuItem();
MenuItem menuItem4 = new MenuItem();
MenuItem menuItem5 = new MenuItem();
MenuItem menuItem6 = new MenuItem();
MenuItem menuItem7 = new MenuItem();
MenuItem menuItem8 = new MenuItem();
MenuItem menuItem9 = new MenuItem();
MenuItem menuItem10 = new MenuItem();

private void initForm()
{
    // ...created by the Forms Designer...
}

/**
 * The main entry point for the application.
 * ...
 */
public static void main(String args[])
{
    Application.run(new Form1());
}
}
```

The *Form1* class maintains two data members. The current squiggle is maintained in a field named *currentList*. This is the *Squiggle* object that the user is currently creating or has just created. This is the only squiggle whose color and width can be modified. The variable *oldLists* consists of a list of the previously drawn squiggles.

The method *Form1_mouseDown()* is essentially two methods in one. If the user presses the left mouse button, the method adds the current squiggle—if there is one—to the list of old squiggles before creating a new current squiggle. When the right mouse button is pressed, the method zeros the *currentList* pointer to remove the current squiggle and then zeros out the old squiggle list by calling *oldLists.setSize(0)*. The call to *invalidate()* repaints the form with the lists removed, thereby clearing the window.

The *Form1_mouseMove()* method handles the mouse drag event by adding the current mouse pointer location to the current squiggle. The call to *invalidate()* repaints the display with the new mouse pointer location added.

The repaint method *Form1_paint()* first draws the *currentList* object by calling the local method *drawList()*. It then iterates through the list of older squiggles, drawing each using *drawList()*.

The method *drawList()* draws a squiggle. It begins by getting the pen stored in the *Squiggle* object and using that pen's settings to set the pen in the *Graphics* object. It then uses a *for* loop to iterate through the points contained in the *Squiggle* object, calling *Graphics.drawLine()* to draw a line between each stored mouse pointer location (i) and the next ($i + 1$). Since the mouse pointer locations stored by the *mouseMove()* method are relatively close together, *drawList()* provides a relatively smooth-looking curve, especially with some of the wider pens.

The *colorItem_click()* method handles the click event for each of the Color menu items. This method uses Java's language reflection capability (discussed in Chapter 6) to find the static member of the *Color* object with the same name as the menu item. It calls *setColor()* to establish this color as the color of the current squiggle before calling *invalidate()* to make the new color visible by repainting the screen. (Remember to attach *colorItem_click()* as the click event for all the Color submenu items.)

The *widthItem_click()* method uses a similar approach in handling the Width menu items. The label on the menu item is converted from a string into a number using the *Integer.parsetInt()* method. This integer value is used to adjust the pen width of the current squiggle by calling *setWidth()*. The call to *invalidate()* makes the change visible. (Remember to attach *widthItem_click()* as the click event for all the Width submenu items.)

Figure 9-3 shows an image drawn with FreeDraw.

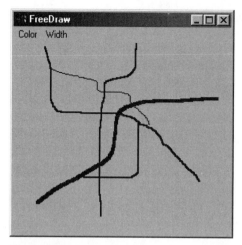

Figure 9-3. *A figure drawn with FreeDraw, showing the highways in and around my hometown.*

DRAWING TEXT

Just as you might find yourself with the need to draw arbitrary shapes to forms, be they handwritten or not, you might also be called upon to output text. Presenting output text to the user in a WFC component environment is easy. You just place an Edit or RichEdit control somewhere on the form, mark it single or multiline, and you're ready to write to it whatever text you want. In an environment ruled by the *Graphics* object and the paint event, displaying this text means drawing the text on the window. Drawing text is a little harder than simply writing it.

Drawing a Single Line

As long as all you are trying to do is draw a simple line of text, using a single font all written at one time, the problem isn't too difficult. It's still useful to divide this application up into the task of drawing a single line and the task of drawing multiple lines.

Drawing in a fixed location

The following simple program, HelloWorld, draws a single line of text—"Hello, world"—in a fixed location on the form. In the Forms Designer, set the form's title to match the name of the program and set *Form1_paint()* to handle the form's paint event. The remaining code appears as follows:

```
import com.ms.wfc.app.*;
import com.ms.wfc.core.*;
import com.ms.wfc.ui.*;
import com.ms.wfc.html.*;

public class Form1 extends Form
{
    public Form1()
    {
        // Required for Visual J++ Form Designer support
        initForm();
    }

    private void Form1_paint(Object source, PaintEvent e)
    {
        Graphics g = e.graphics;

        g.drawString("Hello, world", 80, 40);
    }

    /**
     * NOTE: The following code is required by the Visual J++ form
     * designer.  It can be modified using the form editor.  Do not
     * modify it using the code editor.
     */
    Container components = new Container();

    private void initForm()
    {
        // ...created by the Forms Designer...
    }

    /**
     * The main entry point for the application.
     * ...
     */
    public static void main(String args[])
    {
        Application.run(new Form1());
    }
}
```

This program is very simple. Each time the paint event is generated, the *Form1_paint()* method invokes the *drawString(String, x, y)* method to draw the string "Hello, world". The upper left corner of the string is 80 pixels from the left edge of the form's drawing area (the x offset), and 40 pixels from the top (the y offset). This is demonstrated in the edited output from the program shown in Figure 9-4.

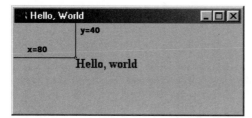

Figure 9-4. *The edited "Hello, world" output, showing the meaning of the x and y offsets.*

Drawing in a variable location

If you look closely at Figure 9-4, you'll notice that the "Hello, world" string appears approximately in the center of the form window and is appropriately sized for that window. This was no accident; I resized the window to make this so. However, suppose we want the text to be centered in the display window and be appropriately sized no matter what size the window is.

The following additions, shown in boldface, to HelloWorld.java do exactly that.

```
import com.ms.wfc.app.*;
import com.ms.wfc.core.*;
import com.ms.wfc.ui.*;
import com.ms.wfc.html.*;

public class Form1 extends Form
{
    public Form1()
    {
        // Required for Visual J++ Form Designer support
        initForm();
    }

    String outString = "Hello, world";
    Point  center    = new Point();
    Point  offset    = new Point();
    Point  outOffset = new Point();
    private void Form1_paint(Object source, PaintEvent e)
    {
        Graphics g = e.graphics;

        // calculate the proper position for the string
        // based on the size of the form and the
        // size of the string in the current font--
        // calculate the center of the form
        Rectangle formSize = this.getDisplayRect();
        center.x = formSize.width  / 2;
        center.y = formSize.height / 2;
```

```
        // to center the string, back up half the length
        // of the string and half of its height
        Point stringSize    = g.getTextSize(outString);
        offset.x = stringSize.x / 2;
        offset.y = stringSize.y / 2;

        // now output the string at the center
        // minus the offset
        outOffset.x = center.x - offset.x;
        outOffset.y = center.y - offset.y;
        g.drawString(outString, outOffset);
    }

private void Form1_resize(Object source, Event e)
{
    // find the size of the display area of the form
    Rectangle size = this.getDisplayRect();

    // get a font size that's about 1/3
    // the vertical size of the form
    int fontHeight = size.height / 3;
    Font oldFont = this.getFont();
    Font newFont = new Font(oldFont,
                            fontHeight,
                            FontSize.PIXELS);

    // make this new font (if there is one) the default
    // font for the form
    if (newFont != null)
    {
        this.setFont(newFont);
    }
}

/**
 * NOTE: The following code is required by the Visual J++ form
 * designer.  It can be modified using the form editor.  Do not
 * modify it using the code editor.
 */
Container components = new Container();

private void initForm()
{
    // ...created by the Forms Designer...
}
```

(continued)

```
/**
 * The main entry point for the application.
 * ...
 */
public static void main(String args[])
{
    Application.run(new Form1());
}
}
```

From the Forms Designer, we set the *Form1_resize()* method to handle the form's resize event. This method's job is to create a font that is proportional in size to the window. To do this, *Form1_resize()* first calls *getDisplayRect()* to find out how big the form's display area is. It then creates *newFont,* which is like the old font in every way except that its height is one-third the height of the form's display area. (One-third was chosen after a very short trial of different values and isn't based on any human response data. In other words, pick whatever size factor you prefer.) *Form1_resize()* then sets this new font to be the default font for the form.

The added code in the *Form1_paint()* method makes that method considerably more complicated than the previous version was. It must calculate the x and y offsets to use in displaying the string, based on the size of the form's displayable area and the size of the string in the current font.

Form1_paint() starts by getting the form's displayable area. It then calculates the coordinates of the center of the screen by dividing the height and width by 2. The result is stored in the variable *center.*

> **NOTE** You might wonder why most of the local variables of *Form1_paint()* are
> created as data members of the class even though they are only used locally to
> the method. Methods such as *Form1_paint()* are called often, and they need to
> execute as fast as possible. Allocating variables such as *center* once at the
> beginning of the program and reusing them, rather than reallocating and then
> abandoning them every time the method is called, can save a considerable
> amount of execution time.

The *Form1_paint()* method must then find out how large the "Hello, world" string is in the current font. Fortunately, the *Graphics* class provides just such a method in *getTextSize()*. Given a string, this method returns a *Point* representing the height and width (in pixels) of the string in the current font. Since we want the center of the string to align with the center of the display area, *Form1_paint()* must divide this *stringSize* value by 2 as well. The result is stored in *offset.*

Subtracting *offset* from *center* gives the coordinates of where *Form1_paint()* should draw the string so that it's correctly centered both vertically and horizontally. Figure 9-5 demonstrates graphically how this works.

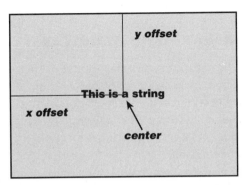

Figure 9-5. *A diagram demonstrating the offsets that* Form1_paint() *uses to center the "Hello, world" text in the form window.*

Figures 9-6 and 9-7 show the output of this program with various window sizes. These figures demonstrate that both the font sizing and centering algorithms work as desired.

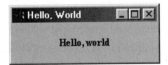

Figure 9-6. *A small form window results in a small font.*

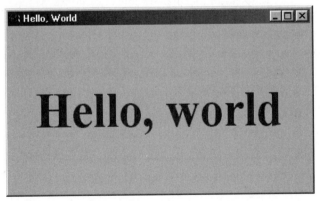

Figure 9-7. *A large form window results in a large, heavy font that is still centered.*

ISN'T THERE AN EASIER WAY TO POSITION TEXT?

When drawing text, you'll often be tempted to take this shortcut: "There are 10 characters in my output string and each character is x pixels wide, therefore the string is 10 times x pixels wide." Unfortunately, this logic doesn't work.

The problem with this solution lies in one of its assumptions. In general, each character isn't x pixels wide. Most fonts are called proportional fonts, meaning each character has a different width. By just reading this page, it should be obvious to you that capital W is given considerably more space than lower-case i. Other characters fall somewhere in between.

This being true, how does the *Graphics.getTextSize()* method calculate the width of a given string? Each font provides a table that lists the width of each character. The *getTextSize()* method iterates through the string you give it, adding up the widths of each character until it arrives at the width of the entire string.

There are a few fonts in which all characters are allocated the same width. These fonts are called monospace or nonproportional fonts and include such fonts as Courier. Monospace fonts are used in applications where you want the characters from different rows to line up in columns; most commonly this is in code listings. (Look closely at the code listings in this book and you'll notice that the characters from different rows align.)

Both proportional fonts and monospace fonts allocate the same amount of vertical space to each character. This isn't to say that the character uses the entire vertical space. Clearly, a capital letter uses more space than a little letter such as an a. However, we as readers really want the bottoms of characters on the same row to line up across the page. (Characters that have descenders, like g, p, q, and y, represent a special case).

Thus, whether the font is monospace or proportional, we can still calculate the vertical offset by multiplying the number of lines times the vertical size of a single line.

Drawing Multiple Lines

You'll often be called upon to draw multiple lines of text. There are two cases that arise. The simpler case is that of drawing multiple rows of left-justified text. A more complicated case involves drawing multiple columns.

Left-justified text

Drawing multiple rows of left-justified text is just a matter of keeping straight what line you're drawing to and how tall your font is. Let me use a previous example program to demonstrate.

In the ConnectTheDots program presented at the beginning of this chapter, it would be interesting to display the coordinates of each dot. The information the application needs to draw in ANSI text from the coordinates of the dots is available in the *paints* list already. The following modifications, shown in boldface, to the *Form1_paint()* method in ConnectTheDots is therefore all that's needed to implement this change.

```
/**
 * Handle repaints of the form by drawing lines
 * between each of the mouse points in the draw list
 * and drawing the coordinates of the mouse points as
 * text.
 */
private void Form1_paint(Object source, PaintEvent e)
{
    // first draw the kaleidoscope
    Graphics g = e.graphics;
    int length = points.getSize();
    for (int i = 0; i < length; i++)
    {
        for (int j = 0; j < i; j++)
        {
            Point p1 = (Point)points.getItem(i);
            Point p2 = (Point)points.getItem(j);

            g.drawLine(p1, p2);
        }
    }

    // now output the coordinates of the points as text:
    // get the height of the current font
    String s = "Number of points = " + length;
    Point size = g.getTextSize(s);
    int height = size.y;

    // loop through the points stored in the list, drawing
    // each as a String;
    // start at vertical offset 10 and increment by the
    // font height plus 2 every line thereafter
    int y = 10;
    g.drawString(s, 10, y);
    for (int k = 0; k < length; k++)
    {
        Point p = (Point)points.getItem(k);
        y += (height + 2);
        g.drawString(p.toString(), 10, y);
    }
}
```

The kaleidoscope section of *Form1_paint()* is unchanged from the earlier version. We have added a section to draw, in text format, the coordinates stored in the *points* list. This section begins by constructing a string *s* consisting of the phrase "Number of points = x" where x is the number of members in *points*. The method then uses the *Graphics.getTextSize()* method to find the height of this string. This value is stored in the variable *height*.

Since *Form1_paint()* doesn't change fonts, it makes the assumption that the height of this line is the same as the height of every subsequent line. (See the sidebar "Isn't There an Easier Way to Position Text?" on page 270.)

Once this height has been captured, *Form1_paint()* displays the string at location {10, 10}. It then iterates through the list *points* calling *getItem()* to return each subsequent *Point* object. At each pass through the list, *Form1_paint()* increments the vertical offset *y* by *height + 2*, which is the height of a line in the current font plus a small increment of 2, to increase the interline spacing to improve the appearance. Finally, the method outputs the *Point* object in *String* format at the calculated vertical offset. Using the same horizontal offset of 10 ensures that all the lines are left-justified.

Figure 9-8 demonstrates the result of this addition to ConnectTheDots.

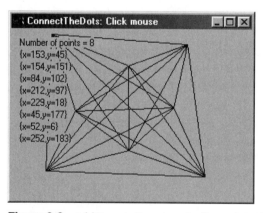

Figure 9-8. *Additions to* Form1_paint() *result in the textual display of the* mouseDown *points.*

Concatenating text

Occasionally the programmer is asked to concatenate two strings on the display. Obviously the easiest approach is to concatenate the strings before drawing them; however, in some cases this isn't possible.

To demonstrate how to approach such problems, let's add one more level of complexity to the ConnectTheDots program. Clearly, if the user clicks many dots, the vertical string of text will eventually trail off the bottom of the window. To avoid this, suppose we make the restriction that each column of text should contain no more than six rows. The coordinates of the seventh point should appear on the first row but begin a new column. Rather than align the second column at a specific location as we did with the first column, however, we want the seventh string to display immediately to the right of the first string.

The following update to *Form1_paint()*, again shown in boldface, implements this new requirement. (By the way, I'm not suggesting that this is the best solution, but merely that this solution demonstrates how to concatenate strings on the display.)

```
/**
 * Handle repaints of the form by drawing lines
 * between each of the mouse points in the draw list
 * and drawing the coordinates of the mouse points as
 * text.
 */
int[] horizontalOffset = new int[6];
private void Form1_paint(Object source, PaintEvent e)
{
    // first draw the kaleidoscope
    Graphics g = e.graphics;
    int length = points.getSize();
    for (int i = 0; i < length; i++)
    {
        for (int j = 0; j < i; j++)
        {
            Point p1 = (Point)points.getItem(i);
            Point p2 = (Point)points.getItem(j);

            g.drawLine(p1, p2);
        }
    }

    // clear out the horizontal offset of each row --
    // start the first row 10 pixels from the left edge
    int maxRows = horizontalOffset.length;
    for (int i = 0; i < maxRows; i++)
    {
        horizontalOffset[i] = 10;
    }

    // now output the coordinates of the points as text;
    // get the height of the current font
    String s = "Number of points = " + length;
    Point size = g.getTextSize(s);
    int height = size.y;
    g.drawString(s, 10, 10);

    // loop through the points stored in the list, drawing
    // each as a String;
```

(continued)

```
// start at an initial vertical offset just beyond
// the first string, an index of 0 and a rowNumber of 0
int initialVO = 15 + height;
for (int k = 0, rowNumber = 0, verticalOffset = initialVO;
    k < length;
    k++, rowNumber++, verticalOffset += (height + 2))
{
    // if the row number exceeds the maximum number of rows...
    if (rowNumber >= maxRows)
    {
        // then reset the row number and vertical offset
        rowNumber = 0;
        verticalOffset = initialVO;
    }

    // get the point, and convert it to a string
    Point p = (Point)points.getItem(k);
    s = p.toString();

    // draw the string at the proper horizontal and
    // vertical offsets for this row
    g.drawString(s,
                horizontalOffset[rowNumber],
                verticalOffset);

    // update the horizontal offset by the width of this
    // string so the next column will appear in the proper
    // place
    horizontalOffset[rowNumber] += g.getTextSize(s).x;
}
}
```

This new version of *Form1_paint()* maintains an array of six integers named *horizonalOffset*, representing the current horizontal offset of each row. Before beginning calculations, the method initializes each member of the *horizontalOffset* array to *10*. This will force each row to begin 10 pixels from the left edge of the display.

Before beginning to display the *Point* objects stored in the *points* list, *Form1_paint()* calculates an initial vertical offset and stores it in the variable *initialVO*. This will become the offset of the first row.

The method then enters the same *for* loop as before, this time initializing the *rowNumber* to *0*, the current *verticalOffset* to *initialVO,* and the index *k* to *0*. Within the *for* loop, the program tests whether the *rowNumber* exceeds the maximum number of rows, in our case 6. If it does, the program resets the *rowNumber* to *0* and resets the *verticalOffset* back to the initial vertical offset, *initialVO*. This has the effect of moving output to the top row of the next column.

Once the program has determined the proper row and column to begin the next string, it retrieves the correct *Point* object from the *points* list and converts it to a text *String* as before. The program then draws the string beginning at the calculated horizontal and vertical offsets.

Before repeating the loop, the program increments the *horizontalOffset* of this *rowNumber* by the length in pixels of the current string. The repeat clause of the *for* loop increments the *rowNumber* by one, the *verticalOffset* by the height of a row (plus 2), and the index *k* by one.

As you can see, the key addition to this program is the array *horizontalOffset*. If you consider just one row, say row 0, *horizontalOffset[0]* starts off with the value 10. After drawing the first string, *horizontalOffset[0]* is equal to 10 plus the length of the first string in pixels. This value is used as the initial horizontal displacement for the seventh string. After drawing the seventh string, *horizontalOffset[0]* is equal to 10 plus the length of the first string plus the length of the seventh string. This cycle repeats for column after column. The results can be seen in Figure 9-9.

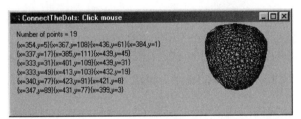

Figure 9-9. *The multicolumn version of ConnectTheDots, demonstrating the results of using* getTextSize() *to concatenate strings on the display.*

DRAWING MORE COMPLEX STRUCTURES

In addition to dots, lines, and text, the *Graphics* class supports the drawing of other types of structures, such as rectangles, circles, ovals, and arcs. There are far too many different structures for me to demonstrate each and every one. I thought that demonstrating one of the more difficult structures—the pie chart—might aid you in drawing pie charts and other structures from within your programs.

The PieChart Application

When used properly, nothing gives users better insight into the relationship of data than the pie chart. Even with the support of the *Graphics* class, the pie chart seems daunting to create at first; however, with the proper use of a few simple trigonometric functions, the pie chart is easily mastered.

The PieChart program presented here accepts any number of numeric arguments that determine the relative size of each pie slice and draws the pie chart on the screen.

In other words, if the user enters *piechart 5 5 5 10,* the PieChart program will draw a pie with three equally sized slices and a fourth slice that is twice as large as the others.

The *drawPie()* method

The key method in drawing a pie chart is the *Graphics* method *drawPie().* In a way, this method is misnamed because it really draws only one pie slice. The first argument to this method is a bounding rectangle. For almost all pie charts, including the one in this example, this rectangle will be a square. (If this isn't a square, the "pie" will be an oval rather than a circle.) The resulting pie chart will be constructed such that it just barely fits within this square.

The next two arguments are the starting and ending points of the pie slice. It's left up to the program to make sure that these points are on the circumference of the pie. As you'll see, this is where trigonometric functions come into play.

The Forms Designer work

Start by creating the PieChart project as a Visual J++ Windows application in the usual way. Set the *text* property of the *Form* object to *Pie Chart.* You should also size the form so it is close to being square, although its exact dimensions aren't critical.

While you have the Forms Designer open, use the Properties window active properties to create two event handlers, one for the paint event and one for the resize event. You can accept the default names for these two methods, *Form1_paint()* and *Form1_resize().* The resize event will be used to set the size of the bounding square for the pie chart and the paint event will be used to draw the pie chart.

The code

The code for PieChart appears as follows:

```
import com.ms.wfc.app.*;
import com.ms.wfc.core.*;
import com.ms.wfc.ui.*;
import com.ms.wfc.html.*;

/**
 * This class can take a variable number of parameters on the command
 * line. Program execution begins with the main() method. The class
 * constructor is not invoked unless an object of type 'Form1' is
 * created in the main() method.
 */
public class Form1 extends Form
{
    // global variables used in the program
    // if there is an error, errorString will be non-null
    String errorString = null;

    // pieBox - the bounding square for the pie chart
    Rectangle pieBox;
```

```
// values - the values to plot; these are read from the
//          command line at startup
double[]  values = null;

// points, brushes - the points and brushes to plot for
Point[]   points;
Brush[]   brushes;

// constants used in the program
static int[] brushstyle = new int[]{
                    BrushStyle.SOLID,
                    BrushStyle.HORIZONTAL,
                    BrushStyle.HOLLOW,
                    BrushStyle.FORWARDDIAGONAL,
                    BrushStyle.DIAGONALCROSS,
                    BrushStyle.CROSS,
                    BrushStyle.BACKWARDDIAGONAL
                    };
static Color[] color = new Color[] {
                    Color.BLACK,
                    Color.CONTROLTEXT,
                    Color.CYAN
                };

public Form1(String[] args)
{
    // Required for Visual J++ Form Designer support
    initForm();

    try
    {
        // read the values in from the arguments
        values = readValues(args);

        // calculate the size of the enclosing box
        pieBox = calculatePieBox();

        // now create the pie chart plot points
        calculatePieChart();
    }
    catch(Exception e)
    {
        // on error, save the error string
        errorString = e.toString();
    }

    // force the window to repaint
    invalidate();
}
```

(continued)

```
/**
 * Read the string arguments into an array of doubles.
 */
double[] readValues(String[] args)
    throws Exception
{
    // there must be at least two arguments
    if (args.length < 2)
    {
        throw new Exception("There must be at least 2 args");
    }

    // create an array of values to plot; the
    // first element should be a 0 and the rest
    // taken from the program argument list
    double[] values = new double[args.length + 1];
    values[0] = 0.0;
    for (int i = 1; i < values.length; i++)
    {
        values[i] = (Double.valueOf(args[i - 1])).doubleValue();
        if (values[i] <= 0)
        {
            throw new Exception("Values must be positive");
        }
    }
    return values;
}


/**
 * Calculate the bounding square for the pie chart
 * based on the minimum dimensions of the form.
 */
Point size = new Point();
Rectangle calculatePieBox()
{
    // find the size of the display area of the form
    Rectangle r = this.getDisplayRect();
    size.x = r.width;
    size.y = r.height;

    // make the bounding square slightly smaller than
    // the form's display area (allow 10 pixels on all
    // sides)
    size.x -= 20;
    size.y -= 20;
    int minSize = Math.min(size.x, size.y);
    return new Rectangle(10, 10, minSize, minSize);
}
```

```
/**
 * Convert the values that were read into pie chart coordinates.
 */
void calculatePieChart()
    throws Exception
{
    // calculate the sum of all the values to plot
    // (each value will be converted into a percentage
    // of this sum)
    double sum = 0;
    for (int i = 1; i < values.length; i++)
    {
        sum += values[i];
    }

    // normalize each value to a number between 0
    // and 2PI
    double[] plotValues = new double[values.length];
    double factor = (2 * Math.PI) / sum;
    sum = 0;
    for (int i = 0; i < values.length; i++)
    {
        plotValues[i] = values[i] * factor;
        sum += plotValues[i];
        plotValues[i] = sum;
    }

    // now convert these values into x,y values
    int radius = pieBox.height / 2;
    points = new Point[values.length];
    brushes = new Brush[values.length];
    for (int i = 0; i < values.length; i++)
    {
        // calculate a point on the radius of a circle
        int xLength = (int)(radius * Math.sin(plotValues[i]));
        int yLength = (int)(radius * Math.cos(plotValues[i]));

        // now move these values relative to the middle of
        // the rectangle
        xLength += radius;
        yLength += radius;

        // now store each value as a point with its own brush
        points[i] = new Point(xLength, yLength);

        // create a brush for this slice
        int colorIndex = i / brushstyle.length;
```

(continued)

```
                colorIndex %= color.length;
                int brushStyleIndex = i % brushstyle.length;
                brushes[i] = new Brush(color[colorIndex],
                                       brushstyle[brushStyleIndex]);
        }
    }

    /**
     * Paint the pie chart based on previously calculated values.
     */
    private void Form1_paint(Object source, PaintEvent e)
    {
        // if there was an error...
        Graphics g = e.graphics;
        if (errorString != null)
        {
            // display the message and quit
            g.drawString("Error: " + errorString, 10, 10);
            return;
        }

        // connect the pie slices
        int length = points.length - 1;
        for (int i = 0; i < length; i++)
        {
            // first draw the slice
            g.setBrush(brushes[i]);
            g.drawPie(pieBox, points[i], points[i + 1]);

            // now draw the value between the two slice points
            // (just take the average of two points)
            String s = Double.toString(values[i + 1]);
            int x = (int)((points[i].x + points[i + 1].x) / 2);
            int y = (int)((points[i].y + points[i + 1].y) / 2);
            g.drawString(s, x, y);
        }
    }

    /**
     * Enforce a minimum size of 100x100 pixels.
     */
    Point minSize = new Point(100, 100);
    protected Point getMinTrackSize()
    {
        return minSize;
    }
```

```
/**
 * Recalculate the pie chart as the form resizes.
 */
private void Form1_resize(Object source, Event e)
{
    try
    {
        // recalculate the plot points based on the
        // new size, and repaint the window
        pieBox = calculatePieBox();
        calculatePieChart();
        invalidate();
    }
    catch (Exception ex)
    {
        errorString = ex.toString();
    }
}


/**
 * NOTE: The following code is required by the Visual J++ form
 * designer.  It can be modified using the form editor.  Do not
 * modify it using the code editor.
 */
Container components = new Container();

private void initForm()
{
    // ...created by the Forms Designer...
}


/**
 * The main entry point for the application.
 */
public static void main(String args[])
{
    Application.run(new Form1(args));
}
}
```

The *PieChart()* constructor starts by invoking *Form1.readValues()* to convert the arguments the user passed to it into an array of numbers named *values*. The constructor then calls *Form1.calculatePieBox()* to calculate the bounding square for the pie chart based on the current size of the form window. Finally, *PieChart()* calls *Form1.calculatePieChart()* to convert the values read into a pie chart within the bounding square. If an exception is thrown from any of these methods, the exception is converted to text and stored in the data member *errorString* for display by the *Form1_paint()* method.

The method *readValues()* converts each argument into a *double* value and stores it into the *values* array starting with index 1. The array value *values[0]* is hard coded to have a value of zero (0). An exception is thrown if any of the values is 0, negative, or not a number.

The method *calculatePieBox()* starts by retrieving the display area of the form. From this it calculates whether the width or the height of the form is smaller. The method creates a bounding square that fits within 10 pixels on both sides of the smaller of these two dimensions. By picking the shorter of the height or width, *calculatePieBox()* ensures that the pie chart won't be bigger than the display area on any side.

The *calculatePieChart()* method is where all the real fun happens. The method begins by adding up all the values to plot and storing the result in a variable named *sum*. In the next step, each value in *values* is converted into a series of angles in the array *plotValues*, such that the first angle starts at 0 and the last angle is 2PI. (2PI is a complete circle in radian.)

You might be wondering why we used a set of example numbers and degrees instead of radian. Suppose that the program has been passed the values 5, 5, and 10. These values are converted into a *values* array of 0.0, 5.0, 5.0, and 10.0. The *for* loop converts these values into *plotValues* of 0, 90, 180, and 360 degree angles. As you can see, in this case we will want to draw the first pie slice from 0 to 90 degrees, the second slice from 90 to 180 degrees, and the last from 180 to 360 degrees.

These angles are converted into a series of points by using this equation:

```
x = radius * sin(angle)
y = radius * cosin(angle)
```

Here, *radius* is the radius of the pie chart. (The radius of the pie chart is the distance to the middle of the bounding square.) This formula converts the angle into an *x* and *y* value on the circumference of a circle.

Finally, these *x* and *y* values are translated to the middle of the bounding square. This is done by adding *radius* to both values before converting them into a *Point* object and storing the values in the *points* array. The *x* and *y* coordinates now vary from 0 to two times *radius*, the edges of the bounding square, rather than varying from −*radius* to *radius*.

A unique *Brush* object is calculated for each pie slice by using the index *i* as a lookup into the array of possible styles called *brushStyle*, and the array of colors called *color*.

The *Form1_paint()* method is fairly simple. This method iterates through each of the pie points. First it sets the drawing brush for the current pie slice by calling *Graphics.setBrush()*. It then calls *Graphics.drawPie()* to draw a pie slice within the bounding square from the first pie point, *points[i]*, to the next pie point, *points[i + 1]*.

The *Form1_paint()* method labels each slice with its value from the *values* array. It uses the crude algorithm of drawing the value midway between the two pie points. This algorithm works fairly well when there are four or more values, especially when these values are roughly equal.

The resize event handler, *Form1_resize()*, is also simple to implement. First it recalculates the size of the bounding square by calling *calculatePieBox()*. Next the method calls *calculatePieChart()* to recalculate a new pie chart that fits within the new bounding square. The final call to *invalidate()* forces the new pie chart to be painted.

One final method, *getMinTrackSize()*, overrides *Component.getMinTrackSize()* to return the minimum size allowed for the form window. In this case, the form can't be shrunk to a size smaller than 100 x 100 pixels.

The result

To execute the program from Visual J++, you must provide the program with an argument list. To do so, from the Project menu select PieChart Properties. On the Launch tab, select Custom and add the desired values to the Arguments box.

When executed with the values shown in Figure 9-10, the program generates the pie chart shown in Figure 9-11 on the following page.

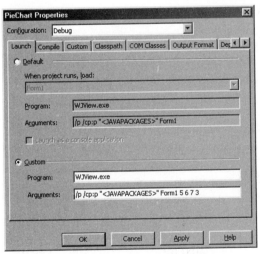

Figure 9-10. *The Project Properties dialog box showing the argument values.*

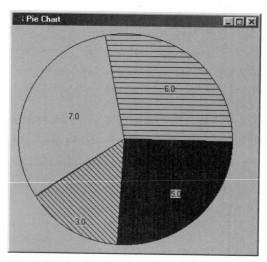

Figure 9-11. *The pie chart resulting from the values shown in Figure 9-10 on the preceding page.*

MIXING GRAPHICS OBJECTS AND WFC COMPONENTS

Up until now, the *Graphics* object and corresponding *paint()* method have been presented as a mutually exclusive alternative to the use of WFC components. There is at least one case, however, where the use of the custom *paint()* method must be mixed with the use of components.

One of the methods of the *Graphics* class, *drawFocusRect()*, is designed to draw a focus rectangle. The focus rectangle is the rapidly updated, dotted rectangle that some software packages use to signify that the user has selected an area of the screen, or to signify that a control has focus.

It might be desirable in some applications to use a focus rectangle to enable the user to select and manipulate WFC components. The following SelectComponents program does exactly that: it allows the user to select a few WFC components and drag them about within the form almost as if they were still under the control of the Forms Designer. The program will also demonstrate that all the while the components are being dragged about, they are still completely functional.

The Forms Designer Work

Create a standard Visual J++ Windows application. Call it SelectComponents. Set the *text* property of the form to *Select Components* to match the name of the application.

We will need to add a few WFC components for the user to select. Arrange four Button controls vertically on the form, leaving the default names for each. Below the four buttons, place an Edit control. Change the *name* property of the Edit control to *edit*. Set the initial *text* property of the control to *Drag mouse to select objects*, to indicate to the user what the purpose of the application is. In addition, set the *click* property of each button to point to a method that will simply display the message "button*x* clicked" in the Edit control, where *x* is the number of the button. We'll use this later to prove that even though they have been moved, the buttons continue to work.

The completed form in the Forms Designer is shown in Figure 9-12.

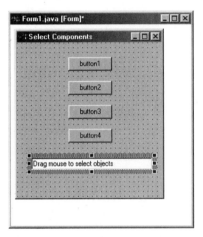

Figure 9-12. *The completed Forms Designer work for SelectComponents.*

The Code

The code for SelectComponents is involved and somewhat lengthy. To simplify the program as much as possible, I have broken the source code up into a number of simpler classes. With the support of these helper classes, the actual Form1.java source listing becomes almost simple.

The *ControlLoc* class

Looking ahead, it's clear that SelectComponents will need to be able to keep track of the *Control* objects the user selects with the focus rectangle.

> **NOTE** I'm not so clever that I can look ahead to determine exactly what I will need in a class. Such development is in practice iterative. I first created *ControlLoc* guessing what I would need. As development progressed, I returned to add capabilities that I hadn't anticipated initially.

To make tracking selected objects easier, create the following *ControlLoc* class.

```java
import com.ms.wfc.ui.*;

/**
 * Retain a control and its original location.
 */
public class ControlLoc
{
    Control c = null;
    Point   originalLoc = null;

    /**
     * Save the control and its original location.
     */
    ControlLoc(Control c)
    {
        this.c           = c;
        this.originalLoc = c.getLocation();
    }

    /**
     * Get the control.
     */
    Control getControl()
    {
        return c;
    }

    /**
     * Get original location of the control.
     */
    Point getOriginalLocation()
    {
        return new Point(originalLoc);
    }

    /**
     * Set the current location of the control.
     */
    void setLocation(Point loc)
    {
        c.setLocation(loc);
    }
}
```

The *ControlLoc* class represents a *Control* object, *c*, and the object's original location on the screen, *originalLoc*. The methods of *ControlLoc* are straightforward. There's a constructor that saves the control and queries its location using the *Control.getLocation()* method, to establish the original location. In addition, the methods *ControlLoc.getControl()* and *ControlLoc.getOriginalLocation()* allow querying of the data members. The method *ControlLoc.setLocation()* updates the current location of the control on the screen.

The *ControlLocList* class

It's also clear that the *ControlLoc* objects created to keep track of the controls selected by the focus rectangle will need to be maintained in a list. To simplify this chore, create the following *ControlLocList* class.

```java
import com.ms.wfc.ui.*;
import com.ms.wfc.util.List;

/**
 * Maintain a list of ControlLoc objects.
 */
public class ControlLocList
{
    List list = new List();

    /**
     * Add a control.
     */
    public void addControl(Control c)
    {
        list.addItem(new ControlLoc(c));
    }

    /**
     * Reset the list to empty.
     */
    public void reset()
    {
        list.setSize(0);
    }

    /**
     * Retrieve a ControlLoc by index.
     */
    public ControlLoc getControlLoc(int index)
    {
        return (ControlLoc)list.getItem(index);
    }
```

(continued)

```
    /**
     * Get the number of ControlLocs in the list.
     */
    public int getSize()
    {
        return list.getSize();
    }
}
```

This class uses the *List* class to maintain the actual list. The methods *addControl()*, *reset()*, *getControlLoc()*, and *getSize()* provide simplified access to this list of *ControlLoc* objects.

The *SelectedControls* class

Now that we have a class for maintaining information about a selected control and a class for maintaining a list of the selected controls, we can set about writing a class for selecting control objects. This class *SelectedControls* appears as follows:

```
import com.ms.wfc.ui.*;

/**
 * Selected controls are those WFC controls that fall
 * within the focus rectangle.
 */
public class SelectedControls
{
    // create a container for selected controls
    private ControlLocList selectedControls =
                                    new ControlLocList();

    /**
     * Add the controls that hang off the parent and are
     * within the rectangle r to the list of selected
     * controls. (Mark them by setting them to boldface.)
     */
    public void findControls(Control parent, Rectangle r)
    {
        // first clear out the list
        selectedControls.reset();

        // now add back all the objects within the rectangle
        add(parent, r);
    }

    private void add(Control parent, Rectangle r)
    {
        int limit = parent.getControlCount();
        for (int i = 0; i < limit; i++)
```

```
    {
        // get the bounding rectangle for this control
        Control child = parent.getControl(i);
        Rectangle childR = child.getClientRect();
        Point loc = child.getLocation();
        childR.x = loc.x;
        childR.y = loc.y;

        // if it's within the focus rectangle...
        if (isWithin(childR, r))
        {
            // mark it and add it to the list
            setHighlight(child, true);
            selectedControls.addControl(child);
        }
        else
        {
            setHighlight(child, false);
        }

        // add any components hanging off this component
        add(child, r);
    }
}

/**
 * Either highlight or unhighlight the Control c.
 */
private void setHighlight(Control c, boolean on)
{
    Font font = c.getFont();
    if (font == null)
    {
        return;
    }
    // if highlight is on...
    if (on)
    {
        // set the font to bold;...
        font = new Font(font, FontWeight.BOLD,
                        false, false, false);
        c.setFont(font);
    }
    // otherwise,...
    else
    {
        // set to normal
```

(continued)

```
                    font = new Font(font, FontWeight.NORMAL,
                                    false, false, false);
                c.setFont(font);
            }
        }


        /**
         * Move the selected objects by delta.
         */
        Point controlPt = new Point();
        public void move(Point delta)
        {
            int size = selectedControls.getSize();
            for (int i = 0; i < size; i++)
            {
                ControlLoc cl = selectedControls.getControlLoc(i);
                controlPt = cl.getOriginalLocation();
                controlPt.x += delta.x;
                controlPt.y += delta.y;
                cl.setLocation(controlPt);
            }
        }


        /**
         * Return true if first rectangle is completely within second.
         */
        static boolean isWithin(Rectangle childR, Rectangle parentR)
        {
            if (childR.x < parentR.x)
            {
                return false;
            }
            if (childR.y < parentR.y)
            {
                return false;
            }
            if ((childR.x + childR.width) > (parentR.x + parentR.width))
            {
                return false;
            }
            if ((childR.y + childR.height) > (parentR.y + parentR.height))
            {
                return false;
            }
            return true;
        }
    }
```

The *findControls(parent, r)* method is perhaps the most important of the methods in this class. This method searches all of the WFC controls that are attached to the *parent* control object. Each of the controls it finds that are completely within the focus rectangle *r* is added to the *ControlLocList* data member called *selectedControls*.

The *findControls()* method starts by first resetting the *selectedControls* list to empty. It then calls the *SelectedControls.add()* method. The *add()* method loops through all of the child controls of *parent* using the method *Control.getControl()*. For each child that it finds, *add()* calculates the smallest rectangle that surrounds the child component. This is the bounding rectangle. The *add()* method calls *SelectedControls.isWithin()* to determine whether the child's bounding rectangle is completely within the focus rectangle *r*. If it is, the control is highlighted by calling *SelectedControls.setHighlight()* and the control is added to the *selectedControls* list.

The *isWithin(childR, parentR)* method returns *true* if the rectangle *childR* is completely within the focus rectangle *parentR*. The logic is straightforward, although a little monotonous. If the child rectangle's left edge is to the left of the parent's left edge (*childR.x < parentR.x*), the method returns *false*. Likewise, if the child rectangle's upper edge is above the parent's (*childR.y < parentR.y*), the method returns *false*. Similar checks are made of the right and bottom edges. After all edges have been checked, if the method still hasn't found any part of the child rectangle to be outside the parent rectangle, the method returns *true*. This is demonstrated in Figure 9-13.

As you can see in the Figure 9-13 example, component A is outside the focus window W because *childR.x* is less than *parentR.x*. Component B is outside W because *childR.y* is less than *parentR.y*. In the case of component C, both *(childR.x + childR.width)* is greater than *(parentR.x + parentR.width)* and *(childR.y + childR.height)* is greater than *(parentR.y + parentR.height)*. Component D is completely within the focus window.

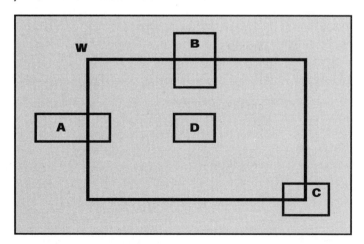

Figure 9-13. *Only control D is within the focus window W.*

The method *setHighlight()* either highlights or unhighlights a control to indicate to the user whether the control has been selected. Although there are several possible ways to indicate a selection, I chose to boldface the control's font (if the control has a font).

Finally, the method *move()* is provided to move all of the selected controls by some delta. This method will prove important once the user has selected several controls with the focus rectangle and wants to move them.

The *FocusRectangle* class

The final support class is *FocusRectangle*. As its name implies, this class helps maintain the focus rectangle itself. The code for this class appears as follows:

```
import com.ms.wfc.ui.*;

/**
 * Represent a focus rectangle.
 */
public class FocusRectangle
{
    // the actual rectangle
    private Rectangle frame;

    // the mouse location at the time the rectangle
    // was started
    private Point originalLoc;

    // the upper left corner of the focus
    // rectangle prior to it being moved
    private Point upperLeft;

    /**
     * Create a focus rectangle at the specified
     * mouse location.
     */
    public FocusRectangle(Point mouseLoc)
    {
        originalLoc = new Point(mouseLoc);
        upperLeft   = new Point(originalLoc);
        frame = new Rectangle(mouseLoc.x,
                              mouseLoc.y,
                              0,
                              0);
    }

    /**
     * Move the focus rectangle by the specified amount.
     */
    public void move(Point delta)
```

```
{
    frame.x = upperLeft.x + delta.x;
    frame.y = upperLeft.y + delta.y;
}


/**
 * Resize the frame based on mouse movement.
 */
public void resize(Point mouseLoc)
{
    // if mouse moved down...
    if (mouseLoc.y > originalLoc.y)
    {
        // then keep the top of the focus area set
        // to the first mouse location and move the bottom down
        frame.y      = originalLoc.y;
        frame.height = mouseLoc.y - originalLoc.y;
    }
    // if mouse moved up...
    else
    {
        // set the top to the current mouse location and
        // calculate the bottom of the frame to be the first
        // mouse location
        frame.y      = mouseLoc.y;
        frame.height = originalLoc.y - mouseLoc.y;
    }


    // repeat for width
    if (mouseLoc.x > frame.x)
    {
        frame.x     = originalLoc.x;
        frame.width = mouseLoc.x - originalLoc.x;
    }
    else
    {
        frame.x     = mouseLoc.x;
        frame.width = originalLoc.x - mouseLoc.x;
    }


    // update the upper left corner
    upperLeft.x = frame.x;
    upperLeft.y = frame.y;
}


/**
 * Retrieve the rectangle.
 */
```

(continued)

```
public Rectangle getRectangle()
{
    return frame;
}
```

The program creates the focus rectangle as soon as the user holds down the left mouse button and begins to drag it within the form. Accordingly, the *Focus-Rectangle()* constructor saves the starting location of the mouse in *originalLoc*. It also creates at that location a rectangle called *frame* that has a height and width of 0.

The *FocusRectangle.resize()* method is called as the user drags the mouse to resize the focus rectangle. The logic for this method is slightly more complicated than you might expect, because it must take into consideration the fact that the user might create a focus rectangle by dragging the mouse in any direction: up or down, and left or right. (The logic would be much simpler if the user were forced to start at the upper left corner and drag the mouse down and to the right in order to create a focus rectangle.)

Like the *SelectedControls* class, the *FocusRectangle* class provides a *move()* method that will be needed to move the focus rectangle—once it has been created—together with the components that it encompasses.

The *Form1* class

With all of these support classes, the actual *Form1* class is fairly small, consisting primarily of event handlers.

```
import com.ms.wfc.app.*;
import com.ms.wfc.core.*;
import com.ms.wfc.ui.*;
import com.ms.wfc.html.*;

import com.ms.wfc.io.*;

public class Form1 extends Form
{
    public Form1()
    {
        // Required for Visual J++ Form Designer support
        initForm();
    }

    // the following represents the focus rectangle
    FocusRectangle focusRectangle = null;
    Point mouseLoc              = new Point();

    // members to support the moving of the selected objects
    boolean   controlsMoving           = false;
```

```
Point      mouseOriginalLoc       = null;
SelectedControls selectedControls = new SelectedControls();

/**
 * Start the building of the focus area, or if there is
 * already a focus area and the mouse is within it, start
 * moving the objects within the focus area.
 */
private void mouseDown(Object source, MouseEvent e)
{
    // ignore anything but left mouse button
    if ((e.button & MouseButton.LEFT) == 0)
    {
        return;
    }

    // if there is a focus area...
    if (focusRectangle != null)
    {
        // and the mouse is within the focus area...
        Rectangle r = new Rectangle(e.x, e.y, 0, 0);
        if (SelectedControls.isWithin(
                        r,
                        focusRectangle.getRectangle()))
        {
            // start dragging the objects within
            // the focusRectangle
            controlsMoving    = true;
            mouseOriginalLoc = new Point(e.x, e.y);
            return;
        }
    }

    // we aren't dragging; start building a focus area
    mouseLoc.x = e.x;
    mouseLoc.y = e.y;
    focusRectangle = new FocusRectangle(mouseLoc);
}

/**
 * If we are in drag control mode, then drag the controls.
 * If we are in focus mode, then resize the focus area.
 */
private void mouseMove(Object source, MouseEvent e)
{
    if ((e.button & MouseButton.LEFT) == 0)
    {
```

(continued)

```
            return;
        }

        if (controlsMoving)
        {
            dragControls(e);
            return;
        }

        if (focusRectangle != null)
        {
            dragFocusArea(e);
        }
    }

    /**
     * If we have been moving an object, then restart the
     * focus area. Restart dragging the selected objects.
     */
    private void mouseUp(Object source, MouseEvent e)
    {
        if (controlsMoving)
        {
            focusRectangle = null;
        }
        controlsMoving = false;
        invalidate();
    }

    /**
     * Drag the selected controls.
     */
    Point mouseDelta = new Point();
    private void dragControls(MouseEvent e)
    {
        // calculate how far the mouse has moved since
        // the dragging started
        mouseDelta.x = e.x - mouseOriginalLoc.x;
        mouseDelta.y = e.y - mouseOriginalLoc.y;

        // first move the selected controls
        selectedControls.move(mouseDelta);

        // now move the focus area
        focusRectangle.move(mouseDelta);

        // repaint the form
        invalidate();
    }
```

```
/**
 * Resize the focus area as a result of mouse movement.
 */
void dragFocusArea(MouseEvent e)
{
    // resize the focusRectangle
    mouseLoc.x = e.x;
    mouseLoc.y = e.y;
    focusRectangle.resize(mouseLoc);

    // find out which objects are enclosed
    selectedControls.findControls(this,
                        focusRectangle.getRectangle());

    // now force a repaint to update the focus rectangle
    invalidate();
}

/**
 * Repaint current form.
 */
private void Form1_paint(Object source, PaintEvent e)
{
    // if there is a focus rectangle...
    Graphics g = e.graphics;
    if (focusRectangle != null)
    {
        // then draw it
        g.drawFocusRect(focusRectangle.getRectangle());
    }
}

/**
 * Output the button's name to the edit window.
 */
private void button_click(Object source, Event e)
{
    Button button = (Button)source;
    String name = button.getText();
    edit.setText(name + " clicked");
}

/**
 * NOTE: The following code is required by the Visual J++ form
 * designer.  It can be modified using the form editor.  Do not
 * modify it using the code editor.
 */
```

(continued)

```
Container components = new Container();
Button button1 = new Button();
Button button2 = new Button();
Button button3 = new Button();
Button button4 = new Button();
Edit edit = new Edit();

private void initForm()
{
    // ...created by the Forms Designer...
}


/**
 * The main entry point for the application.
 */
public static void main(String args[])
{
    Application.run(new Form1());
}
}
```

When the user clicks the left mouse button, the system is in one of two states. One state is when there is no focus rectangle, in which case the SelectComponents program assumes the user is creating one. A second state is when there is a focus rectangle already created by a previous *MouseDown* event, in which case the program assumes the user is trying to move the focus rectangle and the components that it encompasses.

This dichotomy is reflected in the *Form1.mouseDown()* method. If there is a focus rectangle already (*focusRectangle!=null*), and the mouse pointer location is within it, *mouseDown()* sets the *controlsMoving* flag to *true* in order to start the drag process. If there is no focus rectangle, the method creates one. This method begins the creation and resizing of the focus rectangle.

Similarly, *Form1.mouseMove()* has two parts. The method first checks the *controlsMoving* flag. If this is set, *mouseMove()* calls *Form1.dragControls()*, which calls *selectedControls.move()* and *focusRectangle.move()* to move the focus rectangle and any selected controls. If a focus rectangle exists and the *controlsMoving* flag is false, *mouseMove()* calls *Form1.dragFocusArea()*. The *dragFocusArea()* method resizes the focus rectangle and then recalculates which controls are now included within the resized focus rectangle by calling *selectedControls.findControls()*.

The *Form1.mouseUp()* method clears the *controlsMoving* flag to indicate that the user is no longer moving the controls. If the *controlsMoving* flag was set, it also clears the *focusRectangle* to make the focus rectangle disappear.

The *Form1_paint()* method is simple. The WFC controls that are on the form know how to repaint themselves. All that *Form1_paint()* must draw is the focus rectangle, if it exists.

The *button_click()* method was created to handle the click event for each of the buttons, to demonstrate that these buttons still work even after the user has moved them about.

The Results

Figure 9-14 shows the SelectComponents application running with the focus rectangle, which has been drawn to encompass two of the four buttons. Figure 9-15 shows the buttons after being dragged to a new location. Even in their new locations, all four of the buttons remain functional.

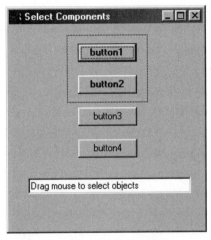

Figure 9-14. *Creating a focus rectangle encompassing the top two buttons.*

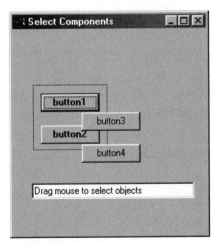

Figure 9-15. *Moving the button controls by dragging the focus rectangle.*

NOTE   To drag the focus area, the user must click on an area within the focus rectangle but outside any of the controls. If you click within a control such as the button, WFC will field the mouse down event before *SelectComponts* gets a chance to interpret it.

CONCLUSION

This chapter has demonstrated how to use the *Graphics* class and the paint event handler to draw arbitrary shapes. You have seen the drawing of points, of text, and of more complicated features. Finally, you have seen the combination of graphics drawing and WFC controls in the same application.

In the next chapter, you'll see the use of some remaining utility classes such as timers, threads, and idle event handlers, which are all part of the WFC application package.

Chapter 10

The WFC Application Package

There is one Microsoft Windows Foundation Classes for Java (WFC) package we have yet to examine: the Application package *com.ms.wfc.app*. This package consists of an assortment of classes that at first appear to be unrelated. This chapter concentrates on time-related classes, the multithreading classes, and the *Registry* class. You'll find the code for the sample files in this chapter in the Windows Applications subfolder on the companion CD.

THE *TIME* AND *TIMER* CLASSES

There are two time-related classes in the Application package: the class *Time* and the class *Timer*. Microsoft Visual J++ provides the *Time* class to find out the current time in terms of fractions of seconds since a fixed time in the past. The *Timer* class is used to generate an event periodically. The purpose of these two classes is analogous to a watch that beeps every hour: the *Time* class is the watch, and the *Timer* class is the trigger for the beep.

In this section, we'll use the *Time* class to create a simple clock, and then add a *Timer* object to make the clock reflect real time.

The *Time* Class

The following TimeDemo application will demonstrate the *Time* class. This simple application contains a button and an output edit box. When the user clicks the button, the application displays the current date, time, and day of the week.

The Forms Designer work

To create the TimeDemo application, you start by creating a Windows Application. After setting the form's *text* property to *Time Demo*, add an Edit control from the Toolbox. Clear the *text* property of the Edit control, and set the *name* property to *outputEdit*. Set the *readOnly* property to *true* to keep the user from changing text in the Edit control, which the application uses for output only. This control will display the time.

Now add a Button control to the form. Set the *text* property to *Display Time*. Then double-click the button to establish a button click event handler.

To account for changes the user might make to the size of the form, anchor the Edit control to the top, left, and right edges of the form and anchor the Button control to the bottom, left, and right edges.

The code

The code for the TimeDemo application appears as follows:

```
import com.ms.wfc.app.*;
import com.ms.wfc.core.*;
import com.ms.wfc.ui.*;
import com.ms.wfc.html.*;

/**
 * This class demonstrates the Time class.
 */
public class Form1 extends Form
{
    public Form1()
    {
        // Required for Visual J++ Form Designer support
        initForm();
    }

    ⋮

    /**
     * Define the days of the week.
     */
    private final static String[] daysOfWeek = new String[]
                                               {
                                               "illegal",
                                               "Mon",
```

```
                                                "Tues",
                                                "Wed",
                                                "Thur",
                                                "Fri",
                                                "Sat",
                                                "Sun"
                                                };

/**
 * Display the time in the output control.
 */
void displayTime(Time time, Control output)
{
    // fetch the date with the month spelled out
    String dateString = time.formatLongDate();

    // now fetch the time
    String timeString = time.formatLongTime();

    // get the day of the week (use the daysOfWeek
    // array to convert the number into a string)
    String wdString   = daysOfWeek[time.getDayOfWeek()];

    // display the results
    output.setText(dateString + " " +
                   timeString + "(" +
                   wdString   + ")");
}

private void button1_click(Object source, Event e)
{
    displayTime(new Time(), outputEdit);
}

/**
 * NOTE: The following code is required by the Visual J++ form
 * designer.  It can be modified using the form editor.  Do not
 * modify it using the code editor.
 */
Container components = new Container();
Edit outputEdit = new Edit();
Button button1 = new Button();

private void initForm()
{
    // ...created by Forms Designer...
}
```

(continued)

```
/**
 * The main entry point for the application.
 */
public static void main(String args[])
{
    Application.run(new Form1());
}
}
```

Since TimeDemo doesn't do anything until the user clicks the Display Time button, the *Form1()* constructor doesn't do anything other than call *initForm()*. The *button1_click()* method, which is attached to the Display Time button, calls *displayTime()* to display the current date and time in the *outputEdit* Edit control.

The *displayTime()* method begins by creating a *Time* object. This object records the time it was created. Oddly enough, this time is recorded in the number of units of 100 nanoseconds since midnight, A.D. 100. The unit 100 nanoseconds equals one-tenth of a microsecond or 10^{-7} seconds.

The *Time* class provides a number of methods for converting the *Time* object's value into meaningful text. The TimeDemo program uses one of these methods, *formatLongDate()*, to create a date string. The LongDate part of the method name refers to the fact that the month in the returned date is spelled out as characters. (A short date format would use only numbers.) Next the *formatLongTime()* method returns a string representation of the time of day in the *Time* object's value.

There is no method to generate a text representation of the day of the week; the *Time.getDayOfWeek()* method returns a value from 1 to 7, with 1 representing Monday. TimeDemo uses the value returned by *getDayOfWeek()* as an index into the string array *daysOfWeek*. The *daysOfWeek* array returns the string that corresponds to the index value and stores it in the *wdString* variable.

NOTE The first value in the *daysOfWeek* array is the string "illegal". This is just a placeholder because the smallest value that *getDayOfWeek()* returns is 1 rather than 0, and arrays in Visual J++ are zero-based. Thus, *daysOfWeek[0]* isn't used.

The three strings *dateString*, *timeString*, and *wdString* are then concatenated and displayed in the *outputEdit* object. The result is shown in Figure 10-1.

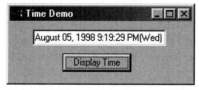

Figure 10-1. *The output from TimeDemo shows the format generated by the* formatLongDate() *and* formatLongTime() *methods, with the day of the week added to the end.*

The *Timer* Class

An inconvenient feature of the TimeDemo application is that the user must choose the Display Time button to see the current time. It would be much more convenient if the time display updated periodically on its own.

To do this, the program could sit in a *for* loop repeatedly creating the current time string and displaying it in the *outputEdit* Edit control. However, not only would this be a bad idea—it would consume a considerable amount of CPU processing power for such a simple task—it also wouldn't work. The problem is that the *outputEdit* Edit control would never get a chance to display the output results. A much better approach would be to update the display once per second. To do this, we need a timer, and this is exactly what the *Timer* class is for.

The following TimerDemo application demonstrates the use of the *Timer* class. This demo displays the time and date in the same format as TimeDemo, and it automatically updates the time display once per second. In addition, TimerDemo adds a stopwatch feature.

The Forms Designer work

The TimerDemo application requires two Edit controls: one to display the date and time, and the other to display the stopwatch value. The application also requires two Button controls: one to start the stopwatch and one to stop it. Take a second to look ahead to Figure 10-2 on page 310 to see how these objects are laid out on the form.

Use the Properties window to change the *name* property of the upper Edit control to *dateOutputEdit*. Set this Edit control's *readOnly* property to *true*, and set its *text* property to empty. Since this control is uppermost in the form, set its *anchor* property to top, left, and right.

Now set the *name* property of the lower Edit control to *secsOutputEdit*. As we did with *dateOutputEdit*, set the *readOnly* property to *true* and the *text* property to empty. Anchor this control to the left, right, and bottom sides of the form, and set its *textAlign* property to *Right*. Create a Label control just to the right of this Edit control, set the label's *text* property to *secs*, and anchor the label to the bottom and right sides of the form to match the *secsOutputEdit* object.

Now name the leftmost button *startClock* and label it *Start Clock*. You will need to anchor it to the bottom and left of the form. Name the rightmost button *stopClock*, and label it *Stop Clock*. Anchor this button to the bottom and right of the form. Finally, use the active properties window to create a click event handler for each button.

The code

The code for the TimerDemo application is shown on the following page.

```
import com.ms.wfc.app.*;
import com.ms.wfc.core.*;
import com.ms.wfc.ui.*;
import com.ms.wfc.html.*;

/**
 * This class demonstrates the Timer class by
 * creating a clock with a built-in stopwatch.
 */
public class Form1 extends Form
{
    // the following Timer object clicks every second
    // to update the display
    Timer timer;

    public Form1()
    {
        // Required for Visual J++ Form Designer support
        initForm();

        // create a timer to be used to update the
        // clock periodically
        timer = new Timer(this.components);
        timer.addOnTimer(new EventHandler(this.handleClockTick));

        // start the clock to click every 100th of a second
        timer.setInterval(10);
        timer.setEnabled(true);
    }

    /**
     * Form1 overrides dispose so it can clean up the
     * component list.
     */
    public void dispose()
    {
        super.dispose();

        // turn the timer off to make sure that it can be
        // disposed of with the rest of the form's container
        timer.setEnabled(false);

        // now dispose of the contents of the container
        components.dispose();
    }

    /**
      * Define the days of the week.
     **/
```

```
        // array unchanged from TimeDemo application...

/**
 * Display the current time in the outputEdit window.
 */
private void displayTime(Time time, Control output)
{
    // unchanged from TimeDemo application...
}


/**
 * Display the elapsed time from startTime in
 * the output control.
 */
public void displayElapsedTime(Time startTime,
                               Time currentTime,
                               Control output)
{
    // now get the difference between the
    // current time and the start time
    long deltaTime = currentTime.toLong() -
                     startTime.toLong();

    int deltaMilliSeconds =
        (int)(deltaTime / Time.UNITS_PER_MILLISECOND);
    float deltaSeconds =
                ((float)deltaMilliSeconds) / 1000.0F;

    // display the delta time
    output.setText(Float.toString(deltaSeconds));
}

// save the start time for the stopwatch
Time startTime = null;

// only update the time display when the second
// changes
long lastSecond = 0;

/**
 * Handle the 1-millisecond clock tick.
 */
private void handleClockTick(Object source, Event e)
{
    // capture the current time
    Time currentTime = new Time();
```

(continued)

```
            // if the second has changed...
            long second =
                currentTime.toLong() / Time.UNITS_PER_SECOND;
            if (second != lastSecond)
            {
                lastSecond = second;

                // update the date and time display
                displayTime(currentTime, dateOutputEdit);
            }

            // if the stopwatch is enabled...
            if (startTime != null)
            {
                // then display the elapsed time
                displayElapsedTime(startTime, currentTime,
                                    secsOutputEdit);
            }
    }

    private void startClock_click(Object source, Event e)
    {
        // start the stopwatch by noting the current time
        // as the start time
        startTime = new Time();
    }

    private void stopClock_click(Object source, Event e)
    {
        // stop the stopwatch by erasing the start time
        startTime = null;
    }

    /**
     * NOTE: The following code is required by the Visual J++ form
     * designer.  It can be modified using the form editor.  Do not
     * modify it using the code editor.
     */
    Container components = new Container();
    Edit dateOutputEdit = new Edit();
    Edit secsOutputEdit = new Edit();
    Label label1 = new Label();
    Button startClock = new Button();
    Button stopClock = new Button();

    private void initForm()
    {
        // ...this code created by the Forms Designer...
    }
```

```
/**
 * The main entry point for the application.
 */
public static void main(String args[])
{
    Application.run(new Form1());
}
}
```

Once the *TimerDemo()* constructor has called *initForm()* to set up the WFC controls, it creates a *Timer* object. This object is attached to the same *components* container that holds the controls we built with the Forms Designer, such as the output *Edit* objects and the buttons.

> **TIP** You are not required to attach your *Timer* objects to a *Container* object. It's a good idea, however, because if you do the resources associated with the *Timer* object are automatically disposed of when the *Container* object's *dispose()* method is invoked.

TimerDemo then creates an *EventHandler* object to handle the timer event. In this case, *EventHandler* points at the method *handleClockTick()*. Once the timer event handler has been established by a call to *addOnTimer()*, the constructor sets the tick interval to 10. This causes the *Timer* object to create a timer event every 10 milliseconds. Finally, calling *setEnabled(true)* enables the timer.

> **NOTE** Timers are created in a stopped state. The program should not start the timer until it has established the timer interval and event handler.

The *dispose()* method, which I normally haven't been showing in the program listings in this book (although it is in the code on the companion CD), is automatically created by the Forms Designer. This code shows *dispose()* edited so that it turns off the timer by calling the *setEnabled(false)* method. Once the timer is disabled, the *dispose()* method calls *components.dispose()* to release the resources of the objects—including the timer—that are attached to the *components* container.

> **NOTE** The resources associated with a timer can't be disposed of as long as the timer is active.

The date and time are updated by the timer event handler, so the methods *startClock_click()* and *stopClock_click()* are very short. The *startClock_click()* method simply sets the stopwatch's *startTime* variable to the current time, and *stopClock_click()* sets the variable to *null*. This signals to the timer event handler that the stopwatch is active or inactive, respectively.

The *handleClockTick()* method that handles the timer event is the heart of this application. This method begins by noting the current time in tenths of a millisecond. It then converts this time into seconds. If the resulting *second* variable value is different from the *lastSecond* variable value, the application updates the date and time display in the *dateOutputEdit* Edit control by calling *displayTime()*. The trick of comparing *second* to *lastSecond* keeps the *handleClockTick()* method from needlessly updating the date and time every 10 milliseconds when the control displays the time only to the nearest second.

The *handleClockTick()* method continues by checking the *startTime* object. If it contains a *null* value, the stopwatch is stopped. Otherwise, it contains the start time of the stopwatch. In this case, *handleClockTick()* invokes *displayElapsedTime()* to display the stopwatch value in the *secsOutputEdit* Edit control.

The *displayTime()* method and the *daysOfWeek* array are identical to those of the same name in the TimeDemo application.

The *displayElapsedTime()* method sends to the output Edit control the difference in seconds between *currentTime* and *startTime*. It begins by calculating the difference between the two timer values and converting the resulting long delta value into an integer variable *deltaMilliSeconds*. The value of *deltaMilliSeconds* is divided by 1000, converting milliseconds to seconds, and assigned to *deltaSeconds*. The *deltaSeconds* variable is of float type so that it can retain the fractional part of the computation results—that is, the 10ths and 100ths of a second. Finally, the *deltaSeconds* value is converted into a string and displayed in the output Edit control.

The result is shown in Figure 10-2.

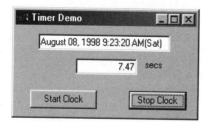

Figure 10-2. *The TimerDemo application automatically updates the date and time display every second, plus it creates a user-controlled stopwatch accurate to one 100th of a second.*

MULTITHREADING

Visual J++ provides another set of capabilities through the *com.ms.wfc.app* package together with the standard Java classes: multithreading. This section will demonstrate different ways of implementing multithreading and provide some guidelines for when to use each approach. In addition, I will touch on some of the dangers of multithreading. Let me begin by explaining the attraction of multithreading.

What is Multithreading?

There are many times when you want your program to do more than one thing at the same time. You saw a hint of that in the previous TimerDemo application. While the clock was being updated in the upper box, the user was able to turn the stop-watch on and off. Even though both controls are tightly bound by the working of the *handleClockTick()* method, to the user the two windows appear to function independently.

To understand multithreading, you should first understand why TimerDemo works this way. It's critical that the event handler, *handleClockTick()*, perform its task and return control to WFC quickly. During the time *handleClockTick()* is running, the TimerDemo program is unresponsive to all other input—that is, if the user clicks one of the buttons during the time that the program is in the middle of the *handleClockEvent()* method, the click event is queued up. This event isn't processed until *handleClockEvent()* completes and returns control to the program.

> **NOTE**   Of course, all events originate from Windows messages that are queued up and handled by the event loop. When the timer expires, for example, it generates a WM_TIMER message that is queued up with any other messages for processing. Once the timer message bubbles to the top of the queue, WFC creates the timer event and passes it to the *handleClockEvent()* method for processing.

As long as *handleClockEvent()* doesn't take too long, the user won't perceive any delay between clicking the mouse button and the program responding. The user would suddenly become aware of unresponsiveness on the part of the program, however, if *handleClockEvent()* were to go off and perform some extended processing such as read a file or perform an extended calculation. The user will think that the program has crashed if the delay is long enough. It's important that an event handler not perform any function that will take very long.

Another way that TimerDemo performs its magic is by placing both the clock and timer capabilities in the single *handleClockEvent()* method. This programming practice is justifiable in simple cases, especially when two features are closely related. When the features are unrelated, however—a word processor might have methods to perform text entry, spell checking, and reformatting of text—placing them into a single method is both difficult and error prone.

So what do you do if a user action results in a request for a feature that takes a long time to perform? The best tactic is to branch off to a new thread of execution. This new thread appears to execute parallel to the original thread. The original thread can return to Visual J++ to continue processing event requests while the new thread performs the lengthy operation. These secondary threads are commonly called *background threads*, because they continue to execute behind the user interface thread.

> **NOTE**   Several background threads already exist in your Visual J++ application without your creating any. One is the garbage collection thread, which searches for objects that are no longer in use and returns them to the memory pool.

How does multithreading work?

A thread that has control of the CPU is said to be in the RUNNING state. Realize that multiple threads only *appear* to work in parallel. Since there is only one CPU, in reality only a single thread can execute at any given time. Therefore, only one thread can be in the RUNNING state.

> **NOTE** Machines running under Microsoft Windows NT can have more than one CPU. Because each CPU can run only a single thread, there can be as many threads in the RUNNING state as there are CPUs in the machine.

A thread waiting for something to happen, like for a file read request to complete, is said to be BLOCKED.

> **NOTE** The thread that reads the Windows message queue is in effect BLOCKED on the message queue.

A thread that is neither BLOCKED nor RUNNING is said to be READY.

In Visual J++, each thread is assigned a priority ranging from 9 (high priority) to 1 (low priority). A thread in the RUNNING state retains control of the CPU until one of three things happens:

■ The RUNNING thread becomes BLOCKED. This happens when the current thread reads a file, for example. In this event, another READY thread of the same priority is given control. If no READY threads have the same priority, control passes to the highest-priority READY thread.

■ A higher-priority thread that was BLOCKED becomes READY. This happens when a BLOCKED thread's file read request is completed, for example. In this event, control passes to the higher-priority thread, leaving the current thread in the READY state.

■ The RUNNING thread has had control of the CPU for a given amount of time, and there are other READY threads of the same priority. In this event, control passes to the next thread. Control passes between threads of the same priority in circular fashion, giving each thread equal access to the CPU.

As an example, Figure 10-3 shows three threads running concurrently on one CPU. Each thread is allowed a certain amount of time to run. When time is up for the running thread, any thread with the same priority runs until its time slice is over. You can see in Figure 10-3 that Thread 1 runs until its time is up, and then control moves to Thread 2 because Thread 2 has the same priority as Thread 1. This process continues in a loop until either Thread 1 or Thread 2 is BLOCKED. If Thread 1 is BLOCKED, Thread 2 runs continuously until Thread 1 is unBLOCKED and Thread 2's time runs out.

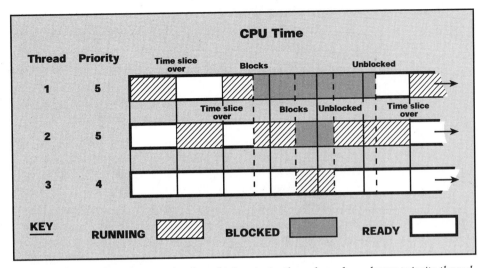

Figure 10-3. *An example of two high-priority threads and one lower-priority thread sharing the CPU.*

If Threads 1 and 2 are both BLOCKED, the lower-priority Thread 3 finally gets its chance to run. Thread 3 stops running and returns to the READY state as soon as a higher-priority thread is unBLOCKED.

When a thread loses control of the CPU—meaning it changes from the state RUNNING to any other state—it's said to be *suspended*.

Each thread has associated with it a data structure that can hold all the information needed to store the state of a thread. (This information consists mostly of the contents of the CPU registers.) When the thread is suspended, this data structure stores the CPU data. When the thread next gains control of the CPU, this data is restored and the thread continues executing from where it left off the last time it lost control. The thread is completely unaware of the break in execution.

What multithreading is not

Multithreading isn't a way to gain extra performance from your CPU. If a given process is slow, breaking it into multiple threads won't make it faster. It will actually make the process slower, because using multiple threads adds the extra overhead of switching control from one thread to another. Multithreading is a way to do these things:

- Give control to a higher-priority thread while relatively lengthy threads execute in the background.

- Allow the program to respond quickly to user input while relatively lengthy threads execute in the background.

The second item is of course a special case of the first item.

The dangers of multithreading

Multithreading does carry with it certain dangers. Consider the following unlikely but possible banking example.

Suppose I have a balance in my checking account of $1000 (this is a purely fictional example, I assure you). I am at an ATM with my bank card in hand, making my usual $40 quick cash withdrawal. I put in my card, type in the password, and choose the quick cash button. The bank computer registers my request, reads my balance, and subtracts $40. Before the program can store the results back into my account, however, the thread handling my transaction is suspended.

Unbeknownst to me, my wife is at this moment in the bank making a deposit of $1000 to the checking account. A separate bank computer program now gets control from my suspended thread. It reads my bank balance and adds the deposit, leaving a bank balance of $2000.

What happens next will leave me very happy and the bank distressed, or will leave me quite distressed and the bank happy, depending on the vagaries of thread timing. If my wife's program continues, my bank balance will be updated to $2000 in the bank's database. Once her program terminates or is suspended, my ATM thread will continue and store the post-withdrawal result of $960 into the database, thereby wiping out any record of my wife's deposit. (Unless I can find her deposit slip, which is very unlikely, I am very unhappy.)

If, on the other hand, my wife's program is somehow suspended—perhaps because it has used up its time slice—and my ATM thread gets control, then my balance of $960 is written to the bank's database only to be overwritten with the $2000 balance calculated by my wife's program. (The bank is now very unhappy, and I'm delirious.)

Such so-called *race conditions* or *thread collisions* are common occurrences in multithreaded programs. An area where a race condition can occur is called a *critical section*. In our example, the critical section in both the withdrawal and deposit programs begins when the program reads the balance from the accounts database and ends when the program completes writing the balance back.

> NOTE For a race condition to occur, all that has to happen is for more than one thread to update a resource such as a memory location. If only one thread writes to the memory location—even if multiple threads read from it—there is no race condition.

How Java handles race conditions

The Java language contains built-in support to avoid race conditions. Marking a method as *synchronized* means that only one thread can execute the method at a time. If thread A is suspended while in the middle of executing a synchronized method and thread B attempts to invoke that method, thread B will instantly become BLOCKED until thread A can regain control and exit from the method.

If the critical section involves only a small part of the method, say the updating of a data member, you might mark a block of code in the method as synchronized in the following way:

```
int pay;

void calculateRaise(float evaluation)
{
    // use some method to calculate the raise
    // based on the evaluation
    :
    // entering a critical section; synchronize it to
    // avoid a collision; obj is some object
    synchronized (obj)
    {
        pay = pay * raise;
    }

    // method continues unsynchronized
}
```

HOW DOES JAVA SYNCHRONIZE METHODS?

Visual J++ implements the synchronization of methods through a mutex. The mutex is checked and set upon entry into the method and cleared upon exit. Java maintains one mutex per object and another for the entire class. Method objects use the object mutex, and static methods use the class mutex.

Suppose that *obj1* and *obj2* are objects of the same class and *m()* is a non-static synchronized method in that class. When thread A makes the call *obj1.m()*, thread A grabs the object mutex before entering *m()*. When thread B calls *obj1.m()* (or any other nonstatic synchronized method using the same object *obj1*), it's BLOCKED as it attempts to grab the object's mutex. Since object *obj2* has it's own mutex, it's perfectly okay for thread A to call *obj1.m()* while thread B calls *obj2.m()*. If *m()* were a static method, only one thread would be able to call it, no matter which object it's calling from.

Mutexes are counters: it's okay for thread A to call one synchronized method from within another synchronized method. Synchronized methods are also recursive. Each time a synchronized method is invoked, the mutex is incremented. Upon each return, the mutex is decremented. The mutex isn't unBLOCKED until it returns to 0.

If an exception occurs from within a synchronized method, the mutex is decremented automatically as control passes from the method.

Here we can see that only the section updating the *pay* variable is synchronized. The mutex of the object *obj* is used to implement the synchronization. (A *mutex*— or mutual exclusion flag—is a special flag that allows one thread mutually exclusive access to critical areas.) In general, the object *this* can be used as the synchronizing object as long as *this* doesn't refer to the *Thread* object (since each thread has its own *Thread* object).

Using the *Thread* class

The easiest way to create a new thread is to create a class that extends the class *Thread*. To start the new thread, the parent thread must first create an object of the new class and then invoke the *start()* method. The *start()* method causes execution to begin with the method *run()*.

```
/**
 * Start a new thread.
 */
void parentMethod()
{
    Thread thread = new MyThread();
    thread.start();
}


/**
 * Implement a new thread of execution.
 */
class MyThread extends Thread
{
    // execution starts here as soon as
    // the parent thread calls start()
    public void run()
    {
    }
}
```

Extending the class *Thread* means that *MyThread* can't extend some other class. To avoid this unfortunate side effect, the Java standard library defines a second mechanism for creating new threads. Any class that implements the interface *Runnable* can have a thread wrapped around it. The *Runnable* interface has only one member—the method *public void run()*. In practice, this thread creation mechanism appears as follows:

```
/**
 * Start a new thread.
 */
void parentMethod()
{
    // wrap my class in a thread
```

```
    Thread thread = new Thread(new MyClass());

    // now start the thread
    thread.start();
}

/**
 * Implement a class that can be wrapped in a thread.
 */
class MyClass extends MyBaseClass implements Runnable
{
    // execution starts here as soon as
    // the parent thread calls start()
    public void run()
    {
    }
}
```

The following demonstration program uses the Java *Thread* class to implement a common multithreading problem.

The MultiThread1 Application

The following MultiThread1 demonstration application continuously calculates prime numbers while remaining responsive to user input. Just to prove the point, this application calculates two sets of prime numbers "simultaneously."

The Forms Designer work

The Forms Designer work for MultiThread1 consists primarily of creating two sets of matching output Edit controls, each with a label, a start button, and a stop button. (See Figure 10-4 on page 324.) Start the forms work with the first Edit control. Set the name to *outputEdit1*. Clear the *text* property value box. Now anchor the Edit control to the left, top, and right edges of the form. Add a Label control above the Edit control, and set the label text to *Last Prime Number Calculated (#)*. The program will replace the pound sign with the priority of the background task. Anchor the label to the left, top, and right edges of the form. Below the *outputEdit1* control, add two buttons: one labeled *Start* and one labeled *Stop*. Anchor the Start button to the top and left, and anchor the Stop button to the top and right edges of the form. Double-click each button to create the click event handlers.

Now repeat the process for a second set of controls immediately below the first.

The Background.java code

The code for MultiThread1 consists of two .java files, the usual Form1.java and also the file Background.java. (Select Add Class from the Project menu to add Background.java.) The Background.java file appears beginning on the following page.

```
import com.ms.wfc.ui.*;

/**
 * Thread that calculates primes and reports
 * them to output control.
 */
public class Background extends Thread
{
    // number of primes
    int numberOfPrimes = 0;

    // output control
    Control output;

    // stopped == true -> thread stopped
    boolean stopped;

    /**
     * Create a background process in the stopped state.
     */
    public Background(Control output)
    {
        this.output = output;
        stopped = true;
    }

    /**
     * Test next number for prime.
     */
    boolean isPrime(long number)
    {
        // test all the multiples from 2 to the
        // square root of the number (increment
        // to handle potential round-off problems)
        long max = (long)Math.sqrt(number)+ 1;
        for (long test = 2; test <= max; test++)
        {
            // if number is evenly divisible by test...
            long remainder = number % test;
            if (remainder == 0)
            {
                // then it can't be prime
                return false;
            }
        }

        // made it through; it must be prime
        return true;
    }
```

```java
/**
 * Start the Background thread.
 */
public void run()
{
    try
    {
        // keep calculating prime numbers
        // until we wrap around
        for (long i = 0; i >= 0; i++)
        {
            // give up control
            Thread.yield();

            // while stopped, keep giving up control
            while (stopped)
            {
                Thread.sleep(100);
            }

            // now calculate a new prime
            if (isPrime(i))
            {
                // count it
                numberOfPrimes++;

                // output prime number to control
                // specified
                output.setText("#" +
                            toString(numberOfPrimes) +
                            "- " +
                            toString(i));
            }
        }
    }
    catch(Exception e)
    {
        output.setText(e.getMessage());
    }
}

/**
 * Convert a number into a string with commas.
 */
private String toString(long value)
{
    // convert the long into a string
```

(continued)

```
        String s = Long.toString(value);

        // now add commas to that string
        StringBuffer sb = new StringBuffer(20);
        int offset = 0;
        for(int length = s.length();
            length > 0;
            length--)
        {
            // every 3 digits from the right side...
            if ((length % 3) == 0)
            {
                // but not at the beginning...
                if (offset != 0)
                {
                    // put a comma
                    sb.append(',');
                }
            }

            // now add another digit
            sb.append(s.charAt(offset++));
        }
        return sb.toString();
    }


    /**
     * Activate the background process.
     */
    public void activate(boolean active)
    {
        stopped = !active;
    }
}
```

The class *Background* extends the class *Thread*. The constructor for *Background* takes one argument, the WFC control to which *Background* will output its prime numbers as it calculates them. The program sets one other variable, *stopped*, to *true*. This flag will be used later to signal *Background* to stop calculating primes.

The parent thread creates an object of class *Background* and then calls the object's *start()* method. (See the *Form1* code that follows.) As soon as it does, Visual J++ creates a new thread. After some setup, this new thread will call *Background.run()*. The *Background.run()* method sits in an essentially infinite loop. (The loop increments a long variable and terminates when the variable contains a negative number).

The new thread immediately invokes the rescheduler by calling *Thread.yield()*. If this is the only thread that is ready to run, it will instantly get control back.

Once it has given another thread a chance, *run()* then enters another loop. As long as *stopped* is *true*, *run()* continues to call *Thread.sleep()* in a loop. (The *stopped* variable gets changed in the *Background.active()* method, explained below.) The argument 100 indicates that the thread should block for 100 milliseconds.

Once *stopped* is *false*, *run()* continues by calling *isPrime(i)* to check whether *i* (the counter in the *for* loop) is prime or not. If it is, *run()* increments the prime number count and outputs both the prime number count and the prime number to the *output* WFC control that was passed to the *Background()* constructor. The method *Background.toString()* does nothing more than insert commas every three digits from the end to increase the readability of the resulting number.

The *Background.isPrime()* method uses a different algorithm than does the Sieve of Eratosthenes benchmark presented in Chapter 1. This version checks the candidate *number* by calculating the modulo of *number* with respect to each whole number from 2 up through the square root of *number*. If the modulo is zero, *number* is evenly divisible by that number and therefore can't be a prime number. If *isPrime()* makes it all the way through the loop without finding an even denominator, *number* must be prime and *isPrime()* returns *true*.

The *Background* method *activate(boolean)* sets the *stopped* variable to *true* or *false*. (The *activate()* method is called from the parent program, in this case *Form1*.) By referring to *run()*, you can see that setting this variable in effect turns the *Background* thread off and on.

The Form1.java code

Most of the real work for the MultiThread1 application is done in the *Background* class; the *Form1* class is straightforward:

```
import com.ms.wfc.app.*;
import com.ms.wfc.core.*;
import com.ms.wfc.ui.*;
import com.ms.wfc.html.*;

/**
 * This class demonstrates background processing using threads.
 */
public class Form1 extends Form
{
    // define two background threads
    Background bg1;
    Background bg2;

    public Form1()
    {
        // Required for Visual J++ Form Designer support
        initForm();
```

(continued)

```
        // create a thread of normal priority
        bg1 = new Background(outputEdit1);
        bg1.setPriority(Thread.NORM_PRIORITY);

        // update the label to reflect the priority
        setLabel(bg1, label1);

        // repeat for a second thread
        bg2 = new Background(outputEdit2);
        bg2.setPriority(Thread.NORM_PRIORITY - 1);
        setLabel(bg2, label2);

        // start both processes (note that both
        // start in the inactive state)
        bg1.start();
        bg2.start();
    }

    /**
     * Update the specified label with the priority of thread.
     */
    private void setLabel(Thread thread, Label label)
    {
        int priority = thread.getPriority();
        String priString = Integer.toString(priority);
        char priChar = priString.charAt(0);
        label.setText(label.getText().replace('#', priChar));
    }

        :

    private void button1_click(Object source, Event e)
    {
        bg1.activate(true);
    }

    private void button2_click(Object source, Event e)
    {
        bg1.activate(false);
    }

    private void button3_click(Object source, Event e)
    {
        bg2.activate(true);
    }

    private void button4_click(Object source, Event e)
    {
```

```
        bg2.activate(false);
}


/**
 * NOTE: The following code is required by the Visual J++ form
 * designer.  It can be modified using the form editor.  Do not
 * modify it using the code editor.
 */
Container components = new Container();
Edit outputEdit1 = new Edit();
Label label1 = new Label();
Button button1 = new Button();
Button button2 = new Button();
Edit outputEdit2 = new Edit();
Label label2 = new Label();
Button button3 = new Button();
Button button4 = new Button();


private void initForm()
{
    // ...created by the Forms Designer...
}


/**
 * The main entry point for the application.
 */
public static void main(String args[])
{
    Application.run(new Form1());
}
}
```

Once control returns from the *initForm()* method, the *Form1* constructor creates a *Background* object *bg1* and passes it the *outputEdit1* object for output. The constructor then sets the priority to the normal priority for a Visual J++ thread. *Form1()* then updates the *label1* Label control text with this priority. The *setLabel()* method replaces the # character in the label with an ANSI representative of the priority.

NOTE Visual J++ thread priorities range from 1 to 9, with 5 being a normal priority.

The *Form1()* constructor repeats this process to create a second *Background* object called *bg2* and to attach it to the *outputEdit2* Edit control. The *Form1()* constructor sets the priority of the *bg2* thread to be one less than the priority of *bg1*. Next *Form1()* calls *bg1.start()* and *bg2.start()* to start the two *Background* threads running on their own.

The *button_click()* methods simply call *Background.activate()* and pass *true* or *false* to *bg1* or *bg2,* depending on which thread the button is trying to stop or start.

Executing MultiThread1 generates output as shown in Figure 10-4. What doesn't come across in this static screen capture is the dynamic aspect of the application. With both threads enabled, the upper box updates so rapidly that the user can't possibly read individual values, and the lower box updates slowly if at all. While the upper box is updating, however, the user can resize and move the form window without much apparent effect. (The main window repaints slightly slower; you can see that rapidly moving the window generates window trails similar to mouse trails).

As soon as the user pauses the higher-priority thread, however, the lower-priority thread snaps into gear and updates at the same high rate as the higher-priority thread did previously.

NOTE   When you pause the higher priority thread (*bg1*), the priority of the lower priority thread (*bg2*) doesn't change. If you had other threads at the same priority as *bg1* that were not BLOCKED, the increase in *bg2*'s performance would not be that pronounced.

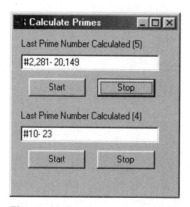

Figure 10-4. *The two boxes in the MultiThread1 application update rapidly with the calculated prime number, while still allowing the user to perform routine actions like minimizing, maximizing, and moving the window.*

Using the WFC *createThread()* Method

One inconvenience of the approach demonstrated in MultiThread1 is the requirement to create a separate class in order to create a new thread. WFC supports an alternative approach by enabling you to create a new thread around a delegate. (Refer back to Chapter 5 for a discussion of delegates.) The following MultiThread2 application demonstrates the use of this strategy. Since this application is a minor variation on MultiThread1, the Forms Designer work is the same.

The MultiThread2 code

The code for MultiThread2 is as follows. (Methods duplicated from MultiThread1 are partially or completely removed from this listing; the entire version of MultiThread2 appears on the companion CD-ROM.)

```
import com.ms.wfc.app.*;
import com.ms.wfc.core.*;
import com.ms.wfc.ui.*;
import com.ms.wfc.html.*;

/**
 * This class demonstrates the Application.createThread() method.
 */
public class Form1 extends Form
{
    /**
     * Control the flow of the threads we form.
     */
    class FlowControl
    {
        private boolean active = false;

        boolean isActive()
        {
            return active;
        }

        void setActive(boolean active)
        {
            this.active = active;
        }
    }

    // create a flow control for each thread
    // (this is used to start and stop the calculation)
    FlowControl flowControl1 = new FlowControl();
    FlowControl flowControl2 = new FlowControl();

    /**
     * Delegate is used to create background thread.
     *
     * @param flowControl - starts and stops background thread
     * @param control - control to accept primes
     */
    delegate void Background(FlowControl flowControl,
                            Control     control);
```

(continued)

```java
public Form1()
{
    // Required for Visual J++ Form Designer support
    initForm();

    // execute delegate in its own thread
    Thread thread1 =
      Application.createThread(new Background(this.run),
                                  new Object[]{flowControl1,
                                                 outputEdit1},
                                  Thread.NORM_PRIORITY);
    setLabel(thread1, label1);


    // repeat the process for the second thread at
    // a lower priority
    Thread thread2 =
      Application.createThread(new Background(this.run),
                                  new Object[]{flowControl2,
                                                 outputEdit2},
                                  Thread.NORM_PRIORITY - 1);
    setLabel(thread2, label2);
}


/**
 * Increment the prime number counter.
 */
synchronized void countPrimeNumber()
{
    numberOfPrimes++;
}


/**
 * Start the Background thread.
 */
public void run(FlowControl flowControl, Control output)
{
    try
    {
        // keep calculating prime numbers
        // until we wrap around
        for (long i = 0; i >= 0; i++)
        {
            // give up control
            Thread.yield();

            // while not active, keep giving up control
            while (!flowControl.isActive())
            {
```

```
                    Thread.sleep(100);
                }

                // now calculate a new prime
                if (isPrime(i))
                {
                    // count it
                    countPrimeNumber();

                    // output prime number to control
                    // specified
                    output.setText("#" +
                                   toString(numberOfPrimes) +
                                   "- " +
                                   toString(i));
                }
            }
        }
        catch(Exception e)
        {
            output.setText(e.getMessage());
        }
    }

    private String toString(long value)
    {
        ⋮
    }

    private void button1_click(Object source, Event e)
    {
        flowControl1.setActive(true);
    }

    private void button2_click(Object source, Event e)
    {
        flowControl1.setActive(false);
    }

    private void button3_click(Object source, Event e)
    {
        flowControl2.setActive(true);
    }

    private void button4_click(Object source, Event e)
    {
        flowControl2.setActive(false);
    }

    // ...from here the same as MultiThread1...
}
```

The most important difference between MultiThread2 and its MultiThread1 cousin is the use of the *Application.createThread()* method to create the new threads.

The first argument to *createThread()* is a delegate object of class *Background*. The delegate declaration of *Background* defines two arguments: an object of the inner class *FlowControl* and an output WFC *Control* object. These arguments are necessary since there is no thread class constructor to save the values these arguments contain. The *Background* delegate returns a *void* as a requirement for being called by *createThread()*. Any delegate used with *createThread()* must return a *void* because *createThread()* doesn't return to the caller.

In this case, the delegate is created using the method *Form1.run()*. It is at this method where execution of the new thread begins. The number and type of arguments plus the return type of *run()* must match the declaration of the delegate *Background*. If they don't, an error is generated at compile time.

The second argument to *createThread()* is an array of objects to be passed to *run()*. Again, the number and type of these arguments must match the declaration of *run()*, which means they also match the declaration of the delegate *Background*. If they don't, a run-time exception is generated as soon as the new thread tries to start.

The final argument to *createThread()* is the priority.

NOTE   When you use *createThread()*, there is no need to call *start()*. The thread is created in an active state.

It's necessary to create the inner class *FlowControl* to contain the *active* flag. This is because *run()* needs a reference back to the same *active* flag that the *button_click()* methods are accessing. Had the program passed *active* directly, *run()* would have simply received the value of the member, either *true* or *false*.

Is *createThread()* worth the trouble?

After comparing the two versions of MultiThread, we are left with the question of whether it's actually worth it to use *createThread()* to avoid creating a new subclass of *Thread* (or a new class that implements *Runnable*). I tend to think no. After all, the delegate *Background* is a new class.

Although I haven't seen the inner workings of the *Thread* class, I imagine that it invokes *createThread()*. Or perhaps *Thread* and *createThread()* both access the same Windows API functions to create a Windows thread. Either way, the net effect of the two techniques is the same. Using the *Thread* class seems the simpler of the two approaches to me.

Synchronizing access to *numberOfPrimes*

Notice how MultiThread2 allows both threads to use the same variable, *numberOf-Primes*. I did this as a demonstration rather than because of any overriding requirements of the program.

Since both threads in MultiThread2 update the same *numberOfPrimes* variable by incrementing it, access to *numberOfPrimes* must be controlled. The program does this by defining a new synchronized method, *countPrimeNumber()*, to perform the incrementation. The statement that incremented *numberOfPrimes* in *run()* is replaced in this example by a call to *countPrimeNumber()*. Since *countPrimeNumber()* is synchronized, the race condition problem is avoided.

Notice that a few statements later, *run()* accesses *numberOfPrimes* directly when it passes its value to *toString()*. This doesn't represent a race condition because the statement doesn't update the value, it only reads it. It's possible for the *numberOfPrimes* variable to be updated by some other thread between the time that it's incremented and the time that it's read. The following subset of *run()* uses a synchronized block to avoid this possibility. (Both variations appear in the version of Multi-Thread2 on the companion CD-ROM, with one commented out):

```
// now calculate a new prime
if (isPrime(i))
{
    // count it
    synchronized(mutex)
    {
        numberOfPrimes++;

        // output prime number to the control
        // specified
        output.setText("#" +
                    toString(numberOfPrimes) +
                    " - " +
                    toString(i));
    }
}
```

Here the object *mutex* is defined to be of the empty inner class *Mutex* as follows:

```
/**
 * Define a dummy class to use as a mutex.
 */
class Mutex
{
}
Mutex mutex = new Mutex();
```

Defining a class object *mutex* provides the block of code with a unique mutex to synchronize on.

> **NOTE** In this example, I could not use the *this* object. Each thread is a separate instance of *Background*. Thus, each thread has a different mutex. Synchronizing on the *this* object would not keep one thread from interfering with another.

The MDIThread Application

Although you can create a Multiple Document Interface (MDI) application without creating multiple threads, using multiple threads is common.

> **NOTE** An MDI interface has several child forms residing within a single parent form. These child forms might refer to different documents—hence the name MDI—but this isn't required. A common example of an MDI application is Microsoft Word.

When the different child forms within an MDI application don't refer to the same document, it's convenient to operate them in separate threads. This allows them to operate independently of each other.

To demonstrate the point, I created an application, MDIThread, in which each thread operates in its own child form.

The Forms Designer work

The trick in laying out MDIThread is to modify *Form1* so that it contains a single label, output control, start button, and stop button, instead of two sets of controls as defined in the MultiThread applications above. In addition, you double-click the active property *closing* to create the method *Form1_closing()*. (I'll explain this method later.) *Form1* will be the child form.

In addition to *Form1*, it's necessary to create a new form to act as the MDI parent. To do so, click the Add Item toolbar button or choose Add Form on the Project menu. Select Form from the list of objects to add and give it the name *MDIParent* before clicking the Open button. This creates a new form class, *MDIParent*, contained in the file MDIParent.java. Visual J++ adds the new .java file to the project automatically.

Change the *text* property of the *MDIParent* form to *Calc Primes Parent* or something equally meaningful. Now add a MainMenu control from the Toolbox. To the main menu, add the menu item PrimeCalc. Under the PrimeCalc menu, add the menu items New and Exit, in that order. Change the *name* property of the New item to *newMI* and the Exit item to *exitMI*. Now double-click both of these menu items to create the menu item event handlers.

Since the *Background* class is unchanged from the MultiThread1 example, simply copy the Background.java file from the MultiThread1 directory to the MDIThread directory. Visual J++ automatically adds the file to the project.

Finally, choose MDIThread Properties from the Project menu. Select the Launch tab, and under the label When Project Runs, Load, select MDIParent from the dropdown list. Now select OK. Since *MDIParent* is the main form, execution starts there.

The code for Form1

The code for the Form1.java file appears as follows:

```java
import com.ms.wfc.app.*;
import com.ms.wfc.core.*;
import com.ms.wfc.ui.*;
import com.ms.wfc.html.*;

/**
 * Implement a child form to the MDI parent MDIParent.
 */
public class Form1 extends Form
{
    // the background Thread object
    Background bg;

    public Form1(Form parent,
                 int bgPriority)
    {
        // Required for Visual J++ Form Designer support
        initForm();

        // attach this form to our parent form
        this.setMDIParent(parent);

        // make ourselves visible
        this.setVisible(true);

        // create a thread of specified priority
        bg = new Background(outputEdit1);
        bg.setPriority(bgPriority);

        // update the label to reflect the priority
        setLabel(bg, label1);

        // start the background thread
        bg.start();
    }

    /**
     * Update the specified label with the priority of thread.
     */
    private void setLabel(Thread thread, Label label)
    {
        // ...same as in MultiThread examples...
    }

    private void button1_click(Object source, Event e)
    {
        bg.activate(true);
    }
```

(continued)

```
        private void button2_click(Object source, Event e)
        {
            bg.activate(false);
        }

        private void Form1_closing(Object source, CancelEvent e)
        {
            // don't close the entire application
            e.cancel = true;

            // but do kill the background thread...
            bg.stop();

            // and dispose of the current form
            this.dispose();
        }

        /**
         * NOTE: The following code is required by the Visual J++ form
         * designer.  It can be modified using the form editor.  Do not
         * modify it using the code editor.
         */
        Container components = new Container();
        Edit outputEdit1 = new Edit();
        Label label1 = new Label();
        Button button1 = new Button();
        Button button2 = new Button();

        private void initForm()
        {
            // ...created by Forms Designer...
        }
}
```

This version of *Form1* has been modified in several ways. First, there is no *main()* method anymore. The application starts with the *MDIParent* class.

In addition, this program adds two arguments to the *Form1()* constructor: a reference to the MDI parent form, and the priority of the background thread. After the form has set itself up by calling *initForm()*, *Form1()* calls the method *setMDIParent(parent)*. This establishes the current form as an MDI child of the parent form *parent*. Next the form makes itself visible by calling *setVisible(true)*. Visual J++ creates forms as invisible so that the user won't see the individual objects get added to the form. The *Application.run()* call in *main()* normally saves you the trouble of making the form visible.

Finally, *Form1()* sets up the background thread using the same *Background* thread class as in MultiThread1.

The remainder of *Form1* is unchanged from the previous version except for the addition of the *Form1_closing()* method. This method is invoked before the form closes. Unfortunately, the default action of a form when closing is to dispose of itself and then call *Thread.exit()*, which terminates the entire application. All we want is the form to close itself. Setting the *cancel* flag in the *CancelEvent* object *e* to *true* (the default is *false*) tells the *Form.closing()* method not to do anything—that we will do it all. The next thing that *Form1_closing()* does is call *bg.stop()*. This kills the background thread and disposes of its resources. Finally, *Form1_closing()* calls *dispose()* to close the current form and dispose of its resources.

The MDIParent code

The code for the *MDIParent* class is reasonably straightforward:

```
import com.ms.wfc.app.*;
import com.ms.wfc.core.*;
import com.ms.wfc.ui.*;
import com.ms.wfc.html.*;


/**
 * Act as an MDI parent to Form1.
 */
public class MDIParent extends Form
{
    public MDIParent()
    {
        // Required for Visual J++ Form Designer support
        initForm();

        // set this form to be an MDI container
        setIsMDIContainer(true);
    }

    :

    private void newMI_click(Object source, Event e)
    {
        // create a child form object of slightly
        // less priority than we are
        Thread thread = Thread.currentThread();
        int priority = thread.getPriority() - 1;
        Form form = new Form1(this, priority);
    }

    private void exitMI_click(Object source, Event e)
    {
        Application.exit();
    }
```

(continued)

```
/**
 * NOTE: The following code is required by the Visual J++ form
 * designer.  It can be modified using the form editor.  Do not
 * modify it using the code editor.
 */
Container components = new Container();
MainMenu mainMenu1 = new MainMenu();
MenuItem menuItem1 = new MenuItem();
MenuItem newMI = new MenuItem();
MenuItem exitMI = new MenuItem();

private void initForm()
{
    // ...created by the Forms Designer...
}

/**
 * The main entry point for the application.
 * ...
 */
public static void main(String args[])
{
    Application.run(new MDIParent());
}
}
```

The method *main()* executes the *MDIParent* form in the usual way. The constructor for *MDIParent* invokes *initForm()* and then calls *setIsMDIContainer(true)* to designate this form as an MDI container form.

The interesting code is in the two menu click event handlers. The *newMI_click()* method is invoked when the user chooses New from the PrimeCalc menu. The *newMI_click()* method creates a new *Form1* child form with a background thread priority that is one less than the priority of the current thread. The *exitMI_click()* method terminates the current application by calling *Application.exit()*.

The result

I find the result of this relatively simple program to be quite interesting. Figure 10-5 shows MDIThread after I have selected New from the PrimeCalc menu three times to create three independent child forms. Each of the child forms executes independently of the rest. You can also see that one of the child forms (the first one created) is currently the active child.

The user can close any one of the child forms—by clicking on the close icon in the upper right corner of that form—with no noticeable effect on the other two forms (except for a slight acceleration in both of them). In addition, since the background threads are executing at a lower priority than the parent thread, the child

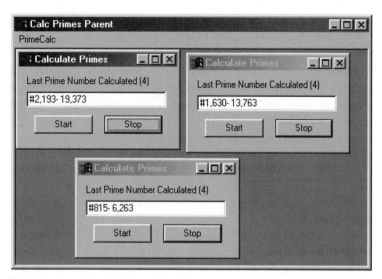

Figure 10-5. *The MDIThread application executing with three active child forms.*

threads have no noticeable effect on the responsiveness of the parent form; the child threads tend to slow down or stop running as soon as the user moves the parent window.

Using the Idle Event to Perform Background Processing

Setting the priority of a thread lower than the main application's priority ensures that the background threads will have minimal negative impact on the performance of the main thread. However, the *Application* class offers a technique for creating a "thread" that is guaranteed to have no impact on the performance of any other thread.

As I have mentioned earlier, all user input is conveyed to the application in the form of Windows messages that Visual J++ converts into events. When the message queue is completely empty—that is, when there is absolutely no user input to process—Visual J++ invokes the idle event.

You can use the idle event to perform simple functions that you don't want to impact system performance. Since the idle event is a "one-shot" event (that is, it occurs once), it's basically not suitable for running in a loop such as our prime numbers loop. We can get around this one-shot problem relatively cleanly, however. (In any event, the problem will be fixed in an even better way in the next chapter.)

The following IdleEvent1 application uses the idle event to calculate prime numbers when there is no user input to process. In addition, IdleEvent1 adds a crude drawing program like that shown in Chapter 9 to demonstrate that the idle process has no deleterious effect on the responsiveness of the system to user input.

The Forms Designer work

First create the application IdleEvent1. Using the Forms Designer, update *Form1* to look much like the child form in the MDIThread application. Now add a large panel on the bottom of the form below the buttons. Set the *name* property of the panel to *paintPanel*. Set the *borderStyle* property to *Fixed 3D* to enhance the appearance. Switch to the active properties, and double click the *paint* property to create the paint event handler *paintPanel_paint()*.

The Form1 code

The code for Form1 appears as follows:

```
import com.ms.wfc.app.*;
import com.ms.wfc.core.*;
import com.ms.wfc.ui.*;
import com.ms.wfc.html.*;

import com.ms.wfc.util.*;

/**
 * This class demonstrates the use of idle processing using
 * the onIdle() process.
 */
public class Form1 extends Form
{
    // define holder for the idle process handler
    IdleProcess idle;

    public Form1()
    {
        // Required for Visual J++ Form Designer support
        initForm();

        // Create an onIdle process
        idle = new IdleProcess(outputEdit);
    }

        ⋮

    private void button1_click(Object source, Event e)
    {
        idle.setActive(true);
    }

    private void button2_click(Object source, Event e)
    {
        idle.setActive(false);
    }
```

```
// The code from this point forward that handles
// the drawing of squiggles in the panel is not
// shown in this listing in the interest of brevity.
// The complete program appears on the companion CD-ROM.

/**
 * NOTE: The following code is required by the Visual J++ form
 * designer.  It can be modified using the form editor.  Do not
 * modify it using the code editor.
 */
Container components = new Container();
Edit outputEdit = new Edit();
Label label1 = new Label();
Button button1 = new Button();
Button button2 = new Button();
Panel paintPanel = new Panel(components);

private void initForm()
{
    // ...created by the Forms Designer...
}

/**
 * The main entry point for the application.
 */
public static void main(String args[])
{
    Application.run(new Form1());
}
}
```

The majority of the source code to *Form1* pertains to handling the painting of squiggles in the panel. Since this is similar to the FreeDraw application in Chapter 9, this code is not shown here in the interest of saving space.

The relevant section of *Form1* is in the *Form1()* constructor where the *IdleProcess* object is passed. The *outputEdit* argument indicates the object to which prime numbers are to be written.

The start and stop button click event handlers turn the idle process on and off.

The IdleProcess code
Add a class named IdleProcess to your project. Here is the code for that class:

```
import com.ms.wfc.app.*;
import com.ms.wfc.core.*;
import com.ms.wfc.ui.*;
```

(continued)

```
/**
 * Calculate primes "in the background" by attaching
 * to the idle event.
 */
public class IdleProcess
{
    // the WFC control to use for outputting primes
    Control output;

    // note whether idle loop is active or not
    boolean active = false;

    // the following timer is used to periodically "kick"
    // the system into invoking the idle loop
    Timer timer;

    // number of primes found and the last
    // candidate for 'primehood'
    int    numberOfPrimes = 0;
    int    lastCandidate  = 0;

    /**
     * Create an idle process that reports primes back
     * to the parent through the output control.
     */
    public IdleProcess(Control output)
    {
        // save the parent
        this.output = output;

        // assign an on idle event handler
        Application.addOnIdle(new EventHandler(this.onIdle));

        // set a timer to prompt system
        timer = new Timer();
        timer.setInterval(20);
        timer.setEnabled(true);
    }


    /**
     * Turn the idle process on and off.
     */
    public void setActive(boolean active)
    {
        this.active = active;
    }
```

```
/**
 * Invoked when the system is idle.
 */
public void onIdle(Object sender, Event e)
{
    // if we're active...
    if (active)
    {
        // note the start time
        Time startTime = new Time();
        Time endTime = startTime.addMillis(10);

        // work until timer exits the loop
        while(true)
        {
            // if current time is greater than end time...
            Time currentTime = new Time();
            if (Time.compare(currentTime, endTime) > 0)
            {
                // get out of the loop and return
                break;
            }

            // loop for 100 candidates or so
            for (int i = 0; i < 100; i++)
            {
                // try the next number
                if (isPrime(++lastCandidate))
                {
                    // it's prime - count it
                    numberOfPrimes++;

                    // report results back to parent
                    output.setText(
                        toString(numberOfPrimes) +
                        "-" +
                        toString(lastCandidate));
                }
            }
        }
    }
}

/**
 * Test next number for prime.
 */
boolean isPrime(long number)
```

(continued)

```
    {
        // ...identical to earlier versions...
    }

    /**
     * Convert a number into a string with commas.
     */
    private String toString(long value)
    {
        // ...identical to earlier versions...
    }
}
```

The *isPrime()* and *toString()* methods are identical to earlier versions. The remainder of the *IdleProcess* class has a completely different flavor.

The constructor for *IdleProcess()* saves the WFC *Control* object to which prime numbers are to be written. That done, *IdleProcess()* creates an *EventHandler* around the *onIdle()* method and assigns it to process the idle event. Finally, the constructor sets a *Timer* object to trigger every 20 milliseconds for reasons I'll explain later.

The actual *onIdle()* method is structured differently than the *run()* methods of the previous multithreaded examples. This is because the calculation of prime numbers in this example is occurring in the same thread as the main program; it's just that at the moment the main thread has nothing else to do. This has two implications:

- The *onIdle()* handler can't attempt to do too much. During the time that *onIdle()* is executing, the program thread is unresponsive to user input.

- The *onIdle()* handler must be able to remember where it was the last time it executed. In this case, that means it must save the last number candidate it passed to *isPrime()* to be checked.

The *onIdle()* method begins by first checking the *active* flag. If *active* is *false*, the prime calculation process is suspended and the *onIdle()* method returns without taking any action. If *active* is *true*, *onIdle()* continues by noting the current time and calculating an *endTime* some 10 milliseconds into the future. I arbitrarily decided that the *onIdle()* processor could work for 10 milliseconds at a time without anyone noticing.

The *onIdle()* method then enters a loop that periodically checks the time until the *currentTime* exceeds the *endTime*. As long as the *endTime* isn't exceeded, *onIdle()* calculates and reports prime numbers using the same algorithm as in earlier versions. The program checks 100 prime number candidates before rechecking the time, to increase performance. The computer can check 100 candidates in much less than 10 milliseconds. It's a waste to check the time after every candidate.

Once 10 milliseconds have gone by, *onIdle()* returns control to the application, saving the position in *lastCandidate* and the number of primes found so far in *numberOfPrimes*.

> **NOTE**   It's critical that the *onIdle()* event handler finish processing, or be able to save sufficient information to allow it to pick up where it left off the next time it runs. Saving its position is called *saving the state*.

Why set a timer?

One curious feature of IdleEvent1 is the *Timer* object created in the *IdleProcess* constructor. This is especially interesting since I never defined a *timerEvent* handler to do anything with the timer event once it occurred.

This *Timer* object solves a problem inherent with any repetitive idle event handler. Each time the process goes idle, the idle event occurs only once. Once the *onIdle()* method returns to the caller (after the first 10 milliseconds), the main thread is blocked to give time to other, lower-priority threads. For many applications, this is okay. In our case, however, we want to continue to calculate primes as long as the system isn't busy.

The *Timer* object sort of "kicks" the main thread by forcing the thread to process a "do nothing" timer event. After every timer event, if the application is still idle, the system passes control to the *onIdle()* process again.

So if the *onIdle()* process executes for 10 milliseconds, why is *Timer* set for 20 milliseconds? If *Timer* were set for the same 10 milliseconds that *onIdle()* uses, the *onIdle()* method would keep the main thread busy all the time, thereby never giving control to any lower-priority threads.

THE REGISTRY

There is another pair of classes in the WFC *app* package that can be very useful to the application programmer. The classes *Registry* and *RegistryKey* allow the application to save values from one execution to another. For example, your application might store the current directory before it exits so that the next time it's executed it can start in that directory.

> **NOTE**   The Windows registry is a hierarchical database within Windows, which is saved to disk when Windows exits and restored when Windows starts back up.

The RegistryDemo application beginning on the following page demonstrates how an application can access the registry from Visual J++.

The RegistryDemo Application

The RegistryDemo application attempts to read the time of last execution from the registry. If no time is found stored there, the application displays the appropriate message. If a time is found, it's displayed in text format. RegistryDemo then stores the current time into the registry so that it can be read the next time the application runs.

To further enhance the demonstration, I have added a Clear Registry button to remove the time from the registry and a ReRead Registry button to read and store the time as if the application were just starting.

The Forms Designer work

After creating the RegistryDemo application as a Windows Application, open Form1.java in the Forms Designer. Change the form's *text* property to *Registry Demo*. Now add an Edit control. Rename the control to *outputEdit*, and anchor it to the top, left, and right edges of the form. Now add a Label control with the text *Application last executed on:* above the Edit control.

Add two buttons immediately below *outputEdit*. Label the left button *Clear Registry* and the right button *ReRead Registry*. Anchor the left button to the left and bottom edges and the right button to the right and bottom edges of the form. Finally, double-click each button to create the *button_click()* methods.

The code

The code for the RegistryDemo application is contained in the following Form1.java file:

```
import com.ms.wfc.app.*;
import com.ms.wfc.core.*;
import com.ms.wfc.ui.*;
import com.ms.wfc.html.*;

/**
 * Demonstrate the storing of information in the registry.
 */
public class Form1 extends Form
{
    public Form1()
    {
        // Required for Visual J++ Form Designer support
        initForm();

        // read time from registry, and then update registry
        readAndUpdateRegistry(outputEdit);
    }

    /**
     * Read the time of last execution from the registry,
```

```
 * and write it to the output control; then update the
 * registry with the current time.
 */
public void readAndUpdateRegistry(Control output)
{
    // get the time of last execution from the registry
    Time time = getRegistryTime();

    // if it's null...
    if (time == null)
    {
        // then application hasn't executed before
        output.setText("Application never run before");
    }
    else
    {
        // otherwise, convert the time into long format
        // and display it
        String sTime = toString(time);
        output.setText(sTime);
    }

    // now store the current date and time into the
    // registry for next time
    setRegistryTime(new Time());
}

/**
 * Display the specified time in the output control.
 */
String toString(Time time)
{
    String sDate = time.formatLongDate();
    String sTime = time.formatLongTime();
    return sDate + " " + sTime;
}

/**
 * Get the Time object stored in the registery; if there
 * is none, return a null.
 */
public Time getRegistryTime()
{
    try
    {
        // get the string representation of the time
        // last executed out of the registry
```

(continued)

```
                RegistryKey appKey = getAppKey();
                String sTime = (String)appKey.getValue("Time");

                // now convert this into a Time object
                Time time = new Time(sTime);
                return time;
            }
            catch(Exception e)
            {
            }

            // in the event of an error (e.g., if there is no
            // time stored), return null
            return null;
        }

        /**
         * Store the specified time into the registry.
         */
        public void setRegistryTime(Time time)
        {
            // store the string representation of time into
            // the "Time" subkey of our application's registry entry
            RegistryKey appKey = getAppKey();
            appKey.setValue("Time", time.toString());
        }

        /**
         * Delete the registry time.
         */
        public void deleteRegistryTime()
        {
            try
            {
                RegistryKey appKey = getAppKey();
                appKey.deleteValue("Time");
            }
            catch(Exception e)
            {
            }
        }

        /**
         * Return the registry key for this application.
         */
        private RegistryKey getAppKey()
        {
            return Registry.CURRENT_USER.createSubKey(
                        "Software\\ProgrammingJava\\RegistryDemo");
        }
```

```
private void button1_click(Object source, Event e)
{
    deleteRegistryTime();
}


private void button2_click(Object source, Event e)
{
    readAndUpdateRegistry(outputEdit);
}


/**
 * NOTE: The following code is required by the Visual J++ form
 * designer.  It can be modified using the form editor.  Do not
 * modify it using the code editor.
 */
Container components = new Container();
Edit outputEdit = new Edit();
Label label1 = new Label();
Button button1 = new Button();
Button button2 = new Button();

private void initForm()
{
    // ...created by the Forms Designer...
}


/**
 * The main entry point for the application.
 */
public static void main(String args[])
{
    Application.run(new Form1());
}
}
```

After calling *initForm()*, the *Form1()* constructor calls *readAndUpdateRegistry()*.

The *readAndUpdateRegistry()* method starts by invoking *Form1.getRegistry-Time()* to fetch a *Time* object containing the time of last execution from the registry. If *getRegistryTime()* returns *null*, the program outputs the message "Application never run before". If a *Time* object is returned, the *Time* object is converted in long format into a *String* object by invoking the local *toString()* method. Next the *String* is written to the output control. Finally, the current time is passed to the *Form1.setRegistryTime()* method to be stored into the registry.

The *setRegistryTime(time)* method starts by fetching a *RegistryKey* object for the current application by calling *Form1.getAppKey()*. The *getAppKey()* method returns the registry key "CURRENT_USER\Software\ProgrammingJava\RegistryDemo". The *setRegistryTime()* method converts *time* into a *String* and stores that string under the subkey "Time" using the *setValue()* method.

The *getRegistryTime()* method calls *getAppKey()* to retrieve the *RegistryKey* for this application. Then *getRegistryTime()* calls *RegistryKey.getValue()* to return the time string stored earlier under the subkey "Time". This string, *sTime*, is then converted into a *Time* object that is returned to the caller. If an exception is thrown at any point (for example, if there is no "Time" subkey), *getRegistryTime()* returns *null*.

Finally, *Form1.deleteRegistryTime()* calls *RegistryKey.deleteValue()* to delete the "Time" subkey in the application's registry entry.

The Clear Registry button handler (*button1_click()*) invokes the method *deleteRegistryTime()*, and the ReRead Time button handler (*button2_click()*) simply calls *readAndUpdateRegistry()*.

The result

Figure 10-6 shows the output from RegistryDemo the first time it runs (or the first time that it's run after pressing the Clear Registry button). Figure 10-7 shows the previous execution time when I ran RegistryDemo a subsequent time.

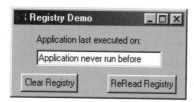

Figure 10-6. *The output from RegistryDemo the first time the program runs.*

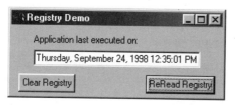

Figure 10-7. *The output from the RegistryDemo application the second time I ran the program.*

CONCLUSION

The WFC Application package *com.ms.wfc.app* is an eclectic mix of useful classes. In this chapter, you've seen the *Time* and *Timer* classes, the multithreading classes including the idle event support, and the *Registry* and *RegistryKey* classes.

In the next chapter, you'll see how the J/Direct feature allows you to add Java support for Windows methods when Visual J++ just doesn't seem to have the class you need.

Chapter 11

J/Direct

No matter how large Microsoft Visual J++'s libraries are, there will always come a time when you can't find the exact function you want in either the Windows Foundation Classes for Java (WFC) or the Abstract Windowing Toolkit (AWT) library. When you are faced with this situation, you might discover that the function you need is a native function residing in an existing Dynamic-Link Library (DLL), such as the Win32 API.

NOTE A *native function* is a function that is written in the machine language of the host machine. These functions are almost invariably written in C.

Prior to Visual J++ 6, you had to use Sun Microsystem's Java Native Interface (JNI) or Microsoft's Raw Native Interface (RNI) to access a native function from Java. Of these two interfaces, RNI is better optimized for accessing Windows functions, but it is not supported by Sun Microsystem's Java. JNI is more standard across the Java landscape, but is not supported by Visual J++ or Microsoft Internet Explorer.

Both JNI and RNI have serious drawbacks. Both require you to convert the Java data types to and from the corresponding C or C++ data types, which takes considerable effort. In addition, RNI limits you to calling functions that fit certain naming conventions. Further, with both JNI and RNI you must be careful to explicitly disable and enable garbage collection at the appropriate times. The net effect of these drawbacks is that to use RNI or JNI to invoke existing DLL functions (including Windows API functions), you must write a shell to perform the necessary conversions.

To address the problem of calling native functions from Java, Visual J++ 6 includes a new mechanism called J/Direct. (J/Direct was introduced as part of the Microsoft Software Development Kit (SDK) for Java version 2.01.) J/Direct provides you with convenient access to native functions. J/Direct performs any data conversions that might be necessary and deals with details concerning memory pointers and garbage collection. With J/Direct, you can use native functions in the same way that you use normal Java methods. Visual J++ 6 pounds the final nail into the RNI/JNI coffin by including a tool, named the J/Direct Call Builder, that builds the necessary J/Direct commands for the functions that make up the Win32 API.

In this chapter, you'll learn how to use J/Direct and the J/Direct Call Builder. This chapter starts out with a simple application called Beep, which attaches itself to a Win32 API function to generate a short beep on the PC. The chapter then moves up to a slightly more complicated example that involves passing structures to and from a Win32 API call. In addition, I'll show you how to access functions from DLLs that you might write yourself. Finally, you'll learn how to use J/Direct to generate a new and better solution to the idle event problem that we worked on in Chapter 10. (The code for all the examples in this chapter is on the companion CD in the Windows Applications subfolder.)

LIMITATIONS TO THE USE OF J/DIRECT

Before we start working with J/Direct, I'll present a few caveats. First, any application written using J/Direct is by definition specific to the Win32 API, and is probably also specific to Intel processors. This implies that it would be unconscionable to use JNI, RNI, or J/Direct to write an applet that is designed to run on the Internet.

Second, although this chapter refers specifically to C structures, J/Direct also supports C++ structures. However, J/Direct doesn't support C++ classes.

Third, J/Direct and RNI can be used in the same program, but you should not intermix J/Direct and RNI calls. You shouldn't pass to a J/Direct call a reference to an object returned from RNI, and you shouldn't pass to an RNI call a reference to an object returned from J/Direct. Because of J/Direct's ease of use, I recommend that you simply not use RNI.

Fourth, because of the security checks, stack checking, and automatic data conversions that J/Direct performs for you, J/Direct calls are slightly slower than RNI calls. This speed difference should almost never be an issue. The time it takes for a program to make a function call is almost always insignificant, compared with the time it takes to execute the function. I doubt that the performance penalty would be noticeable, unless your program sits in a tight loop repeatedly calling small native functions.

USING THE J/DIRECT CALL BUILDER

J/Direct works through a set of what I'll call J/Direct *directives*. These directives are built into the comments that immediately precede each function definition or structure definition, in the same way that the Javadoc comments (described in Chapter 1) work. (Perhaps this is so that Microsoft's J/Direct directives won't conflict with any new Java keywords that might be introduced in the future by Sun Microsystems or by some future Java standards committee.)

It's possible, and not all that difficult, to write J/Direct directives manually; however, in most cases, the J/Direct Call Builder makes this unnecessary.

> **NOTE** The J/Direct Call Builder is currently limited to Win32 API functions. This limitation isn't based on any technical grounds, but is based on the fact that only Win32 API calls are documented in the text file that the J/Direct Call Builder uses to identify the functions and structures a program can access. Presumably, in the future, Microsoft will make text files available for more APIs in order to expand the number of functions accessible from the J/Direct Call Builder.

Using J/Direct: The Beep Application

In this section, I'll demonstrate J/Direct and the J/Direct Call Builder with an extremely simple example. From there, we'll graduate to a slightly more complicated example involving the passing of an object reference from the Win32 API to Visual J++.

The problem

In the Beep application, our needs are simple. All we'll do is write an application with a single button that, when pressed, causes the computer to generate a beep and send the beep to the speaker.

> **NOTE** The standard Java library contains a function that causes the computer speaker to sound a beep, so we don't really need to resort to J/Direct for this application. However, we can use a Win32 API function in order to learn how to use J/Direct.

Finding the right function

Before you can call a function, you have to know that it exists and what arguments it expects. Microsoft Visual Studio's online help system provides this information for Win32 API functions.

To find the function you need, open the MSDN Library for Visual Studio 6, which comes with Visual J++. You can do this by using the Visual J++ Help menu, or by using the Programs item on the Windows Start menu. Select the Index tab in the left pane of the help window, and type the word *beep*. Choose the keyword Beep (not beep), and you should get results similar to those shown in Figure 11-1.

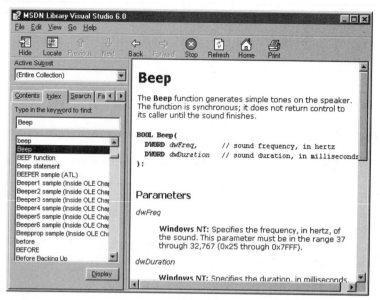

Figure 11-1. *The Visual J++ documentation describes the Windows API function* Beep().

NOTE   When I'm writing Visual J++ code, I normally have the MSDN Library Active Subset option set to Visual J++ so that my searches don't end up finding functions belonging to other languages. When using J/Direct, make sure to change the Active Subset setting to (Entire Collection) or at least to some subset that includes the Win32 API help topics.

By looking at the Beep help topic, we can see that the function *Beep()* appears to be exactly what we want: a Windows API function that generates a beep through the sound card (assuming a sound card is available). Under Microsoft Windows NT, *Beep()* can even determine the frequency and duration of the beep. However, in the Remarks section of the *Beep()* help topic, we learn that the frequency and duration arguments are ignored under Microsoft Windows 95 and Microsoft Windows 98. It would be nice to be able to control the frequency and duration of the beep in all versions of Windows, but we'll have to live without these extra features in all systems but Windows NT.

The arguments to *Beep()* are all intrinsic data types, like integers, which are easier to handle than class objects. You'll see how to pass class objects in the next example.

NOTE   You'll notice that there are several options displayed when you enter the keyword *beep* in the help index. The options other than Beep are actually Microsoft Visual Basic and script functions that are merely providing access to the Windows API *Beep()* function. One distinction between help topic options is that Win32 API functions always begin with an initial capital letter, whereas Java methods and many C++ functions start with a lowercase letter (although Visual Basic statements and methods also begin with an initial capital letter).

Accessing *Beep()* through the J/Direct Call Builder

Using the Visual J++ Windows Application option, create an application called Beep. Now open the J/Direct Call Builder by choosing Other Windows from the View menu and selecting J/Direct Call Builder.

> **CAUTION** Don't confuse the J/Direct Call Builder Options command on the Tools menu with the J/Direct Call Builder command. The J/Direct Call Builder Options command enables you to specify the options for the code that the J/Direct Call Builder generates; it doesn't provide access to the J/Direct Call Builder.

Since the *Beep()* function takes two integers as arguments, and since it returns a simple *boolean* value, we aren't interested in the Win32 structures or Win32 constants. In the J/Direct Call Builder, clear the Structs and Constants check boxes to reduce the number of items you must search through. Scroll down until the function *Beep()* becomes visible. Figure 11-2 shows the J/Direct Call Builder window with the *Beep()* function selected.

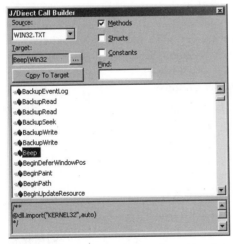

Figure 11-2. *The J/Direct Call Builder showing the Windows* Beep() *function.*

When you examine the window at the bottom of Figure 11-2, you can see the Javadoc-style comments that are the essence of J/Direct. The *dll.import()* directive indicates the name of the DLL that contains the selected function. This *dll.import()* directive indicates that *Beep()* resides in Kernel32.dll. As the name implies, Kernel32 is one of the core DLLs that Windows loads at startup and keeps resident at all times.

You can also see from Figure 11-2 that the Target edit window contains the name and path of the .java file J/Direct is about to create. The default is …\Win32.java. You can change this file name by entering a new .java file name or by selecting an existing .java file name by means of the browser. Since you probably don't particularly care about the name of the file, leave the default file name.

Now choose the Copy To Target button. Since the Win32.java file doesn't yet exist, a dialog box appears asking whether you want Visual J++ to create the file. Select Yes to create the following Win32.java file, which is automatically added to the project.

```
public class Win32
{
    /**
     * @dll.import("KERNEL32",auto)
     */
    public static native boolean Beep(int dwFreq, int dwDuration);
}
```

You can see that the J/Direct Call Builder has created a declaration for a *public static Beep()* function that matches the Win32 API *Beep()* function with respect to arguments and return type. Declaring the function *public* gives all calling methods access to it. The function is *static* because there is no object involved. Since the Win32 API is C-based, it's not object-oriented.

The only part of the declaration that is unique to Visual J++ is the *native* keyword. This keyword indicates that the *Beep()* function is written in machine code. (It was actually written in C, but the C code is compiled into machine code rather than into Java Virtual Machine byte code. How the function ended up being compiled into machine code is irrelevant to our discussion.) The methods that are declared *native* contain no code, because the code resides in the DLL.

You'll also notice the *dll.import()* directive described earlier, which tells Visual J++ where to find the *Beep()* function.

The Forms Designer work

The Forms Designer work for the Beep application is particularly simple. Open Form1.java in the Forms Designer. Shrink the form to make it only slightly larger than an average-sized button. Now change the form's *text* field to *J/Direct Beep Test* to match the purpose of the application.

Add a button to the middle of the form. Label the button *Beep*, and anchor it to the top, bottom, left, and right edges of the form. Finally, double-click the button to create the *button1_click()* event handler.

The code

The code for this application is as follows:

```
import com.ms.wfc.app.*;
import com.ms.wfc.core.*;
import com.ms.wfc.ui.*;
import com.ms.wfc.html.*;
```

```
/**
 * This method demonstrates the J/Direct Call Builder.
 */
public class Form1 extends Form
{
    public Form1()
    {
        // Required for Visual J++ Form Designer support
        initForm();
    }

    ⋮

    private void button1_click(Object source, Event e)
    {
        // invoke the Win32 Beep() function
        Win32.Beep(400, 1000);
    }

    /**
     * NOTE: The following code is required by the Visual J++ form
     * designer.  It can be modified using the form editor.  Do not
     * modify it using the code editor.
     */
    Container components = new Container();
    Button button1 = new Button();

    private void initForm()
    {
        // ...created by Forms Designer...
    }

    /**
     * The main entry point for the application.
     */
    public static void main(String args[])
    {
        Application.run(new Form1());
    }
}
```

The *button1_click()* method simply calls the *Beep()* method that was created by the J/Direct Call Builder. The *Win32.Beep()* syntax is consistent with the fact that *Beep()* is a static method of the class *Win32*. The arguments indicate a 400-Hz tone (equivalent to the middle C note, I believe) of 1-second duration.

The results

When the user chooses the Beep button, the computer generates a 1-second, 400-Hz tone under Windows NT, or a standard system beep under Windows 95 and Windows 98. (This is not very exciting, I admit, but it's what we asked for.)

As an aside, I'll mention that the Win32 *Beep()* function is already available in the WFC package *com.ms.win32*. This package organizes subpackages by DLL, so you would refer to *Beep()* as *com.ms.win32.Kernel32.Beep()*.

Passing Objects Using J/Direct: The SetSystemTime Application

The Beep application is impressive—to me, anyway—not in what it does, but because it demonstrates how easy it is to create an application that accesses the Win32 API. The Forms Designer did all the work in creating the form, and the J/Direct Call Builder, together with J/Direct, did the work of creating a bridge between Visual J++ and the C-based Win32 API.

The Beep application is simple for another reason: the arguments passed to and from the *Beep()* function are all intrinsic data types. The application passes two short integers to the function, and the function returns a *boolean* value. But what happens when the arguments being passed are class objects?

The SetSystemTime example demonstrates how to invoke object-passing Win32 functions by means of J/Direct. You'll see that accessing such functions with the J/Direct Call Builder is only slightly more difficult than accessing Win32 functions that pass intrinsic data types.

The problem

In the SetSystemTime application, we'll want to be able to read and modify the computer's clock. Imagine a small form with an edit box across the top, and a Get Time button and Set Time button at the bottom. The time the edit box displays should be in an easy-to-read format similar to the format generated by the *Time* class we discussed in Chapter 10.

Finding the right function

An index search of the MSDN Library Visual Studio 6 topics for the keyword settime reveals two possible candidates in the list: setTime and SetTime. Names that begin with lowercase letters—such as setTime—are generally methods of a class and are therefore not useful for our purposes.

> **NOTE** Since the Win32 API is a C interface, Win32 API functions are never methods of a class.

Very often, methods whose names begin with a lowercase letter are Java functions. Further examination of the *setTime()* method reveals that, in fact, *Date.setTime()*

and *Time.setTime()* are Java methods. The *SetTime()* function is more likely to be what we are looking for.

Selecting SetTime in the help topic list and choosing Display opens a dialog box that offers two topic options: CDateTimeCtrl::SetTime and COleDateTime::SetTime. Neither function looks right; however, I'm certain that the second function is incorrect. Any function with the word "Ole" embedded in it is an OLE function, and our application has nothing to do with OLE.

NOTE   The name in front of the double colon (::) is the name of the class in C++ and the name after the double colon is the name of the method. The Java equivalent to the double colon is the dot (.) after a Java class name.

The *CDateTimeCtrl* class in the first help topic option indicates that this *SetTime()* function is a method of a Microsoft Foundation Class library (MFC) class. MFC classes begin with a capital "C" followed by a capital letter. MFC classes are the C++ analog to WFC classes. The fact that this function is part of MFC doesn't sound very good, since we can't access MFC from the J/Direct Call Builder; however, it's still worth looking into, because some of the MFC functions are a thin shell over the corresponding Win32 API function.

Selecting the CDateTimeCtrl::SetTime help topic and choosing Display reveals the topic shown in Figure 11-3.

You can see in the right pane that MFC provides three different *CDateTime-Ctrl::SetTime()* methods. We can reject the first method immediately, because it refers to OLE. The second method, *SetTime(CTime*)*, is not a likely candidate either,

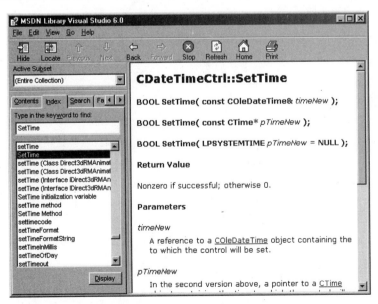

Figure 11-3. *The MSDN Library documentation for the available* SetTime() *methods.*

because *CTime* appears to be an MFC class. The third method, *SetTime(SYSTEMTIME*)*, is a definite possibility, because SYSTEMTIME is obviously not part of MFC—its name is all capitals letters and it doesn't start with "C". Choosing the SYSTEMTIME hot link reveals that SYSTEMTIME is a simple C structure. Things are looking up.

NOTE   The Win32 API uses C structures to pass information.

Now you can refer back to the J/Direct Call Builder window and enable the Methods and Structs options. A quick search of the J/Direct Call Builder options confirms the existence of a *SetSystemTime()* method and a SYSTEMTIME structure. Another quick check shows the *GetSystemTime()* method is also represented. Bingo!

The J/Direct Call Builder work

To begin writing SetSystemTime, create the Windows application SetSystemTime in the conventional manner. To create the J/Direct declarations for the *SetSystemTime()* function, follow the same steps you used in the previous example for creating the J/Direct declaration for *Beep()*: select SetSystemTime from the list of methods, and then choose Copy To Target. Repeat this process to create the J/Direct declaration for the *GetSystemTime()* function.

Neither of these functions is much use without the SYSTEMTIME structure. Fortunately, creating the J/Direct declaration for a class is the same process as creating a J/Direct declaration for a method: select SYSTEMTIME from the list of Structs, and choose Copy To Target.

The final Win32.java file is as follows:

```
public class Win32
{
    /**
     * Set the system time.
     *
     * @param lpSystemTime - a reference to object containing the time
     * @dll.import("KERNEL32",auto)
     */
    public static native boolean SetSystemTime(
                        com.ms.win32.SYSTEMTIME lpSystemTime);

    /**
     * Get the system time.
     *
     * @param lpSystemTIme - object to receive the system time
     * @dll.import("KERNEL32",auto)
     */
    public static native void GetSystemTime(
                        com.ms.win32.SYSTEMTIME lpSystemTime);
}
```

```
/**
 * The system time in Win32 API format.
 * @dll.struct()
 */
public static class SYSTEMTIME
{
    public short wYear;
    public short wMonth;
    public short wDayOfWeek;
    public short wDay;
    public short wHour;
    public short wMinute;
    public short wSecond;
    public short wMilliseconds;
}
```

The *SetSystemTime()* and *GetSystemTime()* definitions resemble the definition of the earlier *Beep()* function, except that they reference an object rather than an intrinsic. The J/Direct Call Builder also created a definition for the class *SYSTEMTIME*, which contains the members described in the MSDN Library for Visual Studio 6. The J/Direct *dll.struct()* directive indicates that the following class is the description of a C structure. I added the comments and *param* statements manually.

The Forms Designer work

The Forms Designer work for this application is similar to the work for other Windows applications you've seen. Change the *text* property of the form to *J/Direct Time Structure Test*.

Next add an Edit control to the upper half of the form. Enlarge the Edit control to make it long enough to hold the date and time in long format. (See Chapter 10 for an example of long format.) Delete the contents of the *text* field, and change the *name* property setting to *timeEdit*. Anchor the Edit control to the top, left, and right edges of the form.

Below the Edit control, add two buttons. Label the button on the left *Get Time*, and set its *name* property to *getTime*. Label the other button *Set Time*, and set its *name* property to *setTime*. Anchor the left button to the left and bottom edges of the form and anchor the right button to the right and bottom edges of the form. Finally, double-click each button to create its click event.

The code

The code for SetSystemTime is shown here:

```
import com.ms.wfc.app.*;
import com.ms.wfc.core.*;
import com.ms.wfc.ui.*;
import com.ms.wfc.html.*;
```

(continued)

```
/**
 * Demonstrate the use of J/Direct calls that pass objects
 * by accessing the GetSystemTime() and SetSystemTime()
 * functions of the Win32 API.
 */
public class Form1 extends Form
{
    // retain the SYSTEMTIME in a data member
    com.ms.win32.SYSTEMTIME time =
                        new com.ms.win32.SYSTEMTIME();
    public Form1()
    {
        // Required for Visual J++ Form Designer support
        initForm();

        // start with the current time
        getTime_click(null, null);
    }

    :

    private void getTime_click(Object source, Event e)
    {
        // get the UTC time using J/Direct
        Win32.GetSystemTime(time);

        // convert into a Time object
        Time t = new Time(time);

        // convert the Time object into local time
        Time lt = t.toLocalTime();

        // use the local Time object to generate a text format
        timeEdit.setText(lt.formatLongDate() +
                        " " +
                        lt.formatLongTime());
    }

    private void setTime_click(Object source, Event e)
    {
        try
        {
            // get the contents of the time field
            String s = timeEdit.getText();

            // now convert this into a Time object
            Time lt = new Time(s);
```

```
            // convert the Time object into a UTC time
            Time t = lt.toUniversalTime();

            // from there generate a SYSTEMTIME object
            time = t.toSystemTime();

            // now use the J/Direct call to set the system time
            Win32.SetSystemTime(time);
        }
        // in the event of an error...
        catch(Exception ex)
        {
            // restore the existing time
            getTime_click(null, null);
        }
    }


    /**
     * NOTE: The following code is required by the Visual J++ form
     * designer.  It can be modified using the form editor.  Do not
     * modify it using the code editor.
     */
    Container components = new Container();
    Edit timeEdit = new Edit();
    Button getTime = new Button();
    Button setTime = new Button();

    private void initForm()
    {
        // ...created by the Forms Designer...
    }


    /**
     * The main entry point for the application.
     */
    public static void main(String args[])
    {
        Application.run(new Form1());
    }
}
```

The *getTime_click()* method begins by reading the system time using the newly created *Win32.GetSystemTime()* native method. Fortunately, one of the constructors of the *Time* class accepts an object of class *SYSTEMTIME*. This will allow the program to use the substantial formatting capability of the *Time* class for output.

NOTE   Were there no way to create a *Time* object from the *SYSTEMTIME* class, the program would have to convert each field within *SYSTEMTIME* into a *String* for output. You'll get a taste of such a situation in the example of a user-defined DLL at the end of this chapter.

Since the time returned by *GetSystemTime()* is in Universal Time Coordinate (UTC)—previously known as Greenwich Mean Time (GMT)—it is necessary to convert the returned time to the local time zone by calling *Time.toLocalTime()*. The resulting time is then output to the *timeEdit* object using the *Time* class's *formatLongDate()* method and *formatLongTime()* method.

The *setTime_click()* method works almost in reverse of the *getTime_click()* method but has one additional behavior: the *Time(String)* constructor throws an exception if it can't parse the string that it receives into a valid time—for example, if the value in the month field is misspelled or if the value in the day field is greater than the number of days in the specified month. If the method throws an exception, the program catches the exception and restores the *timeEdit* value to the current time to indicate to the user that he or she entered an incorrect value.

NOTE   If the user enters in the edit box a long date that includes the day of the week, such as Tuesday, October 06, 1998, an exception will be thrown. The user must remove the day of the week for *SetTime()* to accept the date.

J/DIRECT REVEALED

As simple as the two previous applications might seem to the Java programmer, J/Direct performed several important and nontrivial tasks to make our Beep and SetSystemTime examples execute properly. Let's talk about the steps that J/Direct must perform to enable a call from a Visual J++ 6 program to a C function residing in a DLL.

DLL Loading

The most obvious problem that J/Direct solves is the otherwise difficult task of loading the necessary DLLs. A DLL is a library of routines that isn't necessarily resident in memory. A DLL is loaded into memory immediately before a program that needs it begins to run. The memory occupied by the DLL can be reclaimed by the operating system when the DLL is no longer referenced by any currently running application. (This might seem obvious to Windows programmers, but there was no equivalent to the DLL in operating systems developed prior to Windows.)

As explained previously, the Win32 API functions J/Direct accesses are located within Windows DLLs. J/Direct can also be instructed to access user-defined functions, as long as these functions reside within a DLL. In both cases, J/Direct can't assume that a target DLL is memory-resident. Therefore, before J/Direct can perform the conversion call from Visual J++ 6 to C or C++, it must make sure that the target DLL is memory-resident.

Thus, when the *button1_click()* method invokes *Win32.Beep()* in the previous Beep application, J/Direct checks whether KERNEL32.DLL is already memory-resident. (Remember that *Win32.Beep()* is part of KERNEL32.DLL.) If KERNEL32.DLL isn't in memory, J/Direct makes the system calls necessary to load it.

Marshaling

Once J/Direct has loaded the proper DLL into memory, and before J/Direct can call the C function from Visual J++ 6, J/Direct must convert any arguments to the function from the Java data type to the equivalent C or C++ data type. Once the call to the C or C++ function is complete, J/Direct must convert these arguments plus the return value back into Java data types. This process of converting data types from the calling language to the target language and back is called *marshaling*.

The following table shows the data type conversions J/Direct performs to marshal arguments from Java to C and back. The capitalized native data types are common Windows *#define* constants for intrinsic C types. (Calls to C++ functions work the same as calls to C functions, but calls to C++ methods aren't supported by J/Direct.)

CONVERSION OF DATA TYPES BETWEEN JAVA AND 32-BIT NATIVE FUNCTIONS

Java Data Type	*Native Function Data Type*	*Comments*
void	*void*	This is a return type only. However, J/Direct does handle functions that have no arguments.
byte	*BYTE* or *char*	
short	*short* or *WORD*	
int	*int, unsigned int, long, unsigned long, UINT, ULONG,* or *DWORD*	J/Direct maps signed and unsigned to the same type because Java doesn't support unsigned.
char	*unsigned short, TCHAR*	A C char value is normally 8 bits; a TCHAR corresponds to the Unicode style 16-bit char value.
long	*__int64*	*__int64* is a special Visual C++ 64-bit type.
float	*float*	
double	*double*	

(continued)

CONVERSION OF DATA TYPES BETWEEN JAVA AND 32-BIT NATIVE FUNCTIONS, *continued*

Java Data Type	Native Function Data Type	Comments
boolean	*int, BOOL*	C uses the rule that 0 is false and all else is true.
String	*const TCHAR*, LPCTSTR*	Not allowed by J/Direct as a return type.
StringBuffer	*TCHAR*, LPTSTR*	Not allowed by J/Direct as a return type. Set the *StringBuffer* capacity to hold the largest possible return value.
java[]	*C**	*java* is the Java intrinsic type, and *C* is the C intrinsic type; that is, int[] maps to DWORD*
Object	*struct**	J/Direct maps a pointer to a C structure to a reference to a static class; J/Direct can't handle the passing of structures by value.
com.ms.dll.Callback	function pointer	

To marshal an intrinsic type, such as a *char* to a *short*, J/Direct simply casts the argument from one type to the other. There are numerous problems with marshaling more complex objects, and these problems are outlined in the following sections.

Passing Pointers

Many C functions return a value to the caller by using pointers to intrinsic values as arguments. Let's call these types of pointers *intrinsic pointers* (in contrast to pointers to structure objects). For example, functions like the following aren't uncommon in C:

```
void divideInt(int numerator, int denominator,
            int* pResult, int* pRemainder)
{
    *pResult    = numerator / denominator;
    *pRemainder = numerator % denominator;
}
```

The function *divideInt()* accepts two simple integers and two pointers to integers. The results of dividing *numerator* by *denominator* are returned to the caller through the intrinsic pointers *pResult* and *pRemainder*. Java has no direct equivalent to the C intrinsic pointer—the nearest match is an array of length 1. If the *divideInt()* function were part of the MATH.DLL dynamic-link library, the following Java *isPrime()* function would call the *divideInt()* function, properly receiving the returned integer values in the arrays *result* and *remainder*:

```
class MyMath
{
    /** dll.import("MATH") */
    private static native void divideInt(int numerator,
                                         int denominator,
                                         int[] result,
                                         int[] remainder);

    public static boolean isPrime(int n, int d)
    {
        int[] result    = new int[1];
        int[] remainder = new int[1];

        // make the call
        divideInt(n, d, result, remainder);

        // prime if remainder is 0
        return remainder[0] == 0;
    }
}
```

Declaring the variables *result* and *remainder* to be arrays of length 1 signals J/Direct to pass these references as pointers and to allocate space for the integer returned. The value returned is always in array element zero.

Handling C Structures

A C structure presents J/Direct with a number of problems. The Java class doesn't correspond directly to the C structure. When a Visual J++ 6 method passes to a C function a reference to a class object, J/Direct must take the following steps:

1. It creates a C structure that has the same data members as the Visual J++ 6 class. (We'll talk more about this later.)

2. It assigns to each data member from the Java class the corresponding data member in the C structure.

3. It passes a pointer to the C structure.

4. It reverses the process on the way back from the native function to Visual J++ 6.

As simple as this sounds, several problems that we'll discuss in the following sections can arise during the creation and assignment steps.

Handling Strings

The *String* class is the most commonly used class in the Java library. Unfortunately, the Java *String* object is quite different from the C ASCIIZ string. The Java *String* class contains not only the string itself but a length data member. In addition, Java assigns no particular meaning to any given character. In contrast, the C string has no length. Instead, C strings use the character 0x0 to indicate the end of the string. When converting a Java string into a C ASCIIZ string, J/Direct must add a 0x0 character to the end of the character string data before passing it to the C function. (The application code must make sure that none of the characters in the string are 0x0.) Upon return, J/Direct counts the number of characters up to the 0x0 character and uses this as the length of the *String* object.

In addition, the Java *String* class always refers to Unicode characters. In contrast, C strings can be Unicode or ANSI characters.

> **WARNING**   The Win32 TCHAR is a 16-bit character type. J/Direct doesn't support the conversion of a *String* object to simple 8-bit *char** type C strings. For this conversion, the programmer should convert the *String* object into a byte array using the *String* method *getBytes()*, and then pass the byte array rather than the *String*.

Finally, the Win32 API defines different functions to handle ANSI TCHAR strings than to handle Unicode TCHAR strings. By default, J/Direct assumes the ANSI version. Thus, when Java calls the following method, J/Direct converts the *String* object into a null-terminated ANSI character array:

```
/** @dll.import("USER32") */
static native int MessageBox(int hwnd, String text,
                            String title, int sytle);
```

There are three different types of Win32 functions. Older Win32 functions carry a generic name such as *MessageBox()*. This generic function handles ANSI character arrays. More recent Win32 functions come in two forms. A function with a name like *MessageBoxA()* also processes an ANSI character array. A function like *MessageBoxW()* handles the equivalent task for Unicode character arrays.

The *dll.import()* directive by default accepts the ANSI version, so by default you can use *MessageBox()* or *MessageBoxA()*. The *dll.import()* directive also enables you to specify the *MessageBoxW()* Unicode API version by using the following code:

```
/** @dll.import("USER32", unicode) */
static native int MessageBox(int hwnd, String text,
                            String title, int sytle);
```

Unfortunately, neither the ANSI version nor the Unicode version is ideal for all Win32 platforms. ANSI mode is required by Windows 95 and Windows 98, which don't support Unicode, but it is inefficient for Windows NT, which defaults to Unicode. (Windows NT does grudgingly support ANSI mode.)

The *dll.import()* directive's *auto* modifier provides a way out of this ANSI vs. Unicode problem. The *auto* modifier directs J/Direct to use the optimum type of conversion for the current operating system, as shown in the following code:

```
/** dll.import("USER32", auto) */
public static native void MessageBox(int hwndOwner, String text,
                                     String title, int style);
```

For example, the following method *openMB(String text)* calls the method *MessageBox()* to display the specified text using the optimum method for the host version of Windows.

```
class ShowMessageBox
{
    public static void openMB(String text)
    {
        MessageBox(0, text, "Message", 0);
    }

    /** dll.import("USER32", auto) */
    private static native int MessageBox(int hnd, String text,
                                         String title, int style);
}
```

Since this character mode decision is made at run time, a Visual J++ 6 program written using the *auto* directive always invokes the most efficient Win32 API function for the current version of Windows.

Matching C Structure Details

The C programmer has more control over the layout of C structures than the Java programmer does. Fortunately for Java programmers, Visual J++ accounts for this situation with modifiers to the *dll.struct()* directive.

Packing

One consideration in laying out C structures is *packing*. Most CPUs can only access memory one word at a time, and different processors in the Intel series define "word" differently. Pentium processors and faster processors access memory on 4-byte (32-bit) boundaries. If an integer is located on an address that is a multiple of 4 bytes, the entire integer can be read in a single memory read. This is called an *aligned read*. If the integer is stored at an address that isn't a multiple of 4 bytes, the CPU must perform two reads and combine the necessary parts of these two words into one. This is called an *unaligned read*. Obviously, an unaligned read is slower than an aligned read.

To avoid this slowdown, the Microsoft Visual C++ compiler enables you to specify that integers be packed on 4-byte boundaries. To see the results of this decision, consider the structure definition on the following page.

```
struct X
{
    char a;
    int  b;
};
```

Suppose char *a,* which is 1 byte in length, is at address 100. You might think that int *b* would be at address 101, but this normally is not the case. By default, the Visual C++ compiler would put *b* at address 104, thereby ensuring word alignment and optimum access performance.

The down side of packing for performance is that it wastes space. Thus, Visual C++ enables you to change the packing size to decrease the memory storage requirements. This option might be important when a program contains a large number of structure objects that are accessed infrequently. In such a case, the memory concerns outweigh the performance degradation.

Java has no such control over the packing size. With Java, you must live with whatever the packing rules might be. At the same time, J/Direct must allow the Visual J++ 6 programmer to access a Visual C++ structure no matter how it is packed.

The *pack* modifier enables you to match J/Direct conversion to the packing of the structure in memory:

```
/** @dll.struct(pack = n) */
```

In this code, *n* is either 1, 2, 4, or 8, and the unit of *n* is byte. The default value of *pack* is 8, to match the *pack* pragma default in Visual C++. The default value of *pack* for structures within the Win32 API is also 8.

Fixed length arrays within a structure

A second problem in converting Java classes to C and C++ structures lies in the way Java and C create data members. It's possible in C to declare a fixed-length array within a structure, whereas in Java you declare a reference to an array. J/Direct handles this discrepancy with the *dll.structmap()* directive. Consider the following example, which demonstrates the use of *dll.structmap()*. The C structure is defined as follows:

```
structure Sample
{
    TCHAR array1[32];
    float array2[15];
};
```

You would use the *dll.struct()* directive with *dll.structmap()* to describe this structure to J/Direct:

```
// example class name
class Win32
{
    /** dll.struct() */
```

```
class Sample
{
    /** @dll.structmap([type=TCHAR[32]]) */
    String array1;

    /** @dll.structmap([type=FIXEDARRAY, size=15]) */
    float[] array2;
};
}
```

The data member *array1* is declared as a 32-character *String,* while *array2* is declared as a fixed array containing 15 elements of *float* data type.

Accessing Win32 Error Codes

Most Win32 API functions return error codes as an integer value, with 0 indicating that no error occurred. Some Win32 API functions signal an error by returning a value of *false*—indicating the operation failed—and storing the integer code into a global variable called *errno* to indicate the specific error that occurred. (This is particularly true of the older functions that make up the C function library.)

When calling functions that use *errno,* you should not attempt to access the global error indicator directly. After the error has occurred, J/Direct might make further Win32 calls that could write over the error indicator in *errno* before returning control to your Visual J++ 6 method.

The *dll.import()* directive modifier *setLastError* instructs J/Direct to capture the error code immediately after it invokes the Win32 API call. When using the *setLastError* modifier, the static method *com.ms.dll.DllLib.getLastWin32Error()* returns the error code.

The *setLastError* modifier

The following code is a short example of how to use the *setLastError* modifier.

```
class Win32
{
    /** @dll.struct() */
    class WIN32_FIND_DATA
    {
        ...define the structure here...
    }

    /** @dll.import("KERNEL32", setLastError) */
    static native boolean FindNextFile(int hFindFile,
                                       Win32.WIN32_FIND_DATA wfd);
}
```

(continued)

```
class MyCode
{
   // declare the WIN32_FIND_DATA structure
   Win32.WIN32_FIND_DATA wfd = new Win32.WIN32_FIND_DATA();

   // keep the error code
   int errCode;

   /**
    * Find the next file by using a Win32 API call; set error code.
    */
   boolean findNextFile(int hFindFile)
   {
       // assume no error
       errCode = 0;

       // invoke the method
       boolean f = Win32.FindNextFile(hFindFile, wfd);

       // if it didn't work...
       if (f == false)
       {
           // capture the error code from Win32 call
           errCode = com.ms.dll.DllLib.getLastWin32Error();
       }
       return f;
   }
}
```

In this example, the class *WIN32_FIND_DATA* was either created by the J/Direct Call Builder or carefully constructed by hand to match the WIN32_FIND_DATA structure declared in the windows.h include file. The structure's contents aren't listed here. The Win32 API function *FindNextFile()* is declared to accept the integer variable *hFindFile* (the variable's meaning and purpose are irrelevant for this example) and a *WIN32_FIND_DATA* object. In addition, the function declaration instructs J/Direct to capture any error that might occur while calling the API function.

The class *MyCode* contains a method, *findNextFile()*, which invokes the Win32 API call *FindNextFile()* using the *WIN32_FIND_DATA* object *wfd*. If *findNextFile()* returns *false* indicating that an error occurred in the C function *FindNextFile()*, the method *findNextFile()* captures the error code by calling *com.ms.dll.DllLib.getLastWin32Error()*.

> **NOTE**   Don't capture the Win32 API error code if the value returned indicates that the function worked properly. Many API calls do not set the error code unless something goes wrong.

Garbage Collection

There are several other problems that J/Direct must overcome when calling a C function from Visual J++ 6 and that are unrelated to class and struct issues. One problem is Java's garbage collector.

The garbage collector is a background process that returns unused objects to the pool of unused memory. This pool is called the *heap* in both the Java and C++ languages.

To make more efficient use of the heap, Java moves objects around in memory during the garbage collection process. When an object is moved in memory, the garbage collector updates the references to the object accordingly. This makes the change in an object's memory address invisible to other Java classes.

C has no concept that corresponds with garbage collection. You are expected to direct your program to return objects once they are no longer in use. In addition, C expects its objects to stay put in memory. C would consider moving objects about in memory to be decidedly unfriendly.

J/Direct solves this problem by storing interface objects in a special section of the heap where objects aren't repacked by the garbage collector.

Name Mangling

Another concern in accessing C or C++ functions is that the name of a C or C++ function is different in the source file than it is in the object file. C simply adds an underscore to the name of the function when it puts the function in the object file. Thus, *myFunction(int)* in the source file becomes *_myFunction* in the object file. In the case of C++, the differences in function names are more severe. Thus, *myFunction(int)* might become *myFunction$i*. The suffix *$i* in the C++ function name indicates the number and the types of the function arguments.

This process of changing function names is called *name mangling*. Fortunately, J/Direct understands the way C and C++ mangle names and takes care of tracking function names for you.

Aliasing

Aliasing enables you to assign Java-like names to Win32 API functions. You or the creators of the language might have established naming conventions for the names of methods. For example, by convention Java method names begin with a small letter, and Java class names begin with a capital letter. The names of Win32 API functions begin with a capital letter.

You can change the name of the C function you are calling to a name more to your liking by creating an alias, as shown in the code on the following page.

```
/** dll.import("USER32", auto, entrypoint="MessageBox") */
public static native int messageBox(int hnd, String text,
                                        String title, int style);
```

Handling Callbacks

It's not uncommon for C functions to make use of what is known as a *callback function*. This concept is explained in the following section.

Declaring callbacks in C

Consider the following C example of a generic sort routine. (This example shows neither the struct MO nor the *#define LENGTH*.)

```
// the order function can put an array of MO objects in any order
// as long as you can provide a pointer to a function that compares
// the objects. This pointer to a function is often called a
// callback.
void order(int (*pCompare)(MO* p1, MO* p2), MO* pArray, int length);

// compareMO - compare two MO objects
int compareMO(MO* p1, MO* p2)
{
    ⋮
}


void myProg()
{
    struct mo[LENGTH];
    ⋮
    // order the array of MO objects
    order(compareMO, mo, LENGTH);
}
```

In this code, the *order()* function sorts an array of *MO* objects using the *compareMO()* function to establish the sequencing of objects.

To be more specific, the first argument to *order()* is a function that takes two pointers to *MO* objects and returns an *int* value that indicates whether or not *p1* comes before *p2* in the sorted list.

When calling *order()*, the *myProg()* function provides a pointer to the function *compareMO()*, whose declaration matches exactly the declaration of the pointer required by *order()*. Somewhere within its logic, the *order()* function will invoke this programmer-provided *compareMO()* function indirectly through the function pointer provided.

NOTE   The C callback is similar in concept to the Visual J++ 6 delegate. A delegate is the Visual J++ 6 analog to a function pointer. The delegate is associated with a method before it is passed to an *addX()* method such as *addOnClick()*. When the *onClick()* event occurs, Visual J++ 6 invokes the delegate method.

The term callback comes from the fact that the *order()* function calls back to the *compare()* function.

NOTE There are many other uses for callback functions, but they all involve passing a pointer to a function to another function.

Handling callbacks in J/Direct

The following example demonstrates how to declare a function in Visual J++ 6 that accepts a callback function:

```
// some application programmer defined class
class MyDLL
{
    /** @dll.struct() */
    static class MO
    {
        int value;
    }

    /** @dll.import("MyDLL") */
    static native void order(com.ms.dll.Callback compare,
                             MO[] objs, int length);
}
```

In this example, *compare* is a callback method that is being passed to the C function *order()*.

The callback function must be a nonstatic method named *callback()*. It must be a method of a class that extends the class *Callback*. The arguments to the method *callback()* must match those required by the calling function—in this case, *order()*:

```
class MyCallbackClass extends com.ms.dll.Callback
{
    int callback(MyDLL.MO mo1, MyDLL.MO mo2)
    {
        // ...whatever comparison...
    }
}
```

A Visual J++ program would invoke the *order()* function as follows:

```
MyDLL.order(new MyCallbackClass(), MyDLL.MO, MyDLL.MO.length);
```

In this case you, the Visual J++ 6 programmer, have passed an object of class *MyCallbackClass* to J/Direct. J/Direct constructs a callback function which it passes on to the C function *order()*. When *order()* calls the provided callback function, J/Direct passes the call on to *MyCallbackClass.callback()*.

Callback example

The following example shows a class *MyFunc*, whose constructor declares an array of *MyDLL.MO* objects. The constructor then sorts the objects using the native method *order()* by means of a Java callback function:

```
class MyFunc extends com.ms.dll.Callback
{
    // declare an array of MO objects
    MyDLL.MO[] mo = new MyDLL.MO[]
                        {
                            new MyDLL.MO(),
                            new MyDLL.MO(),
                            new MyDLL.MO()
                        };

    /**
     * Sort the MO objects using the native order function.
     */
    public MyFunc()
    {
        // sort the array mo using the method callback()
        // to perform the comparisons (this is legal since
        // the current class extends Callback)
        MyDLL.order(this, mo, mo.length);
    }

    /**
     * Provide the callback function that performs the comparison.
     * (This function must match exactly the requirements of
     * the callback function as defined by order().)
     */
    int callback(MyDLL.MO mo1, MyDLL.MO mo2)
    {
        if (mo1.value > mo2.value)
        {
            return 1;
        }
        if (mo1.value < mo2.value)
        {
            return -1;
        }
        return 0;
    }
}
```

ACCESSING YOUR OWN DLLS

Up to this point, our J/Direct examples have accessed only functions from the Win32 API. It is also possible to access DLLs of your own making. In this section, we'll build a DLL in C and then access this DLL from Visual J++.

> **NOTE** You'll need Visual C++ in order to create the C DLL in this example. Although the steps provided are specific to Visual C++ 6, you can use earlier versions of Visual C++ to create this DLL (keeping in mind the options might differ slightly). If you don't have Visual C++, you can use the CPP_DLL.dll file from the Windows Applications\CPP_DLL subdirectory on the companion CD to perform the rest of the example.

The Problem

In this section, we'll solve a problem by using a user-defined DLL. Although this problem could easily be handled in Java alone, it's a good vehicle for learning about user-defined DLLs. We'll create a Visual J++ 6 application that displays a form with a button and an edit box. When the user chooses the button, the application causes the computer to beep and then displays in the output edit box the hours, minutes, and seconds in UTC.

What makes this application instructive is that both the function that sends a beep to the speaker and the function that retrieves the current system time will be contained in a user-defined DLL.

The CPP_DLL Dynamic-Link Library

Before we can access a user-defined DLL from Visual J++ 6, we must build our own DLL. In this section, we'll build the DLL named CPP_DLL.

The Forms Designer work

To create a DLL in Visual C++, choose New from the File menu and then select the Win32 Dynamic-Link Library option from the New dialog box. Do not select the MFC AppWizard (dll) option—this will create a DLL that incorporates MFC.

Enter CPP_DLL as the Project Name, and choose OK. Select An Empty DLL Project from the AppWizard window that appears, and choose Finish. This will create a project with the proper options set but won't create any source files. Choose New from the File menu again. This time, select the Files tab and select Text File. Make sure the Add To Project check box is checked, and insert the file name CPP_DLL.c. Choose OK. Visual C++ 6 will add the CPP_DLL.c file to the project. (Under earlier versions of Visual C++, you had to add the file manually.)

The code

Open the CPP_DLL.c file and enter the following:

```
// CPP_DLL - user-defined DLL

// windows.h contains the prototype declarations for the Win32
// API functions including Beep() and GetSystemTime()
#include <windows.h>

// the following prototype declaration declares beepSpeaker
// to be an entry point for the DLL
__declspec(dllexport) void beepSpeaker(int freq, int duration);

// the following structure and prototype declares
// a function that returns the time of day in Universal
// Time Coordinate
struct UTCTime
{
    WORD hour;
    WORD minute;
    WORD second;
};
__declspec(dllexport) void getUTCTime(struct UTCTime*);

// beepSpeaker - invoke the Beep() Win32 API function
void beepSpeaker(int freq, int duration)
{
    Beep(freq, duration);
}


// getUTCTime - use the GetSystemTime Win32 API function
//              to fetch the current UTC time of day
//              and return it in the argument provided
void getUTCTime(struct UTCTime* pUTCTime)
{
    // get the SYSTEMTIME using the Win32 API call
    SYSTEMTIME systemTime;
    GetSystemTime(&systemTime);

    // now get the time of day from the SYSTEMTIME
    // structure and save it in the UTCTime structure
    // passed to the function
    pUTCTime->hour   = systemTime.wHour;
    pUTCTime->minute = systemTime.wMinute;
    pUTCTime->second = systemTime.wSecond;
}
```

CPP_DLL.c begins by including windows.h. This gives CPP_DLL.c access to the Win32 API calls.

NOTE The C *#include* directive is roughly equivalent to the Java *import* directive.

A prototype declaration for *beepSpeaker()* follows the *#include* directive. This declaration specifies the arguments *freq* and *duration* to be of type integer. The *__declspec(dllexport)* part of the declaration exports the *beepSpeaker()* method. Exporting the method makes it accessible from outside the DLL (similar to the Java *public* directive).

The second method, *getUTCTime()*, communicates with the calling function by means of a locally defined structure called *UTCTime*. This method is also exported by means of a *__declspec(dllexport)* modifier.

The code for the *beepSpeaker()* method is trivial; it calls the Win32 API *Beep()* method and passes the two arguments *freq* and *duration*. (The fact that *beepSpeaker()* calls a Win32 API is irrelevant. The point is that *beepSpeaker()* is a user-defined method.)

The code for *getUTCTime()* is only slightly more complicated. It begins by reading the system time by means of *GetSystemTime()*. It then populates the locally defined *UTCTime* structure with the hour, minute, and second fields of the returned system time.

The result

Choose Set Active Configuration from the Build menu and choose the option CPP_DLL - Win32 Release. Now select Build CPP_DLL.dll from the Build menu. Building this project file generates a Release subdirectory containing a DLL with the name CPP_DLL.dll. Once you have built the DLL, close Visual C++.

CAUTION It's important that this file be compiled as a C program and not as a CPP program. (The name of the DLL reflects the fact that it originated from the Visual C++ module of Visual Studio.) The default option is for all .C files to be compiled as C programs. If you have changed that option, you'll need to set it back for this test.

The CustomDLL Application

Now that we have a DLL to access, let's create an application named CustomDLL to access it.

The Forms Designer work

First, create a Visual J++ Windows application named CustomDLL. Open the Form1.java file in the Forms Designer. Resize the form to hold a single button below a standard-sized Edit control. Set the form's *text* property to *CustomDLL Application* to change the program's name in the form's title bar.

Add an Edit control to the form. Set its name to *timeEdit*. Use the property window to clear the control's *text* property so that *timeEdit* initially appears blank.

Now add a Button control immediately below the Edit control, and label it *Get UTC Time*. Anchor the Edit control to the top, left, and right edges of the form, and anchor the Button control to the bottom, left, and right edges of the form.

Double-click the Button control to create its click event handler.

> **NOTE**   Now is a good time to copy the CPP_DLL.dll file into your CustomDLL directory. Alternatively, you can copy the DLL into the Windows\System directory. You must do this before you can execute the application; otherwise, CustomDLL won't be able to find CPP_DLL.dll.

The MyDLL code

First we'll need to add a *MyDll* class to provide the interface to the C functions included in the CPP_DLL dynamic-link library.

Choose Add Item from the Project menu. Now select Class and give it the name MyDLL. This will create the file MyDLL.java and add it to the project. Update the blank Java file as follows:

```
/**
 * Define access methods for CPP_DLL.dll.
 */
public class MyDLL
{
    /**
     * The beepSpeaker() method beeps the speaker.
     * @dll.import("CPP_DLL")
     */
    public static native void beepSpeaker(int freq, int duration);

    /**
     * The UTC time structure.
     * @dll.struct()
     */
    public static class UTCTime
    {
        public short hour;
        public short minute;
        public short second;
    }

    /**
     * The getUTCTime() method retrieves the UTC time of day.
     * @dll.import("CPP_DLL")
     */
    public static native void getUTCTime(UTCTime utcTime);
}
```

The class *MyDLL* defines two static native functions. Both follow the pattern for J/Direct declarations we have seen earlier.

The first *dll.import()* directive declares *beepSpeaker()* to be a member of the CPP_DLL dynamic-link library. Following this is the prototype declaration for the *beepSpeaker()* function. It's important that the declaration match the C declaration in CPP_DLL.c exactly.

The *dll.struct()* directive defines a relatively straightforward C structure called *UTCTime*. The declaration for *getUTCTime()* declares the function's argument to be a reference to *UTCTime*.

> **NOTE** Compare the Visual J++ 6 prototype declaration *static void getUTC-Time(UTCTime utcTime)* to the C declaration *void getUTCTime(struct UTCTime* pUTCTime)*. J/Direct can't pass a structure to a C function by value.

The Form1.java code

The Form1.java code is straightforward.

```
import com.ms.wfc.app.*;
import com.ms.wfc.core.*;
import com.ms.wfc.ui.*;
import com.ms.wfc.html.*;

/**
 * Demonstrate the use of the user-defined DLL.
 */
public class Form1 extends Form
{
    public Form1()
    {
        // Required for Visual J++ Form Designer support
        initForm();
    }

    /**
     * Make sure that the time string is 2 digits.
     */
    String padTime(String time)
    {
        // if time is already 2 digits...
        if (time.length() == 2)
        {
            // just return it; otherwise...
            return time;
        }

        // tack a 0 onto the front
        return "0" + time;
    }
```

(continued)

```
private void button1_click(Object source, Event e)
{
    // get the time of day
    MyDLL.UTCTime time = new MyDLL.UTCTime();
    MyDLL.getUTCTime(time);

    // now display it, making sure each
    // field is 2 digits wide
    String hour = Integer.toString(time.hour);
    hour = padTime(hour);

    String minute = Integer.toString(time.minute);
    minute = padTime(minute);

    String second = Integer.toString(time.second);
    second = padTime(second);

    // display the result in the Edit control
    timeEdit.setText("UTC time:" +
                    hour   + ":" +
                    minute + ":" +
                    second);

    // now send a beep to the speaker
    MyDLL.beepSpeaker(400, 1000);
}


/**
 * NOTE: The following code is required by the Visual J++ form
 * designer.  It can be modified using the form editor.  Do not
 * modify it using the code editor.
 */
Container components = new Container();
Edit timeEdit = new Edit();
Button button1 = new Button();

private void initForm()
{
    // ...created by the Forms Designer...
}


/**
 * The main entry point for the application.
 */
public static void main(String args[])
{
    Application.run(new Form1());
}
}
```

The *button1_click()* method begins by creating an object *time* of class *MyDLL.UTCTime*. The method then invokes *getUTCTime()* to populate the *time* object with the current UTC time.

Each of the data members of *time* is converted into a string and then passed to *padTime()*, to make sure that the value in each field is two characters long. (In other words, "1" should be displayed as "01".) Once all the data members have been converted into two-character strings, the strings are concatenated with a colon in between. The result is displayed in the *timeEdit* object using *Edit.setText()*. Before returning, *button1_click()* calls *MyDLL.beepSpeaker()* to send a beep to the speaker.

Results

The results of executing CustomDLL are shown in Figure 11-4.

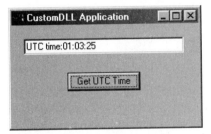

Figure 11-4. *The UTC time of day displayed by CustomDLL.*

It's interesting to see which system DLLs are loaded when CustomDLL executes. Choose About from the Visual J++ Help menu. Now choose System Info to bring up the Microsoft System Information window. Under the Software Environment folder, select 32-bit Modules Loaded. This window enables you to look at a list of the DLLs that are currently in memory. After scrolling through a long list of names, you'll come upon our own CPP_DLL as shown in Figure 11-5.

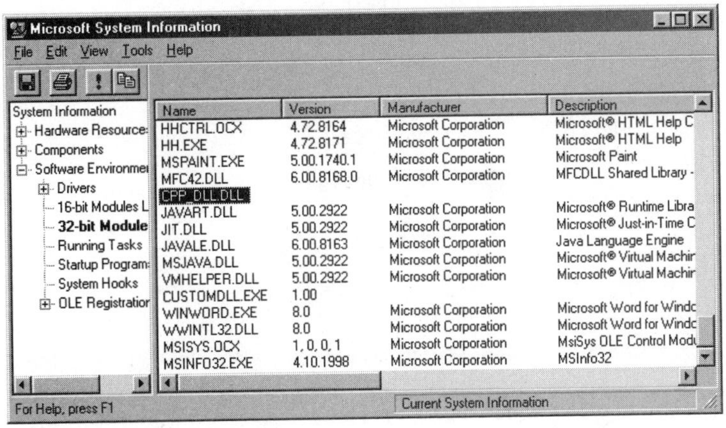

Figure 11-5. *The System Information display showing our CPP_DLL among the list of 32-bit DLLs currently loaded.*

Now exit CustomDLL. Scroll through the 32-bit Modules Loaded list again and you'll notice that the CPP_DLL dynamic-link library is gone.

An aside

You might be tempted to think that the CustomDLL program is no different than the earlier applications that invoked the Win32 API functions directly. From the calling program's standpoint, it isn't. After all, the user-defined DLL doesn't do anything more than call the necessary Win32 API. However, the CPP_DLL.dll functions could have done a lot more than simply call a single Win32 API. By following the pattern demonstrated in CustomDLL, you can create your own dynamic link libraries to do anything you like.

USING J/DIRECT TO IMPLEMENT IDLE EVENT PROCESSING

You can use J/Direct to implement an efficient idle event handler. All Windows events pass through a message queue in the form of Windows messages. When the message queue is empty, Visual J++ 6 calls the idle event handler to perform whatever background processing the application requires. During the time that the event handler is running, the application can't read a message from the message queue, which makes the application unresponsive to user input. Therefore, it is important that most idle event handlers execute for only a short time before giving up control.

However, if the idle event handler could peek into the message queue, it could retain control as long as no message were waiting in the queue to be processed. As soon as the event handler detected a message, it could give up control to allow the system to pick up the message and process it. Once all messages had been processed, Visual J++ 6 would pass control back to the event handler.

In fact, the Win32 API function *PeekMessage()* enables a calling function to check whether the Windows message queue is empty. J/Direct gives us access to this *PeekMessage()* function.

> NOTE   Here is a case where no Visual J++ 6 library method exists that is the equivalent to the Win32 API function.

The Problem

Let's create a new prime number generator to demonstrate the *PeekMessage()* API background processing method. We'll call this version IdleEvent2. This application will have an edit box to display prime numbers as it calculates them. In addition, there will be Start and Stop buttons to turn background processing on and off. Finally, to demonstrate that the application's performance is not affected by the idle processing, we'll outfit the IdleEvent2 application with a simple drawing function.

OUR PREVIOUS SOLUTION

Back in Chapter 10, we created an application called IdleEvent1 that uses the idle event to perform background processing. That application performs idle-time processing for a certain length of time, and then gives up control to allow other events to be processed. If the time the idle event handler method spends executing is not kept short, the application execution becomes jerky.

The problem with that application is that as soon as the event handler returns WFC assumes that the application is done. Thus, IdleEvent1 has to generate some event for the program to process to prod WFC into calling the idle event handler again. IdleEvent1 sets a WFC timer to send a timer event every 100 milliseconds. I remarked at the time this example was discussed that there had to be a better way. The *PeekMessage()* Win32 API method is that better way.

The Forms Designer Work

Choose New Project from the Visual J++ 6 File menu, and create a new Windows application. Name the new project IdleEvent2. Use the Project Explorer to examine the new project.

Open Form1.java in the Forms Designer. Create the same form display that we created in the IdleEvent1 application in Chapter 10. You can see the final display in Figure 11-6 on page 390. The idle process will output prime numbers in the edit box at the top of the form while the user draws in the panel at the bottom.

The Code for Form1

The following code represents the Form1.java code.

```java
import com.ms.wfc.app.*;
import com.ms.wfc.core.*;
import com.ms.wfc.ui.*;
import com.ms.wfc.html.*;

import com.ms.wfc.util.*;

/**
 * This class demonstrates the use of idle processing using
 * the idle process.
 */
public class Form1 extends Form implements IdleParent
{
    // define holder for the idle process handler
    IdleProcess idle;
```

(continued)

```java
public Form1()
{
    // Required for Visual J++ Form Designer support
    initForm();

    // create an idle process
    idle = new IdleProcess(this, this);
}


/**
 * Set the current prime in the current application.
 */
public void setPrime(int numberOfPrimes,
                     long prime)
{
    outputEdit.setText(toString(numberOfPrimes) +
                       "-" +
                       toString(prime));
}


/**
 * Convert a number into a string with commas.
 */
private String toString(long value)
{
    // convert the long into a string
    String s = Long.toString(value);

    // now add commas to that string
    StringBuffer sb = new StringBuffer(20);
    int offset = 0;
    for(int length = s.length();
        length > 0;
        length--)
    {
        // every 3 digits from the right side...
        if ((length % 3) == 0)
        {
            // but not at the beginning...
            if (offset != 0)
            {
                // put a comma
                sb.append(',');
            }
        }

        // now add another digit
        sb.append(s.charAt(offset++));
    }
```

```
        return sb.toString();
}

/**
 * Form1 overrides dispose so it can clean up the
 * component list.
 */
public void dispose()
{
    super.dispose();
}

/**
 * Turn idle processing on.
 */
private void button1_click(Object source, Event e)
{
    idle.setActive(true);
}

/**
 * Turn idle processing off.
 */
private void button2_click(Object source, Event e)
{
    idle.setActive(false);
}

/**
 * Allow the user to draw within the paint panel while
 * the background onIdle processor continues to operate.
 */
List squiggles = new List();
List squiggle  = null;
private void paintPanel_mouseDown(Object source, MouseEvent e)
{
    // if the right mouse button is clicked...
    if ((e.button & MouseButton.RIGHT) != 0)
    {
        // clear the list of squiggles and trash
        // the current squiggle
        squiggles.setSize(0);
        squiggle = null;

        // now repaint the blank screen
        paintPanel.invalidate();
    }
```

(continued)

```
        // if the left mouse button...
        if ((e.button & MouseButton.LEFT) != 0)
        {
            // create a new squiggle
            if (squiggle == null)
            {
                squiggle = new List();
            }
        }
    }

    /**
     * As the mouse moves along with the left button held down,
     * add each reported point to the current squiggle.
     */
    private void paintPanel_mouseMove(Object source, MouseEvent e)
    {
        if ((e.button & MouseButton.LEFT) != 0)
        {
            squiggle.addItem(new Point(e.x, e.y));
            paintPanel.invalidate();
        }
    }

    /**
     * When the user releases the mouse button, save
     * the current squiggle in the list of squiggles.
     */
    private void paintPanel_mouseUp(Object source, MouseEvent e)
    {
        // if there is a current squiggle...
        if (squiggle != null)
        {
            // add it to the squiggle list and
            // start the current squiggle over
            squiggles.addItem(squiggle);
            squiggle = null;
        }
    }

    /**
     * Paint the squiggles the user has created so far.
     */
    private void paintPanel_paint(Object source, PaintEvent e)
    {
        Graphics g = e.graphics;
```

```
        // draw the current squiggle
        if (squiggle != null)
        {
            drawSquiggle(g, squiggle);
        }

        // iterate through previously saved squiggles,
        // drawing each one
        IEnumerator iter = squiggles.getItemEnumerator();
        while (iter.hasMoreItems())
        {
            List list = (List)iter.nextItem();
            drawSquiggle(g, list);
        }
    }

    /**
     * Draw a squiggle. A squiggle is a list of point segments.
     */
    private static void drawSquiggle(Graphics g, List squiggle)
    {
        try
        {
            // get the list of all squiggles
            Object[] list = squiggle.getAllItems();
            int length = list.length;

            // draw from each point to the next
            Point previous = (Point)list[0];
            for (int i = 1; i < length; i++)
            {
                Point current = (Point)list[i];
                g.drawLine(previous, current);
                previous = current;
            }
        }
        catch(Exception e)
        {
        }
    }

    /**
     * NOTE: The following code is required by the Visual J++ form
     * designer.  It can be modified using the form editor.  Do not
     * modify it using the code editor.
     */
    Container components = new Container();
```

(continued)

```
Edit outputEdit = new Edit();
Label label1 = new Label();
Button button1 = new Button();
Button button2 = new Button();
Panel paintPanel = new Panel();

private void initForm()
{
    // ...generated by Forms Designer...
}

/**
 * The main entry point for the application.
 */
public static void main(String args[])
{
    Application.run(new Form1());
}
}
```

The majority of this code is dedicated to user drawing. The *mouseDown* event handler is the *paintPanel_mouseDown()* method. When the right mouse button is clicked while the mouse pointer is in the drawing panel, *paintPanel_mouseDown()* clears the drawing panel. When the left mouse button is clicked, *paintPanel_mouse-Down()* creates a squiggle object that will contain a list of mouse locations. The *mouseMove* event handler continues to add mouse locations to the current *squiggle* object as long as the left mouse button is held down. The *mouseUp* event handler terminates the squiggle, and adds the *squiggle* object to a container of *squiggle* objects. The *paintPanel_paint()* method draws the squiggles one at a time, by drawing a line between each consecutive point in a squiggle.

The *Form1()* constructor creates an object of the user-defined class *IdleProcess*, which we'll look at in a moment. This object represents the background processing element. In addition, the *Form1* class contains a *setPrime()* method that displays the prime number data in the *outputEdit* object. The *setPrime()* method is required because *Form1* implements the *IdleParent* interface.

The *IdleParent* interface is defined as follows:

```
public interface IdleParent
{
    // the following method is called
    // to report a change in the current
    // prime number
    public void setPrime(int numberOfPrimes,
                         long prime);
}
```

A class that implements the *IdleParent* interface accepts a prime number along with the number of primes detected to date via the *setPrime()* method.

The Code for the J/Direct Interface

Before we can write the *IdleProcess* background process, we'll need access to the *PeekMessage()* Win32 API function.

Open the J/Direct Call Builder (choose Other Windows from the View menu). Clear the Structs and Constants check boxes, leaving only the Methods check box selected. Scroll down through the list of API functions. Select PeekMessage and choose Copy To Target.

The J/Direct Call Builder creates the Win32.java file. Edit the file to look like the following code:

```
public class Win32
{
    /**
     * Peek into the message queue to see if there's anything to do.
     * @dll.import("USER32",auto)
     */
    public static native boolean PeekMessage(com.ms.win32.MSG lpMsg,
                                             int hWnd,
                                             int wMsgFilterMin,
                                             int wMsgFilterMax,
                                             int wRemoveMsg);
    public static final int PM_NOREMOVE = 0x0000;
    public static final int PM_NOYIELD = 0x0002;
}
```

The *PeekMessage()* function takes a number of arguments. The first argument is the message that's at the top of the event queue. IdleEvent2 doesn't care what that message is; all it cares about is whether there is one. The *hWnd* argument is the window handle for the main form. (We haven't discussed window handles so far, and we won't now. Suffice it to say that the *Form* class provides a *getHandle()* method to retrieve the form's window handle.) The min filter and max filter arguments enable the program to look for a particular message or range of messages. Setting both to 0 indicates that the program is interested in all messages. The last flag indicates whether the message should be removed from the queue. (For this program it shouldn't, so the flag will pass *PM_NOREMOVE*).

The Code for the *IdleProcess* Class

We can now create the background process class, which we'll call *IdleProcess*. Choose Add Item from the Project menu. From the list of available items, select Class. Enter the name *IdleProcess,* and choose Open.

Update the *IdleProcess* class to implement the *onIdle* background processing so the code looks as follows:

```
import com.ms.wfc.app.*;
import com.ms.wfc.core.*;
import com.ms.wfc.ui.*;

/**
 * Implement processing in the background by attaching
 * to the idle event.
 */
public class IdleProcess
{
    // parent object
    IdleParent parent;

    // variable necessary to use the PeekMessage call:
    // window handle of the parent form
    int hWnd;
    // a dummy message
    com.ms.win32.MSG dummyMsg = new com.ms.win32.MSG();

    // idle event handler
    EventHandler idleHandler;

    // note whether idle loop is active or not
    boolean active = false;

    // number of primes found and the last
    // candidate for 'primehood'
    int     numberOfPrimes = 0;
    int     lastCandidate  = 0;
    int     lastPrime      = 0;

    /**
     * Create an idle process that reports back
     * to the parent through the IdleParent interface.
     */
    public IdleProcess(IdleParent parent, Form form)
    {
        // save the parent
        this.parent = parent;

        // assign an onIdle event handler
        Application.addOnIdle(new EventHandler(this.onIdle));

        // save the window handle of the parent form
        hWnd = form.getHandle();
    }
```

```java
/**
 * Turn the idle process on and off.
 */
public void setActive(boolean active)
{
    this.active = active;
}


/**
 * Invoked when the system is idle.
 */
private void onIdle(Object sender, Event e)
{
    // if we're active...
    if (active)
    {
        // work until the system has something to do
        while(!Win32.PeekMessage(dummyMsg,
                    hWnd, 0, 0,
                    Win32.PM_NOREMOVE | Win32.PM_NOYIELD))
        {
            // try the next number
            if (isPrime(++lastCandidate))
            {
                // it's prime, so count it
                numberOfPrimes++;
                lastPrime = lastCandidate;

                // report the results back to parent
                parent.setPrime(numberOfPrimes,
                            lastPrime);
            }
        }
    }
}

/**
 * Test next number for prime.
 */
private boolean isPrime(long number)
{
    // ...same as in earlier prime number processes...
}
}
```

We've added two data members to the *IdleProcess* class in IdleEvent2 that were not in IdleEvent1: *hWnd*, which holds the form's window handle, and *dummyMsg*, which will receive the message from the *PeekMessage()* method. The data type of *dummyMsg* is chosen to match the prototype for *PeekMessage()* in Win32.java. The constructor for *com.ms.win32.MSG()* creates a message object to store the message that is read.

The *bWnd* data member is initialized in the *IdleProcess()* constructor with the window handle of the current form, by invoking the *form.getHandle()* method. (Again, it doesn't matter what a window handle is, because we won't use it for anything except to call *PeekMessage()*.)

The *IdleProcess()* constructor assigns the *onIdle()* method to handle the idle event. The *button1_onClick()* and *button2_onClick()* methods use the *IdleProcess-.setActive()* method to turn background idle processing on and off.

The *IdleProcess.onIdle()* method starts by checking the *active* flag. If the *active* flag is set to *false*, meaning that background processing has been turned off, *onIdle()* returns immediately without taking any action. If *active* is set to *true*, *onIdle()* enters a loop to constantly check the Windows message queue.

The *onIdle()* method continues to loop as long as *PeekMessage()* returns *false*, which indicates that the message queue is empty. The two flags passed to *Peek-Message()* that were copied from the windows.h file—*Win32.PM_NOREMOVE* and *Win32.PM_NOYIELD*—indicate that the program is not to remove any message it finds in the queue nor yield control to some other thread as a result of the call. As soon as *PeekMessage()* returns *true*, *onIdle()* exits to allow the message to be processed. Within the loop, *onIdle()* calculates prime numbers and displays them using the *setPrime()* method provided by the parent class.

The Results

Figure 11-6 shows the IdleEvent2 application in action. IdleEvent2 runs about the same as IdleEvent1, but is considerably faster. In addition, the user drawing panel in

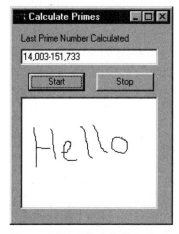

Figure 11-6. *The IdleEvent2 application supports user drawing while calculating prime numbers during idle time.*

IdleEvent2 updates more rapidly, resulting in smoother squiggles that update more rapidly. This is because the amount of time spent calculating prime numbers in the *onIdle()* event handler is synchronized with external activity.

> **CAUTION**   There is a certain danger in this approach. Since *onIdle()* doesn't yield control until a message appears in the Windows message queue, if Visual J++ 6 or any other part of your program defines a second idle event handler, the second handler will never get control.

CONCLUSION

WFC together with the basic Java library provides a powerful set of functions. In those rare cases when Win32 doesn't provide the function you need, the J/Direct Call Builder provides easy access to practically the entire Win32 API. J/Direct also provides access to commercially provided DLLs and to DLLs that you might write yourself.

In this chapter, you've seen how to use the J/Direct Call Builder to access the Win32 API, and you've seen the problems that J/Direct solves. You've also seen a few restrictions on calls to DLL functions that are due to problems J/Direct can't solve.

You've learned how to write your own DLL and how to access it through J/Direct, a technique that provides you access from Visual J++ 6 code to functions you would rather write in a different language.

Finally, you learned how to use J/Direct to solve a problem that was only partially solved in an application from Chapter 10. J/Direct is a powerful package that extends Visual J++ 6 into practically every capability the Win32 operating system and many commercial applications provide.

This chapter ends Part II and our discussion of Windows applications. Part II has discussed a number of topics regarding Visual J++ 6 windowed applications. You've seen how to write generic windowed applications using the Abstract Windowing Toolkit (AWT), how to extend AWT capabilities with WFC, and how to access DLLs directly. The next part of this book will demonstrate a number of new capabilities provided by Visual J++ 6.

Part III

Special Topics

Parts I and II of Programming Microsoft Visual J++ 6 demonstrate how to write generic and Microsoft Windows–based applications. Both of these parts are laid out in a logical progression, with each chapter building on previous chapters. After reading these first two parts, you should have a rich understanding of how to write generic and Windows-based applications.

By comparison with the first two parts, Part III consists of a set of unrelated topics. With the exception of Chapter 14 and Chapter 15, which talk about applets, each of the chapters in this part can be understood by itself without reference to the other chapters within this part.

The fact that the topics in Part III are unrelated to each other does not diminish their importance in any way. Understanding features such as database access, applet generation, ActiveX controls, and Dynamic HTML will add significantly to your capabilities as a Visual J++ 6 programmer.

Chapter 12

Accessing Databases

Chapter 3, The Windows Foundation Classes Utilities Package, described the Windows Foundation Classes for Java (WFC) Input/Output *io* package, which allows Microsoft Visual J++ programs to read from files, write to files, and copy files. One task not described in that chapter—one that Visual J++ 6 programmers will invariably find themselves faced with—is the accessing of data from a database. This chapter deals with that task.

THE SQL LANGUAGE

Most databases today use Structured Query Language, commonly referred to as SQL (pronounced "see quell"). This common language enables a Visual J++ 6 program to access almost any database using the same source code. In fact, as you'll see, Visual J++ 6 programs can access different types of databases from the same .EXE file.

What is SQL, and how did it come to be?

The Roots of SQL

There are many different types of databases. In earlier times, each database company defined its own command set. This made accessing databases more costly than it is now, for several reasons. Companies had to train programmers in a unique database language when they hired them, and train them again if the company moved from one type of database to another. In addition, unique internal data storage formats made moving data from one database type to another almost impossible. Database companies didn't seem to mind this state of affairs, because the use of unique languages and formats meant the cost of changing from one type of database to another was prohibitive. Companies tended to get stuck with one database type whether or not it proved to be the best one over time.

This situation might have continued, were it not for pressure from the user community to standardize. At the same time that different database suppliers were using their own unique languages, university database researchers invented an extremely powerful yet simple database command language called Structured Query Language (SQL). (The acronym SQL has become so common that the phrase "SQL language" is part of the programming vernacular, even though the word "language" is redundant.)

SQL is so simple and powerful that once the first database provider adopted it, the user community forced other database companies to follow. Most database companies that refused to adopt SQL disappeared. Microsoft supports SQL in its database tools, including Microsoft Access and Microsoft SQL Server.

DATABASE INTERNAL FORMATS

The use of the common SQL command set doesn't imply that different database providers have adopted a common internal format—far from it. I would wager that no two database companies use the same internal format to store data.

This lack of common internal structure is actually a benefit to the user community. No one database structure can be best at everything. Different internal formats means that database companies can optimize their offerings to serve different requirements. A database format might be optimized to minimize the amount of disk space required to store data, the effort required to maintain the database, or the time required to access the data, to name just a few possibilities. This is why Microsoft offers both Access and SQL Server.

Even with different internal formats, SQL enables companies to move both programmers and data from one database type to another with minimal effort. The programmer queries data from one database using SQL commands and stores it back into another database using the same type of SQL commands.

SQL Databases

There are many commands that make up the SQL command set. Entire databases can be created and destroyed using SQL commands. The average Visual J++ 6 user, however, will use a tool such as Microsoft Access or SQL Server to create the database. A Visual J++ program that is able to read, write, insert, and delete a record from the database is sufficient for most purposes. First, you'll need to reach a fundamental understanding of the way a SQL database is organized—at least, when viewed from the outside world. The internal details are unimportant.

Every database has a name. In most cases, the name of the database is the same as the name of the file that contains it. Thus, the Access file MyCompany.mdb contains the database MyCompany.

A database can include any number of tables, and each table carries a name. For example, the table named Customers might contain the names and phone numbers of different customers of the company MyCompany.

Each table is conceptually arranged like a grid. The columns—often referred to as *fields*—represent the various categories of information. The horizontal rows—often referred to as *records*—represent the entries in the table. For example, the following table shows a possible layout for the Access table named Customers.

Customer ID Number	Contact First Name	Contact Last Name	Phone
1	Stephen	Davis	(212) 555-1234
2	Kinsey	Davis	(212) 555-2345
3	Christa	Hvidsten	(512) 555-6789
4	Charlene	Eller	(713) 555-3456
5	Pip	Combs	(416) 555-4567
6	Zak	Gibson	(416) 555-5678
7	Chris	Gibson	(416) 555-6789
8	Boiky	Navias	(503) 555-7890
9	Bill	Wilcoxson	(202) 555-8901

You can access the entire table, but it's more common to address a single row at a time. This format also enables you to pull out and analyze individual columns within a row, or individual columns within the entire table.

SQL Commands

The simplest SQL command is the *DELETE* command. For example, using Access to delete the row in the Customers table containing the name Stephen Davis, you would enter the following SQL command:

```
DELETE FROM CUSTOMERS
WHERE CONTACTFIRSTNAME = 'Stephen' AND CONTACTLASTNAME = 'Davis';
```

The command *DELETE FROM CUSTOMERS* says that we want to delete one or more rows from the Customers table. The *WHERE* clause specifies which row to delete. Notice that because SQL uses a space to delineate commands, Access converted the row named "Contact First Name" to *ContactFirstName*.

NOTE   SQL commands aren't case sensitive.

You can delete multiple rows with the following command:

```
DELETE FROM CUSTOMERS WHERE CONTACTLASTNAME = 'Davis';
```

In this case, every row in which the Contact Last Name value is *Davis* (in this example, the first two rows) is removed from the table.

What if you want to retrieve the rows of the database? For this, you need the *SELECT* command. The following command selects the entire Customers table:

```
SELECT * FROM CUSTOMERS;
```

What this command returns is essentially the entire Customers table, although Visual J++ 6 contains commands that can access one row returned from the *SELECT* command at a time.

Of course, you might not want to process every row in the table. Suppose, for example, that you wanted to single out the rows in which the last name value is *Davis* (undoubtedly for special recognition):

```
SELECT * FROM CUSTOMERS WHERE CONTACTLASTNAME = 'Davis';
```

Finally, suppose you don't want to select an entire row, but merely a few columns of the row. For example, suppose you wanted the customer id and the phone number for the Gibson twins and you want the results sorted in alphabetical order by the first names:

```
SELECT CUSTOMERID, PHONENUMBER FROM CUSTOMERS
    WHERE CONTACTLASTNAME = 'Gibson'
    ORDER BY CONTACTFIRSTNAME;
```

Although numerous other commands—including variations on the *SELECT* command—exist, this is all the SQL you'll need to know for the rest of this book.

These SQL commands are great for accessing a SQL database from a command tool like Access, but what about accessing these tables from a Visual J++ program?

ACTIVEX DATA OBJECTS

The balance of this chapter deals with the use of Microsoft ActiveX Data Objects (ADO) and the relationship of ADO to Visual J++ and SQL.

What is ADO?

As I mentioned earlier, the internal data structure might (and in fact, generally does) vary from one database to another. This isn't a problem when you are entering commands from a SQL tool, but it's a problem when accessing these databases from Visual J++.

As part of the Windows Open System Architecture (WOSA), Microsoft defined the Open Database Connectivity (ODBC) application program interface (API). The current 32-bit version, ODBC32, replaces the older 16-bit version.

ODBC32 provides an API that database vendors implement by means of ODBC drivers specific to their particular database. Your program uses this API to call the ODBC32 Driver Manager, a dynamic-link library that passes the calls to the appropriate driver. The driver, in turn, interacts with the database using SQL.

As a Windows standard, there is an ODBC32 driver for almost every common database in existence. Unfortunately, the ODBC32 API is somewhat complicated and is not optimized for Visual J++. To address the ODBC32 complexity problem, version 6 of the development environment for the Microsoft Visual Studio languages introduces the ADO 2.0 interface. This interface is an API that is ideal for object-oriented languages like Visual J++: it has fewer classes and a simpler interface than ODBC32. Since ADO is built on top of the 32-bit version of ODBC, the ADO classes can be used with any database for which an ODBC32 driver exists.

Visual J++ 6 also contains a number of Toolbox tools for adding database interaction capabilities to your application. While these tools certainly simplify the job, you still must have some knowledge of ADO to develop applications that use databases.

Approaches to ADO

In this chapter, we'll cover three basic approaches to writing ADO applications: writing the application manually; using the Application Wizard; and using the Toolbox data tools.

I have always felt that a person needs to know how to multiply by hand before using a calculator. With that in mind, we'll begin by manually creating a simple example application that accesses a small database by means of ADO. From there, we'll move to an application built by the fully automatic but inflexible Application Wizard. The chapter wraps up with a demonstration of a slightly more complicated but much more flexible approach. We'll use the Toolbox data tools and learn how to access databases on PCs connected to your PC by means of a LAN.

MANUAL ADO

This first example ADO application is built manually without the aid of the Visual J++ tools. The purpose of this application is to demonstrate the principles of this manual approach, rather than to perform a serious function.

The Problem

This example program, ManualADO, accesses the Customers table of the Access database MyCompany.mdb described previously. Although this database was created with Microsoft Access, the database format doesn't matter as long as there is an ODBC32 driver for the type of database you want to use.

> **NOTE** ODBC32 drivers for Access, SQL Server, Microsoft FoxPro, Microsoft Visual FoxPro, Oracle, formatted text files, and several other storage formats are built into Windows. Other vendors provide their own ODBC32 drivers for their products.

ManualADO reads the first name, last name, and phone number from a row in the Customers table and combines them into one string that is displayed in an edit box along the top of a form. In addition, ManualADO provides a Next and a Previous button so the user can navigate through the database records.

The Setup Work

Start by creating a new directory named Windows Database Applications, to hold all the data applications we'll create in this chapter. In addition, you'll need to create an Access database named MyCompany. Add to the database a table called Customers that contains columns named CustomerID, CustomerFirstName, CustomerLastName, and PhoneNumber, and add some data to the table. Place the database in a Databases subdirectory of the Windows Database Applications directory.

> **NOTE** It would be simpler and less error prone for you to use the database MyCompany.mdb from the companion CD instead of creating it yourself from scratch. This is true even if you want to add new records using Microsoft Access. The database and all the examples in this chapter are in the Windows Database Applications subfolder on the companion CD.

Create a conventional Visual J++ Windows application project in the directory Windows Database Applications. Name the project ManualADO.

The Forms Designer Work

From Project Explorer, open Form1.java in the Forms Designer. Using the Properties window, change the form's *text* property from *Form1* to *Manual ADO*. Resize the default form to roughly half its original height and two-thirds its original width (the exact size isn't critical).

Place an Edit control along the top of the form. Size the Edit control to be almost as wide as the form. Rename the Edit control *nameEdit* and anchor it to the left, right, and top sides of the form. Since this simple application has no writing capability, set the Edit control's *readOnly* property to *true*. Finally, erase the initial value in the *text* property.

Now add two Button controls side by side and immediately below the Edit control. Name the left button *previousButton* and set its *text* property to *Previous*. Anchor *previousButton* to the left and bottom sides of the form. Name the right button *nextButton* and set its *text* property to *Next*. Anchor *nextButton* to the right and bottom sides of the form. Finally, double-click both buttons in order to create an event handler for each.

The Code

For simplicity's sake, I have broken the code into two public classes, ManualADO.java and Form1.java. The *ManualADO* class contains all of the ADO-related functions, and the *Form1* class concentrates solely on the mundane output functions.

The *ManualADO* class

The following code is the source code for the *ManualADO* class:

```
import com.ms.wfc.app.*;
import com.ms.wfc.core.*;
import com.ms.wfc.ui.*;

import com.ms.wfc.data.*;

/**
 * This class gives the user convenient access to a database
 * via the ActiveX Data Objects API.
 */
public class ManualADO
{
    // an ADO connection to the database
    Connection con = new Connection();

    // a recordset returned from a query
    Recordset rs   = new Recordset();

    // the name of the fields within the recordset to access
    String[] fields;

    /**
     * Create the ManualADO object that will
     * be used to perform the actual ADO calls.
     */
```

(continued)

```
        public ManualADO(String    dbType,    // database information
                         String    dbPath,
                         String    dbName,
                         String    userID,
                         String    password,
                         String    table,      // table information
                         String[]  fields,
                         String    sortField)
    {
        // save the table information
        this.fields  = fields;

        // combine the database fields into one string;
        // this string will be used to make the connection
        String sDB = createDatabaseString(dbType,
                                          userID,
                                          password,
                                          dbPath + dbName);

        // now build a SQL query from the fields
        String SQL = buildSQL(table, sortField, fields);

        // open the database
        dbQuery(sDB, SQL);
    }


    /**
     * Create a complete database string from the parts.
     * @param type of database (DSN)
     * @param user id
     * @param user password
     * @param path to database file
     */
    public static String createDatabaseString(String dsn,
                                              String userID,
                                              String psswd,
                                              String db)
    {
        String s = "PROVIDER=MSDASQL;";

        // add the DSN
        s += "dsn=" + dsn + ";";

        // now the user id and password
        s += "uid=" + userID + ";";
        s += "pwd=" + psswd + ";";
```

```
        // now the path to the database itself
        s += "DBQ=" + db;

        // return the result
        return s;
    }


    /**
     * Build a SQL query.
     * @param the table name to query
     * @param the order field (null->don't sort)
     * @param the fields to extract
     */
    public static String buildSQL(String sTable,
                                  String sOrder,
                                  String[] fields)
    {
        // always start with SELECT
        String queryString = "SELECT ";

        // now add in the field names separated by commas
        int index = 0;
        while(true)
        {
            queryString += fields[index];

            if (++index >= fields.length)
            {
                break;
            }

            queryString += ", ";
        }

        // add the table name
        queryString += " FROM " + sTable;

        // if there is a sort order, add that too
        if (sOrder != null)
        {
            queryString += " ORDER BY " + sOrder;
        }

        return queryString;
    }
```

(continued)

```
/**
 * Perform a query on specified database.
 * @param fully qualified database name (use createDatabaseString)
 * @param the SQL query to execute
 */
public void dbQuery(String s, String queryString)
    throws AdoException
{
    // first create a Connection on specified database
    con.setConnectionString(s);
    con.setCursorLocation(AdoEnums.CursorLocation.CLIENT);
    con.open();

    // now open a Recordset with the SQL query
    rs.setActiveConnection(con);
    rs.setSource(queryString);
    rs.setCursorType(AdoEnums.CursorType.STATIC);
    rs.setCursorLocation(AdoEnums.CursorLocation.CLIENT);
    rs.setLockType(AdoEnums.LockType.OPTIMISTIC);
    rs.open();
}


/**
 * Return the contents of an individual field from a recordset.
 */
public String getField(String fieldName)
    throws AdoException
{
    Field f = rs.getField(fieldName);
    return f.getString();
}


/**
 * Update the fields within the current recordset.
 * @param commit true->update the database table
 */
public void setField(String field, String value, boolean commit)
{
    Field fld = rs.getField(field);
    fld.setString(value);

    if (commit)
    {
        rs.update();
    }
}
```

```
/**
 * Move to the previous record; return false if at
 * beginning of table.
 */
public boolean movePrevious()
{
    // if already at beginning of file (the table),
    // don't go any further
    if (rs.getBOF())
    {
        return false;
    }

    // move to the previous entry
    rs.movePrevious();

    // BOF now?
    return !rs.getBOF();
}


/**
 * Move to the next record; return false if at end of table.
 */
public boolean moveNext()
{
    // if already at the end of the table, don't go any further
    if (rs.getEOF())
    {
        return false;
    }

    // OK, move to the next entry
    rs.moveNext();

    // end of table now?
    return !rs.getEOF();
}


/**
 * Close the current database connection.
 */
public void close()
{
    rs.close();
    con.close();
}
}
```

The *ManualADO* class begins with the constructor. This constructor appears more complicated than it really is, because it accepts each part of the connection string (explained below) as a separate argument. In fact, the first four arguments merely describe the database.

In our case, the *dbType* is *MS Access 97 Database*, the *dbPath* is the path to the database directory, and the *dbName* is *MyCompany.mdb*. Normally, the *userID* and *password* arguments are *null*—unless the database is secured.

The remaining arguments to the constructor are *table*, which in our case has the value of *Customers; fields*, which is an array of strings that contain the names of the fields in which we are interested; and *sortField*, which is the name of the field (column) in *Customers* by which the data is to be sorted. The sort field might or might not be one of the members of *fields*.

The *ManualADO()* constructor begins by calling *createDatabaseString()* to combine the database name information into an ADO connection string. A typical ADO connection string might look like the following:

PROVIDER=MSDASQL; dsn= MS Access 97 Database; uid=; pwd=; DBQ=\databases\MyCompany.mdb

From there, *ManualADO()* calls *buildSQL()* to build the SQL *SELECT* statement. Again, a typical *SELECT* statement might be something like this:

```
SELECT CONTACTLASTNAME, CONTACTFIRSTNAME FROM CUSTOMERS
    ORDER BY PHONENUMBER
```

Finally, *ManualADO()* invokes *dbQuery()* to open a connection to the database and read its contents.

The *dbQuery()* method starts by opening a *Connection* object using the connection string built by *createDatabaseString()*. As the name implies, a *Connection* object is a connection to the database. Once the connection has been established, the program initializes the *Recordset* object *rs*.

First, *rs* is attached to the open *Connection* object. The SQL query string built earlier is then passed to *rs.setSource()*. The final call to *rs.open()* performs the query of the database and populates the recordset with information from the database. If anything goes wrong with the query, *dbQuery()* throws an *ADOException*.

NOTE The cursor to which the *Connection* and the *Recordset* objects refer is the index of the current row in the SQL database.

The remaining methods are relatively simple. The *getField()* method queries the recordset for the value of the specified field in the current record by getting a *Field* object and then fetching the *String* contents.

The *setField()* method is almost the reverse of *getField()*. The only difference is that it isn't until the argument *commit* is *true* that the updated data in the recordset is written back to the current row of the database. In this way, a program can update all of the fields that have changed within a single row before committing the result to the database. This is much faster than writing to the database every time each field is updated.

The *movePrevious()* and *moveNext()* methods move the cursor to the previous and next row of the table, respectively. Both return *true* if the operation was successful and *false* if the beginning of the table or end of the table was encountered. Both methods guard against moving past the beginning-of-file and the end-of-file, because these would throw an exception.

Finally, *close()* closes the recordset and the connection to the database. This operation is similar to writing the database to disk and exiting Access.

The *Form1* class

With the bulk of the work done by the *ManualADO* class, the *Form1* class is relatively simple:

```
import com.ms.wfc.app.*;
import com.ms.wfc.core.*;
import com.ms.wfc.ui.*;

public class Form1 extends Form
{
    // the ManualADO class makes the actual
    // ADO connections
    ManualADO ado;

    // define the fields to extract from the database table
    String[] fields = new String[]
                        {"ContactFirstName",
                         "ContactLastName",
                         "PhoneNumber"};

    public Form1()
    {
        // Required for Visual J++ Form Designer support
        initForm();

        // create an ADO connection
        String db = "C:\\ProgramVJ\\" +
                    "Windows Database Applications\\Databases\\";
        ado = new ManualADO(
                    "MS Access 97 Database", // type of database
                    db,                // path to database file
                    "MyCompany.mdb",       // name of database file
                    "",                // user id (normally "")
                    "",                // password (normally "")
                    "Customers",       // name of table
```

(continued)

```
                               fields,         // array of fields to extract
                               null);          // sort field (null -> don't sort)

          // now update the edit field with the first entry
          updateField(nameEdit);
      }


      /**
       * Update the outputEdit field with the current row.
       */
      void updateField(Edit outputEdit)
      {
          // fetch the field contents for the current row
          String[] outFields = getStrings(fields);

          // convert the phone number into xxx-xxx-xxxx format
          outFields[2] = phoneToString(outFields[2]);

          // generate output string
          String s = outFields[1] + ", " +
                     outFields[0] + " (" +
                     outFields[2] + ")";

          // now output it
          outputEdit.setText(s);
      }


      /**
       * Return the database fields from the current recordset
       * as strings.
       * @return array of strings
       */
      String[] getStrings(String[] fields)
      {
          // allocate enough strings to hold all the fields
          String[] s = new String[fields.length];

          // now loop through the fields, fetching their values
          for (int i = 0; i < fields.length; i++)
          {
              // get the string version of each column
              // of the current row
              s[i] = ado.getField(fields[i]);
          }
          return s;
      }
```

```
/**
 * Update the current database entry.
 */
void setStrings(String[] fields, String[] values)
{
    // the last field in the list is at this offset
    int last = fields.length - 1;

    // update all of the fields except the last w/o commit
    for (int i = 0; i < last; i++)
    {
        ado.setField(fields[i], values[i], false);
    }

    // now update the last field and commit it
    ado.setField(fields[last], values[last], true);
}


/**
 * Convert a phone number into a string in the format xxx-xxx-xxxx.
 */
static String phoneToString(String phoneNumber)
{
    String sAC = phoneNumber.substring(0, 3);
    String sEx = phoneNumber.substring(3, 6);
    String sPh = phoneNumber.substring(6);
    return sAC + "-" + sEx + "-" + sPh;
}


/**
 * Form1 overrides dispose so it can clean up the
 * component list.
 */
public void dispose()
{
    super.dispose();
    components.dispose();

    ado.close();
    ado = null;
}

private void previousButton_click(Object source, Event e)
{
    if (!ado.movePrevious())
    {
        nameEdit.setText("Beginning of database");
    }
```

(continued)

```
        else
        {
            updateField(nameEdit);
        }
    }

    private void nextButton_click(Object source, Event e)
    {
        if (!ado.moveNext())
        {
            nameEdit.setText("End of database");
        }
        else
        {
            updateField(nameEdit);
        }
    }

    /**
     * NOTE: The following code is required by the Visual J++ form
     * designer.  It can be modified using the form editor.  Do not
     * modify it using the code editor.
     */
    Container components = new Container();
    Edit nameEdit = new Edit();
    Button previousButton = new Button();
    Button nextButton = new Button();

    private void initForm()
    {
        // ...built by Forms Designer...
    }

    /**
     * The main entry point for the application.
     */
    public static void main(String args[])
    {
        Application.run(new Form1());
    }
}
```

The data member *fields* contains an array of strings that represent the fields within the Customers table that *Form1* is to read and display. After the *Form1()* constructor has initialized the form, *Form1()* creates a *ManualADO* object to access the data within the Customers table of the Access database MyCompany.mdb. (Note that the only reason that the path *db* is broken in two is to allow each part to fit on a single line on the page. Also, if the path to MyCompany.mdb on your machine isn't the path shown here, you'll need to change this path before this program will work.)

The final call, to *updateField()*, causes the current record of the table (the first record) to be displayed in the *Edit* object *nameEdit*.

The *updateField()* method works by first fetching the desired fields from the current record, using the local method *getStrings()*. The phone number field is converted from its stored format into that of a U.S. telephone number (xxx-xxx-xxxx) using the local method *phoneToString()*. Finally, *updateField()* concatenates the fields into a single string and displays the string in the *Edit* object specified in the argument to *updateField()*.

The *getStrings()* method accepts an array of field names and returns the field values in an array of *String* objects. The *getStrings()* method begins by allocating the output *String* array to be the same size as the input *fields* array. The method then enters a *for* loop, in which it calls *ado.getField()* on the current record for each field passed in the *fields* array, and saves the result in the output array. The *setStrings()* method is the analogous output method, which isn't used in this example but is included as a demonstration.

The *dispose()* method has been updated from the system-generated code to also close the *ado* object. Closing the *ado* object closes the database.

The *previousButton_click()* and *nextButton_click()* methods move the current record pointer to the previous record or next record, respectively. If the current record pointer is already before the first record in the recordset or after the last record in the recordset, then the associated method displays an appropriate message. If the current record pointer is at a record, then the local *updateField()* method displays the new record values in the *nameEdit* field.

The Result

The result of your hard work should look something like Figure 12-1. The output form is simple, but it does allow you to navigate back and forth within the Customers table of the MyCompany.mdb database.

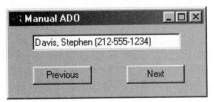

Figure 12-1. *The appearance of the ManualADO demonstration application when used on the simple Customers table of the MyCompany.mdb Access database.*

Adding more capability—for example, adding new Insert, Delete, and Update buttons—is just a matter of your adding methods to the *ManualADO* class. Each new method would invoke the proper *Recordset* method for the corresponding button and tie it back to the event handler of the button. The code for an Update button is already present in ManualADO.

If you decide to add an Insert button, you'll need to add data to all of the fields within a row or else the new entry won't be complete. In addition, it's much easier to parse user input if you provide a separate edit box for each entry, but it's not as attractive.

It's surprisingly simple to access different data from ManualADO. For example, you can add records to the Customers table by opening the MyCompany database from Access and selecting the Customers table.

To access a new table within MyCompany.mdb, create a table with Access, define the fields you want, and add data to the table. Within the ManualADO code, update the fields array and change the table name, which is the sixth argument, in the call to the *ManualADO()* constructor within Form1.java.

To access a different database, create a new database with Access and then follow the same steps as for accessing a new table. In addition, update the third argument to the *ManualADO()* constructor call to the new database name.

To access a different type of database, such as a Microsoft Visual FoxPro database, you'll need to change the data source name (DSN) specification in addition to changing the database, table, and field names. It's easy to figure out what this new DSN specification should be by looking at the DSN for an Access database: MS Access Database. If you have any questions about changing the DSN, create a simple application using the Visual J++ Application Wizard as described in the next section, and look to see what DSN the wizard came up with.

THE APPLICATION WIZARD

Now that you've created an ADO application manually, it's time to give Visual J++ a chance to automatically build an application to your specifications. The following example application, AutoADO, reads the MyCompany.mdb file and generates a window where the user can delete or update entries in the Customers table. Of course, it's possible to include other button controls, database options, and table options, but let's keep it simple for now.

The Wizard Work

Choose New Project from the File menu, as usual. This time, select Application Wizard instead of Windows Application. In the wizard, supply the project name AutoADO. When you choose the Open button, the wizard presents you with a window asking whether you want to load a previously stored profile. (I'll explain profiles soon.) Since you have no stored profiles yet, leave the profile name as the default (None) and choose the Next button.

The second window is critical to creating this application. Make sure that you choose the Form Based Application With Data radio button, as shown in Figure 12-2. The default is for the form not to be attached to data, which would lead you down a completely different path.

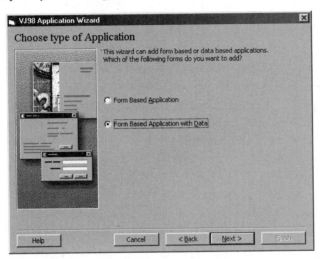

Figure 12-2. *The second window of the Application Wizard showing the Form Based Application With Data option selected.*

The third wizard window asks whether you want to use ODBC to access your data file, or instead use a more direct access method unique to Access databases. Choose ODBC.

The fourth window is intimidating at first glance. First (if you don't remember from the ManualADO example), as soon as you click the DSN drop-down menu it will quickly become clear that this field refers to the type of database you want to use. Select MS Access 97 Database. As soon as you make this selection, the bottom two options are deselected since they no longer apply. You already know from previous experience in this chapter that you'll normally want to leave the User ID and Password blank. Now fill in the Database entry. You can do this by clicking on the ellipses button at the far right of the edit box. From there, you can navigate to the MyCompany.mdb database. When you have made these changes to the fourth window, it should look like Figure 12-3. Choose Next.

You can accept the defaults in the fifth window, so choose Next again.

The sixth window presents you with a list of the columns in the Customers table. This table was chosen automatically, because it's the first (and only) table in the database. Double-click the ContactFirstName, ContactLastName, and PhoneNumber columns to move them from the list of available columns to the list of columns to be displayed. That done, choose Next.

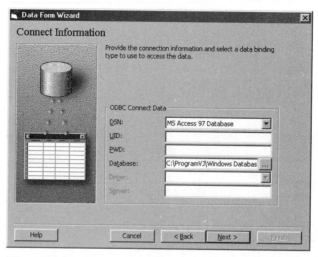

Figure 12-3. *The completed fourth window in the Application Wizard.*

The seventh window enables you to select the buttons you want in your application. The wizard will add a button and the associated event handler function for each option that you select. Select the Delete Button, Update Button, Close Button, and Data Navigator options. The resulting window looks as shown in Figure 12-4.

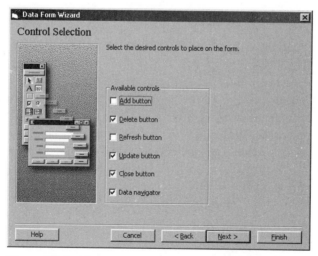

Figure 12-4. *Choosing the buttons in the seventh window of the Application Wizard.*

Choosing the Next button takes you to the eighth wizard window. Here, you select the type of output you want. The default is an .EXE file, which is what we want. Choosing Next takes you to the ninth and final wizard window. Here, you are given the option of saving this profile for future use. (Remember that you were given the option of reading a profile back in the first window when the wizard started.) You can save it, if you want to, by supplying a profile file name; however, whether you save the profile isn't critical to this demonstration application.

Just to make sure that the settings you made with the wizard are correct, select View Report in this last wizard window. Your results should look like that shown in Figure 12-5. If they don't, choose Back until you reach the window whose settings differ, and start over again. If all of the options match, choose Finish to allow the wizard to build a complete application to your specifications.

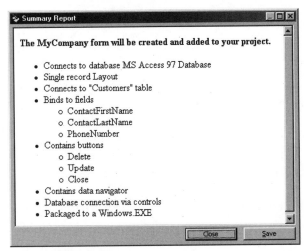

Figure 12-5. *The summary report for the AutoADO demonstration application.*

The Application Wizard Result

To see the result of your wizardly work, compile and execute the program. The results are shown in Figure 12-6.

> **WARNING** When you first try to compile the wizard-generated code in AutoADO, you'll get the following compile-time error:
>
> Undefined name m_bAddnew
>
> This error is the result of a bug in the Visual J++ 6 Application Wizard. In order to compile the program, you need to edit the *btnUpdate_Click()* method. Delete the following section of code from *btnUpdate_Click()*:

```
if( m_bAddNew )
{
    this.setCursor( Cursor.DEFAULT );
    return;
}
    else
```

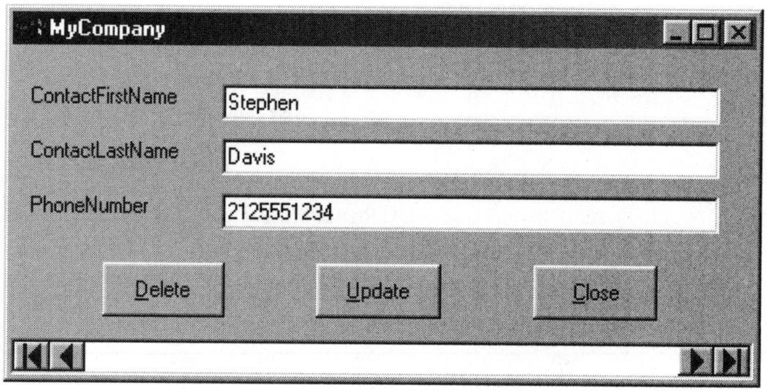

Figure 12-6. *The output from the Application Wizard.*

The wizard created a separate edit box for each field you selected in the sixth wizard window. The user can navigate through the records in the Customers table using the buttons at the bottom of the form.

This application was easy to build, and it's functional for quickly accessing a database; however, I find the results rather ugly. You can make it look slightly better by using the Forms Designer to adjust the size and position of the controls.

A worse problem is the unusual display of the phone number field. To be fair, I choose to store the phone number data as simple numbers, but other formats are available. Later in this chapter, I'll demonstrate how to customize this field to look like the phone number displayed in the ManualADO application.

The Code

Let me start by displaying a portion of the code created by the Application Wizard. I will then explain it.

The code generated by the Application Wizard is lengthy but interesting. A highly edited version of this code that shows only the interesting parts—including the code for one of the buttons—is shown here:

```
//MyCompany.java

import com.ms.wfc.app.*;
import com.ms.wfc.core.*;
import com.ms.wfc.ui.*;
import com.ms.wfc.data.*;
import com.ms.wfc.data.ui.*;

public class MyCompany extends Form
{

    public void btnDelete_Click(Object sender, Event evt)
    {
```

```
    try
    {
        dataSource1.getRecordset().delete(AdoEnums.Affect.CURRENT);
        if( !dataSource1.getRecordset().getEOF() )
            {
                dataSource1.getRecordset().moveNext();
                if( dataSource1.getRecordset().getEOF() )
                    dataSource1.getRecordset().movePrevious();
            }
    }
    catch (Exception e)
    {
        handleADOException(e);
        dataSource1.getRecordset().cancelBatch();
    }
}

    ⋮


void handleADOException(Exception e)
{
    e.printStackTrace();
    MessageBox.show( e.toString(), "MyCompany" );
}

    ⋮


Container components = new Container();
DataSource dataSource1 = new DataSource(components);
DataBinder dataBinder1 = new DataBinder(components);
    ⋮
DataNavigator dataNavigator = new DataNavigator();

private void initForm()
{
    ⋮
    // the following has been edited by dividing the
    // strings up and then concatenating them back
    // together using '+' signs to keep the strings
    // from wrapping on the page
    dataSource1.setConnectionString(
        "PROVIDER=MSDASQL;dsn=MS Access 97 Database;" +
        "uid=;pwd=;" +
        "DBQ=C:\\ProgramVJ\\" +
        "Windows Database Applications\\Databases\\MyCompany.mdb");
    dataSource1.setCommandText(
        "select ContactFirstName, ContactLastName, " +
```

(continued)

```
            "PhoneNumber from Customers");
        ⋮
        dataBinder1.setDataSource(dataSource1);
        dataBinder1.setBindings(new DataBinding[] {
            new DataBinding(editContactFirstName, "Text",
                        "ContactFirstName"),
            new DataBinding(editContactLastName, "Text",
                        "ContactLastName"),
            new DataBinding(editPhoneNumber, "Text",
                        "PhoneNumber")});

        ⋮
        btnDelete.setText("&Delete");
        btnDelete.addOnClick(new EventHandler(this.btnDelete_Click));

        ⋮

        dataNavigator.setDataSource(dataSource1);


        this.setNewControls(new Control[] {
                        dataNavigator,
                        btnDelete,
                        btnUpdate,
                        btnClose,
                        panel1,
                        labelContactFirstName,
                        editContactFirstName,
                        labelContactLastName,
                        editContactLastName,
                        labelPhoneNumber,
                        editPhoneNumber});

        panel1.setNewControls(new Control[] {
                        btnDelete,
                        btnUpdate,
                        btnClose});

        dataSource1.begin();
        dataBinder1.begin();

        ⋮

    }
```

The *initForm()* method

The first thing you'll notice is the lack of a *Connection* or a *Recordset* object anywhere within the program. However, if you look at the declarations for the *initForm()* method, you'll see an object of class *DataSource*. The role of the *DataSource* class is similar to that of the *ManualADO* class defined earlier. This is made obvious by the arguments to the *setConnectionString()* and the *setCommandText()* methods. Apparently, the first method creates the *Connection* and *Recordset* objects, and the second method sets the SQL call within the *Recordset*.

If you look at the next block of code within *initForm()*, you'll see an object of class *DataBinder*. The *DataBinder.setDataSource()* method binds the *DataBinder* object to the *DataSource*. The next call is to the method *setBindings()*. This method receives an array of objects of class *DataBinding*. Each *DataBinding* object ties a field within the Customers table to an edit box in the form.

Farther down in the code, the *DataNavigator.setDataSource()* method call ties an object of type *DataNavigator* back to the *DataSource* class. In the final method call shown—the call to *setNewControls()*—the *DataNavigator* object is listed as one of the controls.

Explanation of *initForm()*

As mentioned earlier, the *DataSource* class is a more sophisticated version of the *ManualADO* class that was defined in the ManualADO example. It creates the *Connection* and the *Recordset* with the associated SQL query.

The *DataBinder* and *DataBinding* classes are completely new since our previous example. The *DataBinder* class, along with its *DataBinding* class members, allows the program to display an entry in the table by using a single call. This call would have to go through the following steps to display the current record from the table:

1. Read the current record from the *DataSource* object.

2. Extract the field name contained in the *DataBinding* object.

3. Display the returned data in the edit box that is contained in the same *DataBinding* object.

4. Increment to the next *DataBinding* object within the *DataBinder* object and return to Step 2, until all of the *DataBinding* objects have been processed.

The process is similar when performing other operations on the table such as update and delete.

The delete operation

Towards the bottom of the *initForm()* method, you can see that the Delete button is tied to the *btnDelete_Click()* event handler. This method starts by deleting the CURRENT record from the *Recordset* contained in the *DataSource* that contains the *Connection* object. The *btnDelete_Click()* method then moves the CURRENT record pointer to the next member of the recordset by calling *moveNext()*.

The *moveNext()* method also updates the display using the *DataBinding* objects attached to the *DataBinder* object for this *DataSource*, as in the display steps described above. The remaining code in *btnDelete_Click()* ensures that we don't read beyond the end of the table.

Any exception thrown during this process—which would probably be because of an error in the database—is handled by the *handleADOException()* internal method. This method first calls *printStackTrace()*, which displays a trace in the debugger of the methods called if the program was executed from within the Visual J++ Integrated Development Environment (IDE). (The *printStackTrace()* method does nothing if the program wasn't running in the IDE.) The *handleADOException()* method then displays a *MessageBox* to the user.

The *DataNavigator* object

The *DataNavigator* object is the control that appears at the bottom of the form. This control uses the *moveNext()*, *movePrevious()*, *moveFirst()*, and *moveLast()* methods of the *DataSource* object to change the *CURRENT* record pointer within the *Data-Source* object. Each of these move methods displays the results using the *DataBinder* as explained above. The *DataNavigator* is convenient, but not necessary to the workings of the *DataSource*, *DataBinder*, and *DataBinding* classes. A similar control, the *DataGrid* object, displays the table data in tabular form using the same data classes.

USING THE DATA TOOLBOX CONTROLS

While the Application Wizard was easy to use, the output was less than spectacular in appearance and difficult to customize. Another approach is to use the *DataSource* and *DataBinder* objects contained in the WFC Controls section of the Toolbox.

The manual approach presented at the beginning of this chapter allowed you to completely control output, but it was difficult to program. The completely automated Application Wizard approach was easy to use, but inflexible in its output. The Toolbox method shown here is a compromise. While slightly more complicated than the fully automated approach, it's much simpler than the totally manual method and still allows you almost total control of the output.

The Problem

The problem this demonstration application solves is similar to the problem solved by the ManualADO application: allow the user to navigate back and forth through the Customers table using two buttons. Because of the way that the *DataBinder* object works, however, this time the ContactFirstName, ContactLastName, and PhoneNumber fields must appear in separate edit boxes as they did in the AutoADO example.

The Forms Designer Work

The Forms Designer work for this application consists of two different types of tasks. The first type of forms work involves the manipulation of conventional controls; the second type involves the DataSource and DataBinder controls.

Conventional controls

Create a normal Windows Application project (don't use the Application Wizard this time). Name the project ToolboxADO. Open the Form1.java file in the Forms Designer.

Rename the form by changing the *text* property to *Toolbox ADO*. Now add three Label controls containing the text *Customer First Name, Customer Last Name*, and *Telephone Number*. Place the labels so they are equally spaced vertically and aligned horizontally on the left side of the form.

Add an Edit control to the right of each label. Align the three Edit controls horizontally. Name them *firstNameEdit, lastNameEdit*, and *phoneNumberEdit*. Set the *readOnly* property to *true* for each.

Add two buttons below the Label and Edit controls. Label the left button *Previous* and change its *name* property to *previousButton*; label the right button *Next* and change its *name* property to *nextButton*. Double-click each button to create the event handlers that we'll need later.

Resize the form until it accommodates the controls without excessive space on either side. This time, as a change, rather than anchor the controls to the different edges of the form, set the form's *borderStyle* property to *Fixed Toolwindow*. This will retain the appearance of the form by rendering it nonresizeable.

Creating a file DSN

It's easier to define a DSN to which the *DataSource* object can refer before you start creating the *DataSource* object. To create a DSN, start by opening the Windows Control Panel.

Double-click the ODBC (32bit) icon to bring up the ODBC Data Source Administrator. Select the User DSN tab, and select MS Access 97 Database as the type of DSN to create.

Now select the File DSN tab. Select the Add button to create a new DSN for our database. The first window to appear is the Create New Data Source window, which lists all of the ODBC Data Drivers that are installed on your system. Select Microsoft Access Driver (*.mdb); this is the ODBC driver for .mdb files like ours. (If this driver isn't available, it's because you didn't select it when you installed Visual J++.) Choose Next and enter *MyCompany.dsn* as the name of the DSN to create. Now choose Next to see a summary of your choices, and then choose Finish to complete the creation of the DSN.

An Access DSN must be attached to an Access database. After you've created the DSN, the ODBC Microsoft Access 97 Setup window appears. Choose Select to specify the database file to attach to this DSN. Use the Select Database window to navigate to MyCompany.mdb, as shown in Figure 12-7. Choose MyCompany.mdb and then choose OK to attach the database to the DSN.

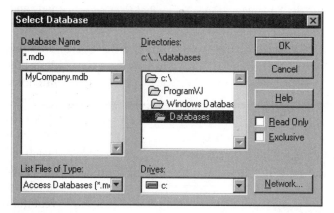

Figure 12-7. *The Select Database window of the ODBC Microsoft Access 97 Setup editor.*

Finally, choose OK to close the ODBC Microsoft Access 97 Setup window.

You can now see on the File DSN tab of the ODBC Data Source Administrator that MyCompany.dsn has been defined. Choose OK to close the ODBC Data Source Administrator. You can now close the Control Panel.

The DataSource control

Drag a DataSource control from the Toolbox and drop it onto the form. (The data controls are at the bottom of the WFC Controls list of Toolbox controls.) Rename the object to *dataSource*.

Click the three dots to the right of the *connectionString* property to display the Data Link Properties window. Now choose the Provider tab. From the OLE DB Provider(s) list, select Microsoft OLE DB Provider For ODBC Drivers. On the Connection tab, choose the Use Connection String option. Now choose the Build button to reveal a list of DSNs, including MyCompany.dsn, in the Select Data Source window. Select MyCompany.dsn and choose OK. The ODBC Microsoft Access 97 Setup window is displayed again, giving you a second chance to select a database. Since you've already attached a database to the DSN, choose OK to close the window.

Before exiting the Data Link Properties window, you should choose the Test Connection button on the Connection tab to test the connection to the MyCompany.mdb database. If the connection is good, a message box appears indicating that the test connection succeeded. With the *connectionString* property setting established, select OK to exit the Data Link Properties window.

Now choose the *commandText* property and enter the following SQL command:

SELECT ContactFirstName, ContactLastName, PhoneNumber FROM Customers

The DataBinder control

Drag a DataBinder control from the Toolbox and drop it onto the form. Rename the object to *dataBinder*. Change the *dataSource* property to *dataSource*.

> **NOTE** You can use the drop-down list for the *dataSource* property and select from a list (of one) of data sources defined in the form.

To set up the data bindings, click the value box for the *bindings* property. Click the three dots to the right of the box to open up the DataBinding Editor. Choose the Add button three times to add three data bindings, and then choose OK. (The DataBinding Editor is really not much of an editor—it's more of a creator. The editing is done back in the Properties window of the *DataBinding* object.)

You'll notice that the *bindings* property has a plus sign to its left. Choose the plus sign to reveal the three binding objects. Click the plus sign for each binding object (not the plus sign in front of the *All* property) to reveal its properties. Under the *binding0* property, click the *fieldName* property. Notice that a small arrow appears in the value field immediately to the right. Click the arrow to reveal the field names within the Customers table. Select *ContactFirstName*. Now click the *target* property. From the drop-down list, select *firstNameEdit*. Finally, select *text* as the *propertyName*. Repeat the process for *binding1*, this time selecting *ContactLastName*, *lastNameEdit*, and *text*. Repeat the process one last time for *binding2* by selecting *PhoneNumber*, *phoneNumberEdit*, and *text*.

When you're finished, your *dataBinder* Properties window should look like Figure 12-8.

Figure 12-8. *The completed properties for the* DataBinder *object for the* ToolboxADO *application.*

NOTE   As you create each binding, the corresponding value for the first record in the database appears in the form's Edit control. For example, as soon as you tie the ContactFirstName field to the *firstNameEdit* object and set the *text* property, the name *Stephen* appears in the top Edit control.

Test the controls

Before continuing any further, test the data controls you have established by saving, compiling, and executing the ToolboxADO application. The program should display the first record in the database, as shown in Figure 12-9.

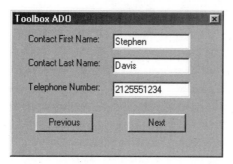

Figure 12-9. *The ToolboxADO application with the Toolbox data controls established.*

Building the event handler methods

Open the form in the Forms Designer again. Open the active properties of the Properties window. Now select the *phoneNumberEdit* object and double-click the *textChanged* property. The resulting method will read the contents of the *phoneNumberEdit* object whenever the contents change, and update the value to the standard U.S. (xxx) xxx-xxxx format.

The Code

With the Toolbox data controls doing most of the work, all that is left is to write the button event handlers to call *Recordset.moveNext()* and *Recordset.movePrevious()*, and the phone number display code, much like we did back in ManualADO:

```
import com.ms.wfc.app.*;
import com.ms.wfc.core.*;
import com.ms.wfc.ui.*;

import com.ms.wfc.data.*;
import com.ms.wfc.data.ui.*;

/**
 * This class can take a variable number of parameters on the command
 * line. Program execution begins with the main() method. The class
 * constructor is not invoked unless an object of type 'Form1' is
```

```
 * created in the main() method.
 */
public class Form1 extends Form
{
    public Form1()
    {
        // Required for Visual J++ Form Designer support
        initForm();

        // make sure that the first field is updated
        phoneNumberEdit_textChanged(null, null);
    }

    /**
     * Form1 overrides dispose so it can clean up the
     * component list.
     */
    public void dispose()
    {
        super.dispose();
        components.dispose();
    }

    /**
     * Update the phone number passed in as a string to appear
     * in the standard U.S. format of (xxx) xxx-xxxx.
     */
    private String updatePhone(String s)
    {
        // if it's not the right number of digits
        // (including if it's already been updated)...
        if (s.length() != 10)
        {
            // then don't update
            return s;
        }

        // break the phone number up into parts
        String s1 = s.substring(0, 3);
        String s2 = s.substring(3, 6);
        String s3 = s.substring(6, 10);

        // now put it back together again with punctuation
        s = "(" + s1 + ") " + s2 + "-" + s3;

        // and return to caller
        return s;
    }
```

(continued)

```java
/**
 * Navigate backward in the Customers table.
 */
private void previousButton_click(Object source, Event e)
{
    // get the recordset
    Recordset rs = dataSource.getRecordset();

    // if the database is empty...
    if (rs.getDataMemberCount() == 0)
    {
        // return without action
        return;
    }

    // move to the next record
    rs.movePrevious();

    // if at end-of-file...
    if (rs.getBOF())
    {
        // move back to the first record
        rs.moveFirst();
    }
}

/**
 * Navigate forward in the Customers table.
 */
private void nextButton_click(Object source, Event e)
{
    // get the recordset
    Recordset rs = dataSource.getRecordset();

    // if the database is empty...
    if (rs.getDataMemberCount() == 0)
    {
        // return without action
        return;
    }

    // move to the next record
    rs.moveNext();

    // if at end-of-file...
    if (rs.getEOF())
    {
        // move back to the last record
```

```
            rs.moveLast();
    }
}


/**
 * Invoked when the phone number edit box is updated by the
 * DataBinder; update the phone number to the (xxx) xxx-xxxx format.
 */
private void phoneNumberEdit_textChanged(Object source, Event e)
{
    // get the contents of the phone number edit box
    String s = phoneNumberEdit.getText();

    // update the phone number
    s = updatePhone(s);

    // and put it back into the edit box
    phoneNumberEdit.setText(s);
}


/**
 * NOTE: The following code is required by the Visual J++ form
 * designer.  It can be modified using the form editor.  Do not
 * modify it using the code editor.
 */
Container components = new Container();
Label label1 = new Label();
Label label2 = new Label();
Label label3 = new Label();
Edit firstNameEdit = new Edit();
Edit lastNameEdit = new Edit();
Edit phoneNumberEdit = new Edit();
Button previousButton = new Button();
Button nextButton = new Button();
com.ms.wfc.data.ui.DataSource dataSource =
            new com.ms.wfc.data.ui.DataSource(components);
com.ms.wfc.data.ui.DataBinder dataBinder =
            new com.ms.wfc.data.ui.DataBinder(components);


private void initForm()
{
    // ...create by Forms Designer...
}


/**
 * The main entry point for the application.
 *
```

(continued)

```
 * @param args Array of parameters passed to the application
 * via the command line.
 */
public static void main(String args[])
{
    Application.run(new Form1());
}
}
```

ToolboxADO.java must import the *wfc.data* and *wfc.data.ui* packages—in addition to those packages already imported by the Windows Application Wizard—in order to gain access to the *DataBinder* and *DataSource* classes. The program accesses the Customers database table through the *DataSource* class. The connection between the *DataSource* class and the database was established when we added the DataSource control to the application form in the Forms Designer and initialized the control. The connection between the DataSource control and the individual fields was created by the DataBinding control, which also came from the Toolbox.

The *updatePhone()* method here is identical to the *updatePhone()* method in the ManualADO program. This routine takes a phone number written as a string of numbers and converts it into the U.S. standard (xxx) xxx-xxxx format.

The *previousButton_click()* method is invoked when the user chooses the Previous button. This method begins by retrieving the *Recordset* object from the *DataSource*. If the recordset isn't empty, then *previousButton_click()* calls *movePrevious()* to move the current record pointer back one record. If a beginning-of-file condition is encountered, then the function moves the current record pointer back to the beginning of the recordset. The process is similar for the *nextButton_click()* method, only the method calls *moveNext()* rather than *movePrevious()* and checks for an end-of-file condition.

When the user chooses the Previous or Next button, the *DataBinder* object attached to the *Recordset* object automatically detects that the current record pointer has moved. The *DataBinder* object automatically updates the edit boxes that are bound to the *Recordset* by means of the *DataBinding* objects.

Customizing edit box output

The *updatePhone()* method isn't really necessary to the execution of the program; however, it demonstrates how you can insert your program into the data binding update process to customize output to the edit boxes. Without *updatePhone()*, a phone number is displayed as a 10-digit integer: 1234567890.

The *phoneNumberEdit_textChanged()* method is invoked whenever the contents of the *phoneNumberEdit* control object change. Since *phoneNumberEdit* is read-only, the contents change only when the *previousButton_click()* or the *nextButton_click()* methods update the customer data. The *phoneNumberEdit_textChanged()* method retrieves the string contents of the *phoneNumberEdit* object, calls *updatePhone()* to convert the string into the proper format, and then saves the resulting string back into the object. The *Form1()* constructor calls *phoneNumber-Edit_textChanged()* to convert the phone number of the first record displayed.

The Results

Figure 12-10 shows the results of executing ToolboxADO. The output doesn't differ significantly from the results of the ManualADO program, even though the Toolbox-ADO program is much easier to generate (once you get used to the Forms Designer steps). ToolboxADO isn't quite as easy to create as the wizard-generated AutoADO program, but the output from ToolboxADO is considerably more attractive and flexible than the output generated by the wizard.

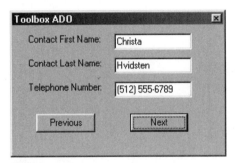

Figure 12-10. *The output of ToolboxADO is much like that of ManualADO with less work.*

ACCESSING DATABASES OVER THE LAN

Accessing a database over a LAN is essentially no different than accessing a database on your local machine. The only difference is this: the path for a database on the LAN is of the form \\ *MACHINENAME\ directorypath\ database.ext,* where *MACHINENAME* is the name assigned to the remote computer by the user of that machine (for example, my machine is named RANDY); *directorypath* is the path to the database; and *database.ext* is the name of the database (MyCompany.mdb in our example).

If you don't know the name of the remote machine, look in the Network Neighborhood section of Windows Explorer. There, you'll find a list of all the machines on your LAN.

CONCLUSION

In this section, you have seen how to access database information in a variety of ways. The chapter began with a fully manual process, which involved manipulating ADO connections and recordsets. The second example demonstrated the use of the Application Wizard to generate data-capable applications quickly. However, the output from these first two applications is unattractive and relatively inflexible. The final example—my personal preference—used the DataSource and DataBinder Toolbox controls to create the connections to the database, which leaves the button click event handlers up to the programmer (you).

Chapter 13

Creating Controls

The Microsoft Visual J++ 6 Toolbox contains a number of Microsoft Windows Foundation Classes for Java (WFC) controls. In fact, the majority of Part II was devoted to demonstrating the power and flexibility of WFC controls. There might come a time, however, when you'll need some exotic control that isn't in the Visual J++ Toolbox. For example, you might want to create a clock object with hands that sweep out the minute and hour, or a button with rounded edges. Fortunately, Visual J++ 6 allows you to create your own controls and add them to the Toolbox.

You can create two types of controls in Visual J++:

■ Local WFC-style controls

■ Remote ActiveX controls

For the remainder of this chapter, I'll refer to these two types of controls as WFC-style controls and ActiveX controls.

NOTE ActiveX controls are actually no more remote than local WFC-style controls. Unlike local controls, however, they are available outside Visual J++.

You can create your own WFC-style control to perform the same types of tasks as a Label control, an Edit control, a Button control, and so on. A user-defined WFC-style control looks and acts like the controls that are already in the WFC Controls section of the Toolbox. In fact, once you've created your own WFC-style control, you can add it to the Toolbox. Essentially, there is no difference between your WFC-style control and the controls that Visual J++ provides.

You can easily turn WFC-style controls into ActiveX controls. You can then add these ActiveX controls to the Visual J++ Toolbox, although you'll lose some of the editing capability you had when they were WFC-style controls. You can also add

ActiveX controls to the toolbars of other Microsoft Visual Studio 6 languages, such as Microsoft Visual Basic 6.

In this chapter, we'll create our own WFC-style control. This control will have the same type of data and active properties as WFC controls, and will support both a data property and an event that we create. We'll add this control to the Toolbox, and use it in a very simple example program to demonstrate how it works.

Once we've created our WFC-style control, we'll turn it into an ActiveX control. We'll first use this ActiveX control in a Visual J++ 6 program and then in a Visual Basic 6 program.

> **NOTE**   The WeightEdit control developed throughout this chapter is included on the companion CD in the Custom Controls subdirectory. The control is built in stages, so you'll find each version of the control located in a separate subdirectory within the Custom Controls subdirectory. Because only one copy of the WeightEdit class files can be in the \Windows\Java\Classes directory (explained later), you'll find WeightEditTest.exe in the same directory as WeightEdit for test purposes.

WFC-STYLE CONTROLS

Let's write a new control that we'll call WeightEdit. This control will look like an Edit control, but it will include a new property, *weight*. The *weight* property will have three possible values: Light, Normal, and Bold. Initially, we'll require the user to enter an integer value to indicate his or her preference: *0* for Light, *1* for Normal, and *2* for Bold. Any other value will be ignored. Later on, we'll be sophisticated enough to offer the user a drop-down list from which to choose the values *Light*, *Normal*, and *Bold*.

To keep things simple, the WeightEdit control will support only a single line of text, and the other properties of the Edit control won't be supported. (Later in this chapter, you'll find out how you can waive this restriction.)

The Integer WeightEdit Control

Let's begin with the integer-based WeightEdit control. The plan is first to create a form for our WeightEdit control. After that, we'll need to define the *weight* property and add an *onPaint()* method capable of displaying the value of the *text* property in a Light, Normal, or Bold font, based on the value of *weight*. In this initial version of our WeightEdit control, the *weight* property will contain an integer value.

We'll add the *weight* property to the Properties window to allow the application programmer to set the value of this newly created property at design time. To complete the WeightEdit control, we'll add an edit capability to allow the user to modify the text displayed in the control.

To demonstrate our WFC-style WeightEdit control, we'll add it to the Toolbox and then use it in a test application.

Creating the control framework using the Control Wizard

Begin by choosing New Project from the Visual J++ File menu. Select Components from the Visual J++ Projects folder in the left pane of the New Project window. From there, select Control in the right pane and name the project WeightEdit. Your window should look like the one shown in Figure 13-1.

Once your window looks like the one in Figure 13-1, click Open to create the project for the WeightEdit control. Opening the project using the Project Explorer reveals a single file with the rather nondescriptive name Control1.java. Double-clicking this file opens a form much like the one that the Windows Application Wizard generates. Close the form before proceeding to the next section.

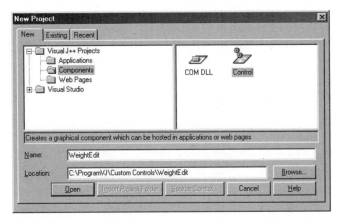

Figure 13-1. *You can create a WFC-style control by starting the Control Wizard from the New Project window.*

The code

To open the Control1.java file, select Code from the View menu. You'll notice three significant differences between this source file and the source files that we have seen in previous chapters:

- There is no *main()* method because this file is intended never to run by itself, but always to run as part of a larger program.

- An ActiveX-style globally unique identifier (GUID) appears commented out as the last line of *Control1*'s header comments.

- The class *Control1* extends the class *UserControl,* rather than extending the class *Form* as a Windows EXE program would. The class *UserControl* extends the class *Control,* so any new class we create that extends *User-Control* will be a WFC-style control.

The GUID is a number that would uniquely identify this control were we to convert it into an ActiveX component. Because we plan to leave WeightEdit as a WFC-style control, however, we can leave the GUID commented out.

Creating the WeightEdit framework

Rather than stick with the name Control1.java, let's rename the file to match the name of the project. First close the source listing. Now rename Control1.java by right-clicking the file in the Project Explorer window and choosing Rename. Change Control1.java to WeightEdit.java.

Open the WeightEdit file again. Within the source file window, rename the class *WeightEdit*. Change the name of the constructor to match. Also change the line *this.setText("Control1")* in the *initForm()* method to *this.setText("WeightEdit")*. Save the file.

Double-click WeightEdit in Project Explorer to open the control in the Forms Designer. The title bar of the Forms Designer will have the title WeightEdit.java [Form]. This form will be the basis of our new control.

Because our WeightEdit control supports only a single line of text, resize the form to the height of a normal font (or slightly larger) and to the length of about half that of the default length of the Forms Designer window. The actual size is unimportant because the final WeightEdit control will be resizeable. Leave the remaining properties in the Properties window at their default values.

The resulting code so far should look like this:

```
import com.ms.wfc.core.*;
import com.ms.wfc.ui.*;


/**
 * This class is a visual component. The entry point for class execution
 * is the constructor.
 *
 * This class can be used as an ActiveX control. Check the checkbox
 * for this class on the Project Properties COM Classes tab, or remove
 * the // from the next line:
// * @com.register ( clsid=xxx, typelib=xxx )
 */
public class WeightEdit extends UserControl
{
    public WeightEdit()
    {
        // Required for Visual J++ Form Designer support
        initForm();

        // TODO: Add any constructor code after initForm call
    }
```

```
/**
 * NOTE: The following code is required by the Visual J++ form
 * designer.  It can be modified using the form editor.  Do not
 * modify it using the code editor.
 */
Container components = new Container();

private void initForm()
{
    this.setSize(new Point(267, 28));
    this.setText("WeightEdit");
}
// NOTE: End of form designer support code

public static class ClassInfo extends UserControl.ClassInfo
{
    // TODO: Add your property and event infos here
}
}
```

Notice that the *clsid* and *typelib* values have been replaced with *xxx* in this listing because these values are unique for each instance of *WeightEdit*.

To make sure that everything still works, build the project. No errors should occur. (Of course, our control doesn't do anything yet!)

Defining the *weight* property

To support the *weight* property, we'll need to define an integer data member named *weight* within the *WeightEdit* class. For convenience, let's add three constants representing the three legal values of *weight*. Set *LIGHT* to *0*, *NORMAL* to *1*, and *BOLD* to *2*. Add the following code to the *WeightEdit* class to define the *weight* property:

```
public class WeightEdit extends UserControl
{
    // the different legal values of weight
    private final static int LIGHT  = 0;
    private final static int NORMAL = 1;
    private final static int BOLD   = 2;

    // the weight control value - start with weight NORMAL
    private int weight = NORMAL;

    public WeightEdit()
    {
    :
}
```

Displaying text using the proper weight

To change the way an object displays text, we'll need to write our own *onPaint()* method using the font weight specified by the local *weight* value. (For now, let's not worry about how the *weight* value is updated.) The following *onPaint()* method— added to our *WeightEdit* class—paints text using our *weight* value:

```
// handle changes to the control
protected void onPaint(PaintEvent pe)
{
    Graphics g = pe.graphics;

    // set the font for the display
    Font f = this.getFont();
    int w;
    switch(weight)
    {
        case LIGHT: w = FontWeight.EXTRALIGHT;
                    break;
        case BOLD:  w = FontWeight.BOLD;
                    break;
        default:    w = FontWeight.NORMAL;
    }

    Font fw = new Font(f, w, false, false, false);
    g.setFont(fw);

    // get the text to display
    String s = this.getText();

    // draw text in the middle of a rectangle
    // of the specified size
    Rectangle r = getClientRect();
    g.drawString(s, r,
                TextFormat.HORIZONTALCENTER|
                TextFormat.VERTICALCENTER);
}
```

This *onPaint()* method starts just as any other *onPaint()* method does, by re-trieving the *Graphics* object from the *PaintEvent*. From there, this method sets the value *w* to the appropriate font weight, depending on the weight values specified by the *weight* property. A new font, *fw*, is created from the existing font but with the new font weight. The *Graphics* object is then updated with this font using the method *setFont()*.

The call to *Control.getText()* retrieves the current string. The *onPaint()* method then displays the text in the middle of the rectangle specified by the size of the *WeightEdit* control.

Saving the user-entered text

Fortunately, the *Control* class has a *text* property. Although the *text* property means different things to different types of controls, we can use this property to save the text the user entered. As we saw in the *onPaint()* method, the *Control* class contains a *getText()* method that we can use without customizing it. However, we'll need to override the *setText()* method to add a call to *invalidate()*. The method *invalidate()* will force the new text string to be repainted with our *onPaint()* method, which reflects the weight factor. We'll also want to override the *onResize()* method to repaint the text, to keep the user-entered text in the middle of the control's area:

```
/**
 * Display the string again whenever it changes.
 */
public void setText(String s)
{
    super.setText(s);

    invalidate();
}

/**
 * Repaint the window when it is resized.
 */
protected void onResize(Event e)
{
    super.onResize(e);
    invalidate();
}
```

Updating the weight value

It's all very nice to define a *weight* property, but a property isn't much use if the user can't set it. To allow the user to set the property, add the following access methods:

```
//---------the following defines the property methods----

/**
 * Return the font weight.
 */
public int getWeight()
{
    return weight;
}

/**
 * Set the font weight.
 */
```

(continued)

```
public void setWeight(int w)
{
    // if the new font weight is valid...
    if (w >= LIGHT && w <= BOLD)
    {
        // update the weight
        this.weight = w;
    }

    // make sure the display is updated with the
    // current weight
    this.invalidate();
}

/**
 * Reset the weight to its default value.
 */
public void resetWeight()
{
    weight = NORMAL;
}
```

The Visual J++ 6 property editor uses access methods that follow the pattern *getX()* and *setX()* to access the property *x*. The *resetX()* method sets the initial value of the *x* property.

Adding weight to the property editor

If you look toward the bottom of the WeightEdit source file, you'll see an inner class named *ClassInfo*. This class is the key to adding a property or set of properties to the property editor. Update the *ClassInfo* class as follows:

```
public static class ClassInfo extends UserControl.ClassInfo
{
    // add our property to the property list
    public static final PropertyInfo weightProperty
        = new PropertyInfo
                    (
                    WeightEdit.class,
                    "weight",
                    int.class
                    );
    public void getProperties(IProperties props)
    {
        super.getProperties(props);
        props.add(weightProperty);
    }
}
```

The first line defines a static data member of class *PropertyInfo*. This object ties the property named *weight* to the current class file, WeightEdit.class, and defines this property to be of type *int*. This object definition tells the property editor the name to display in the Properties window (*weight*), the name of the class (*WeightEdit*) that contains the *getWeight()* and *setWeight()* methods, and the type of the *weight* property (*int*).

The class *ClassInfo* overrides the method *getProperties()*. The *getProperties()* method is what the property editor calls to find the properties to display in the Properties window. This new version of *getProperties()* starts by retrieving the previously defined properties through the call to *super.getProperties()*. To this list of properties, *getProperties()* adds the newly created property *weightProperty*.

Supporting user input

So far, what we've really defined is a control equivalent to a label. We now need to add some code that will allow the user to edit the control.

Open *WeightEdit* in the Forms Designer. Select the WeightEdit control, and in the Properties window double-click the active properties *keyPress*, *click*, *mouseEnter*, and *mouseLeave*. Update the resulting event handlers as follows:

```
// ----the following code creates the actual property editor---

    // maintain a flag indicating whether the user has clicked
    // within the control and whether or not the mouse is still there
    boolean selected = false;
    boolean clicked = false;
    private static final char BACKSPACE = (char)8;

    /**
     * Process the keypress by adding the key to the
     * displayed text if the control is currently active.
     */
    private void WeightEdit_keyPress(Object source, KeyPressEvent e)
    {
        // if the object is selected...
        if (clicked)
        {
            // then update the string
            String s = this.getText();
            char c = e.getKeyChar();
            if (c == BACKSPACE)
            {
                int length = s.length();
                s = s.substring(0, length - 1);
            }
```

(continued)

```
            else
            {
                s = s + c;
            }
            setText(s);
        }
    }

    /**
     * If the mouse is within the control,
     * then set the clicked flag.
     */
    private void WeightEdit_click(Object source, Event e)
    {
        if (selected)
        {
            clicked = true;
        }
    }

    /**
     * Set the selected flag, indicating that the mouse is
     * within the area of the control.
     */
    private void WeightEdit_mouseEnter(Object source, Event e)
    {
        selected = true;
    }

    /**
     * Clear the selected and clicked flags as the mouse leaves
     * the control to indicate that the control is no longer active.
     */
    private void WeightEdit_mouseLeave(Object source, Event e)
    {
        selected = false;
        clicked = false;
    }
```

Let's start our discussion of the preceding code with the *WeightEdit_mouse-Enter()* method. The *WeightEdit_mouseEnter()* method is called when the mouse pointer enters the area designated as the WeightEdit control. This method sets the *selected* data member to *true*, indicating that the mouse pointer is within the control. The method *WeightEdit_mouseLeave()* is invoked when the mouse pointer leaves the control. This method sets *selected* to *false* to indicate that the mouse pointer has left the WeightEdit control. (It also sets *clicked* to *false*, but we won't go over the significance of that until later in this discussion.)

When the user clicks the mouse, the method *WeightEdit_click* first checks the flag *selected*. If this flag is set to *true*, the method sets the flag *clicked* to *true*. Thus, the *clicked* flag is set to *true* when the mouse is clicked within the control and the mouse pointer has yet to leave the area of the control.

The *WeightEdit_keyPress()* method is invoked when the user presses a key. If the *clicked* flag isn't set, the key input is ignored. If *clicked* is set, *WeightEdit* processes the character. This control is a very simple editor (hardly worthy of the name editor): any character entered is appended to the string no matter where the user clicks within the WeightEdit control. The only character that gets special attention is the Backspace key, which deletes the last character in the string, again regardless of where the user clicks within the control. (The point of this editor is to show you the principles of creating a control. We don't want to get bogged down in detailed editor code.)

The string created by *WeightEdit_keyPress()* is displayed in the WeightEdit editor control by calling *setText()*. Keep in mind that our overriding *setText()* method updates the *text* field in the *Control* class before invalidating the display so that the *onPaint()* method displays the resulting string to the user.

Viewing the total result

In case you're confused, I'll show you the entire WeightEdit listing here:

```
import com.ms.wfc.core.*;
import com.ms.wfc.ui.*;

import com.ms.lang.*;

/**
 * The WeightEdit class extends Control by adding the
 * weight property.
// * @com.register ( clsid=xxx, typelib=xxx )
 */
public class WeightEdit extends UserControl
{
    // the different legal values of weight
    private final static int LIGHT  = 0;
    private final static int NORMAL = 1;
    private final static int BOLD   = 2;

    // the weight control value - start with weight NORMAL
    private int weight = NORMAL;

    public WeightEdit()
    {
        // Required for Visual J++ Form Designer support
        initForm();
    }
```

(continued)

```
/**
 * Display the string again whenever it changes.
 */
public void setText(String s)
{
    super.setText(s);

    invalidate();
}

/**
 * Repaint the window when it is resized.
 */
protected void onResize(Event e)
{
    super.onResize(e);
    invalidate();
}

/**
 * Reflect the weight property.
 */
// handle changes to the control
protected void onPaint(PaintEvent pe)
{
    Graphics g = pe.graphics;

    // set the font for the display
    Font f = this.getFont();
    int w;
    switch(weight)
    {
        case LIGHT: w = FontWeight.EXTRALIGHT;
                    break;
        case BOLD:  w = FontWeight.BOLD;
                    break;
        default:    w = FontWeight.NORMAL;
    }

    Font fw = new Font(f, w, false, false, false);
    g.setFont(fw);

    // get the text to display
    String s = this.getText();

    // draw text in the middle of a rectangle
    // of the specified size
    Rectangle r = getClientRect();
```

```
        g.drawString(s, r,
                    TextFormat.HORIZONTALCENTER|
                    TextFormat.VERTICALCENTER);
}


//---------the following defines the property methods----


/**
 * Return the font weight.
 */
public int getWeight()
{
    return weight;
}


/**
 * Set the font weight.
 */
public void setWeight(int w)
{
    // if the new font weight is valid...
    if (w >= LIGHT && w <= BOLD)
    {
        // then update the weight
        this.weight = w;
    }

    // make sure the display is updated with the
    // current weight
    this.invalidate();
}


/**
 * Reset the weight to its default value.
 */
public void resetWeight()
{
    weight = NORMAL;
}


// ----the following code creates the actual property editor---

// maintain a flag indicating whether the user has clicked
// within the control and whether or not the mouse is still there
boolean selected = false;
boolean clicked = false;
private static final char BACKSPACE = (char)8;
```

(continued)

```
/**
 * Process the keypress by adding the key to the
 * displayed text if the control is currently active.
 */
private void WeightEdit_keyPress(Object source, KeyPressEvent e)
{
    // if the object is selected...
    if (clicked)
    {
        // update the string
        String s = this.getText();
        char c = e.getKeyChar();
        if (c == BACKSPACE)
        {
            int length = s.length();
            s = s.substring(0, length - 1);
        }
        else
        {
            s = s + c;
        }
        setText(s);
    }
}


/**
 * If the mouse is within the control,
 * set the clicked flag.
 */
private void WeightEdit_click(Object source, Event e)
{
    if (selected)
    {
        clicked = true;
    }
}


/**
 * Set the selected flag, indicating that the mouse is
 * within the area of the control.
 */
private void WeightEdit_mouseEnter(Object source, Event e)
{
    selected = true;
}


/**
 * Clear the selected and clicked flags as the mouse leaves
 * the control to indicate that the control is no longer active.
 */
```

```
private void WeightEdit_mouseLeave(Object source, Event e)
{
    selected = false;
    clicked = false;
}


/**
 * NOTE: The following code is required by the Visual J++ form
 * designer.  It can be modified using the form editor.  Do not
 * modify it using the code editor.
 */
Container components = new Container();

private void initForm()
{
    this.setBackColor(Color.CONTROL);
    this.setSize(new Point(235, 28));
    this.setText("");
    this.addOnClick(new EventHandler(this.WeightEdit_click));
    this.addOnKeyPress(
            new KeyPressEventHandler(this.WeightEdit_keyPress));
    this.addOnMouseEnter(
            new EventHandler(this.WeightEdit_mouseEnter));
    this.addOnMouseLeave(
            new EventHandler(this.WeightEdit_mouseLeave));
}
// NOTE: End of form designer support code

/**
 * Add weight to the properties defined for this control.
 */
public static class ClassInfo extends UserControl.ClassInfo
{
    // add our property to the property list
    public static final PropertyInfo weightProperty
        = new PropertyInfo
                    (
                    WeightEdit.class,
                    "weight",
                    int.class
                    );
    public void getProperties(IProperties props)
    {
        super.getProperties(props);
        props.add(weightProperty);
    }
}
}
```

Adding the WeightEdit control to the Toolbox

Once you've compiled the *WeightEdit* class, you must still add the control to the Toolbox before other programs can use it. Before closing *WeightEdit*, select the General section in the Toolbox. (You can put the WeightEdit tool in any section of the Toolbox, but I prefer to place newly created tools within the General area.)

Right-click within the Toolbox, and choose Customize Toolbox. Select the WFC Controls tab in the Customize Toolbox window. You'll see a list of WFC controls that you can add to the Toolbox. Controls that are checked already appear in the Toolbox. These are the WFC controls that you've been using in the examples in this book up until now.

Scroll toward the bottom of the list. Somewhat remarkably (at least to me), there it is, our WeightEdit control, at the bottom of the list. Select the check box next to the WeightEdit entry as shown in Figure 13-2, and then choose OK to add the control to the Toolbox. (It will appear in the Toolbox as an outline of a WFC-style control icon—without a target program, this control and all others are not selectable.)

NOTE   If the control doesn't appear in the Customize Toolbox window, try closing the WeightEdit solution by choosing Close All from the File menu and then reloading the solution.

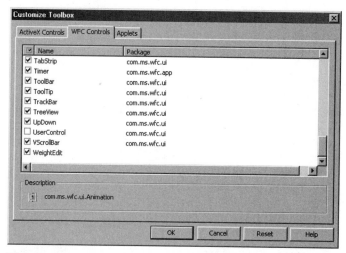

Figure 13-2. *The Customize Toolbox window shows our WeightEdit control being added to the Toolbox.*

HANDLING ERRORS IN USER-DEFINED CONTROLS

I've found that changes to a user-defined control often don't take effect until the project containing the control has been closed and reopened. I've also found that if I've made a mistake in creating a control such as WeightEdit, I might not discover it until I've tried to use the control in an application. The most common error that occurs in creating user-defined controls is forgetting to provide both a *getX()* and a *setX()* method, or providing one that is declared incorrectly (for example, declaring a *void setX()* method instead of the correct *void setX(int)*). Unfortunately, if you do have such an error when using a user-defined control, the Forms Designer gets confused and removes the declaration from the form's *initForm()* method.

For example, let's say that your *initForm()* method originally looked like this:

```
Control control = new Control();
WeightEdit weightEdit1 = new WeightEdit();
void initForm()
{
    ⋮
}
```

After the usage error, your form code will look like this:

```
Control control = new Control();
void initForm()
{
    ⋮
}
```

The references to *weightEdit1* within the *initForm()* code remain, however, so not only does the application code not compile but you can't even open the form in the Forms Designer. (You get this "helpful" message: "Unable to show the form designer...Fix the error, and then try to view the form again.")

Thus, if you make a mistake in your user-defined control, you'll need to take three steps to fix the error:

1. Fix the problem in the user-defined control code.

2. Close and reopen the project containing the control.

3. Add the declaration of the user-defined control object back into the *initForm()* code.

Using this roundabout solution, you'll be able to fix any problems that arise in the code generated by the Forms Designer.

Using the WeightEdit control within the Forms Designer

To add the WeightEdit control to a program, you'll first need to create a program. With the WeightEdit solution still open, choose Add Project from the File menu, and then select Windows Application. Enter the name *WeightEditTest*, make sure the Add To Current Solution option is selected, and choose Open. You've just added a new project to the solution.

> **NOTE** A solution consists of one or more projects. Each of these projects acts as an independent program, with one exception: Only one project can contain the *main()* method with which to start. You must indicate which project contains this method by using the Project Properties dialog box.

Open the WeightEditTest project in Project Explorer to reveal a conventional Windows executable-style Form1.java file. Double-click this file to open the form in the Forms Designer.

Once you've opened the form, return to the General section of the Toolbox. Notice that WeightEdit is now available. Drop a WeightEdit control onto the form. The resulting form window should look like the one shown in Figure 13-3.

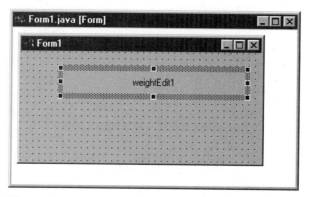

Figure 13-3. *The WeightEdit control looks like this in an application.*

Now open the Properties window, and select the WeightEdit control. Notice that the *text* property displays the default display text for the control. Also notice the appearance of our newly added *weight* property with the initial value of *1*. (The default of 1 came from the control's *resetWeight()* method.) The Properties window with these settings is shown in Figure 13-4.

The *text* property in the Properties window is synchronized with the text displayed within the WeightEdit control. To demonstrate this synchronization, click the WeightEdit control on the form and begin typing. (Be sure to leave the mouse pointer within the control while you're typing.) Notice that the *text* property within the Properties window automatically updates. Now click the *text* property and type something new. Notice that the contents of the WeightEdit control update as you type. This automatic updating is a direct result of using the *getText()* and *setText()* methods of the *Control* class to retrieve and update the text.

Figure 13-4. *The Properties window shows an updated* text *property and the new* weight *property.*

While still in the Forms Designer, and with the WeightEdit control selected, set the *weight* property in the Properties window to *2*. The display immediately converts to Bold. Now set the value to *0*, and the display turns to Light. (Some display drivers can't display the text with a Light font type to look any different than text with a Normal font type.)

Using the WeightEdit control

Set the WeightEdit control to whatever initial text and weight you prefer. Now compile the Form1 application. We're going to run the application from within the integrated development environment (IDE), but first you must tell Visual J++ which project within the solution contains the application. Point at the WeightEditTest project in Project Explorer, and hold down the right mouse button. From the drop-down menu, choose Set As StartUp Project.

When you run WeightEditTest, you'll see a WeightEdit control appearing within the form with the text you entered at the weight you specified in the Properties window. Click the text with the mouse pointer, and begin typing (or hitting the Backspace key) with the mouse pointer still at the position where you clicked. Whatever you type is appended to the text. (Remember that the text is appended to the end no matter where in the string you click. I warned you this control wasn't much of an editor, but it does demonstrate the principles of creating and using a user-defined control.)

Figure 13-5 shows the program with text displayed in the WeightEdit control in the middle of the form.

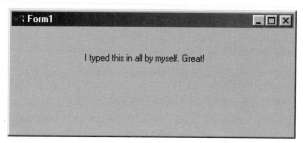

Figure 13-5. *The WeightEditTest program runs with our newly defined WeightEdit control.*

Making the WeightEdit control available in other solutions

The WeightEdit control was available to WeightEditTest from within the IDE because the two were built together as part of the same project. It would be clumsy if we had to include the WeightEdit project within a solution every time we wanted to use the control. In addition, if you attempt to run the test application by double-clicking the WeightEditTest.exe file, you'll notice that the program fails and displays an error message indicating that it couldn't find the WeightEdit.class files.

When a Visual J++ application begins, it looks in a number of different places for the .class files needed to run Toolbox controls. It always looks in the current directory first. If it doesn't find the .class files there, it next looks in the directory \Windows\Java\Classes.

To see how this works, copy the two .class files from the WeightEdit directory to the \Windows\Java\Classes directory. WeightEditTest.exe now runs properly directly from Windows or from the IDE. In addition, you can now remove the WeightEdit project from the common solution we've been working with, and recompile and run the result. WeightEditTest continues to run from the IDE even without WeightEdit in the same solution.

> **NOTE**   You'll find this version of the WeightEdit control on the companion CD in the subdirectory Custom Controls\Integer WFC-Style WeightEdit.

The Enumerated WeightEdit Control

As neat as the integer version of the WeightEdit control is, it would be that much better if the user were provided with the options *Light*, *Normal*, and *Bold* rather than the integer values *0*, *1*, and *2*. In this section, we'll change the integer version of the WeightEdit control so that it uses an enumerated *weight* property.

Exposing the *weight* property values

In the integer version of the WeightEdit control, we defined the different legal values of the *weight* property in a set of *static final* integers that were private to the *WeightEdit* class. By being private, no outside program could access these values.

To make the weight constants available to the Properties window, we'll need to make these properties public. Even this isn't enough. The class that contains the properties must also extend the class *Enum*.

NOTE Recall that the class *Enum* provides enumerated sequences of values.

Because the enumerated weight class must be declared public, and because two public classes can't reside in the same source file, we'll need to create a separate Visual J++ source file in the WeightEdit project. To create a new public class under the WeightEdit project, choose Add Class from the Project menu and name this new class *WeightValues* (though the name isn't really important).

Open the new class in Visual J++, and append the *extends Enum* statement to the class declaration. You'll need to import *com.ms.wfc.core.Enum* to access the *Enum* class. Now move the weight constants that were defined in the *WeightEdit* class to this new class and change their declarations from private to public. In addition, add the public static method *valid()*. This new method returns *true* if the integer passed to it is a legal weight value and *false* otherwise. The Properties window and user programs use this method to filter out illegal input from the user.

Once you're finished, the *WeightValues* class should look like this:

```
import com.ms.wfc.core.Enum;

/**
 * Define the names of the different weights.
 */
public class WeightValues extends Enum
{
    // the different legal values of weight
    public final static int LIGHT  = 0;
    public final static int NORMAL = 1;
    public final static int BOLD   = 2;

    public static boolean valid(int i)
    {
        return (i <= LIGHT) && (i <= BOLD);
    }
}
```

Making changes to the *WeightEdit* class

All references within the *WeightEdit* class to these constants must now be changed to refer to this class. For example, you must change the previous reference to *NORMAL* (or 1) to *WeightValues.NORMAL*. You can also use the new *valid()* method to replace the line *if (w >= LIGHT && w <= BOLD)* in the *setWeight()* method with the line *if (WeightValues.valid(w))*.

The only other change we need to make is to the *PropertyInfo* object within the *WeightEdit* class. You must edit the *ClassInfo* inner class to appear as follows:

```
public static class ClassInfo extends UserControl.ClassInfo
{
    // add our property to the property list
    public static final PropertyInfo weightProperty
        = new PropertyInfo
                        (
                        WeightEdit.class,
                        "weight",
                        WeightValues.class
                        );
    public void getProperties(IProperties props)
    {
        super.getProperties(props);
        props.add(weightProperty);
    }
}
```

Nothing has changed within *ClassInfo,* other than the fact that the *weightProperty* declaration now refers to *WeightValues.class* for the type of values to expect rather than to *int.class.* The class passed to the *PropertyInfo* constructor is where the property editor looks to find the names of the enumerated constants.

Using the enumerated WeightEdit control

Return to the Toolbox, and remove the WeightEdit control by right-clicking it and selecting Delete Item. (Don't worry, the file won't be deleted.) Now recompile the entire solution. (The WeightEditTest project will be recompiled, too, which is unnecessary but doesn't hurt.) Close the solution, and then reopen it to make the changes take effect.

> **NOTE**   Keep in mind that you might need to close the solution and reopen it before changes to user-defined controls take effect.

Reopen the *WeightEditTest* class in the Forms Designer. Select the Properties window, and then select the WeightEdit control. (If you've deleted the control, just add it to the form again.) If you examine the *weight* property, rather than seeing the value *1,* as you did before, you'll see the enumerated value *Normal.* Even better, if you select the *weight* property, a drop-down list that displays the valid values for *weight* in text form appears, as shown in Figure 13-6. Other than that, the enumerated WeightEdit control works exactly the same as the integer WeightEdit control.

> **NOTE**   You'll find this version of the WeightEdit control on the companion CD in the subdirectory Custom Controls\Enumerated WFC-Style WeightEdit.

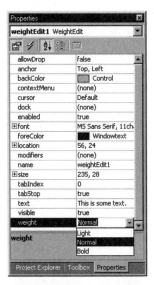

Figure 13-6. *Enumerated weight values are passed on to the* **Properties** *window.*

Adding Events to WeightEdit

Not only can you add properties, such as *weight,* to a user-defined control, but you can also add user-defined events, using a technique similar to the one we've just discussed for adding properties. Let's add a *WeightEvent* event that occurs when the weight changes.

Adding a new event involves the following steps:

1. Create the event class.

2. Define a delegate for the event class.

3. Add the event to the Properties window.

4. Update the WeightEdit control to generate the new event.

Defining the *WeightEvent* class

Before we can start, we must define an event class and a purpose. Let's call this class *WeightEvent* and say that we want it to report changes in the font weight of a Weight-Edit control.

Because user code must be able to access *WeightEvent,* we must declare the class public. Therefore, we must define *WeightEvent* in its own WeightEvent.java file. In addition, if the user code is to access the value of the new weight, we must also declare the *weight* property public. (If you prefer, you can leave the *weight* property private, and provide a public *getWeight()* method.)

Select the WeightEdit project in Visual J++ Project Explorer. Now choose Add Class from the Project menu. Name the class *WeightEvent*. Update the class as follows:

```java
import com.ms.wfc.core.Event;

/**
 * This event is thrown when the weight of
 * the WeightEdit class changes.
 */
public class WeightEvent extends Event
{
    // the new weight
    public int weightChange;

    /**
     * Create an event to announce a change
     * in the weight property.
     * @param weightChange - the new weight value
     */
    public WeightEvent(int weightChange)
    {
        this.weightChange = weightChange;
    }
}
```

WeightEvent is a true event because it extends the *Event* class. The *Event* class contains no data, and its constructor takes no arguments. The *WeightEvent* class has one data member, *weightChange*, to store the new weight, and its constructor accepts one argument, the value to be stored in *weightChange*.

Defining a *WeightEvent* delegate

Each new event requires a set of access methods in the same way that a new data property requires a pair of *getX()* and *setX()* methods. If you examine the event methods already supported by different types of controls in the Visual J++ 6 subset of the MSDN help library, you'll notice that for each event type *X* there is an *addOnX* method, a *removeOnX()* method, and sometimes an *onX()* method.

The *add* method adds a delegate to the list of delegates prepared to handle the event. The *remove* method removes the specified delegate from the list.

NOTE   A delegate is an object that contains a reference to a method. All delegates are subclassed from the abstract class *Delegate*.

The *onX()* method calls each of the registered delegates, passing them the *X* event. Our new *WeightEvent* is no different.

NOTE   The order in which the delegates are invoked isn't specified and isn't the order in which they are added. In addition, if one of the delegate methods throws an exception, execution of the delegate list is halted. Control passes up the stack until the first error-handling catch of the proper type to match the thrown object is encountered.

Following the same pattern, we'll need to add the methods *addOnWeight-Event()*, *removeOnWeightEvent()*, and *onWeightEvent()* to our *WeightEdit* class. Before we can do this, however, we need to define a *WeightEventDelegate* class. We must declare this delegate class public; if we don't, the user-created delegate functions won't be able to process the events sent to them. As mentioned earlier, because *WeightEvent* is public, we are forced to create a new source file, WeightEventDelegate.java, that contains the public *WeightEventDelegate* class.

Here is the *WeightEventDelegate* class file:

```
/**
 * Handle the WeightEvent.
 */
import com.ms.wfc.core.*;

public final multicast delegate
    void WeightEventDelegate(Object sender, WeightEvent e);
```

As you can see, this file is nothing more than the declaration of a multicast delegate designed to handle the *WeightEvent* class. The delegate must be declared *multicast* to support the distinct possibility that two or more delegates will attach themselves to the *WeightEvent* event.

Adding the *WeightEvent* handlers to *WeightEdit*

In some ways, the changes we need to make to our principal class, *WeightEdit*, to incorporate the new event are predictable. As mentioned earlier, *WeightEdit* must provide an *addOnWeightEvent()* method, a *removeOnWeightEvent()* method, and an *onWeightEvent()* method. These methods are shown in the following code, which is extracted from the full *WeightEdit* code listing:

```
// initially, the WeightEvent has no existing handlers;
// these are added by calling addOnWeightEvent()
private WeightEventDelegate allWeightDelegates = null;

/**
 * Provide a method to add new delegates to the list of
 * delegates to notify of the WeightEvent.
 */
public void addOnWeightEvent(WeightEventDelegate addHandler)
{
    allWeightDelegates = (WeightEventDelegate)
                        Delegate.combine(
                            allWeightDelegates,
                            addHandler);
}
```

(continued)

```
/**
 * Remove a WeightEvent handler.
 */
public void removeOnWeightEvent(WeightEventDelegate rmvHandler)
{
    if (allWeightDelegates != null)
    {
        allWeightDelegates = (WeightEventDelegate)
                                 Delegate.remove(
                                     allWeightDelegates,
                                     rmvHandler);
    }
}

/**
 * Run the WeightEvent handler.
 */
protected void onWeightEvent(WeightEvent event)
{
    // if there is any WeightEvent delegate...
    if (allWeightDelegates != null)
    {
        // then process it
        allWeightDelegates.invoke(this, event);
    }
}
```

The data member *allWeightDelegates* is a listing of all the method delegates that are interested in receiving the *WeightEvent* event. Initially, this list is *null*. Although the name of this data member isn't important, the names of the following three methods are critical.

The *addOnWeightEvent()* method takes a *WeightEventDelegate* object as its argument. The *addOnWeightEvent()* method adds the argument *addHandler* to the list *allWeightDelegates* by passing both a reference to the list, and the new delegate *addHandler,* to the *Delegate.combine()* method. The result is a new list containing the previous delegates plus *addHandler*. This list is saved back into *allWeight-Delegates*. We declare the *addOnWeightEvent()* method public so that all classes have access to it.

NOTE The *Delegate* class is part of the Microsoft Software Development Kit (SDK) for Java. The class has few methods, all of which are devoted to event-type operations, such as the *combine()* method used in our *addOnWeightEvent()* method. The *Delegate* class is included in the package *com.ms.lang,* which means that you'll need to add the statement *import com.ms.lang.** to the beginning of *WeightEdit*.

Similarly, *removeOnWeightEvent()* uses the *Delegate.remove()* method to remove a *WeightEventDelegate* object from the list. You also need to declare this method public.

The *onWeightEvent()* method is invoked when the *WeightEvent* occurs. This method starts by examining the *allWeightDelegates* delegate list. If *allWeightDelegates* is not *null*, *onWeightEvent()* calls *allWeightDelegates.invoke()*, which invokes each attached *WeightEventDelegate* object.

Adding *WeightEvent* to the active properties list

Adding the *addWeightEvent()*, *removeWeightEvent()*, and *onWeightEvent()* methods to *WeightEdit* is necessary but insufficient to allow user programs to implement these methods. We must also add the *weightEvent* property to the active properties displayed in the Properties window. To do this, we need to add another property to the *ClassInfo* inner class, as we did when we added the *weight* data property to the Properties list.

The following listing is the entire *ClassInfo* class containing the code for the new property addition:

```
public static class ClassInfo extends UserControl.ClassInfo
{
    //-----------------add the data properties-------------
    // add our property to the property list
    public static final PropertyInfo weightProperty
        = new PropertyInfo
                        (
                        WeightEdit.class,
                        "weight",
                        WeightValues.class
                        );
    public void getProperties(IProperties props)
    {
        super.getProperties(props);
        props.add(weightProperty);
    }

    //-----------------add the event properties----------
    public static final EventInfo weightEvent
                = new EventInfo(
                        WeightEdit.class,
                        "weightEvent",
                        WeightEventDelegate.class
                        );

    public void getEvents(IEvents events)
    {
        super.getEvents(events);
        events.add(weightEvent);
    }
}
```

The data properties section is completely unchanged from the code we added earlier to the *WeightEdit* class. Following that, however, is the declaration of a *weightEvent* object of class *EventInfo*. The *EventInfo* constructor attaches the event named *weightEvent* to the *WeightEdit* class, which contains the *weightEvent* handler. The last argument specifies the delegate that will handle the *weightEvent*.

When Visual J++ calls the *getEvents()* method to get the list of events, *getEvents()* adds our *weightEvent* object to those events already defined.

Updating *WeightEdit* to generate a *WeightEvent* event

Creating a new *weightEvent* object means nothing if *WeightEdit* doesn't generate it when the weight is updated. Let's consider this question for a moment: When would an event to inform the system that the weight has changed be sent? The answer is, obviously, when the weight is changed, which is in the *setWeight()* method. The following change (shown in boldface) to *setWeight()* is all that is needed to send the *WeightEvent* event notification to the system:

```
/**
 * Sets the font weight.
 */
public void setWeight(int w)
{
    // if the new font weight is valid...
    if (WeightValues.valid(w))
    {
        // update the weight
        this.weight = w;

        // notify the world of the change in weight
        onWeightEvent(new WeightEvent(w));
    }

    // make sure the display is updated with the
    // current weight
    this.invalidate();
}
```

As you can see, the only change to *setWeight()* is the addition of a call to *onWeightEvent()* if the weight changes. Even if the value hasn't changed, you should still call *onWeightEvent()* to inform other classes that a weight change was attempted.

The call to *onWeightEvent()* passes an object of class *WeightEvent*—which contains the new weight *w*—to all classes that have previously declared their interest in this event by calling *addOnWeightEvent()*. Refer to the *WeightEvent* constructor and the *onWeightEvent()* method if this line of code isn't clear.

Adding the new WeightEdit control to the Toolbox

Save the modified files, and compile the solution. In the General section of the Toolbox, right-click to open the context menu and choose Customize Toolbox. To add the WeightEdit control to the Toolbox, select WeightEdit from the list of available controls on the WFC Controls tab of the Customize Toolbox dialog box.

Viewing *weightEvent* in the active Properties window

To know whether our *WeightEvent* works as planned, we must first check the list of events in the Properties window to make sure that our event is included.

First open the *WeightEditTest* form in the Forms Designer. Now open the Properties window. Select the WeightEdit control in the middle of the *WeightEditTest* form. (If you've previously deleted the *WeightEdit* object from the form, just add it back and select it.) Now examine the list of active properties. You should be able to find the *weightEvent* event listed among the other events. (Events are easier to find if you list them in alphabetical order.)

Figure 13-7 shows the event properties for the WeightEdit control. Our new weight event appears in the list. So far, so good.

Figure 13-7. *This list of event properties for the* WeightEdit *class shows our new* weightEvent *event.*

Using *WeightEvent* in a program

Now comes the final test. Let's process the weight event in our test program.

Still looking at the *WeightEditTest* form, open the Properties window and select the *WeightEdit* object. Now double-click the *weightEvent* property. This should create an empty method in your *WeightEditTest* class as shown on the following page.

```
void weightEdit1_weightEvent(Object source, WeightEvent e)
{

}
```

Save the form, and then look through the code the Forms Designer generated. You'll find a new call to *addOnWeightEvent()*. This method adds a *WeightEventDelegate* object that references the newly created *weightEdit1_weightEvent()* method to the list of delegates interested in processing the weight event.

To prove that *weightEdit1_weightEvent()* does get invoked when the weight changes, let's add a call to *setText()* that changes the text in the WeightEdit control to a description of what the new weight value is. This will make it instantly obvious that the *weightEdit1_weightEvent()* method is called. Remember that it's *setWeight()*, not *setText()*, that invokes the *WeightEvent* event.

> **NOTE**   If the event handler makes a call to a method that invokes the event being processed, the program will hang in an endless loop until it eventually runs out of stack and crashes.

The following code should do the trick:

```
/**
 * Update the text to reflect the new weight whenever a
 * weightEvent occurs.
 */
private void weightEdit1_weightEvent(Object source, WeightEvent e)
{
    int newWeight = e.weightChange;
    weightEdit1.setText("Weight changed to " +
                        newWeight);
}
```

This code is fine for processing the *WeightEvent* when it occurs, but something has to trigger the event. In other words, some method has to change the *weight* property.

Even though this technique isn't very sophisticated, let's just add a double-click method to the *WeightEditTest* code to update the weight. With the WeightEdit control selected in Forms Designer, double-click the *doubleClick* active property to create the *weightEdit1_doubleClick()* method. Next modify the method as follows:

```
/**
 * Change the weight whenever the user double-clicks the
 * WeightEdit control (simply to test the weightEvent
 * active property).
 */
private void weightEdit1_doubleClick(Object source, Event e)
{
    int w = weightEdit1.getWeight();
```

```
    w++;
    if (w > 2)
    {
        w = 0;
    }
    weightEdit1.setWeight(w);
}
```

This version gets the current weight of the *weightEdit1* object by calling *get-Weight()*. From there, it increments the weight until it becomes larger than 2, at which point it resets the weight back to 0. It then calls *setWeight()* to update the weight with the new value. This call to *setWeight()* generates a *WeightEvent* that the previously registered *weightEdit1_weightEvent()* method should process. Now recompile the entire solution.

Giving the final test

Run the WeightEditTest program. Change the *weightEdit1* text in your form to something like that shown in Figure 13-5 on page 450. Make note of the font weight. Now double-click the *weightEdit1* object. The weight changes instantly. Even more important, the text changes to display a string indicating the new weight. This test proves that our *weightEdit1_weightEvent()* method is being invoked as planned. My results are shown in Figure 13-8.

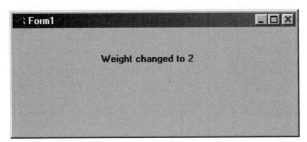

Figure 13-8. *The* weightEdit1 *object looks like this after it's been double-clicked.*

Double-click the object again, and you'll notice that both the value and the weight continue to change. The user-defined WeightEdit WFC control works.

> **NOTE** You'll find this version of the WeightEdit control on the companion CD in the subdirectory Custom Controls\Active WFC-Style WeightEdit.

CUSTOM ACTIVEX CONTROLS

The WeightEdit WFC-style control is available to other Visual J++ 6 applications. (Remember to copy the .class files to the Windows\Java\Classes directory so that the .EXE files generated using the WeightEdit control can find them.) However, only Visual J++ can use WFC controls. Is there any way to make the WeightEdit control more universally available?

Turning the WeightEdit control into an ActiveX control makes it available to other Visual Studio 6 languages, not to mention any other ActiveX-capable application. (It's doubtful that any application other than a programming language would know what to do with the WeightEdit ActiveX control.)

Turning WeightEdit into an ActiveX Control

Once you've created a WFC-style control, the remaining steps needed to create an ActiveX control are straightforward:

1. Uncomment the *@com.dll* directive.

2. Repackage the .class files and type library (.tlb) file into a COM package.

3. Rebuild the project.

4. Register the COM package as an ActiveX component.

5. Add the ActiveX control to the Toolbox.

Preparing the WFC-style control

There's no reason to retain the WeightEditTest project in the solution, because it won't be made part of the ActiveX control. Right-click the WeightEditTest project in Project Explorer, and select Remove Project. Removing the project doesn't delete the files or the directory that make up the project.

You might also want to change from the Debug configuration to the Release configuration, which will reduce the size of the eventual .class files by removing the debug information. Right-click the project, and select WeightEdit Properties. Select Release from the Configuration drop-down list.

> **NOTE** We could have done this at any point during the creation of the WFC-style control.

Uncommenting the DLL directive

Edit the WeightEdit.java file, and remove the // comment bars that precede the *@com.register* directive. This assigns the control a GUID, which uniquely identifies our WeightEdit control.

Repackaging the project

The control will need all of the .class files that are part of the WeightEdit project. To make sure that all the .class files are included, open the WeightEdit Properties dialog box again. In the COM Classes tab, check each of the classes present. Figure 13-9 shows the resulting display.

Now click the Output Format tab. Check Enable Packaging. From the Packaging Type drop-down list, select COM DLL. Figure 13-10 shows the WeightEdit Properties dialog box with these settings selected.

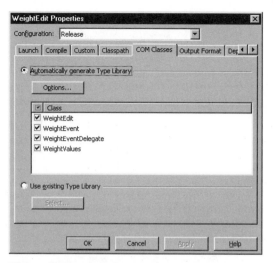

Figure 13-9. *The COM Classes tab allows you to select which classes you want to include in the ActiveX control.*

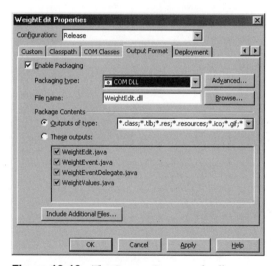

Figure 13-10. *The Output Format tab allows you to bundle the necessary files into a single COM DLL.*

Now close the Properties window and rebuild the project. The *@com.dll* directive tells Visual J++ 6 to register the WeightEdit COM DLL as an ActiveX component.

Adding the ActiveX control to the Toolbox

To add the new control to the Toolbox, right-click within the General section of the Toolbox. From the context menu, select Customize Toolbox. The steps so far are the same as those for creating a WFC-style control.

Click the ActiveX Controls tab rather than the WFC Controls tab we used in the previous section. Scroll down to the bottom of the list of available ActiveX controls to find our WeightEdit control, as shown in Figure 13-11. Check the box to create the new Toolbox control. A new icon will appear on the Toolbox immediately below the WFC control icon (assuming you haven't already removed the WFC-style control icon from the Toolbox). The ActiveX control appears disabled because there is no application in which to use the control.

NOTE   The ActiveX control icon is slightly different than the WFC-style control icon. This difference distinguishes the two types of controls for the user.

You can now close the WeightEdit solution.

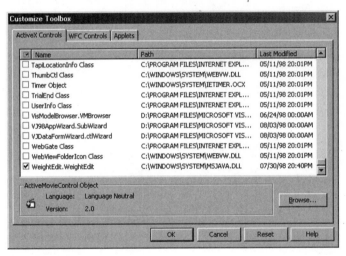

Figure 13-11. *The Customize Toolbox dialog box shows the available ActiveX controls.*

Using the New ActiveX Control

We can use the new WeightEdit ActiveX control in much the same way as we used the WFC-style control we created earlier in the chapter. The main difference between the WFC-style control and the ActiveX control is that Visual J++ 6 creates a set of interface classes with which to access the ActiveX control.

To demonstrate this difference, create a new Windows application named WeightEditTest. Double-click Form1.java in Project Explorer to open the class in the Forms Designer (if it isn't open already). Open the Toolbox. Now that an application is open, the WeightEdit ActiveX control is enabled. Drag the control and drop it in the middle of the WeightEditTest form.

You should notice the large amount of disk activity as soon as you drop the WeightEdit ActiveX control onto the form. (By comparison, adding the WFC-style control was much quicker.) This activity is due to the creation of the interface classes mentioned previously.

Look at the project with Project Explorer. Figure 13-12 shows just a subset of new files added to the project. Each of these small .java files represents an active property in the WeightEdit ActiveX control.

Open the Properties window, and select the WeightEdit control within Form1. As before, both the *weight* and *weightEvent* properties are present. Build and run the WeightEditTest application. The WeightEditTest application runs in the same way it did before, although it takes somewhat longer to begin running because of the increased access to the operating system ActiveX components require. If you examine the WeightEditTest.exe file, you'll notice that it weighs in at over 100 KB—large for a Java application, but still much smaller than a C or C++ program.

There is one difference between the WFC-style control and the ActiveX control. Select the WeightEdit control in the Forms Designer. Now begin typing. Rather than update the control, the Properties window immediately appears in the foreground. Whatever text you enter appears in the *text* property. The text that appears in the ActiveX control doesn't update until you finish updating the *text* property.

> **NOTE**   You'll find this version of the WeightEdit control on the companion CD in the subdirectory Custom Controls\ActiveX WeightEdit.

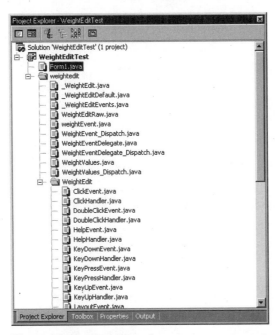

Figure 13-12. *Visual J++ 6 generates a separate interface class for each event handler in the WeightEdit ActiveX control.*

Using the ActiveX Control in Visual Basic 6

As mentioned earlier, an ActiveX control written in Visual J++ 6 is available to all other Visual Studio 6 languages. To demonstrate this versatility, I created the default Windows EXE program under Visual Basic 6 using the following steps. (If you own Visual Basic 6, you can follow along; if not, you'll just have to trust me.)

Open Visual Basic 6. Create a new Standard EXE. Open Form1 within Project1 in the Forms Designer.

You'll need to add the WeightEdit control to the Visual Basic 6 Toolbox before you can use it. Right-click within the Visual Basic Toolbox. From the context menu, choose Components to bring up the Components dialog box. The WeightEdit ActiveX component is at the bottom of the list, as shown in Figure 13-13. Check the WeightEdit component, and choose OK to close the window. A new control appears in the Visual Basic Toolbox.

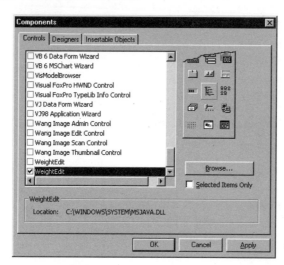

Figure 13-13. *Visual Basic allows you to add Visual J++ controls to the Toolbox.*

NOTE   The display on my computer reflects the fact that I had already created a different WeightEdit component. Your display might list only a single Weight-Edit component. In any case, you want to use the component that references MSJAVA.DLL, as shown in Figure 13-13.

Select the newly added WeightEdit control. Now click somewhere within the form. While holding down the left mouse button, drag the mouse to specify the size of the WeightEdit control. Type within the object to add text and update the *text* property in the Properties window, as shown in Figure 13-14.

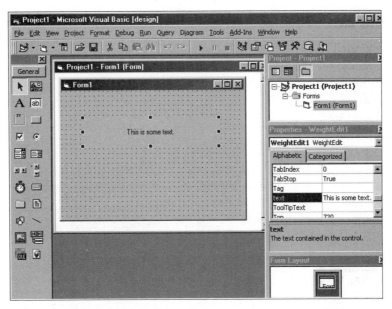

Figure 13-14. *Typing within the WeightEdit control updates the* text *property, just as within Visual J++ 6.*

Scroll down within the Properties window to the *weight* property. Change the weight to Bold. As you can see in Figure 13-15, the text display immediately updates to reflect the change.

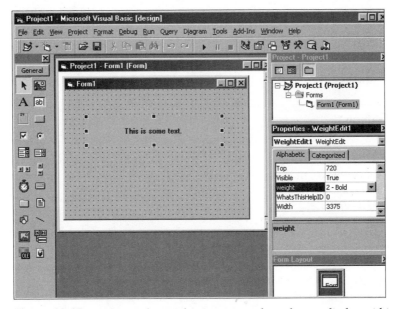

Figure 13-15. *Updating the* weight *property updates the text display within the Form1 window.*

To access the *weightEvent* property, double-click the WeightEdit control. A code window displaying the *WeightEdit1_click()* subroutine appears. Open the drop-down list on the upper right-hand side of the code window. Scroll down the list to find the *weightEvent* property. Selecting that list item creates the *WeightEdit1_weightEvent()* subroutine shown in Figure 13-16.

Finally, from the Run menu, select Start With Full Compile to run the Visual Basic 6 program. As the program runs, a form containing the WeightEdit control appears. Click the control, and begin typing to verify that it functions as designed.

NOTE   You'll find this version of using the WeightEdit control on the companion CD in the subdirectory Custom Controls\Visual Basic Program.

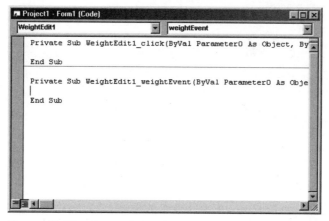

Figure 13-16. *The* weightEvent *property is available in the code editor.*

CONCLUSION

In this chapter, we created a WFC-style control. You saw how to add a new data property to the control and how to tie this property into the data section of the Properties window. From there, you learned how to convert enumerated data properties from simple integer values into a sophisticated drop-down list containing the names of the properties rather than just numbers.

You also saw how to define your own event class and how to send and receive this event and then how to tie this event into the active properties of the Properties window.

Finally, you learned how to convert a WFC control into an ActiveX control and how to use this control both in Visual J++ 6 applications and in other Visual Studio 6 languages, such as Visual Basic.

Chapter 14

Applets

For many years, Java has been associated almost solely with applets, those little programs that run from within Web pages. Microsoft Visual J++ 6 has changed all that by turning the Java language into an application program powerhouse. Both easier to use than C++ and better adapted to large applications than Basic, Java is well suited for whatever application you have in mind.

Just because Visual J++ 6 provides a powerful environment for application development doesn't mean that it doesn't provide significant support for applets. In this chapter and the next, we'll cover a variety of applet-related topics, from simple "Hello, world" applets through the Visual J++ Applet Wizard and right up to multi-threaded applet animation.

APPLET BASICS

In this section, we'll go over applet basics. We'll start with a series of simple examples that demonstrate the principles of applet development. We'll use this opportunity to study such diverse but interrelated technologies as HTML files, browsers, Just-in-Time (JIT) compilers, and machine-independent code. We'll expand on this knowledge in later sections of the chapter.

Overview

You can run Visual J++ 6 .EXE applications on any of the Microsoft Win32 operating systems without the help of external files or tools. By contrast, Java applets exist only in the context of an HTML file. You run an applet by using a Web browser to open an HTML page that is linked to that applet.

THE JAVA VIRTUAL MACHINE

Normal executable files (.EXE files) such as those generated by Microsoft Visual C++ contain machine code designed to run on the base processor; in the case of the PC, this code is 80x86 machine code. The Pentium processor uses the same machine instructions as the other members of the 80x86 family.

All Java compilers, including Visual J++ 6, compile Java source code into a special machine language called Virtual Machine (VM) byte code. This machine language is called *virtual* because the VM doesn't really exist. Instead, each Java-equipped browser has an interpreter inside it capable of executing VM byte codes on the base machine. In other words, a browser for a PC executes the VM byte codes on an 80x86–equipped machine. A Macintosh browser interprets VM byte codes into PowerPC instructions. A browser on a UNIX workstation interprets VM byte codes into the native machine instructions for the workstation's processor.

The use of VM byte codes is almost a necessity for applets to run on the Web, because the applet programmer never knows what type of browser might access the Web page. Using VM byte codes provides platform independence so that the applet executes in the same way no matter what base machine it's running on. In addition, the format of the VM byte codes provides program integrity. If anyone were to place a virus in a .class file stored on the base machine, the browser would instantly detect the fact that the file had been edited and would refuse to execute it.

Finally, VM-based executables are much smaller than normal .EXE files. You might have noticed how small the Visual J++ 6–generated .EXE files are compared to conventional .EXE files such as those generated by Visual C++. This size difference is largely because C++ programs link support functions, such as those that make up the standard C++ library, into the .EXE files. By contrast, Java programs leave the standard Java support classes in the VM environment. All that is contained in the .class file are the instructions the programmer writes. This size difference is important when the .class file is being transmitted through a conventional modem.

The downside of using VM byte codes is that interpreting this virtual language is much slower than executing native code. To address this problem, the Microsoft JIT compiler (which is part of the Java VM) compiles the VM byte codes into 80x86 machine code and then executes the native machine code. Although the JIT compilation process takes a small amount of time, the resulting code is about as fast as a conventional (non-Java) .EXE program.

To further enhance the Visual J++ 6 experience, Microsoft has placed the VM along with the JIT compiler in the Win32 operating system. This allows Visual J++ 6–generated .EXE files to use the same JIT compiler that applets use.

Let's use the simple "Hello, world" applet to examine the relationship between an HTML page, an applet, and you—the programmer.

The "Hello, world" Applet

Our first applet must be the famous "Hello, world" applet. Not only does convention demand this, but also such a simple applet allows us to concentrate on the details of how applets are loaded and executed rather than on how an applet is coded.

It would be easy enough to build the "Hello, world" example using the Visual J++ 6 Applet Wizard. In fact, it's a little tricky to convince Visual J++ not to use the Applet Wizard. However, the applet code the Applet Wizard creates is overkill for an applet as simple as this one. Furthermore, I believe that you should learn to do things manually before using automatic tools. (For example, it's a good idea to learn to multiply by hand before using a calculator.) Without this background, you'll find it difficult to get a feel for what the Applet Wizard is doing for you.

Creating the "Hello, world" project

From the File menu, choose New Project. Select Visual J++ Projects in the left pane of the New Project window to reveal the single option Empty Project in the right pane. Choose Empty Project.

Create a new subdirectory named Applets under the directory in which you're storing your Visual J++ programs. Enter this directory into the Location edit box. (If you prefer, you can use the Browse feature.) Finally, enter the project name HelloWorld. When your window looks similar to the one shown in Figure 14-1 (depending on the path to your Applets directory), click Open. You now have a solution with a single empty project.

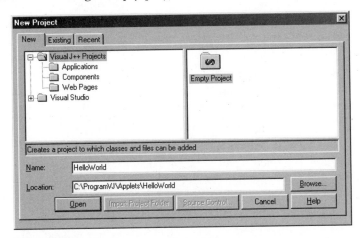

Figure 14-1. *Creating an empty project.*

Adding an applet to the project

Before we can do anything, we need to add an applet to the project. With the Hello-World project highlighted in Project Explorer, choose Add Item from the Project menu. From the New tab in the Add Item window, select Class and enter the class name HelloWorld. Visual J++ 6 adds the file HelloWorld.java, which contains an empty class, to the previously empty project.

Enter the following boldface code into the class you've just created:

```java
import java.applet.Applet;
import java.awt.Graphics;

public class HelloWorld extends Applet
{
    public void paint(Graphics g)
    {
        g.drawString("Hello, world", 10, 10);
    }
}
```

Let's not analyze the code just yet. We'll wait until you've seen it execute.

Creating the "Hello, world" HTML file

To run our new applet, we'll need an HTML file from which it can run. Select Add Item again. This time, select Web Page. Enter HelloWorld.htm in the Name text box, and click Open. A new HTML file–specific editor appears. This editor looks a little like the Forms Designer we've used in earlier chapters. Notice the three tabs along the bottom of the editor: Design, Source, and Quick View.

The purpose of the Design tab is roughly the same for HTML files as the Forms Designer's purpose is for Windows Foundation Classes for Java (WFC)–based applications. It allows you to drag tools from the HTML section of the Toolbox onto the HTML page. (The tools in the HTML section are not the Java tools we've used until now.) As you'll see later, certain aspects of the HTML file limit what the HTML Designer can do.

The Source tab plays the role of the Visual J++ 6 source code editor. It allows you to examine and edit the HTML source statements. And finally, the Quick View tab allows you to view many (but not all) of the features present in the HTML file without the sometimes tedious process of opening a browser.

Notice that in Design view the HTML page appears to be empty. Select Source view, however, and you'll see a series of HTML tags. These default system-generated tags represent merely the framework of an HTML page and have no displayable content.

CAUTION If you're running Visual J++ 6 in SDI mode, you might not see the actual features of the applet displayed in the IDE viewers, especially in the file I/O examples later in this chapter. You might have better luck previewing your applets in MDI mode.

INTRODUCTION TO HTML

Entire books are devoted to HTML. I couldn't possibly cover the whole topic in just a few lines. Fortunately, we need only a few HTML tags for the applets in this chapter. The initial HTML framework Visual J++ 6 creates for us looks like this:

```
<HTML>
<HEAD>
<META NAME="GENERATOR" Content="Microsoft Visual Studio 6.0">
<TITLE></TITLE>
</HEAD>
<BODY>

<P> </P>

</BODY>
</HTML>
```

All HTML tags are bracketed using angle brackets (<>). In addition, tags that surround a block of information in the HTML file begin with a tag and end with the same tag preceded by a slash. Thus, the <HTML> tag at the beginning of the HTML file is bracketed with the </HTML> tag at the end. (The HTML tags in this example are all uppercase, but HTML tags are not case sensitive.)

Any HTML file has two main sections: the head and the body. The head includes only a few tags that apply to the entire file. The <TITLE> tag defines the name that appears in the browser's title bar when the page is displayed. The browser ignores the <META> tag, which informs you and any HTML editor you might use how the HTML file was created. (You might see <META> tags with attributes other than the NAME attribute shown in this code, but the browser universally ignores them.)

The display tags begin after the <BODY> tag. The tag <P> introduces a paragraph, <BR> breaks a sentence (like a newline character), and <HR> draws a horizontal line across the page. Any text that appears outside angle brackets is displayed in the browser.

The HTML-interpreting browser treats all white space the same. White space includes a space, tab, vertical tab, and a new line. Specifically, entering a newline character at the end of a series of text doesn't force the start of a new line (as in a simple text editor) or a paragraph (as in Microsoft Word).

The following HTML file generates the results shown in Figure 14-2.

(continued)

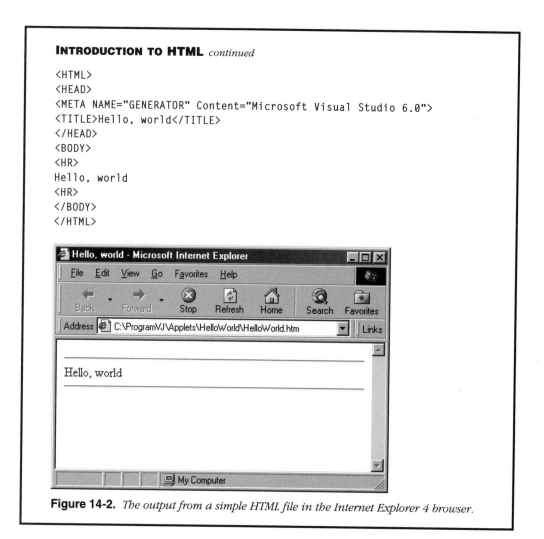

INTRODUCTION TO HTML *continued*

```
<HTML>
<HEAD>
<META NAME="GENERATOR" Content="Microsoft Visual Studio 6.0">
<TITLE>Hello, world</TITLE>
</HEAD>
<BODY>
<HR>
Hello, world
<HR>
</BODY>
</HTML>
```

Figure 14-2. *The output from a simple HTML file in the Internet Explorer 4 browser.*

In the early years of HTML, the <APPLET> tag was used to include calls to applets in an HTML file. Although the <APPLET> tag is still supported, today the more flexible <OBJECT> tag is the preferred way to include applet calls in an HTML file.

To execute our HelloWorld applet, modify the default HTML framework contained in the HelloWorld.htm file so that it looks like the following:

```
<HTML>
<HEAD>
<META NAME="GENERATOR" Content="Microsoft Visual Studio 6.0">
<TITLE>First Applet</TITLE>
</HEAD>
<BODY>
<HR>
```

```
<OBJECT CODE="HelloWorld.class"
        HEIGHT=100
        WIDTH=100>
</OBJECT>
<HR>
</BODY>
</HTML>
```

This <OBJECT> tag specifies that the applet code resides in the file Hello-World.class. (The name of the .class file is case sensitive because Java is case sensitive.) The HEIGHT and WIDTH attributes specify the initial size in pixels of the window in which the applet is to appear (normally referred to as the applet window). The </OBJECT> tag closes the applet command. Later in this chapter, we'll see the types of commands that can appear between the <OBJECT> and </OBJECT> tags.

Executing the result

To execute the applet, we first need to set the launch properties. From the Project menu, choose HelloWorld Properties. In the When Project Runs, Load drop-down list, select HelloWorld.htm and choose OK. Now compile the project by selecting the Build option from the Debug menu. Click Start in the Debug menu to run the program. Visual J++ 6 opens the browser to execute the HelloWorld.htm file. The results are shown in Figure 14-3.

Notice the gray box. This is the 100-by-100-pixel applet window specified within the <OBJECT> tags. The "Hello, world" message appears at the top of this applet window. In addition, the two horizontal lines specified by the <HR> tags in the HTML file surround the applet window.

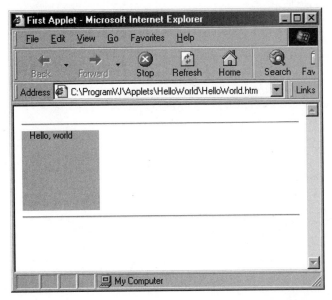

Figure 14-3. *The HelloWorld applet executing within Internet Explorer 4.*

Loading an applet

Let's go through the steps involved in loading and executing the HelloWorld applet. First the browser loads the HelloWorld HTML file. The <OBJECT> tag within the HTML file indicates to the browser that it is to load an executable file. The CODE attribute indicates that the name of the file to load is HelloWorld.class and that it contains VM byte codes. Unless told otherwise, the browser assumes that the .class file is located in the same directory on the same server as the HTML file.

Once the HelloWorld.class file is loaded, the browser begins executing it. In Microsoft Internet Explorer, the .class file is first compiled using the JIT compiler, and the resulting machine code is executed. Other browsers might take the same approach, or they might simply use an interpreter to execute the byte codes directly.

Because the applet refers to other classes, they are loaded as well. The browser begins by looking through the built-in classes that make up the standard Java library. (In the case of machines executing Microsoft VM for Java, these built-in classes include WFC). For example, the *Applet* class is always present on the client side. If the browser can't find the class among the built-in classes, it then inspects the cached files. If the browser can't find the class there either, it looks back on the server for the .class file.

An interesting property of applets is that classes, especially user-defined classes, aren't loaded until execution absolutely requires it. This minimizes the amount of information being passed over a potentially slow modem—there's no need to pass the byte codes for a class that is never accessed.

Examining the HelloWorld applet code

Let's examine the HelloWorld applet source code to see how it works. The *HelloWorld* class extends the *Applet* class. This base class of all applets provides a number of methods that establish the interface between the Java code and the browser.

One of these interface methods is the method *paint()*. Java invokes this method whenever the browser signals that the applet window needs to be redrawn.

When the browser first displays the HTML page, the applet window is invalid and requires repainting. The Java core within the browser invokes the *paint()* method to create the display.

A window can be invalidated in other ways, such as when the user minimizes and then restores the browser. Parts of the applet window might be invalidated even if the user simply scrolls the HTML page.

Our version of *paint()* prints the "Hello, world" message.

NOTE The *paint()* method in applets plays the same role as the *paint()* method in applications, but with applets the browser (instead of Win32) performs the *paint()* calls.

See Chapter 9, The *Graphics* Class, for a discussion of overriding the *paint()* method in WFC applications.

Examining the Visual J++ 6 HTML editor

Now that our applet is compiled and working, let's return to the applet editor. In Design mode, select within the two horizontal lines. An applet window containing the "Hello, world" message appears.

Now switch to Source mode. You can see the normal HTML tags, but again the <OBJECT> tag is replaced by the applet output, as shown in Figure 14-4. (You can select View Controls As Text from the View menu to force the source code editor to display the <OBJECT> tag rather than the applet output.)

Finally, the Quick View mode displays the HTML output very much like it would look in an Internet browser.

> **NOTE** The applet window might initially appear as a blank box. You can make the applet appear in the window by clicking inside this box.

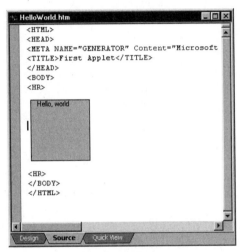

Figure 14-4. *The HTML editor showing the applet output in Source mode.*

Applet Special Methods

All Java applications share one unique method: *public void main(String[])*. Application execution always begins with this method. In effect, this method forms the handoff link from Win32 into the application. (There are many links from the application back into Win32. For example, all the Visual J++ 6 methods that perform Win32 API calls must call into Win32.)

Rather than having just a single *main()* method, applets have numerous methods that the browser can use to hand control to the applet. One example is the *paint()* method we saw in the HelloWorld applet. Four other methods are key to a browser's communication with an applet.

Special methods

The four methods that have particular importance in the birth and death of an applet are *init()*, *start()*, *stop()*, and *destroy()*. The following sequence demonstrates how the browser uses these methods:

1. The browser loads the .class file referenced by the HTML file. The class constructor is invoked immediately after the class is loaded.

2. The browser lays out the objects defined in the HTML file in the browser. This step includes creating the applet window.

3. The browser invokes *init()* to allow the applet to initialize any objects that are to appear in the applet window.

4. The browser invokes *start()* immediately prior to displaying the HTML file that contains the applet.

5. The HTML file is displayed.

6. The browser invokes *stop()* immediately after the HTML page that contains the applet is replace by a new HTML page. (Generally, this replacement occurs because the user has navigated to a new HTML page.)

7. The browser invokes the *destroy()* method prior to stopping the applet and reclaiming the memory occupied by the applet.

At the time the class constructor is invoked, the browser isn't prepared for the program to display any objects. Our applet performs in the *init()* method much of the work our WFC applications performed in the class constructor through the call to *initForm()*.

The dichotomy between the *init()*/*destroy()* and the *start()*/*stop()* methods might not be clear. The browser invokes the *init()* method followed by the *start()* method when the HTML page is first displayed. As the user moves to the next HTML page, the browser invokes the *stop()* method to place the applet in a dormant state; however, the actions taken by the *init()* method remain valid. The browser can hold off calling *destroy()* as long as the HTML file is still on the "back" list.

If the user returns to the HTML page containing the HTML file by clicking the browser's "back" button, the browser calls the *start()* method to "reenergize" the applet. This process saves execution time by avoiding unnecessary calls to the relatively expensive *init()* method.

> **NOTE** Although recommended, this sequence is not enforced. Some browsers call *destroy()* whenever the user leaves the HTML page containing the applet, for whatever reason. These browsers must call *init()* if the user redisplays the HTML page.

Demonstrating the special methods

The use of the special methods *init()*, *start()*, *stop()*, and *destroy()* is demonstrated in the following SpecialMethods applet. Let's create an applet in the Applets subdirectory using the same technique described for the HelloWorld applet: create an empty project and then add a class named *SpecialMethods* and an HTML file named SpecialMethods.htm.

The code

Edit the SpecialMethods.java file so that it looks like the following:

```java
import java.applet.Applet;
import java.awt.*;
/**
 * Demonstrate the special methods init(),
 * start(), stop(), and destroy().
 */
public class SpecialMethods extends Applet
{
    // declare a counter for each method
    public static int inits    = 0;
    public static int starts   = 0;
    public static int stops    = 0;
    public static int destroys = 0;
    public static int paints   = 0;

    /**
     * Display the number of each event.
     */
    public void paint(Graphics g)
    {
        // count the number of paints
        paints++;

        // get the font height
        FontMetrics fm = g.getFontMetrics();
        int height = fm.getHeight();

        // add a tad to the font height and vertically
        // space each line by that much
        height += 5;
        int yOffset = 0;
        yOffset += height;
        g.drawString("inits = "    + inits,    10, yOffset);
        yOffset += height;
        g.drawString("starts = "   + starts,   10, yOffset);
        yOffset += height;
```

(continued)

```
        g.drawString("stops   = "   + stops,    10, yOffset);
        yOffset += height;
        g.drawString("destroys = " + destroys, 10, yOffset);
        yOffset += height;
        g.drawString("paints = "   + paints,   10, yOffset);
    }

    /**
     * The following methods increment the respective
     * counters.
     */
    public void init()
    {
        inits++;
        invalidate();
    }
    public void start()
    {
        starts++;
        invalidate();
    }
    public void stop()
    {
        stops++;
        invalidate();
    }
    public void destroy()
    {
        destroys++;
        invalidate();
    }
}
```

You can see that the four methods at the bottom of the class do nothing more than increment their respective counters and then invalidate the applet window. The *paint()* method displays all these counters and its own counter.

The *paint()* method begins by incrementing its counter. The *paint()* method continues by retrieving the *FontMetrics* object from the *Graphics* object *g* passed to it. This *FontMetrics* object contains an assortment of information about the current font, including its height, width, style (such as italics), and so forth. The *paint()* method takes the font height and adds 5 pixels. This resulting *height* value is used as the interline spacing for each line as *paint()* goes down the list, outputting each counter. (The 5 pixels are added to provide blank space between lines.)

The HTML file

Edit the default SpecialMethods.htm file in Source mode to appear as follows:

```
<HTML>
<HEAD>
<META NAME="GENERATOR" Content="Microsoft Visual Studio 6.0">
<TITLE></TITLE>
</HEAD>
<BODY>

<P>
<OBJECT CODE = "SpecialMethods.class"
        HEIGHT = 150
        Width  = 100>
</OBJECT>
</P>

</BODY>
</HTML>
```

The result

Compile the project, and then view the SpecialMethods.htm file in Internet Explorer 4 or some other browser. The *inits*, *starts*, and *paints* counters are initially displayed as 1, and the *stops* and *destroys* counters appear as 0.

You'll find it encouraging that the paint count displays a value of 1 under Internet Explorer 4. This implies that the applet was painted only a single time during the display of the HTML page. Even as you resize the browser, the *paints* counter value stays at 1, until you resize the browser to the point that the applet window is partially obscured, at which time the *paints* counter value begins to increase. As soon as you stop resizing, the *paints* counter immediately stops updating. Throughout the entire resizing exercise, the *inits*, *starts*, *stops*, and *destroys* counters remain at their initial values.

Navigate to another page and return to the SpecialMethods page using the browser's back button. Figure 14-5 shows the resulting display.

As you can see from the counters, Internet Explorer 4 destroys the applet whenever the user jumps to another page and restarts the applet when the user returns.

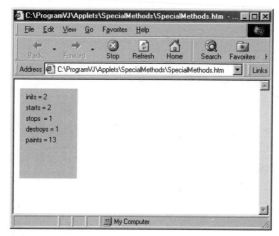

Figure 14-5. *The SpecialMethods applet displaying the number of times that each special method has been invoked.*

Displaying Abstract Windowing Toolkit Objects

In Chapter 4, Generic Windowed Applications, you saw how windowed applications can use the machine-independent Abstract Windowing Toolkit (AWT). AWT is also available for applet use. In fact, you might argue that AWT was designed specifically for applets to use. The classes that make up AWT are already present in every Java-enabled browser.

APPLETS AND WFC

Under normal circumstances, you shouldn't access WFC from applets. WFC is not part of the standard Java library that is accessible to all browsers; WFC is accessible only to Internet Explorer version 4 or higher. Thus, if your applet refers to a WFC class, the browser will be forced to load large sections of the WFC library over the Internet (assuming that you placed the WFC classes in a directory on the server where the browser could find them). The time required to perform such a download would be unacceptable to the user.

Internet Explorer 4 does have access to the WFC classes. Thus, if you have complete control of the user community, such as would be the case in a small intranet community, restricting all users to a single version of a single browser might be acceptable. From my experience on the intranet of even a medium-sized company, however, this restriction is impractical.

AWT use in applets isn't that much different from AWT use in applications. The following AWTApplet applet demonstrates the principle. This applet opens two labeled text fields, one above the other. Below the text fields is a button the user can click to transfer the contents of the upper text field to the lower text field. (For now, the button does nothing; we'll add functionality to it in the next section).

The code

To create the AWTApplet applet, you begin by creating an empty project named AWTApplet1. (We'll add more features to later versions.) Add a class named AWTApplet and an HTML file named AWTApplet.htm. Update the AWTApplet.java source file as follows:

```java
import java.applet.Applet;
import java.awt.*;

public class AWTApplet extends Applet
{
    TextField tfSource = new TextField();
    TextField tfTarget = new TextField();
    Button    button   = new Button("Transfer");

    public void init()
    {
        // create two text field panels
        Panel sPanel = createTextFieldPanel(
                        "Source",
                        tfSource);
        Panel tPanel = createTextFieldPanel(
                        "Target",
                        tfTarget);

        // and a button panel
        Panel bPanel = createButtonPanel(button);

        // set them in a single-column grid layout
        // (this will lay them out vertically)
        GridLayout gridLayout = new GridLayout();
        gridLayout.setColumns(1);
        gridLayout.setRows(0);
        gridLayout.setVgap(10);
        this.setLayout(gridLayout);
        this.add(sPanel);
        this.add(tPanel);
        this.add(bPanel);
    }
```

(continued)

483

```
/**
 * Create a panel with a label and a text field
 * offset from the left and right boundaries.
 */
Panel createTextFieldPanel(String label, TextField t)
{
    Panel panel = new Panel();
    panel.setLayout(new BorderLayout());

    Panel subPanel = new Panel();
    subPanel.setLayout(new BorderLayout());
    subPanel.add("North", new Label(label));
    subPanel.add("South", t);

    panel.add("West", new Label(" "));
    panel.add("East", new Label(" "));
    panel.add("Center", subPanel);

    return panel;
}

/**
 * Create a panel with a single button in the
 * center.
 */
Panel createButtonPanel(Button button)
{
    // establish a 3x3 grid layout
    // (the following is crude, but it does the
    // job without resorting to the more complicated
    // GridBagLayout)
    Panel panel = new Panel();
    panel.setLayout(new GridLayout(3, 3));

    // fill the first row with blanks
    panel.add(new Label("  "));
    panel.add(new Label("  "));
    panel.add(new Label("  "));

    // on the second row, put the button in the center
    panel.add(new Label("  "));
    panel.add(button);
    panel.add(new Label("  "));

    // fill the third row with blanks
    panel.add(new Label("  "));
    panel.add(new Label("  "));
    panel.add(new Label("  "));

    return panel;
}
}
```

The code for this applet looks a lot more complicated than it really is. (This seeming complexity is typical of AWT applets.) The *init()* method begins by creating a panel containing the source *TextField* object and an identical panel containing the target *TextField* object. We'll eventually copy the contents of the source field to the target field. Finally, the applet creates a panel containing the Transfer button.

The *init()* method uses a *GridLayout* layout manager to create the display. The purpose of this layout manager is to create spreadsheet-like grids with columns of equal width and rows of equal height. The *init()* method of our AWTApplet applet specifies a single column, and as many rows as are required (designated by the *setRows(0)* command.). Creating a grid with only a single column creates what is essentially a vertical layout.

The *AWTApplet.createTextFieldPanel()* method is perhaps the most complicated of the methods in this class. This method creates an inner panel (*subpanel*) in which it places the label and the *TextField* object. The method then places this inner panel in the center of an outer panel (*panel*) that contains an empty label on the left and another label on the right. These empty labels place a small space on the left and right between the applet boundary and the label/text field panel.

The *AWTApplet.createButtonPanel()* method is crude but effective. This method creates a 3-by-3 grid layout and places the button in the middle. This placement gives the button a pleasing appearance with suitable space around it in the applet window.

The HTML file

The HTML file for AWTApplet has the standard features you've seen in other applets:

```
<HTML>
<HEAD>
<META NAME="GENERATOR" Content="Microsoft Visual Studio 6.0">
<TITLE></TITLE>
</HEAD>
<BODY>

<P>
<OBJECT CODE = "AWTApplet.class"
        HEIGHT = 200
        WIDTH  = 300>
</OBJECT>
</P>

</BODY>
</HTML>
```

The result

When viewed from the Designer after compiling, the Source window appears as shown in Figure 14-6.

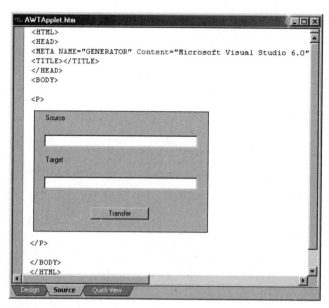

Figure 14-6. *The appearance of the Designer's Source window when viewing AWTApplet.*

Handling Events

Our AWTApplet applet is fine so far, but is somewhat unimpressive because the Transfer button doesn't do anything. To activate the Transfer button, we must add an event handler, which is what we'll do for the AWTApplet2 project.

The code

The code for the event-capable version of the AWTApplet applet is shown below. The majority of the code in this version is the same as that in its predecessor and isn't shown here.

```java
import java.applet.Applet;
import java.awt.*;
import java.awt.event.*;

public class AWTApplet extends Applet
{
    TextField tfSource = new TextField();
    TextField tfTarget = new TextField();
    Button    button   = new Button("Transfer");

    public void init()
    {
        // ...the same as previous version...

        // add the transfer button event code
```

```
        addTransfer();
    }

    ⋮

    /**
     * Add the transfer capability to the specified event.
     */
    void addTransfer()
    {
        // make the target field read-only
        tfTarget.setEditable(false);

        // now add a transfer action listener to perform
        // the transfer
        button.addActionListener(new TransferActionListener());
    }

    /**
     * Implement the ActionListener interface.
     */
    class TransferActionListener implements ActionListener
    {
        /**
         * Transfer text from the source text field to
         * the target text field.
         */
        public void actionPerformed(ActionEvent ae)
        {
            String s = tfSource.getText();
            tfTarget.setText(s);
        }
    }
}
```

The call to *AWTApplet.addTransfer()* in *init()* activates the transfer button. The *addTransfer()* method begins by making the target text field read-only. The method then adds an *ActionListener* interface to the transfer button. An *ActionEvent* object is created when the user clicks the button. The *ActionListener* interface plus the *ActionEvent* are defined in the *java.awt.event* package.

The inner class *TransferActionListener* implements the *ActionListener* interface by providing an *actionPerformed()* method. This method reads the text out of the source text field and stores it into the target text field.

The result

The AWTApplet2 project uses the same HTML as AWTApplet1. Figure 14-7 shows AWTApplet when viewed from the Quick View mode of the Applet HTML editor. To create this display, I entered text into the source text field and clicked the Transfer button to copy the contents of the source text field to the target text field.

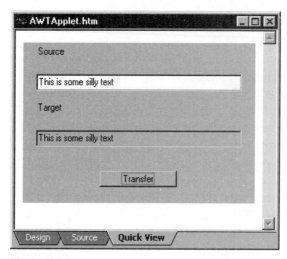

Figure 14-7. *The results of the event-capable AWTApplet.*

LISTENERS

The *ActionListener* approach is a means of event handling we discussed briefly in Chapter 5, Microsoft Windows Applications. WFC prefers the easier-to-use delegate approach. However, AWT uses the listener approach introduced in Java 1.1.

In the listener approach, for every action that can befall an AWT control, there is a method with the following syntax:

```
<control>.add<X>Listener(my<X>Listener)
```

X represents the name of some action type, and *my<X>Listener* represents an object of some locally defined class *My<X>Listener*, which implements the *<X>Listener* interface. An *<X>Listener* interface generally defines a single method of the form *public void <X>Performed(<X>Event)*. The most common value of *<X>* is *Action*, which is demonstrated in the AWTApplet2 code statement shown here:

```
button.addActionListener(new TransferActionListener());
```

The action events are loosely defined as what the control receives when the user activates the control. Therefore, the action event for a button is invoked when the user clicks the button.

This approach to event handling is powerful and flexible. The primary disadvantage of this approach compared with the delegate approach is the need to implement a separate class for each event handled. (Refer to Chapter 5 for more on delegates.)

Passing Arguments to the Applet

As you saw in Part II, you can pass information to applications in several ways. The most straightforward way is through the array of strings passed to *main()* via the command line. An applet has no command line. However, you can pass arguments to the applet from the HTML file via the HTML <PARAM> tag. The <PARAM> tag defines a parameter by name and assigns it a string value. The applet can query this parameter by its name to read the value.

To demonstrate the use of the <PARAM> tag, the following ParamDisplay applet displays the name the HTML file passes to it in the TEXT parameter in the font and point size specified in the FONT and SIZE parameters.

The code

The key to this applet—and any other applet that reads parameter data from the HTML file—is the *getParameter(String name)* method. This method accepts the name of the parameter and returns the corresponding value as a *String*.

If the parameter with the name passed to *getParameter()* isn't in the HTML file, the method returns *null*. Because the applet programmer generally has no control over the HTML files that call the applet, the applet must account for the fact that any given parameter might not be present in the HTML file. If a specific parameter is missing from the HTML file, the applet must assign a default value.

The following ParamDisplay applet demonstrates how this works:

```java
import java.applet.Applet;
import java.awt.*;

public class ParamDisplay extends Applet
{
    // define the names of the parameters
    String textName = "TEXT";
    String fontName = "FONT";
    String sizeName = "SIZE";

    // define the default values for each
    String textDefault = "No text";
    String fontDefault = "Courier";
    int    sizeDefault = 12;

    // now declare the actual values
    String text;
    String font;
    int    size;

    // resulting font
    Font f;
```

(continued)

```java
public void init()
{
    // get the text to display
    text = this.getParameter(textName);
    if (text == null)
    {
        text = textDefault;
    }

    // next the font
    font = this.getParameter(fontName);
    if (font == null)
    {
        font = fontDefault;
    }

    // finally the size, which must be converted
    // from string to integer
    String sSize;
    sSize = this.getParameter(sizeName);
    size = sizeDefault;
    if (sSize != null)
    {
        size = Integer.parseInt(sSize);
    }

    // create a font using those parameters
    Font f = new Font(font, Font.PLAIN,size);
}

/**
 * Paint the text specified in the HTML
 * file with the specified font and size.
 */
public void paint(Graphics g)
{
    if (f != null)
    {
        g.setFont(f);
    }
    int yOffset = size + 10;
    g.drawString(text, 10, yOffset);
}
}
```

If we take the TEXT parameter as an example, the *textName* variable is assigned the value *TEXT.* A default value for this parameter is provided in the string *textDefault.* The resulting string is stored in *text.*

As the applet starts, the browser invokes *init().* This method calls *getParameter()* to retrieve the value of the parameter named *textName* and stores the result in *text.* If the value returned by *getParameter()* is *null, init()* assigns *text* the default value stored in *textDefault.*

This pattern is repeated for each parameter. The only complication is that the font size must be converted from a string into an integer using the static method *Integer.parseInt().*

Once *init()* has read all the HTML parameters, it creates a *Font* object using the values in the *font* and *size* variables. The *paint()* method uses this *Font* object to format the string passed in the text parameter when the string is displayed.

The HTML file

To test ParamDisplay, create the following HTML file:

```
<HTML>
<HEAD>
<META NAME="GENERATOR" Content="Microsoft Visual Studio 6.0">
<TITLE></TITLE>
</HEAD>
<BODY>

<P>
<OBJECT CODE = "ParamDisplay.class"
        HEIGHT = 100
        WIDTH = 400>
<param name = "TEXT" value = "This is the text param">
<param name = "SIZE" value = "28">
</OBJECT>
</P>

</BODY>
</HTML>
```

Most of the HTML file is identical to previous versions. The <OBJECT> tag differs in this HTML file, however, with the addition of the <PARAM> tag for TEXT and SIZE. Notice the absence of the FONT parameter.

The result

The output from ParamDisplay using the previous HTML file appears in Figure 14-8. Here the string size and font size specified in the HTML file are combined with the default font type of *COURIER* to create the applet display shown.

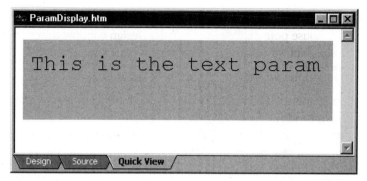

Figure 14-8. *The output from the ParamDisplay applet using specified TEXT and SIZE parameters but default FONT.*

THE APPLET WIZARD

Visual J++ 6 provides an applet wizard named Applet On HTML that simplifies the job of creating applets. Rather than go through the steps of creating an empty project and adding the applet and HTML files manually, the Applet On HTML wizard builds a complete applet framework from which you can begin coding.

An Example Applet on HTML Applet

To demonstrate the strengths and weaknesses of the Applet On HTML wizard compared with the purely manual approach to creating applets we've been using so far in this chapter, let's create AWTApplet3. This applet transfers data from an input text field to an output text field. This problem is the same one we solved in the previous versions of AWTApplet earlier in the chapter.

Creating the project

From the File menu, choose New Project. From the New Project window, select Web Pages under the Visual J++ Projects folder. In the right-hand pane, choose Applet On HTML; type in the project name, AWTApplet3; and choose Open. This process creates a project with two members: Applet1.java and Page1.htm.

The design work

The design work for this applet consists of the following steps:

1. Open the HTML editor by double-clicking the Page1.htm file in Project Explorer.

2. Select the Design tab.

3. Open the Properties window.

4. Select the applet in the Design window. (The applet initially isn't visible. Move the mouse pointer around within the Design window until the mouse pointer turns into a "move" icon, and then click the mouse button.)

5. Resize the applet window to be about two-thirds of its original size.

If you examine the Properties window, you'll notice numerous applet properties that you can modify.

The code

The Applet1.java code appears as follows. (I've left out sections of repetitive wizard-generated code.)

```java
import java.awt.*;
import java.applet.*;

import java.awt.event.*;

/**
 * This class reads PARAM tags from its HTML host page and sets
 * the color and label properties of the applet. Program execution
 * begins with the init() method.
 */
public class Applet1 extends Applet
{
    /**
     * The entry point for the applet.
     */
    public void init()
    {
        initForm();

        usePageParams();

        // create the user panel and add it in the
        // middle of the applet window
        this.add("West",  new Label(" "));
        this.add("East",  new Label(" "));
        this.add("South", new Label(" "));
        this.add("Center", userPanel());
    }

    private    final String labelParam = "label";
    private    final String backgroundParam = "background";
    private    final String foregroundParam = "foreground";
```

(continued)

```
/**
 * Reads parameters from the applet's HTML host and sets applet
 * properties.
 */
private void usePageParams()
{
    final String defaultLabel = "Default label";
    final String defaultBackground = "C0C0C0";
    final String defaultForeground = "000000";
    String labelValue;
    String backgroundValue;
    String foregroundValue;

    /**
     * Read the <PARAM NAME="label" VALUE="some string">,
     * <PARAM NAME="background" VALUE="rrggbb">,
     * and <PARAM NAME="foreground" VALUE="rrggbb"> tags from
     * the applet's HTML host.
     */
    labelValue = getParameter(labelParam);
    backgroundValue = getParameter(backgroundParam);
    foregroundValue = getParameter(foregroundParam);

    if ((labelValue == null) || (backgroundValue == null) ||
        (foregroundValue == null))
    {
        /**
         * There was something wrong with the HTML host tags.
         * Generate default values.
         */
        labelValue = defaultLabel;
        backgroundValue = defaultBackground;
        foregroundValue = defaultForeground;
    }

    /**
     * Set the applet's string label, background color, and
     * foreground colors.
     */
    label1.setText(labelValue);
    label1.setBackground(stringToColor(backgroundValue));
    label1.setForeground(stringToColor(foregroundValue));
    this.setBackground(stringToColor(backgroundValue));
    this.setForeground(stringToColor(foregroundValue));
}
```

```
/**
 * Converts a string formatted as "rrggbb" to an awt.Color object
 */
private Color stringToColor(String paramValue)
{
    // ...created by wizard...
}

    ⋮

Label label1 = new Label();

/**
 * Initializes values for the applet and its components
 */
void initForm()
{
    this.setBackground(Color.lightGray);
    this.setForeground(Color.black);
    label1.setText("label1");
    this.setLayout(new BorderLayout());
    this.add("North",label1);
}

//-------locally defined code-----------
TextField sourceTF;
TextField targetTF;
Button    button;

/**
 * Create the user panel to go below the applet label.
 */
Panel userPanel()
{
    // create a vertical layout with the source text field,
    // target text field, and button
    Panel panel = new Panel();
    panel.setLayout(new GridLayout(0, 1, 50, 10));
    panel.add(sourceTF = new TextField());
    panel.add(targetTF = new TextField());

    // put the button in the middle of a horizontal layout
    Panel subPanel = new Panel();
    subPanel.setLayout(new GridLayout(1, 0));
    subPanel.add(new Label(" "));
    subPanel.add(button = new Button("Transfer"));
    subPanel.add(new Label(" "));
```

(continued)

495

```
        panel.add(subPanel);

        // add an action listener to the button to
        // perform the transfer
        button.addActionListener(new TransferActionListener());

        return panel;
    }

    /**
     * Implement a transfer listener class that transfers
     * text from the source to the target text fields.
     */
    class TransferActionListener implements ActionListener
    {
        public void actionPerformed(ActionEvent ae)
        {
            targetTF.setText(sourceTF.getText());
        }
    }
}
```

The Applet On HTML wizard generated most of the code prior to the comment "locally defined code," except for the import of the *java.awt.event* package. The applet needs this package to gain access to the *ActionListener* class that is used to perform the text transfer operation.

The *init()* method begins with the wizard-generated calls to the *initForm()* and *usePageParams()* methods. I added the series of calls to *add()* at the bottom of the *init()* method.

The *initForm()* code performs the function of the similarly named method the Forms Designer creates for applications in that it sets up some of the basic applet properties. In Visual J++ 6, however, the applet *initForm()* has limited capability.

The *usePageParams()* method reads and implements the parameters defined in the HTML file. These parameters reflect the applet properties set in the Properties window.

The majority of the added code appears at the bottom of the Applet1 file, after the comment "locally defined code." This code is similar to that defined in AWTApplet2, using a vertical grid layout for the source text field, target text field, and button subpanel. The button subpanel uses a horizontal grid layout.

The *TransferActionListener()* method is invoked when the user chooses the Transfer button. This method reads the contents of the source text field and writes it into the target text field.

The result

The output from executing AWTApplet3 is shown in Figure 14-9. (I edited the wizard-generated HTML file to change the title text.)

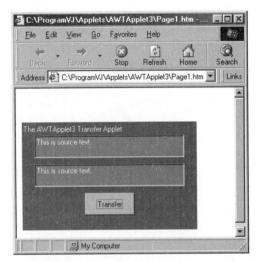

Figure 14-9. *The appearance of the AWTApplet3 applet after transferring a line of text.*

In my opinion, the Applet On HTML wizard doesn't save that much effort. In earlier chapters, we used the Forms Designer to lay out the appearance of Visual J++ 6 applications. The code it generated was both concise and powerful. All that was left to the programmer was to write the code to make the program actually do something. The net result was similar in feeling but more powerful than the advanced design capability of Microsoft Visual Basic.

By comparison, the applet Properties window offers limited capability. The code the Applet On HTML wizard generates is both lengthy and of questionable value. In addition, many of the settings within the Properties window appear to have little effect on the selected applet.

The Applet On HTML wizard shows a lot of promise, but this tool appears to be in need of improvement in future versions.

APPLET INPUT/OUTPUT

Applet I/O is a tricky subject. Applets are designed to execute within the browser of a person who is surfing the Web. Our Web surfer might have no idea what type of Web site he or she is about to encounter. If an applet within one of those Web pages could read and, more important, write to the disk with impunity, Java would be doomed as a Web language. No one would allow potentially dangerous applets to execute on their machine. People would turn off the Java interpreter within their browsers and leave it off.

This disk I/O security problem has led to the oft-heard comment that Java applets can't read or write to the hard disk. Although Java applets must make some concessions to security concerns, they can perform disk I/O.

Client-Side I/O

Writing a Java program to perform disk I/O isn't difficult. Part I contains several examples of applications that read and write files on the disk. To avoid the data-loss problem inherent in I/O-capable applets, Java has adopted a series of security models over time.

Originally, Java didn't allow applets to perform any type of file access. Applets executing within the client's browser had no access to the underlying machine. This security model was known as the *sandbox* model (the idea being that the applet could play with the sand inside the browser all it wanted but it couldn't get out of the box). Although this form of security kept the client safe, it severely limited the usefulness of Java applets.

Even in the initial release of Java, its developers conceded that some type of security model other than the sandbox model was needed. Eventually, Microsoft and the rest of the Java community developed a more advanced security model that allowed various forms of I/O on the client machine at the user's discretion. This security model involved what is known as *applet signing* and is referred to as the *trusted applet* model.

The trusted applet model allows the Java applet to request some level of access from the user. The Java developers realized that it was impossible for the browser to determine access automatically because the browser is unable to differentiate a benign Java applet from an attacker. To the VM, one set of disk write instructions looks like another.

The only form of security that the Java authors could offer was to inform the person running the browser of who the originator of the applet was, and then let the user decide whether to give the applet access to the client computer. The Java developers felt that a programmer would be loath to write attack applets if his or her identity were attached. Therefore, applet authors must electronically sign their applets. Before a programmer can sign an applet, he or she must have a signature. Such a signature must verify the identity of the author. In addition, the signature must be tamperproof.

> **NOTE** An applet whose signature has been accepted by the user is known as a secure applet.

Getting a signature

Several companies dispense electronic signatures. Probably the most popular signature company is VeriSign (*www.verisign.com*). This company sells a number of different types of signatures. The easiest (and cheapest) is a Class 1 signature. The Class 1 signature is meant for an individual programmer. For a Class 1 license, VeriSign verifies data such as an e-mail address, phone number, and mail address.

If a programmer of a Class 1–signed applet intentionally generates an applet that damages someone's data files, that person can contact VeriSign, who can find (and perhaps legally charge) the individual who wrote the applet. In addition, any Internet user presented with an applet request for I/O signed with only a Class 1 license has reason to be suspicious, because Class 1 licenses lack the extra security and identification of higher classes.

Figure 14-10 shows the first page of the VeriSign questionnaire I filled out to receive my Class 1 license.

VeriSign also sells licenses that offer higher levels of security. Class 2 licenses are available to small companies and offer more protection than a Class 1 license does. Class 3 licenses are available only to software companies, not to individuals. Before being granted a license, a company must demonstrate that it is a viable software company, and not some shadow company created for the purpose of generating damaging applets. Applets carrying the signature of a Class 3 license holder are fairly safe. For example, you can assume that an applet signed by Microsoft is safe.

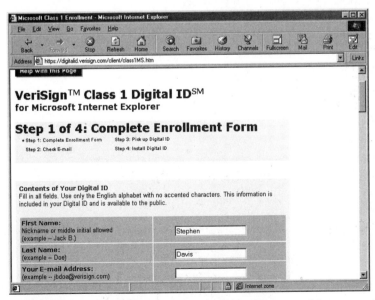

Figure 14-10. *Obtaining an electronic signature involves filling out a detailed questionnaire from a company registered to dispense such signatures.*

Signing an applet

Unfortunately, when the format of the Java .class file was created, no room was allocated for storing a signature. Therefore, before an applet can be signed, the .class file must be wrapped in some other type of file that does allow space for an electronic signature. Visual J++ 6 uses the cabinet (.CAB) file for this purpose.

These .CAB files existed long before Java appeared on the scene. Microsoft uses CAB files to save data in compressed format. The CAB file uses a compression technique similar to that of the ZIP file.

Fortunately, the CAB file is ideal for applet signing. First, the increased compression of the CAB file provides reduced download times. Second, the CAB file allows for the inclusion of user-defined record types. Visual J++ 6 added a new record type to contain the electronic signature.

Prior to Visual J++ 6, generating and electronically signing a CAB file involved a number of commands, all of which had an assortment of mysterious arguments. Fortunately, Visual J++ 6 has automated applet signing to the point that all you need to do is to make a few selections in dialog boxes.

An example secure applet

To demonstrate the process of applet signing, let's create an applet that reads a user-specified file from the local client disk. We'll begin by creating an empty project that we'll name SecureApplet. Use the Add Item command to add the class *SecureApplet* and the HTML file SecureApplet.htm.

The code

The SecureApplet.java file appears as follows:

```
import java.awt.*;
import java.applet.Applet;
import java.io.*;
import java.awt.event.*;

/**
 * The following applet reads a user-specified file
 * from the client's hard disk.
 */
public class SecureApplet extends Applet
{
    // the following objects are used to read
    // the file name and save the data read
    Button button = new Button("Read Text");
    TextArea textArea = new TextArea();
    TextField fileName = new TextField();

    /**
     * Lay out the applet window.
     */
```

```
public void init()
{
    // make the background color white so that
    // it blends in with the browser's default background
    this.setBackground(Color.white);
    Font font = new Font("Arial", Font.PLAIN, 18);
    this.setFont(font);

    // use a slightly smaller font for the text area
    Font textFont = new Font("Arial", Font.PLAIN, 12);
    textArea.setFont(textFont);

    // lay out the text area, label subpanel,
    // and button subpanel
    Panel buttonSubPanel = new Panel();
    Panel labelSubPanel  = new Panel();
    this.setLayout(new BorderLayout());
    this.add("North",  labelSubPanel);
    this.add("Center", textArea);
    this.add("South",  buttonSubPanel);

    // layout label area
    labelSubPanel.setLayout(new BorderLayout());
    labelSubPanel.add("West", new Label("File Name:"));
    labelSubPanel.add("Center", fileName);

    // set the button in an evenly spaced horizontal layout
    GridLayout gl = new GridLayout();
    gl.setVgap(5);
    buttonSubPanel.setLayout(gl);
    buttonSubPanel.add(new Label(" "));
    buttonSubPanel.add(button);
    buttonSubPanel.add(new Label(" "));

    // create an action listener for the button to
    // perform the actual read
    button.addActionListener(new ReadActionListener());
}

class ReadActionListener implements ActionListener
{
    // read the filename specified in the fileName
    // text field, and write it to textArea
    public void actionPerformed(ActionEvent ae)
    {
        // get the name of the file
        String fName = fileName.getText();
        String text;
```

(continued)

```
    try
    {
        // open the file, and read its contents
        // into a byte array buffer
        FileInputStream fis = new FileInputStream(fName);
        int size = fis.available();
        byte[] buffer = new byte[size];
        fis.read(buffer);

        // turn the buffer into a String
        text = new String(buffer);
    }
    catch(Exception e)
    {
        // on failure, set the text to a meaningful message
        text = "Read Failed:" + e.toString();
    }

    // display the text string in textArea
    textArea.setText(text);
        }
    }
}
```

Compared with other applets you've seen in this chapter, this applet is reasonably straightforward. The constructor builds three controls: a *TextField* object in which the user can enter the input filename, a *Button* object to effect the read operation, and a *TextArea* object in which to display the contents of the file read.

The *init()* method begins by setting the font to a pleasingly large 18-point Arial. The font for the text area is set to a somewhat smaller 12-point font to allow more of the display text to be visible. The applet then sets about building subpanels to arrange the three components attractively.

The *ReadActionListener* that's attached to the button begins by retrieving the name of the file to read from the *fileName* text field. A *FileInputStream* object is created using this name, and then the entire contents of the file are read into a byte buffer. Finally, this buffer is converted into a string that is displayed in the text area. If an exception is generated anywhere during the read operation, an error message is displayed instead.

Signing SecureApplet

Before we can execute the SecureApplet applet, we must first compile the project to create the SecureApplet.class file, and then generate a CAB file from the Secure-Applet.class file and sign the CAB file. From the Project menu, choose SecureApplet Properties. Select the Output Format tab. This page allows you to generate a number of different output format types for your applet in addition to the .class format.

Select the Enable Packaging option, and then select CAB Archive (.CAB) from the Packaging Type drop-down list. Select These Outputs in the Package Contents section, and make sure that all of the necessary files are included in the CAB file. (The source .java and .htm files aren't necessary and increase load time.) The resulting Properties window appears in Figure 14-11.

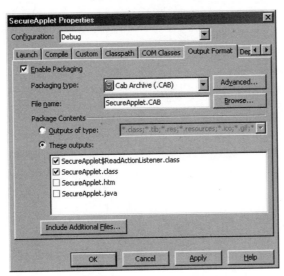

Figure 14-11. *Generating a CAB file via the Output Format tab in the Project Properties window.*

To sign this CAB file, choose the Advanced button on the Output Format tab. The Advanced Properties window is where you can enter your approved signature. This signature consists of two parts: the user-defined private key and the signature provider–generated certificate. I keep my signature files on a floppy disk. Figure 14-12 shows the entries I would use to sign the SecureApplet.cab file.

If you don't have a personal signature file, you can select the Use Test Certificate File button. Selecting this option will sign the applet with a test certificate that doesn't identify the user and that no self-respecting Web surfer would ever accept. (We'll see why later.) Choose OK to close the Advanced Properties window and choose OK again to close the SecureApplet Properties window.

Now rebuild the applet. You should notice that the Visual J++ 6 compiler goes through a couple of extra steps after compilation, called building and signing the CAB file. (You might not notice the Building CAB File step unless you watch the status bar carefully—the step notification goes by quickly.) Your directory should now have a SecureApplet.cab file in addition to the .class file.

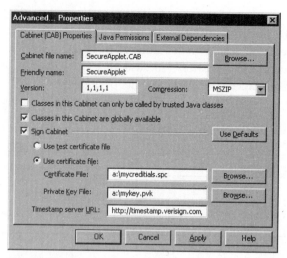

Figure 14-12. *Signing an applet with my electronic signature, which I keep on a floppy disk.*

The HTML page

The HTML page for a signed applet is slightly different from a "normal" applet page. The following HTML page instructs the browser to download the SecureApplet.cab file from the server and then read SecureApplet.class from this file rather than directly from the server.

```
<HTML>
<HEAD>
<META NAME="GENERATOR" Content="Microsoft Visual Studio 6.0">
<TITLE></TITLE>
</HEAD>
<BODY>
<HR>

<OBJECT code=SecureApplet.class
        HEIGHT=200
        WIDTH=300 VIEWASTEXT>
    <PARAM NAME="cabbase" VALUE="SecureApplet.cab">
</OBJECT>
<HR>
</BODY>
</HTML>
```

Notice the extra parameter, *cabbase*. This command tells the browser to download the SecureApplet.cab file. Also, notice that the name of the CAB file is normally the same as the name of the project. In this case, it is also the same as the name of the .java and .class files, but that's not necessary.

The result

Open the HTML file in Design mode. The dialog box generated by the test signature generates the rather dire warning shown in Figure 14-13. A real signature generates a similar dialog box except that it reassures the user that the signature is valid and identifies the signer. Either way, the decision whether or not to trust the applet is still left to the user.

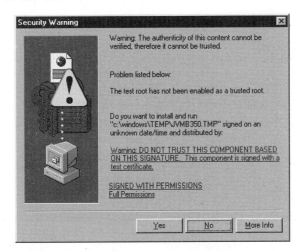

Figure 14-13. *A warning dialog box asking the user whether or not he or she trusts the creator of the applet.*

Figure 14-13 also notes that the applet is requesting Full Permissions. This means that the applet is asking to be able to do anything it wants. Our applet simply reads a file, but the user can't know that from this dialog box.

Because we wrote the applet, we know it's safe, so choose Yes to accept the signature. Switch to Quick View mode. Because the HTML file is a text file, enter SecureApplet.htm in the File Name field and click the Read Text button. You'll need to enter the full path to the file if you're running the applet outside the Visual J++ 6 IDE because the concept of a default client directory has no meaning in the context of a browser. The results should appear as shown in Figure 14-14.

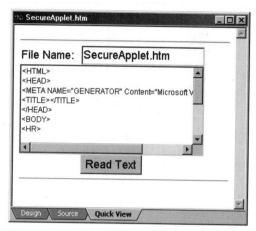

Figure 14-14. *SecureApplet applet displaying the contents of its own HTML file.*

Signing an applet using permissions

Even though applet signing provides the user with some level of reassurance, there's still a problem. Once the user has given the applet full permissions, the applet is capable of doing anything it wants, from reading a file on the disk (as our applet does) to wiping out the hard drive. This level of permission seems a bit severe.

Internet Explorer 4 introduced a new security model: permission-based security. Under permission-based security, an applet can ask for just the permission it needs and no more. Thus, our applet could get by with read permission. A user would certainly feel more comfortable granting read permission than allowing the full permissions the applet requested under the simple trusted applet model.

To request file I/O permission, which includes both read and write capability, return to the Advanced page of the Project Properties Output Format tab. Now select the Java Permissions tab. Select Custom from the Permission Level drop-down list. Clear the Contains ActiveX Controls option, because our applet doesn't have ActiveX capability. Scroll down through the Permissions options if necessary, and click the File I/O option. Choose OK to close the Advanced Properties window, and choose OK again to close the Project Properties window. Now rebuild the applet.

Running the applet again generates a dialog box like the one shown in Figure 14-15. (You might have to close and reopen the .htm file for the permission changes to take effect and this dialog box to appear.) Notice that this time the applet is asking only for File I/O Permission. Select Yes. The applet runs exactly as before.

Try repeating the process but signing the applet with some lesser permissions, such as Printing Permission; this time a similar dialog box appears, requesting print permission. Select Yes. The applet appears as before, but when you click the Read File button, the error message shown in Figure 14-16 appears, warning of a *Security-Exception* because the applet didn't request the capability to perform file I/O. (This is the same error message you would see had you not signed the applet at all.)

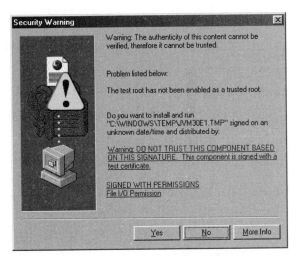

Figure 14-15. *An applet asking only for the permissions that it needs.*

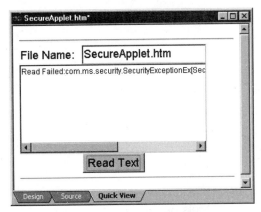

Figure 14-16. *The error message that appears when an applet with the wrong or insufficient privileges attempts to read from the disk.*

Server-Side I/O

Although you might not immediately think about it, one aspect of reading and writing to the disk involves reading and writing to disk files on the server. The applet can read or write to a disk file contained on the computer from which the applet's .class file originated.

Java doesn't hinder this type of I/O in any way. After all, if you want to write an applet that wipes out your own hard drive, so be it. You as the programmer are precluded from damaging data on any server other than your home directory by the protection features built into all Web servers' operating systems. Allowing access to the server's files poses no threat to the client.

At first glance, access to server-side files might not seem all that useful; however, this type of access is what allows applets to read images and sound from the server for output to a browser. (We'll see how to read such images in Chapter 15.) In addition, you could build database files on the server. A program on the server could update this data regularly so that remote applets could read it. The data contained within these files could even be processed by the applet and then written back out to the server. This remote access approach would be very useful to businesspeople on the road.

The problem

The ServerRead demonstration program is very simple. In this case, a fixed-named file, file.txt, is read from the current directory and displayed in a text area.

The code

Begin by creating an empty project named ServerRead. To this project, add the class *ServerRead* and the HTML file ServerRead.htm.

Then edit the ServerRead.java file as follows:

```
import java.applet.Applet;
import java.awt.*;
import java.io.*;
import java.net.*;

/**
 * The following class reads a fixed file from the server.
 */
public class ServerRead extends Applet
{
    // create a fixed-size text area
    TextArea textArea = new TextArea();
    public void init()
    {
        this.setLayout(new BorderLayout());
        this.add("Center", textArea);

        try
        {
            // read a file off the server
            // start by getting the name of the HTML file
            // (full path)
            String base = getDocumentBase().toExternalForm();

            // remove the trailing HTML filename
            int index = base.lastIndexOf("/") + 1;
            String path = base.substring(0, index);
```

```
            // create a URL by concatenating the
            // path to the fixed-file name "file.txt"
            String fileName = "file.txt";
            String totalName = path + fileName;
            URL url = new URL(totalName);

            // open an input stream on the URL
            InputStream connection = url.openStream();

            // now read the file
            int size = connection.available();
            byte[] block = new byte[size];
            connection.read(block);

            String s = new String(block);
            textArea.setText(s);
        }
        catch(Exception e)
        {
            textArea.setText(e.toString());
        }
    }
}
```

The applet begins by creating a display text area and attaching it to the center of the applet window. (If there are no other constraints, this will make the text area take up the entire applet window.)

The applet continues by retrieving the URL path of the HTML file that launched the applet. By searching for the "/" preceding the HTML name, the *substring()* statement effectively removes the HTML file name, leaving just the path. To this path, the program appends the fixed-file name file.txt.

The total name (including both path and file name) is used to create a *URL* object. This *URL* object represents a connection either to the local disk in the form of a *file:://* prefix or to a server in the form of an *http://* prefix. The *openStream()* method opens an *InputStream* object, which can be used like any other input file stream.

The remaining statements simply read the contents of the file and display them in the text area window.

> **NOTE** Keep in mind that we couldn't have used this trick in the SecureApplet example because there's no equivalent to a default client directory when using a browser.

The HTML file

The HTML file is completely conventional:

```
<HTML>
<HEAD>
<META NAME="GENERATOR" Content="Microsoft Visual Studio 6.0">
<TITLE></TITLE>
</HEAD>
<BODY>
<HR>
<OBJECT CODE="ServerRead.class"
        HEIGHT=100
        WIDTH=300 VIEWASTEXT>
</OBJECT>
<HR>
</BODY>
</HTML>
```

The result

The result appears in Figure 14-17 for the simple file.txt file containing "This is an experimental string." We didn't need to turn this .class file into a .CAB file (although it is allowed) or sign it to read the server file.

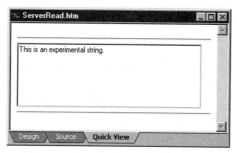

Figure 14-17. *The resulting display from reading the file.txt file from the server.*

CONCLUSION

We've come a long way in this chapter. After starting with the relatively simple technique of overriding the *paint()* method, we continued through displaying an Abstract Windowing Toolkit object and on to adding action through event handlers. After viewing the Applet Wizard output, we examined topics you might not have thought possible: applet I/O both from the client (the computer on which the browser resides) and the server (the computer housing the HTML file).

In the next chapter, we'll continue our study of applets by examining multitasking in applets and using that capability to implement graphic animation.

Chapter 15

Applet Animation

This chapter takes up the topic of applet animation. We'll begin with a discussion of multithreading in applets, because multithreading is a key component in applet animation. We'll move on to examine applets that generate their own data dynamically and that thereby create an artificial animation effect.

Techniques for loading and displaying images are presented next, because image handling is a key part of image animation. The final topic in this chapter is the animation of images that have been loaded from the disk.

MULTITHREADED APPLETS

Multithreading in applets is no different than multithreading in applications. (Chapter 10, The WFC Application Package, discussed multithreading in applications.)

A Quick Review of Java Multithreading

Without access to the Windows Foundation Classes for Java (WFC), an applet can start a new thread in two ways. The first technique is for you to create a new class that extends the class *Thread*. The new class must provide a method named *run()*, which executes in a new thread when the parent class invokes the *start()* method.

```
class MyApplet extends Applet
{
    public void init()
    {
        // include initForm() and other applet methods
    }
```

(continued)

```
    /**
     * Start a new thread.
     */
    public void startThread()
    {
        // create an object of class MyThread
        Thread myThread = new MyThread();

        // now start the thread
        // the new thread begins execution with run()
        myThread.start();
    }
}

class MyThread extends Thread
{
    /**
     * Execution of the new thread begins here.
     */
    public void run()
    {
        ⋮
    }
}
```

The second approach to multithreading is to create a *Thread* object from an object that implements the *Runnable* interface. The object that implements the *Runnable* interface can be the applet object itself, as shown in the following example, MyApplet. The only requirement of the *Runnable* interface is the existence of the *run()* method.

```
// MyApplet implements Runnable by providing a run() method
class MyApplet extends Applet implements Runnable
{
    public void init()
    {
        // include initForm() and other applet methods
    }

    /**
     * Start a new thread.
     */
    public void startThread()
    {
        // create an object of class Thread using this, an object
        // of class MyApplet that implements Runnable
        Thread myThread = new Thread(this);
```

```
      // now start the thread.
      myThread.start();
   }

   /**
    * Execution of the new thread begins here.
    */
   public void run()
   {
         ⋮
   }
}
```

Here we see that since MyApplet implements the *Runnable* interface, its *run()* method can become the starting point for a new thread.

The MultiThread Prime Number Applet

Chapter 10 used the example of a prime number generator to demonstrate multi-threading in Microsoft Visual J++ 6 applications. Let's rewrite the same program here as an applet named MultiThreadApplet to highlight the similarities and the differences between multithreading in applications and multithreading in applets.

The problem

The problem is to create an applet that will spawn two independent threads, each of which will calculate prime numbers. The output of these prime numbers will be displayed in different panels within a single frame.

The setup work

Create an empty project by choosing New Project from the File menu. Select the Visual J++ Projects folder, and then select Empty Project. Name the applet MultiThreadApplet, and choose Open.

Add the applet .java file to your empty project by choosing Add Item from the Project menu and adding a class file named MultiThreadApplet.java. We'll also need a class that implements our prime number calculating thread. Repeat the process to add a class file named PrimeThread.java to our project.

Finally, add the HTML file. Select the Add Item command again. This time, select the Page option from the Web Page folder. Before choosing Open, enter the file name MultiThreadApplet.htm.

APPLET FRAMES

The use of frames in an applet is a technique that we have not seen before. In the applet examples we've seen so far—those in Chapter 14, Applets—all output has been to the applet window. In these cases, the *Applet* object appears (as much as possible) to be a part of the HTML page. To accomplish this functionality, however, the *Applet* class has to give up some important capabilities. For example, the applet window can't be resized, minimized, or closed.

The *Frame* class provides the same capabilities as the application *Form* class does. In contrast to an *Applet* object, a *Frame* object has a title bar that supports minimizing, maximizing, and closing. In addition, the frame boundary supports resizing. The downside of frames is that they are not part of the HTML page. Instead, frames hover over the HTML page. In fact, the user can grab the frame and drag it completely outside the browser window. The only connection between a frame and the HTML page that spawns it is that when the HTML page is closed, the frame closes.

A frame can be used in any applet, and is most commonly used to create a dialog box. There is no connection between a frame and multithreading. However, using a frame enables the applet to look more like the multithreaded application it's mimicking.

The *PrimeThread* code

The key to this applet lies in the *PrimeThread* class code, which extends a *Thread* class and is designed to calculate and display prime numbers:

```java
import java.awt.*;
/**
 * Thread that calculates primes and reports
 * them to output control.
 */
public class PrimeThread extends Thread
{
    // number of primes
    int numberOfPrimes = 0;

    // display controls
    TextField output = new TextField();
    Panel     panel  = new Panel();

    /**
     * Initialize the prime number thread.
     */
```

```
public PrimeThread(String name, int priority)
{
    // create a label object with the name
    Label label = new Label(name);

    // make the output control read only
    output.setEditable(false);

    // set the current thread's priority
    this.setPriority(priority);

    // -----format the thread's display panel-------
    // put space around the outside
    panel.setLayout(new BorderLayout());
    panel.add("West", new Label(" "));
    panel.add("East", new Label(" "));
    panel.add("North",new Label(" "));
    panel.add("South",new Label(" "));

    // create an inner panel with the label and
    // the output text field, and put it in the center
    // of the panel
    Panel innerPanel = new Panel();
    innerPanel.setLayout(new BorderLayout());
    innerPanel.add("North", label);
    innerPanel.add("South", output);
    panel.add("Center", innerPanel);
}

/**
 * Return the panel that contains the prime number
 * thread's output.
 */
Panel getPanel()
{
    return panel;
}

/**
 * Return true if number is prime.
 *
 * @param number - the number to test
 */
boolean isPrime(long number)
{
    // test all the multiples from 2 to the
    // square root of the number (increment
    // to handle potential round-off problems)
```

(continued)

```
        long max = (long)Math.sqrt(number) + 1;
        for (long test = 2; test <= max; test++)
        {
            // if number is evenly divisible by test...
            long remainder = number % test;
            if (remainder == 0)
            {
                // it can't be prime
                return false;
            }
        }

        // made it through, it must be prime
        return true;
    }


    /**
     * Start the background PrimeThread class executing.
     */
    public void run()
    {
        // keep calculating prime numbers
        // until we wrap around
        for (long i = 0; i >= 0; i++)
        {
            try
            {
                // give up control
                Thread.yield();

                // now calculate a new prime
                if (isPrime(i))
                {
                    // count it
                    numberOfPrimes++;

                    // output prime number to the control
                    // specified
                    output.setText("#" +
                                toString(numberOfPrimes) +
                                "- " +
                                toString(i));
                }
            }
            // ignore any exceptions that might occur
            catch(Exception e)
            {
            }
```

```
        }
    }

    /**
     * Convert a number into a string with commas.
     */
    private String toString(long value)
    {
        // convert the long into a string
        String s = Long.toString(value);

        // now add commas to that string
        StringBuffer sb = new StringBuffer(20);
        int offset = 0;
        for(int length = s.length();
            length > 0;
            length--)
        {
            // every 3 digits from the right side...
            if ((length % 3) == 0)
            {
                // but not at the beginning...
                if (offset != 0)
                {
                    // put a comma
                    sb.append(',');
                }
            }

            // now add another digit
            sb.append(s.charAt(offset++));
        }
        return sb.toString();
    }
}
```

The constructor for the *PrimeThread* class takes two arguments. The first argument is the name to be displayed in the thread's output panel. The second argument is the priority of the thread. The *PrimeThread()* constructor begins by creating a *Label* object out of the name passed to it. The constructor continues by setting the properties of the newly created output text field. This text field will be used to display the prime numbers as they are calculated. Next the constructor sets the priority for the current thread. The remainder of the *PrimeThread()* constructor is spent laying out the label and text field objects within a newly constructed panel.

The *getPanel()* method returns a reference to the panel that is created by the constructor. The remainder of the methods, *isPrime()*, *run()*, and *toString()*, are identical to the methods of the same name in the MultiThreadApplet application in Chapter 10.

The *MultiThreadApplet* code

The code for the *MultiThreadApplet* class appears as follows:

```java
import java.applet.Applet;
import java.awt.*;
import java.awt.event.*;

/**
 * This class implements the MultiThreadApplet (prime number)
 * application example from Chapter 10 as an applet.
 */
public class MultiThreadApplet extends Applet
{
    // frame will be used to house the prime number threads' output
    Frame      frame;

    // the two prime number threads (PrimeThread extends Thread)
    PrimeThread pt1;
    PrimeThread pt2;

    /**
     * Create and lay out the display objects.
     */
    public void start()
    {
        // create two thread objects (one with a lower priority
        // than the other); the class PrimeThread also creates the
        // output panels, including display objects
        pt1 = new PrimeThread("Prime #1", Thread.NORM_PRIORITY);
        pt2 = new PrimeThread("Prime #2", Thread.NORM_PRIORITY - 1);

        // display both panels created by PrimeThead in a frame
        frame = new Frame("Applet Prime Number");
        frame.setLayout(new BorderLayout());
        frame.add("North", pt1.getPanel());
        frame.add("South", pt2.getPanel());

        // now display the frame
        frame.setSize(300, 200);
        frame.setResizable(false);
        frame.setVisible(true);

        // the following listener is invoked when the user clicks
        // the frame's close button
        frame.addWindowListener(new FrameCloseAdapter());
```

```
        // start the two threads executing
        pt1.start();
        pt2.start();
    }


    // the following adapter is invoked when the user clicks
    // any of the window dressings
    class FrameCloseAdapter extends WindowAdapter
    {
        /**
         * Handle the window close event.
         */
        public void windowClosing(WindowEvent e)
        {
            // kill the threads
            stop();
        }
    }


    /**
     * Kill the two threads, and return their memory to the heap.
     */
    public void stop()
    {
        // if the frame hasn't already been closed...
        if (frame != null)
        {
            // close the frame, dispose of its
            // resources (returns memory to the heap)...
            frame.setVisible(false);
            frame.dispose();

            // and terminate the two threads
            pt1.stop();
            pt2.stop();
        }

        frame = null;
        pt1   = null;
        pt2   = null;
    }
}
```

The class *MultiThreadApplet* extends the *Applet* class, just like in all other applets. Unlike other applets, however, this applet uses the *start()* method to create the display objects rather than the *init()* method. This is a result of the fact that *MultiThreadApplet* must have a *stop()* method.

The *MultiThreadApplet* class needs a *stop()* method because when the browser continues to other HTML pages, the *PrimeThread*-based threads should be terminated and the frame closed. To accomplish this, we need a *stop()* method to call *Thread.stop()* for each of the threads. In addition, *stop()* closes the frame by calling *Frame.setVisible(false)* and disposes of the frame's memory by calling *Frame.dispose()*.

If the user returns to the MultiThreadApplet HTML page, the *start()* method must rebuild the frame and *PrimeThread* objects. This replaces the objects disposed of by *stop()*.

After creating the two threads of class *PrimeThread*, the *start()* method creates a frame with the title "Applet Prime Number" in the title bar. The *start()* method then creates two panels associated with these two threads and positions them in the top and bottom of the frame. The frame is then resized and displayed.

Finally, *start()* associates the method *windowClosing()* with the window close event through the listener *FrameCloseAdapter*. The *windowClosing()* method is invoked when the user clicks the close button in the frame's title bar. This method calls *stop()*, which stops the threads and disposes of the frame. Setting *frame* to *null* in the *stop()* method keeps the applet from attempting to dispose of the frame twice, which it would try to do were the user to close the applet window and then link to another HTML page. This precaution allows the user to click the close button to close the frame rather than forcing him or her to link to another HTML page to close the frame.

Window adapters

Notice that the object passed to *addWindowListener()* is an object of class *FrameCloseAdapter*. Based on our previous experience, you would expect that *FrameCloseAdapter* would implement the *WindowListener* interface. Instead, *FrameCloseAdapter* extends the *WindowAdapter* class. What's going on?

The *WindowAdapter* class implements the *WindowListener* interface. By extending this class, *FrameCloseAdapter* also implements *WindowListener*. However, the *WindowListener* interface includes six other methods besides *windowClosing()*. These methods handle other window-related events such as window minimizing (iconifying) and restoring (deiconifying).

With so many methods in the interface, the programmer is able to handle a number of different events; however, it also makes implementing the *WindowListener* interface monotonous. Because we don't care about the other six methods, we would need to create six empty "do nothing" methods along with *windowClosing()* to fully implement *WindowListener*. To avoid this unnecessary work, Java provides the class *WindowAdapter*. This class implements the *WindowListener* interface by providing all seven methods, each of which does nothing. *FrameCloseAdapter* extends *WindowAdapter* and overrides the single method *windowClosing()* with a method that actually does something. *FrameCloseAdapter* inherits the remaining methods necessary to implement *WindowListener*.

The HTML file

The HTML for MultiThreadApplet is conventional, with the exception of the size of the applet window. The <OBJECT> tag sets the size to 1 by 1 pixel, which essentially makes the applet invisible. (Setting the size to 0 by 0 pixels makes some browsers do strange things.)

```
<HTML>
<HEAD>
<META NAME="GENERATOR" Content="Microsoft Visual Studio 6.0">
<TITLE></TITLE>
</HEAD>
<BODY>

<HR>
The prime number applet opens a new form for
display.
<P>
<OBJECT CODE="MultiThreadApplet.class"
        HEIGHT=1
        WIDTH=1 VIEWASTEXT>
</OBJECT>
<HR>

</BODY>
</HTML>
```

The result

The MultiThreadApplet program, when run from Microsoft Internet Explorer, results in the output shown in Figure 15-1. The upper output text field of the frame updates rapidly with newly calculated prime numbers, while the lower text field updates much more slowly. What isn't obvious from Figure 15-1 is that the user can drag the prime number frame around in the screen. In addition, the applet frame has its own button on the Microsoft Windows taskbar.

When the user links to a new HTML page, the prime number output frame and the frame's button on the taskbar both disappear immediately. When the user returns to the page, the frame reappears and the threads begin running again. Similar results are obtained when the HTML page is displayed with the HTML editor.

> NOTE   I defined the frame so that it's not resizeable by calling the method *Frame.isResizable(false)*. I did this because Visual J++ 6 has a bug in the *Frame* code. Resizing the frame while the *PrimeThread* methods are running causes the MultiThreadApplet applet to hang.

Figure 15-1. *The output from MultiThreadApplet resembles that of the earlier multithreaded applications.*

ANIMATION

You will find many uses for multithreading in Java applets; however, by far the most popular use is applet animation. There are two distinct types of animation. When most people think of animation, they think of moving video images; however, this is only one type of animation. Animation created by the applet is just as important.

Applet-Generated Animation: The JigglingText Applet

Some applets generate data that the applet uses to update the appearance of the display. Let's call this type of animation *applet-generated* animation.

In a way, the MultiThreadApplet prime number generator presented previously is a type of applet-generated animation; however, the data generated by Multi-ThreadApplet is simply displayed in a text field. In true applet-generated animation, the data created by the applet is used to update the graphic display.

The problem

To demonstrate the concept of applet-generated animation, let's consider the simple example of an applet that displays a string of text in which the characters randomly wiggle about.

The setup work

Create an empty project named JigglingText. To this project, add a class and an HTML file of the same name.

The code

Update the JigglingText.java file to look as follows:

```java
import java.applet.Applet;
import java.awt.*;
import java.util.*;

/**
 * Demonstrate applet-generated animation by displaying a
 * string in the applet window and "jiggling" the characters.
 */
public class JigglingText extends Applet implements Runnable
{
    // random number generator that generates a sequence
    // of random bytes
    Random random = new Random();
    byte[] randomJiggle;

    // the input string broken down into characters
    char[] chars;
    int length;

    // the offset of the string in the display window
    Dimension stringOffset;

    // the average offset to each character
    int[] charOffsets;

    // the font information
    int fontHeight;
    int fontWidth;
    int stringWidth;

    // the thread generating the repaint calls
    Thread thread;

    /**
     * Set up the display.
     */
    public void init()
    {
        String display = this.getParameter("string");
        if (display == null)
        {
            display = "Default String";
        }
```

(continued)

```
        length = display.length();
        chars = new char[length];
        display.getChars(0, length, chars, 0);

        // now allocate a number of random offsets
        randomJiggle = new byte[length];
        for(int i = 0; i < length; i++)
        {
            randomJiggle[i] = 0;
        }

        // allocate a nice font
        this.setFont(new Font("Arial", Font.PLAIN, 18));

        // calculate font information
        Font f = this.getFont();
        fontHeight = f.getSize();
        fontWidth  = (2 * fontHeight) / 3;
        stringWidth= length * fontWidth;

        // from this, calculate the string offset
        stringOffset = this.getSize();
        stringOffset.height = (stringOffset.height - fontHeight) / 2;
        stringOffset.width  = (stringOffset.width  -  stringWidth) / 2;

        // now calculate the offset of each character
        charOffsets = new int[length];
        for (int i = 0; i < length; i++)
        {
            charOffsets[i] = fontWidth * i;
        }
    }

    /**
     * If a refresh thread doesn't already exist, start a new one.
     */
    public void start()
    {
        if (thread == null)
        {
            // begin a thread to update the offsets
            thread = new Thread(this);
            thread.start();
        }
    }
```

```
/**
 * If the refresh thread is running, stop it.
 */
public void stop()
{
    if (thread != null)
    {
        thread.stop();
        thread = null;
    }
}


/**
 * Execute the refresh thread by calculating a random sequence
 * of bytes and using this to update the character string.
 */
public void run()
{
    try
    {
        while(true)
        {
            // recalculate random numbers for character position
            random.nextBytes(randomJiggle);

            // now repaint the applet display
            repaint();

            // wait for a small period
            Thread.sleep(200);
        }
    }
    catch(Exception e)
    {
    }
}


/**
 * Display the character string while shifting the character
 * positions slightly.
 */
public void paint(Graphics g)
{
    // now paint the string a character at a time
    for (int i = 0; i < length; i++)
```

(continued)

```
      {
          // calculate the character offset
          int charOffset;
          charOffset = stringOffset.width + charOffsets[i];
          charOffset+= (fontWidth * randomJiggle[i]) / 256;

          // display each character at its position
          g.drawChars(chars, i, 1, charOffset, stringOffset.height);
      }
   }
}
```

Like all applet classes, the class *JigglingText* extends the class *Applet*. Unlike most applets, *JigglingText* also implements the *Runnable* interface. Implementing *Runnable* will allow *JigglingText* to be used as the basis for a new thread.

The *init()* method begins by reading the parameter *string* from the HTML file. If this parameter exists, it's stored in the string variable *display*. If it doesn't exist, the string *Default String* is stored in *display*. The *display* string is then converted into an array of characters. (As you'll see, the *paint()* method will require such an array rather than a character string.)

The *init()* method then allocates an array of bytes the same length as the input string. The *randomJiggle* array is initialized to all zeroes. This array will eventually contain the randomly calculated "jiggle factors."

After applying an attractive font, *init()* calculates a series of font variables. The font height is easily calculated. Calculating the font width is difficult, because the width of each character is different. Experience with different ratios shows that using two-thirds of the font height as an average character width generates good results. The total *stringWidth* value is calculated as the *fontWidth* value times the number of characters in the string. (The *stringLength()* method can't be used without a *Graphics* object.)

The *init()* method uses the calculated font sizes along with the size of the applet window to calculate the proper offset of the *display* string that is stored in *stringOffset*, an object of type *Dimension*. In addition, the offset of each character in the *display* string is stored in the integer array *charOffsets*. This completes the initialization of the data members that *paint()* will need to implement the jiggling display.

The *start()* method creates a *Thread* object from the current *JigglingText* applet object. The call to *thread.start()* creates a new thread, which begins execution with the method *run()*. As with many animation applets, *run()* executes a loop that calculates some variable values that are required to support the *paint()* method, and then invokes *repaint()* to force a repaint of the applet window. In this case, *run()* calls *Random.nextBytes()*, which fills the array *randomJiggle* with a series of randomly chosen byte values. The call to *sleep()* gives the *paint()* method a chance to do its job and gives the user a chance to view the results.

It's the *paint()* method that actually displays the jiggling string. This method loops through each character in the *chars* array of characters to be displayed. For each character, *paint()* calculates a character offset by first adding the character offset within the string to the offset of the string within the applet window. A small additional factor is then added to the character offset. This factor is based on both the average *font-Width* value and the *randomJiggle* factor calculated in the *run()* method. In no case is this factor greater than one half the *fontWidth* value.

Finally, the character at offset *i* within the character array representing the input string is drawn at the calculated offset. The *paint()* method continues by drawing the next character in the array. The *paint()* method terminates when all of the characters in the string have been drawn.

The HTML file

To test the JigglingText applet, update the HTML file so it looks as follows:

```
<HTML>
<HEAD>
<META NAME="GENERATOR" Content="Microsoft Visual Studio 6.0">
<TITLE></TITLE>
</HEAD>
<BODY>

<OBJECT CODE="JigglingText.class"
        HEIGHT=100
        WIDTH=300 VIEWASTEXT>
<PARAM name="string" value="Display String">
</OBJECT>

</BODY>
</HTML>
```

The parameter *string* causes the message "Display String" to be displayed in the applet window.

The result

The results of executing the JigglingText applet with JigglingText.htm are shown in Figure 15-2.

Figure 15-2. *The JigglingText applet displays a string of characters that jiggle about on the display.*

Loading a Single Image

Image animation occurs when the applet replays in rapid succession a series of images. Of course, before these images can be displayed they must be transferred to the applet. This transfer process is called *image loading*. Before we tackle the problem of loading multiple images, let's build an applet that loads a single image.

Applets understand two different types of images: the GIF (pronounced as either giff with a hard "g," or jiff, like the peanut butter) format and the JPEG (universally pronounced jay-peg) format. Each of these formats has its advantages. GIF files give better color rendition when the number of different colors is small. JPEG files are smaller, but they take longer to decompress.

The *Applet* class contains the method *getImage(url, imageName)*, where *url* is normally equal to the applet code base (the path to the applet's .class files) and *imageName* is the name of the individual image file to load. (This method assumes that the image is in the same directory as the .class file.)

Judging from its name, you might assume that *getImage()* loads an image, but this isn't the case. The *getImage()* method only registers the image to be loaded by the applet. The image isn't loaded until it's needed. Since the loading of an image is a time-consuming process, the Java library provides an *ImageObserver* interface for this task. An object of a class that implements *ImageObserver* can monitor the loading of an image while the applet continues executing.

To demonstrate this principle, let's create a small applet that loads and displays an image of a magnifying glass. (The GIF images used in this section were extracted from FindFile.avi, which is on the Visual J++ 6 CD in the \Common\Graphics\AVIs folder.)

The DisplayImage applet

The DisplayImage applet displays a single GIF file in the applet window. Begin by creating an empty DisplayImage project. Populate the project with a Display-Image.java file and a DisplayImage.htm file. Update the HTML file to load the DisplayImage.class file.

The code for the *DisplayImage* class appears as follows:

```java
import java.applet.Applet;
import java.awt.*;
import java.net.URL;
import java.awt.image.*;

/**
 * This applet displays a single image file find01.gif.
 */
public class DisplayImage extends Applet
{
    // the size of the window
    Dimension windowSize;

    // the find01 image information
    Image image;
    int    imageHeight = 0;
    int    imageWidth = 0;
    boolean imageError = false;

    // use the following image observer to determine
    // when the image load operation is complete
    ImageObserver observer = new Observer();

    /**
     * Set up the image to be loaded by the new
     * thread.
     */
    public void init()
    {
        // set the background color to white
        this.setBackground(Color.white);

        // first calculate the size of the applet window
        windowSize = this.getSize();

        // get the image
        URL url = this.getCodeBase();
        image = this.getImage(url, "find01.gif");
    }
```

(continued)

```
class Observer implements ImageObserver
{
    public boolean imageUpdate(Image dummy,
                               int status,
                               int x, int y,
                               int width, int height)
    {
        boolean returnVal = true;

        if ((status & ImageObserver.HEIGHT) != 0)
        {
            imageHeight = height;
        }
        if ((status & ImageObserver.WIDTH) != 0)
        {
            imageWidth = width;
        }
        if ((status & ImageObserver.ALLBITS) ==
            ImageObserver.ALLBITS)
        {
            returnVal = false;
        }

        if ((status & ImageObserver.ABORT) != 0)
        {
            imageError = true;
            returnVal = false;
        }

        repaint();
        return returnVal;
    }
}

/**
 * If the image has been loaded, display it;
 * otherwise, display an error message.
 */
Dimension offset = new Dimension();
public void paint(Graphics g)
{
    // if an image error has occurred...
    if (imageError)
    {
        // output an error message
        String s = "Image load failed";
        FontMetrics fm = g.getFontMetrics();
```

```
        offset.width = (windowSize.width - fm.stringWidth(s))/2;
        offset.height= windowSize.height/2;

        g.drawString(s, offset.width, offset.height);
        return;
    }

    // draw the image in the middle of the applet window
    g.drawImage(image,
            (windowSize.width - imageWidth)/2,
            (windowSize.height - imageHeight)/2,
            observer);
    }
}
```

As the *DisplayImage* class is constructed, the image height and width are set to zero. In addition, the *imageError* flag is set to *false*. This flag will be set to *true* if the image load process is aborted with an error. In addition, the *DisplayImage* constructor creates an instance of the *Observer* class. Looking ahead in the code, you can see that *Observer* is an inner class that implements the *ImageObserver* interface. I'll explain the significance of this shortly.

The *init()* method begins by setting the background of the applet to white so it blends with the browser background. The method continues by retrieving the window size used by the *paint()* method. Finally, the *init()* method creates an *Image* object from the file find01.gif, which is located at the same URL that the DisplayImage.class file came from. Remember that creating the image object doesn't cause the image to be loaded.

The *paint()* method begins by checking to see if an image load error has occurred. If it has, *paint()* displays the message "Image load failed" in the middle of the applet window, and makes no further attempts to load the image.

If no image load error has occurred, the *paint()* method continues by calling the *drawImage()* method to draw the image contained in the *Image* object in the middle of the applet window. Initially no image is available; however, the *drawImage()* call starts the image-loading process. In addition to passing the x and y coordinates at which to draw the image, *paint()* passes the *observer* object, which implements *ImageObserver*, to *drawImage()*. The image loader uses the *observer* object to inform the DisplayImage applet of the status of the image as it's being loaded.

The internal class *Observer* has one method: *imageUpdate()*. The applet calls this method whenever there is a change in the image status. The *status* argument contains a bit pattern indicating for which values the image status is known. For example, the image width is one of the first values retrieved from the image. As soon as the *ImageObserver.WIDTH* flag is set, *imageUpdate()* can save the *imageWidth* value. The call to *repaint()* at the bottom of the *imageUpdate()* method forces *paint()*

to draw the portion of the image that is already loaded. The *imageUpdate()* method returns *true* to indicate that the image load operation should continue.

The image load operation is complete when the *status* argument's *ALLBITS* bit is set. When this happens, *imageUpdate()* returns *false* to indicate that the image loader should stop loading the image. Similarly, if the *ABORT* bit is set, a fatal error has occurred, indicating that the image load operation should be halted.

The result of executing the DisplayImage applet is shown in Figure 15-3. What isn't obvious from this static display is that the image display is repainted continuously from top to bottom as the image information is loaded.

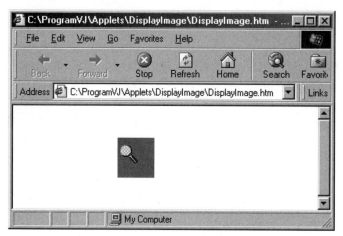

Figure 15-3. *The DisplayImage applet displays the single image contained in find01.gif.*

Loading Multiple Images

Most people, when they think of animation, think of image animation.

> **NOTE**   With the advent of multiple-frame GIF files, image animation in applets is a lot less important than it used to be. A multiple-frame GIF file allows simple image sequences to be displayed within an HTML file without resorting to applet animation.

Although there are variations in how image animation applets work, all image animation applets begin by loading a series of images. The applet then displays these images in sequence within the applet window, pausing between each image. If the pause is sufficiently small, the user's eye perceives the image sequence as smooth motion. (This is the same principle used in movie or television films.)

Images used in applets are normally loaded from the server. If the connection to the server is over a LAN, as would be the case with an intranet, the server connection is of sufficient speed that the image download times for a reasonable number of images are not significant. However, when you are downloading images using a modem, the connections to the server are slow enough that if an image is large or if there are a great number of images, the image download time becomes unacceptable to the user.

(For applications involving a fixed customer base, it might be possible to store the images on the client computer. Loading images from the client is much faster than over a modem or a LAN; however, the applet will need to be trusted. See Chapter 14, Applets, for a discussion of applet I/O.)

The *ImageObserver* interface is great for loading a single image. When it is loading the numerous images required to perform image animation, however, the *ImageObserver* interface quickly becomes unwieldy. To track the load process of multiple images, use the class *MediaTracker*. The following applet demonstrates the *MediaTracker* class.

The ImageAnimation applet

To begin writing the ImageAnimation applet, create an empty project and add the files ImageAnimation.java and ImageAnimation.htm. Create a sequence of frames that together make up an animated sequence. I chose the full sequence of 23 frames from the FindFile.avi file that is contained on the Visual J++ 6 CD. Since this file contains so many images, I stored them in the subdirectory *images*.

Update the *ImageAnimation* class as follows:

```java
import java.applet.Applet;
import java.awt.*;
import java.net.URL;

/**
 * The following class performs animation by flipping rapidly
 * through the images/Findxx frames, where xx is 01 through 23.
 */
public class ImageAnimation extends Applet implements Runnable
{
    // define the image file base name and the number of
    // images in the animation sequence
    final static String BASENAME = "Find";
    final static int NUMFRAMES = 23;

    // define the media tracker used to load the images
    MediaTracker mt;
    boolean imagesLoaded;
    boolean imageLoadError;

    // the following thread both loads the images (using
    // the media tracker) and prompts the paint() method
    // to cycle through the images
    Thread replayThread = null;
```

(continued)

```
        // the images themselves
        Image[] images = new Image[NUMFRAMES];

        // the image number and position of the image
        int imageNumber = 0;
        int imageX = 0;
        int imageY = 0;

        /**
         * Create the media tracker, and load the images into it.
         */
        public void init()
        {
            // create a media tracker to track the loading of
            // images
            mt = new MediaTracker(this);

            // now add the images to the media tracker
            String imageRoot = "Images/" + BASENAME;
            URL url = this.getDocumentBase();

            for(int i = 0; i < NUMFRAMES; i++)
            {
                // create the image names find01, find02, and so on
                int imageNum = i + 1;
                String imageName = new String(imageRoot);
                if (imageNum < 10)
                {
                    imageName += "0";
                }
                imageName += imageNum;
                imageName += ".gif";

                // create an image object from that name
                images[i] = this.getImage(url, imageName);

                // now add each image name to the MediaTracker
                mt.addImage(images[i], 1);
            }
        }

        /**
         * Start the image display process.
         */
        public void start()
        {
            if (replayThread == null)
            {
```

```
        // start the replay thread
        replayThread = new Thread(this);
        replayThread.start();
    }
}


/**
 * Stop the image display process.
 */
public void stop()
{
    if (replayThread != null)
    {
        replayThread.stop();
        replayThread = null;
    }
}


/**
 * Load the images stored in the MediaTracker and
 * then prompt paint() to display them rapidly.
 */
public void run()
{
    // initialize variables
    imagesLoaded = false;

    // start loading the images
    try
    {
        mt.waitForAll();
    }
    catch(Exception e)
    {
        return;
    }
    imagesLoaded = true;

    // get the status of the image load - if not complete
    // there was a load error
    imageLoadError = false;
    if (mt.isErrorAny())
    {
        imageLoadError = true;
        repaint();
        return;
    }
```

(continued)

```
            // now that the images are loaded, calculate
            // the proper display offset
            Dimension size = this.getSize();
            int width = images[0].getWidth(null);
            int height= images[0].getHeight(null);
            imageX = (size.width - width) / 2;
            imageY = (size.height- height)/ 2;

            // prompt paint() to sequence through the images
            try
            {
                while(true)
                {
                    Thread.sleep(200);
                    repaint();
                }
            }
            catch(Exception e)
            {
            }
    }


    /**
     * Display the images.
     */
    public void paint(Graphics g)
    {
        // interpret the load flags
        if (imageLoadError)
        {
            g.drawString("Image load error", 10, 20);
            return;
        }
        if (!imagesLoaded)
        {
            g.drawString("Images loading...", 10, 20);
            return;
        }

        // draw each image from 0 through 22 repeatedly
        g.drawImage(images[imageNumber++],
                    imageX,
                    imageY,
                    null);
        if (imageNumber >= NUMFRAMES)
        {
            imageNumber = 0;
        }
    }
}
```

The *ImageAnimation* class implements the *Runnable* interface in order to be able to spawn a background thread, which we'll see the importance of shortly.

The *init()* method begins by creating a *MediaTracker* object *mt*. The *for* loop within *init()* creates the name of each of the *Find* files in turn: *images/Find01.gif*, followed by *images/Find02.gif*, and so forth. Each of these file names, along with the URL of the HTML file, is passed to the *getImage()* method. The resulting image is stored in the *images* array. In addition, each image is added to the *MediaTracker*.

The *start()* method creates and then starts a new thread out of the *Image-Animation* object.

The *run()* method, which is executed within the new thread, begins by calling *waitForAll()*. This method of *MediaTracker* doesn't return to the caller until all images have been loaded. Once loaded, *run()* sets the *imagesLoaded* flag to *true*. The media tracker monitors the load process. If an error arises, the media tracker sets an error flag that *run()* queries by calling *isErrorAny()*. If no error occurs, *run()* calculates the size of the applet window and the size of the images. (We are assuming all images are the same size.) Using this size information, *run()* calculates the offset to display the images centered within the frame. The *run()* method then sits in a loop, pausing for a fifth of a second (200 milliseconds) and then forcing a repaint of the applet window.

The *paint()* method first checks the *imageLoadError* and *imagesLoaded* flags. If either is set, *paint()* displays a message and returns. If not, *paint()* draws the image at index *imageNumber* from the *images* image array, and increments the *image-Number* value. As soon as the *imageNumber* value is incremented to 23, *paint()* resets the number back to zero.

The 200 millisecond delay between repaints, together with the drawing of the sequence of images in *paint()*, creates the animation effect. A static representation of the result is shown in Figure 15-4.

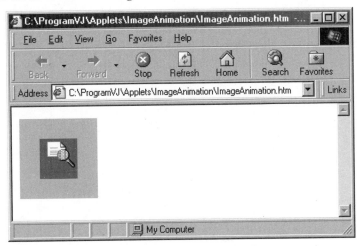

Figure 15-4. *ImageAnimation repaints the same sequence of images rapidly to generate an animation effect.*

ImageAnimation without the flicker

What you can't see in Figure 15-4 is the animation effect. You also can't see that the image within the applet display flickers. At a frame rate of five frames per second, the flicker is barely noticeable. If you increase the rate to 10 frames per second, depending on your machine the flicker might become so bad that the animation is barely visible.

The reason for the flicker lies in the way that *paint()* works. During the repaint sequence, the browser calls the *update()* method. This method first clears the applet window to remove whatever was displayed there during the previous repaint. Once the window has been cleared, *update()* calls *paint()* to update the window with the new information.

For normal operations, this sequence is fine. However, when the applet window is being updated rapidly, the time between each window repaint becomes longer than the time it takes to repaint the window. When the applet reaches this point, the window is blank longer than it's painted.

The reason that *update()* clears the screen doesn't apply to our ImageAnimation routine. There is no reason to clear the applet window when the next image will completely overwrite the current image. To avoid the unnecessary window clearing, we can override the Visual J++ *update()* method with a new version of *update()* that calls *paint()* without first clearing the applet window.

The new version of ImageAnimation, ImageAnimationA, is identical to its predecessor, except for the addition of the *update()* method and some minor changes to the *paint()* method, which are shown here.

```
/**
 * Normally the update() method clears the applet window before
 * calling paint(); in this version, just call paint()--it reduces
 * flicker considerably.
 */
public void update(Graphics g)
{
    paint(g);
}


/**
 * Display the images.
 */
boolean imageFirstPass = true;
public void paint(Graphics g)
{
    // interpret the load flags
    if (imageLoadError)
    {
        g.drawString("Image load error", 10, 20);
```

```
            return;
        }
        if (!imagesLoaded)
        {
            g.drawString("Images loading...", 10, 20);
            return;
        }

        // if this is the first time an image is to be drawn...
        if (imageFirstPass)
        {
            // clear the applet window (this is necessary
            // because update() is no longer doing it)
            g.clearRect(0, 0, getSize().width, getSize().height);
            imageFirstPass = false;
        }

        // draw each image from 0 through 22 repeatedly
        g.drawImage(images[imageNumber++],
                    imageX,
                    imageY,
                    null);
        if (imageNumber >= NUMFRAMES)
        {
            imageNumber = 0;
        }
    }
}
```

This new version of *paint()* adds the call to *Graphics.clearRect()* before displaying the first image. The *clearRect()* method clears some portion of the window—in this case, the entire window. This removes any text written there earlier by *drawString()*. Clearing the window would normally be handled by the *update()* method; however, since this new version of *update()* doesn't clear the window, *paint()* must.

CONCLUSION

In this chapter, you have seen a number of different ways to generate applet animation. The chapter began with a demonstration of multithreading in applets, because applet animation relies so heavily on multithreading.

With a firm knowledge of multithreading in hand, we then examined applet animation, beginning with images constructed by the applet itself. The chapter concluded with demonstrating animation that uses downloaded images.

This is the last chapter in this book that deals with applets. The next chapter will take up the closely related topic of Dynamic HTML generation in Visual J++ 6.

Chapter 16

The WFC Dynamic HTML Package

Conventional Hypertext Markup Language (HTML) pages are static. HTML pages can't read and process user input, nor can they change in appearance once they have been downloaded to a browser. The introduction of the Dynamic HTML (DHTML) standard has changed all that. DHTML tags can be modified even after the browser has downloaded and displayed the page. This ability allows DHTML-based pages to react to user input without external assistance.

Accessing the dynamic features of DHTML has not been easy for the Java programmer. Fortunately, Microsoft Visual J++ 6 eases this burden by providing direct access to the DHTML standard from your Java application.

THE DYNAMIC HTML STANDARD

The World Wide Web has grown and flourished through the use of the HTML standard, as is evidenced by the large number of attractive HTML pages accessible from your browser. However, as the Web has become more sophisticated, limitations in the HTML standard have become increasingly apparent.

The major problem with HTML is that it isn't dynamic. The conventional HTML page can't truly interact with the Web user. Once a browser has interpreted and displayed an HTML page, the page can't change.

Wait a minute, you say. What about search engines that search the Web for keywords entered into an HTML page by the Web user? How is that done? There are a number of ways that user interaction can be simulated in an HTML page.

Adding User Interaction to Conventional HTML Pages

Web-based search engines, such as Yahoo (*www.yahoo.com*), make it clear that HTML includes features that make an HTML page appear to be dynamic. What are the techniques that HTML page developers use to animate their Web sites? This section focuses on the answer to this question.

The applet

Java applets can of course implement user interaction, as was demonstrated in Chapter 14, Applets, and Chapter 15, Applet Animation. A Java applet is started by an HTML page and the applet runs within the browser. Because a Java applet is an application, it can interact with the user in a number of ways. In addition, a Java applet can change its appearance after the HTML page has been displayed.

The major limitation of any applet is that its window is carved out of the HTML page. A Java applet doesn't look like it's part of the HTML page that surrounds it, because a Java applet doesn't play by the same rules as an HTML page does. For example, when the user changes the size of the browser window the Java applet isn't resized like the other HTML objects on the page. In addition, a Java applet can't access the surrounding HTML page. Unless an applet uses scripts, it can do nothing to change the appearance of an image or a field on the HTML page display.

CGI applications

CGI (Common Gateway Interface) is an extension to the browser-to-server interface that defines an interactive—although not dynamic—interface. The HTML standard supports CGI by a feature known as *forms*, identified with the <FORM> tags.

A form defines a span within the HTML page, and also defines an attached URL link. Any number of standard HTML elements can be placed between the <FORM> tags, and the browser renders these elements within the form, just as it would render elements outside the form.

A form can also include user input fields. Each input field carries a name and can be one of various types. Input field types include buttons, check boxes, drop-down list boxes, and text entry fields, to name a few. Each input field also has a value. The possible values for a given input field are determined by the type of field it is. For example, the value of a button is either on or off, and the value of a text field is the text entered by the user.

One and only one of the input fields in a form must be a Submit button. (The label on this button doesn't have to be Submit, but it normally is.) When the user chooses the Submit button, the browser links to the URL address indicated in the form, and sends the URL to the server. Unlike conventional hyperlinks, however, the browser adds to the end of the URL the name and value of each of the input fields defined for the form. This tells the server what values the user entered into each input field.

The URL listed in the form doesn't refer to an HTML page on the server. Instead, the form's URL refers to an application on the server. When the server receives this application link, it passes the data the user entered to the application referenced by the URL. (The details of how this data is passed to the application aren't relevant to this discussion.) The application creates a new HTML page based on the user's input, and sends it back to the server. The server then passes the new HTML page to the browser for display. The browser is unaware that the displayed HTML page was generated by an application rather than by an HTML file.

The CGI concept is extremely powerful. As a CGI programmer, you can create any type of browser output you want in real-time, based on user input. However, the limitations of the CGI interface are numerous. For example, CGI applications are difficult to write, and CGI applications can't save their state from one query to the next.

The most serious problem with CGI, however, is that CGI applications put a significant load on the server. Every CGI request causes the server to begin running an application to process the query. Once the request has been processed, the server must pass the results back to the HTML page and terminate the application. When a large number of concurrent CGI requests occur, the constant starting and stopping of server applications can cause unacceptable delays for the user.

Scripting languages

Netscape addressed some of the difficulties inherent in CGI by defining an HTML scripting language called LiveScript, which was later renamed JavaScript. (The name change to JavaScript was driven more by commercial factors than by any similarity between JavaScript and the Java language.) Microsoft responded with its own version of JavaScript, which it named JScript. (JavaScript and JScript are almost completely compatible.) In addition, Microsoft implemented a completely different scripting language called VBScript, which is based on Microsoft's application macro language.

Script languages enable you to preprocess form data before sending it to the Web server for CGI processing. This preprocessing allows the scripting language to catch obviously incorrect user input, such as no text in a required text input field.

Catching invalid data before sending it over the Web for processing improves the response time to the user and reduces the load on the server. Preprocessing data ensures that the user doesn't wait for a CGI request to make the round trip to the server and back, only to find out that an entry was incorrect. In addition, with preprocessing the server isn't loaded down with erroneous CGI requests.

Although scripting languages can read and process user input before passing it to the server, they have a serious disadvantage. Once the browser has rendered the HTML page, scripting languages are powerless to change the page without server assistance.

DHTML Capabilities

DHTML extends HTML by allowing an HTML page to be modified after the browser has rendered the page. For example, with DHTML, a text field that says "Stopped" when the page is first displayed can be changed to say "Started" when the user clicks a "Go" button. You can make a clock in an HTML page tick automatically, whether the underlying HTML includes a clock directive or not. (DHTML also extends features such as style sheets; however, the focus of this chapter is active changes in the HTML page display.)

DHTML increases the capability of scripting languages immensely. With DHTML, you can use script to implement many programming features that previously required CGI, while at the same time reducing the HTML page response time. In the previous example of changing the contents of a text field from "Stopped" to "Started," the HTML page spends no time requesting a new HTML page from the server and displaying it. The display change is instead made directly by the HTML page. Avoiding CGI requests reduces the time a page takes to respond to user input, and lessens the load on the server.

DHTML also enables you, as a script programmer, to implement features that are impossible to implement with CGI. The CGI application doesn't receive input until the user clicks the Submit button. By comparison, DHTML-based scripts can receive and process an event when the user clicks any button or even when the mouse pointer passes over a button.

While DHTML increases the capability of scripting languages, it does nothing to address other problems inherent in scripts. Because script languages lack the clear structure of Java (or other languages such as C++), scripts of more than a few dozen lines become difficult to write and debug. (Some programmers claim that 100 lines represent a practical upper boundary for a script application.) In addition, script languages have a long learning curve that the Java programmer must surmount.

Visual J++ 6 Access to DHTML

Visual J++ 6 introduces the ability to access the capabilities of DHTML from a Java application. Your control of DHTML features no longer requires you to learn a new scripting language. Your control of DHTML features can also be more sophisticated than before, because Java applications can be larger and more involved than applications written in a script language. In addition, Java access to DHTML introduces capabilities that aren't supported by scripting languages, such as access to database information on the client (the browser) or the server.

DHTML access in Visual J++ 6 is contained in the Windows Foundation Classes for Java (WFC) *wfc.html* package. Visual J++ source code that accesses the *html* package looks amazingly like the code that accesses other WFC objects. The same Visual J++ application can use the *html* package on the client or the server with only minor changes.

CLIENT-SIDE DHTML

Client-side use of the *wfc.html* package provides the Java programmer with significant capabilities, such as the ability to manipulate HTML objects. While the code for client-side applications is similar to that of a WFC applet, the results look and feel like conventional HTML rather than like applet output.

This power comes at a price. The *html* package can be accessed on the client side only by Microsoft Internet Explorer version 4 or later. This means that HTML pages that utilize the *html* package on the client side can't run on the Internet unless you can limit access to Internet Explorer 4 users.

Thus, a company might apply client-side DHTML for intranet pages used by its sales force, because the company can control which Web browsers are used. In such a situation, client-side DHTML can also provide a significant increase in performance for intranet sites. For Internet sites, however, accessing the *html* package from the client side isn't practical.

Client-side DHTML is most easily explained by example. The following Simple-ClientSide example application demonstrates the principles of the *html* package. Following that is a more involved example demonstrating access to a client database.

The SimpleClientSide Application

The SimpleClientSide example application modifies two fields on an existing HTML page while adding two more. The application also demonstrates the user interaction capability for both the existing objects and the added objects.

The HTML editor work

From within the Visual J++ 6 environment, choose New Project from the File menu. In the New Project window, select Web Pages from the Visual J++ Projects folder. Now choose Code-behind HTML. Provide the name *SimpleClientSide* as the project name within a DHTML directory, and choose Open.

From within Project Explorer, open the Page1.htm file. The HTML editor opens in Design mode. In this mode, you can edit the HTML page visually. This initial HTML page display contains a warning that only the Microsoft Virtual Machine for Java beyond a certain version can display client-side DHTML, followed by the string "This is bound text."

Switch the HTML editor into Source mode. In this mode, the editor displays the underlying HTML code. The <BODY> section of our initial HTML file is broken into three parts. The first part contains the version warning, bracketed between <HR> tags. Delete this part. Retain the second part that begins with the <OBJECT> tag, and retain the final part that begins with the HTML comment <!-- Insert HTML here -->.

Return the HTML editor to Design mode, to update the HTML file with your edits. (This time, only the sentence "This is bound text." should be displayed.) Select the

HTML section of the Toolbox. You'll see that all of the HTML tools are enabled. Drag a Line Break control to the editor, and drop it immediately underneath the existing string. (Direct positioning of controls isn't supported by DHTML. The HTML editor does support a special mode called Absolute mode, in which objects can be placed anywhere within the display window by means of a special COM object. In Absolute mode, however, client-side DHTML isn't supported.)

Now drag a Button control to the HTML editor below the Line Break control. With the Button still selected, open the Properties window. Change the *value* property of the Button control to *Change Bound Text.*

Finally, drag a Paragraph Break control to the right of the Button or underneath the Button, to provide extra space following the button and any subsequent objects.

Now switch the HTML editor back to Source mode, and if the space command (* *) is present, delete it. The resulting source code should appear as follows (I have edited this section slightly so that it fits on the book page):

```
<!-- Insert HTML here -->
<SPAN id="bindText">This is bound text.</SPAN>
<BR>
<INPUT id=button1 name="button1" type=button value="Change Bound Text">
<P></P>
```

Display the result in the Quick View mode of the HTML editor. The Quick View mode of the editor provides a rapid way of viewing what the DHTML file will look like when viewed by the Internet Explorer browser. Figure 16-1 shows the result.

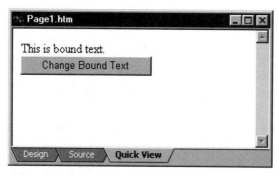

Figure 16-1. *The initial appearance of the edited Page1.htm file.*

Close the HTML editor.

The wizard-generated code

Open the Class1.java file in the Text editor. The code generated by the Code-behind HTML Wizard appears as follows (I have edited the comments to fit within the book page):

```
import com.ms.wfc.html.*;
import com.ms.wfc.core.*;
import com.ms.wfc.ui.*;

public class Class1 extends DhDocument
{
    DhText createdText;
    DhText boundText;

    public Class1()
    {
        // Required for Visual J++ Form Designer support
        initForm();

        // TODO: Add any constructor code after initForm call
    }

    /**
     * Class1 overrides dispose so it can clean up the
     * component list.
     */
    public void dispose()
    {
        super.dispose();
    }

    /**
     * Add all your initialization code here. The code here can add
     * elements, set bindings to existing elements, set new properties
     * and event handlers on elements. The underlying HTML document is
     * not available at this stage, so any calls that rely on the
     * document being present should be added to the onDocumentLoad()
     * function below (client-only).
     */
    private void initForm()
    {
        createdText = new DhText();
        createdText.setText("Created Text");

        boundText = new DhText();
        boundText.setID("bindText");
        boundText.setBackColor(Color.LIGHTGRAY);

        /**
         * setBoundElements() will take a list of elements that already
         * are present in the HTML document, and binds them to the
         * DhElement list.
         */
```

(continued)

```
        setBoundElements(new DhElement[] {boundText});

        /**
         * setNewElements() takes a list of DhElements and adds them
         * to the HTML document.
         */
        setNewElements(new DhElement[] {createdText});
    }

    /**
     * Client-side only.
     *
     * Here, the underlying HTML document is available for inspection.
     * Add any code that wants to get properties of elements or inspect
     * the document in any other way.
     */
    protected void onDocumentLoad(Object sender, Event e)
    {
    }
}
```

Let's examine this code for a second. You can see that the class *Class1* extends the class *DhDocument*. The names of all classes in the *html* package begin with the letters *Db*. For the most part, the remainder of an *html* class name is the same as the WFC equivalent. For example, the class name for an *html* button is *DbButton,* whereas the WFC class name would be *Button.*

The class *DbDocument* describes the HTML document. (The class *DbWindow* describes the browser window in which the document resides. Parallel concepts are found in JScript.)

The *Class1* constructor immediately invokes the *initForm()* method, in much the same fashion as the constructor for a WFC-generated class.

The *initForm()* method contains example code to perform two different tasks: adding objects to the DHTML file and binding the code to objects already present. Unfortunately, the code for these two functions is intertwined in the system-generated listing. Let me display the two tasks separately to better explain each.

Adding DHTML objects is implemented by the following code:

```
private void initForm()
{
    createdText = new DhText();
    createdText.setText("Created Text");

    /**
     * setNewElements() takes a list of DhElements and adds them
     * to the HTML document.
     */
```

```
        setNewElements(new DhElement[] {createdText});
}
```

Here, you can see that *initForm()* creates an object of class *DhText*. This is the
DHTML equivalent of the WFC *Text* object. The *text* property of the *DhText* object is
then set to *Created Text*.

The call to *setNewElements* adds an array of *DhElement* objects to the HTML
display. In this case, the array contains a single element, the *createdText* object. The
class *DhText* extends the class *DhElement,* as do all other *Dh* component classes.

The second task is represented by the following portion of *initForm()*:

```
private void initForm()
{
    boundText = new DhText();
    boundText.setID("bindText");
    boundText.setBackColor(Color.LIGHTGRAY);

    /**
     * setBoundElements() will take a list of elements that already
     * are present in the HTML document, and binds them to the
     * DhElement list.
     */
    setBoundElements(new DhElement[] {boundText});
}
```

This portion begins by creating a *DhText* object just as we did before. Rather
than set the properties of this object directly, however, this code uses the *setID()*
method to attach to the text object *bindText*, which already appears in the Page1.htm
file. Look back to the Page1.htm file on page 546 to see that the initial text string is
contained within <SPAN> tags carrying the *id* value *bindText*.

A string of text doesn't allow for the definition of properties such as the *id*
property. To address this limitation, DHTML allows for the inclusion of the <SPAN>
tags, which can encompass a section of code and which do have an *id* property.
Defining a property within the <SPAN> tags applies that property to the entire span
of DHTML text.

The *setID()* method scans the DHTML document looking for a text span with
the ID *bindText*. Once found, this text is then bound to the *boundText* object. The
boundText.setBackColor() method changes the background color property of the text
span to *LIGHTGRAY*. (This is a rather subtle change. For a more dramatic effect, try
setting a different property, such as font, and redisplaying the result in the Quick View
window. You'll see this type of setting demonstrated later in this section.)

The user-defined code

Edit the Class1.java file so it looks as follows:

```java
import com.ms.wfc.html.*;
import com.ms.wfc.core.*;
import com.ms.wfc.ui.*;

/**
 * Demonstrate html package principles by adding a few
 * simple HTML tags and then updating them dynamically.
 */
public class Class1 extends DhDocument
{
    DhText createdText;
    DhText boundText;

    public Class1()
    {
        // Required for Visual J++ Form Designer support
        initForm();
    }

    /**
     * Class1 overrides dispose so it can clean up the
     * component list.
     */
    public void dispose()
    {
        super.dispose();
    }

    /**
     * Bind to a few existing elements and add a few more.
     */
    private void initForm()
    {
        // attach to the text span and update the font
        boundText = new DhText();
        boundText.setID("bindText");
        Font font = new Font(boundText.getFont(), 18, FontSize.PIXELS);
        boundText.setFont(font);

        // attach to the boundButton id
        DhButton boundButton = new DhButton();
        boundButton.setID("button1");
        boundButton.addOnClick(
                    new EventHandler(this.onBoundButtonClick)
                        );
```

```
    // --- created stuff ---
    // add some initial tags
    DhRawHTML start = new DhRawHTML("<P>");

    // add a new text string
    createdText = new DhText();
    createdText.setText("Created Text");

    // now add a break
    DhRawHTML raw = new DhRawHTML("<BR>");

    // finally attach a button
    DhButton button2 = new DhButton("Say Hello");
    button2.addOnClick(new EventHandler(this.onButtonClick));

    // now attach some ending text
    DhRawHTML end = new DhRawHTML("</P>");

    /**
     * setBoundElements() will take a list of elements that already
     * are present in the HTML document, and binds them to the
     * DhElement list.
     */
    setBoundElements(new DhElement[] {boundText, boundButton});

    /**
     * setNewElements() takes a list of DhElements and adds them
     * to the HTML document.
     */
    setNewElements(new DhElement[] {start,
                                    createdText,
                                    raw,
                                    button2,
                                    end});
}

public void onButtonClick(Object o, Event e)
{
    createdText.setText("Clicked");

}

public void onBoundButtonClick(Object o, Event e)
{
    boundText.setText("Bound clicked");
}
```

(continued)

```
/**
 * Client-side only.
 */
protected void onDocumentLoad(Object sender, Event e)
{
}
}
```

This version of *initForm()* starts out as before, by binding *Class1* to the existing *bindText* object we defined in our HTML file. Rather than set the background color, this version changes the font to an 18-point font, which is much larger than the original font.

The next section of *initForm()* binds an object *boundButton* to the *button1* object we added using the HTML editor. This section adds an event handler *onBoundButtonClick()* to the *boundButton* object. Notice that the mechanism for adding an event handler to a DHTML object is identical to the mechanism used to add an event handler to a WFC object in a Windows application. A newly created *EventHandler* delegate is passed to the *addOnClick()* method. The *onBoundButtonClick()* method must follow the format required by the *EventHandler* delegate.

Looking ahead, the *onBoundButtonClick()* method changes the text of the *boundText* object to "Bound clicked".

The "created stuff" section goes through the steps of creating a *DhText* object and a *DhButton* object, and then attaching an *onButtonClick()* method to the button. The calls to *DhRawHTML()* allow you to create *DhElement* objects containing raw DHTML commands. These objects can be inserted into the DHTML stream along with more sophisticated *html* package objects.

The *setBoundElements()* method adds the bound objects to the *DhDocument* container. The *setNewElements()* method adds the newly created elements to the DHTML file and to the *DhDocument* container.

The result

Build the resulting SimpleClientSide project. Notice that Visual J++ 6 creates and signs the CAB file referenced in the Page1.htm file. Display Page1.htm in the HTML editor in Quick View mode. Before the HTML file is displayed, a dialog box appears to make sure that the user agrees to allow the SimpleClientSide application full access. A page containing client-side DHTML must be accepted as trusted by the user, because the browser doesn't know the intent of the SimpleClientSide.cab object. Choose Yes to proceed.

Figure 16-2 shows the output of the Quick View window as the Page1.htm page appears initially. Figure 16-3 shows the Quick View window after both buttons have been chosen.

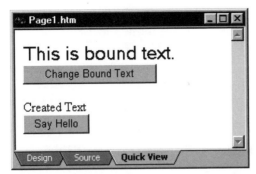

Figure 16-2. *The initial appearance of the SimpleClientSide application window.*

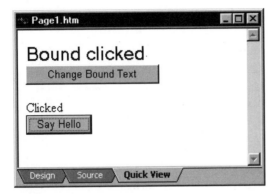

Figure 16-3. *The appearance of the SimpleClientSide application window after both buttons have been clicked.*

The change from Figure 16-2 to Figure 16-3 demonstrates the principles of DHTML better than anything we've seen so far. Choosing either button results in an immediate change in the corresponding HTML text without the aid of the server and without the use of an applet. Try executing Page1.htm from within Internet Explorer, and then view the HTML source code from the browser. You'll see that there is no trace in the source HTML code of the second section of text or the second button, nor is there a trace of the text as modified after you choose either of the buttons—and yet these changes are displayed in the browser. Both of these facts are a result of the ability of the CAB file application to modify the browser display dynamically.

A comment

While the SimpleClientSide application demonstrates that it's possible to create new HTML objects (*createdText = new DhText()*), binding to existing objects (*boundText.setID("bindText")*) seems more fruitful. It's much easier to create an HTML file using your favorite HTML editor than it is to create the code to display HTML pages dynamically. (There is nothing magical about the HTML editor in Design mode. You can use whatever editor you prefer, as long as it assigns each object an ID. Even if the editor doesn't assign each object an ID, you can add it by hand.)

Once the HTML objects have been created, it's relatively simple to bind to them and then add the necessary *addOnX()* methods to support the functionality you want.

(Notice that I have been avoiding using the term "applet" when describing the SimpleClientSide application. SimpleClientSide isn't an applet, even though it's referenced from an HTML page.)

Accessing a Database Using Client-Side DHTML

While it is certainly interesting to see the Dynamic HTML changes in SimpleClientSide, the application doesn't do anything particularly interesting. The following Data-ClientSide application represents a practical use of the *html* package. This application reads a local database at run time, and displays the results in a DHTML table.

The HTML editor work

Use the Code-behind HTML wizard to create the DataClientSide application in your DHTML directory. In Source mode, remove the warning section from the Page1.htm file. Also remove the <SPAN> tag that contains the "This is bound text." string. Leave the <OBJECT> tags.

The database access code

While it would be possible to write the entire DataClientSide application in a single class, the application will be easier for you to grasp if it's divided into at least two classes. Add the following *TableDatabaseConnection* class to your project to provide simple access to a Microsoft Access 97 database. This class is very similar both in concept and structure to those created in Chapter 12, Accessing Databases. (If you don't understand this class, return to Chapter 12 for a more detailed discussion.)

```
import com.ms.wfc.html.*;
import com.ms.wfc.core.*;
import com.ms.wfc.data.*;
import com.ms.wfc.data.ui.*;

/**
 * Extends DataSource to form a convenient database connection to
 * a DhTable object.
 */
public class TableDatabaseConnection extends DataSource
{
    /**
     * Build datasource
     * @param pathName      the path to a Microsoft Access 97 database
     * @param databaseName  the name of the file (including extension)
     * @param tableName     table to extract from the database
```

```
    * @param fields        fields to read from that table
    */
public  TableDatabaseConnection(String    pathName,
                                String    databaseName,
                                String    tableName,
                                String[]  fields)
{
    // construct the connection string to the specified file
    String s = "PROVIDER=MSDASQL;dsn=MS Access 97 Database;" +
               "uid=;pwd=;DBQ="
             + pathName
             + "\\"
             + databaseName;
    setConnectionString(s);

    // set up the query
    setCommandText(buildQuery(tableName, fields));

    // initialize miscellaneous settings
    setCursorLocation(
            com.ms.wfc.data.AdoEnums.CursorLocation.CLIENT);
    setLockType(com.ms.wfc.data.AdoEnums.LockType.OPTIMISTIC);
    setSort(null);
    setStayInSync(true);
    setUserId(null);
    setPassword(null);
}

/**
 * Build a SQL query from the table name and the field names.
 */
static private String buildQuery(String tableName, String[] fields)
{
    // start with select statement
    String s = "select ";

    // now tack on the field names with a comma in between
    // each name (but no comma after the last field)
    int i = 0;
    while(true)
    {
        s += fields[i++];
        if (i >= fields.length)
        {
            break;
        }
        s += ",";
    }
```

(continued)

```
        // add the table name
        s += " from " + tableName;

        // return the SQL select statement
        return s;
    }


    /**
     * Build a DataBinding array that binds the fields in the
     * database table to the columns in the repeater row of the table
     * @param fields  field names from the database table to bind to
     * @param columns columns in the repeater row to bind to
     */
    public static DataBinding[] buildDataBindings(String[] fields,
                                                  DhCell[] columns)
    {
        // create a set of data bindings consisting of
        // a data binding for each field
        DataBinding[] dataBindings = new DataBinding[fields.length];
        for(int i = 0; i < dataBindings.length; i++)
        {
            dataBindings[i] = new DataBinding(columns[i],
                                             "Text",
                                             fields[i],
                                             null);
        }

        // return the data bindings
        return dataBindings;
    }
}
```

The *TableDatabaseConnection* constructor begins by creating an Access 97
access string from the *pathname* and *databaseName* values. (The *databaseName*
value is the name of the database file). This connection string is passed to *Data-
Source.setConnectionString()* to become the command string used by the base
DataSource class to access the database.

The constructor continues by using the *buildQuery()* method to create a SQL
query from the table name and the field names passed to the constructor. The resulting
query is passed to the *DataSource.setCommandText()* method to be used as the
database query. The remaining calls in the constructor set *DataSource* properties.

The *buildQuery()* method takes as arguments the *tableName* string and the *fields*
array of strings containing the field names, and constructs a query from them. Suppose, for example, that the *tableName* value was "A" and that the *fields* array contained the strings "B", "C", and "D". From this, *buildQuery()* would create the following
SQL query:

```
SELECT B,C,D FROM A
```

The final method in the class, *buildDataBindings*, creates and returns an array of *DataBinding* objects. The length of this array is the same as the number of strings in the *fields* array. Each *DataBinding* object binds a field name to a *DhCell* class. (We don't yet know what a *DhCell* class is, but for now suffice it to say that it's the equivalent of a *text* field in the examples in Chapter 12. If you aren't familiar with the concept of a data binding, you can return to Chapter 12 for a more complete discussion.)

The Class1 code

Armed with the *TableDatabaseConnection* class, the DataClientSide *Class1* class is relatively simple. The only new concept presented by this code is the way that HTML tables are constructed using the *DhTable*, *DhRow*, and *DhCell* classes:

```
import com.ms.wfc.html.*;
import com.ms.wfc.core.*;
import com.ms.wfc.data.*;
import com.ms.wfc.data.ui.*;

/**
 * Demonstrate accessing a local database via the WFC html package.
 */
public class Class1 extends DhDocument
{
    // -------------define the database information-----------------
    // path to the database
    String   pathName = "C:\\ProgramVJ\\" +
                            "Windows Database Applications\\Databases";

    // the database name
    String   databaseName = "MyCompany.mdb";

    // define the table name
    String   tableName = "Customers";

    // define the fields to extract from the database table
    String[] fields = new String[]
                            {"ContactFirstName",
                             "ContactLastName",
                             "PhoneNumber"};
    // --------------end of database info---------------------------


    // class constructor
    public Class1()
    {
        // Required for Visual J++ Form Designer support
```

(continued)

```
        initForm();
}


/**
 * Class1 overrides dispose so it can clean up the
 * component list.
 */
public void dispose()
{
    super.dispose();
}


/**
 * Create a table from the contents of a client-side database.
 */
private void initForm()
{
    // create data source designed for connection to
    // a DhTable
    DataSource dataSource = new TableDatabaseConnection(
                                            pathName,
                                            databaseName,
                                            tableName,
                                            fields);


    // --- create a table using that data ---
    // start the table
    DhTable dhtable = new DhTable();
    dhtable.setPageSize(10);
    dhtable.setBorder(3);

    // generate the header row
    DhRow headerRow = new DhRow();
    DhCell headerCol = new DhCell("Header");
    headerCol.setColSpan(3);
    headerCol.setAlign(DhAlignment.CENTER);

    headerRow.add(headerCol);
    dhtable.setHeaderRow(headerRow);

    // now create a template row
    DhRow repeaterRow = new DhRow();
    DhCell[] columns = new DhCell[fields.length];
    for(int i = 0; i < columns.length; i++)
    {
        columns[i] = new DhCell();
        repeaterRow.add(columns[i]);
    }
```

```
      // attach the template row to the table
      dhtable.setRepeaterRow(repeaterRow);

      // attach the data source to the table
      dhtable.setDataSource(dataSource);

      // attach the database to the columns of the table
      DataBinding[] dataBindings =
            TableDatabaseConnection.buildDataBindings(fields,
                                                  columns);

      dhtable.setDataBindings(dataBindings);

      // start the datasource
      dataSource.begin();

      /**
       * setNewElements() takes a list of DhElements and adds them
       * to the HTML document.
       */
      setNewElements(new DhElement[] {dhtable});
   }

   /**
    * Client-side only.
    *
    * Here, the underlying HTML document is available for inspection.
    * Add any code that wants to get properties of elements or inspect
    * the document in any other way.
    */
   protected void onDocumentLoad(Object sender, Event e)
   {
   }
}
```

The data members of *Class1* define the path to the database and the table to access within that database. (This application accesses the same Customers table of the MyCompany database that we used in Chapter 12. Because we're using the same database in this chapter as we used in Chapter 12, you can compare the output of this application with the output of the ToolboxADO example in Chapter 12.) The values in the *fields* array specify that the application is to access the first name, last name, and phone number of each customer in the Customers table.

The only method we modified from its default version is the *initForm()* method. The *initForm()* method begins by establishing a *DataSource* object using the *Table-DatabaseConnection* class described previously. The *initForm()* method continues by creating a *DbTable* object that will access the entries present in the Customers database table.

To understand the way *DhTable* works, you must first understand how an HTML table is constructed. An HTML table is defined with the <TABLE> tag. The first row of the table—the header row—is contained within the span of a <THEAD> tag. The table header is optional. Below the header appears a sequence of rows. Each row is defined by a <TR> tag. Each column within the row is defined by a <TD> tag. The <TD> elements are called *cells* rather than columns, since they really represent a data entry within the row rather than an entire column. Each row can have a different number of cells than its neighbors.

The code for a DHTML table is analogous to the HTML code. The table is defined by the *DhTable* class. In our *Class1* example the first few method calls that follow the creation of the *DhTable* object set the maximum page size to 10 rows, and set the border width to three pixels.

The next block of code defines the header row to consist of a single cell that spans three columns and contains the centered text "Header". As you'll see shortly, since the entire table has only three columns, this effectively places a banner across the top of the entire table.

Normally, the next sequence would be to add a number of *DhRow* objects to the table, each with a set of *DhCell* objects attached. However, building a table with an unknown number of entries adds a certain wrinkle. To handle this case, *DhTable* allows you to define a "repeater" row, sometimes called a *template* row. This row is repeated for each entry in the database up to the page size defined earlier. The *initForm()* method constructs this template row by creating a cell for each entry in the *fields* array. Thus, the ContactFirstName, ContactLastName, and PhoneNumber database fields are each assigned a column in the resulting HTML table. The template row is added to the table using the *setRepeaterRow()* method. (A normal row would be added to a table using the conventional *add()* method.)

Once the repeater row has been defined, the *DataSource* created previously is attached to the HTML table. An array of *DataBinding* objects, one object for each field in the database, is created using the *buildDataBindings()* method defined earlier in the *TableDatabaseConnection* class. This *dataBindings* array is also attached to the table.

Finally the flow of data is started by calling *dataSource.begin()*, and the HTML table is attached to the DHTML page using the *setNewElements()* method.

(You'll notice how the *DhTable* class uses the *DataSource* and the *DataBinding* classes in the same way as the *DataBinder* class did in Chapter 12.)

The result

The result of executing the DataClientSide application in Quick View mode of the HTML editor is shown in Figure 16-4. While the output of this example application lacks the window dressings a real-world DHTML application would have, this example clearly demonstrates the results you can obtain by using the *html* package with a

Figure 16-4. *The DataClientSide application displays the contents of the Customers table with a* DhTable *object.*

client-side database: the DataClientSide application modified an existing DHTML file in real-time in order to display the contents of a client-side database.

SERVER-SIDE DTHML

The "Client-Side DHTML" section of this chapter demonstrated how the *html* package allows applications on the client side to perform dynamic functions like responding to user input and reading client-side database information. DHTML gives applications many of the same capabilities of an applet while remaining in the HTML domain. On the other hand, client-side applications that use the *html* package are only accessible from Internet Explorer.

Applications based on the *html* package can also run on the server. Server-side applications that use DHTML have both advantages and disadvantages as compared to client-side applications that use DHTML.

Server-side DHTML applications have access to the same display features as do client-side DHTML applications. In fact, you can use practically identical source code for a server-side application as for a client-side application. However, since server-side DHTML applications don't run within a browser, server-side applications can't respond to user input. Server-side DHTML-generated HTML pages aren't dynamic.

Server-side DHTML applications can only run on the Microsoft Internet Information Services (IIS) and Personal Web Server (PWS) Web servers, which are the only servers that have access to the *html* package of classes. On the other hand, server-side DHTML-generated HTML pages aren't Internet Explorer-specific. Server-side DHTML pages look like HTML pages that any other Web application might generate. The server-side server restriction is less severe than the client-side browser restriction, because it's much easier to control the type of server than the type of browser.

The net effect of these considerations is that using server-side DHTML is useful under these conditions:

- The programmer wants to create sophisticated HTML pages that aren't interactive with dynamic server-side data.

- The programmer can control the choice of server.

- The programmer can't control the choice of browser.

For normal business applications, you can usually control the choices of server and browser. Thus, server-side DHTML is applicable in situations when the second and third conditions are true, and is acceptable when the first condition is true.

Static Server-Side Applications

Two types of server-side DHTML applications exist: dynamic applications and static applications. In one sense, as I said previously, no server-side DHTML applications are dynamic. No application of this type can respond directly to user input. However, dynamic server-side DHTML applications are able to generate HTML instructions when the user references the application. This is similar to, but more sophisticated than, the CGI applications mentioned earlier in this chapter.

Static server-side DHTML applications run repeatedly at some time interval. These applications write output to HTML files, and these HTML files can be accessed from browsers. The distinction here is that static server-side applications aren't run at the request of the browser.

It might seem at first that static server-side DHTML applications are less useful than dynamic server-side applications, however, static server-side applications are generally more useful. Consider the example of a company with a number of travelling salespeople. A dynamic server-side application might allow the salespeople to access up-to-the-minute information concerning customers and their telephone numbers. It does this at considerable cost to the server, however. Every time a salesperson calls up the telephone directory, the server must run the dynamic server-side application that queries the database. This is wasteful, given that the customer telephone directory doesn't change from day to day, much less change from minute to minute.

By comparison, the static server-side DHTML application might run every day at midnight, when Web traffic is at a minimum. The static application queries the customer database in order to generate the necessary telephone information in the form of HTML pages. The next day, the salespeople access the updated information with static HTML pages. While the data might be up to one day old, accessing the HTML pages generated by static server-side applications doesn't place any more of a load on the server than conventional HTML pages do.

The following DataServerStatic application demonstrates how such an application might work.

The design work

Create the DataServerStatic project in the same DHTML directory you used before, using the Code-behind HTML wizard. Remove the Page1.htm file from the project, because static server-side applications aren't run from a browser at all.

We can use the same *TableDatabaseConnection* class we used in the Data-ClientSide application. Open your DataClientSide folder and copy the TableDatabase-Connection.java file to the DataServerStatic folder. (Be sure to copy the file, not to move it.) Visual J++ 6 adds the file to the DataServerStatic project as soon as the file appears in the DataServerStatic folder.

The code

Amazingly, the *Class1* class for this application is virtually identical to the client-side version of the class. Copy the Class1.java file from the DataClientSide folder to the DataServerStatic folder, and edit the code so it looks as follows:

```java
import com.ms.wfc.html.*;
import com.ms.wfc.core.*;
import com.ms.wfc.data.*;
import com.ms.wfc.data.ui.*;

/**
 * Demonstrate accessing a local database by using the WFC html package.
 */
public class Class1 extends DhDocument
{
    // --------------define the database information-----------------
    // ...identical to the client-side DHTML version...
    // --------------end of database info-------------------------


    /**
     * Class constructor.
     */
    public Class1()
    {
        // Required for Visual J++ Form Designer support
        initForm();
    }
```

(continued)

```
/**
 * Class1 overrides dispose so it can clean up the
 * component list.
 */
public void dispose()
{
    super.dispose();
}

/**
 * Create the same DHTML objects created by the
 * client-side application.
 */
private void initForm()
{
    // ...identical to the client-side DHTML version...
}

/**
 * Run as a Windows console application. Create a Class1
 * object identical to the client-side Class1 object.
 * Rather than display the results, write the corresponding
 * DHTML to standard output.
 */
public static void main(String[] args)
{
    // create the Class1 object
    DhDocument doc = new Class1();

    // wrap the Class1 object in head and body section
    // HTML tags (on the client side this is handled
    // by the DHTML file that invokes the program)
    doc.setGenerateTags(true);
    doc.setTitle("Statically Generated Table");

    // now convert the html package commands into
    // conventional HTML, and write the HTML to standard output
    String s = doc.getHTML();
    System.out.println(s);
}
}
```

The only difference between this application and the DataClientSide application is the addition of a *main()* method. As with all Windows applications, execution begins with *main()*. This method begins by creating a *Class1* object. The *Class1* constructor invokes the same *initForm()* method called by the DataClientSide class constructor. Just as before, *initForm()* queries the database to generate the internal structures necessary to create the HTML instructions displayed by the browser.

However, this time the HTML is captured in a conventional *String* object by call-ing the *DbDocument.getHTML()* method. The resulting string is then written to stan-dard output.

One last step is required before you can run the application. Since DataSer-verStatic will run as a Windows console application, we need to change the deploy-ment format. Save the project, then click the project name with the right mouse button in Project Explorer and choose DataServerStatic Properties from the context menu. In the DataServerStatic Properties dialog box, choose the Launch tab. Select Class1 from the When Project Runs, Load drop-down list, and then select the Launch As A Console Application check box. Now choose the Output Format tab, and change the Packaging Type to Windows EXE.

The result

Running DataServerStatic.exe from the prompt of an MS-DOS window generates the output shown in Figure 16-5.

Figure 16-5. *Running the DataServerStatic application generates this HTML code.*

While this result isn't very pretty, careful examination of the HTML output re-veals the <TR> and <TD> tags that one would expect to see when defining a table.

Now capture the console output and copy it to an HTML file by entering the following DOS command:

```
DataServerStatic > DSS.htm
```

Using Microsoft Windows Explorer, navigate to the DataServerStatic folder and run the DSS.htm file. You'll see the same browser display as that shown in Figure 16-6. The browser window output appears identical to the output from the Data-ClientSide application, but notice that the URL that appears in the Address window is that of the DSS.html file.

Figure 16-6. *The Internet Explorer browser generates a table from the HTML code that is shown in Figure 16-5.*

The same table is generated when you display DSS.htm with the Netscape Navigator browser.

Dynamic Server-Side Applications

In principle, a dynamic server-side DHTML application is the same as the static version. However, there is one significant difference between the two. With the static version, the application must run when the user's browser selects a certain HTML page, and the output must be sent directly to the client's browser. Without resorting to CGI, it isn't possible to send the output to a file using conventional HTML. This is possible, however, from Active Server Pages (ASP).

Active Server Pages are HTML pages that contain commands run by the server prior to sending the page to the client's browser. The browser sees no difference in the resulting HTML from any other HTML page.

Often, the purpose of these ASP applications is as simple as inserting the current time and date into the HTML page as the page is sent from the server. However, the capabilities of ASP code extend to Component Object Model (COM) components that have been registered on the server. We'll use this ability of ASP to use COM objects in the DataServerDynamic application.

(Note the following example borrows heavily from an example appearing in one of Microsoft's tutorials.)

The design work

Create the DataServerDynamic Code-behind HTML project in the DHTML directory. Just as in the DataServerStatic example, remove the Page1.htm file from the project— we won't need it.

The code for this application and the client-based DataClientSide are virtually identical. Copy the Class1.java and TableDatabaseConnection.java source files from the DataClientSide folder to the DataServerDynamic folder.

ASP can only run registered COM objects, so choose DataServerDynamic Properties from the project name's context menu in Project Explorer. Choose the COM Classes tab and select the Class1 check box. Choose OK. If you now open the Class1.java file, you'll notice the addition of a *@com.register* directive to the comment appearing immediately above the *Class1* declaration. This will register as a COM object the CAB file generated by *Class1*.

The code

Edit the Class1.java file copied from DataClientSide so it looks as follows:

```java
import com.ms.wfc.html.*;
import com.ms.wfc.core.*;
import com.ms.wfc.data.*;
import com.ms.wfc.data.ui.*;

/**
 * Demonstrates accessing a local database using the WFC html package.
 * @com.register ( clsid=<GUID>, typelib=<GUID> )
 */
public class Class1 extends DhDocument
{
    // -------------define the database information-----------------
    // ...identical to the client-side DHTML version...
    // --------------end of database info--------------------------


    /**
     * Class constructor.
     */
    public Class1()
    {
    }


    /**
     * Class1 overrides dispose so it can clean up the
     * component list.
     */
```

(continued)

```
public void dispose()
{
    super.dispose();
}

/**
 * Create the same DHTML objects created by the
 * client-side application.
 */
private void initForm()
{
    // ...identical to the client-side DHTML version...
}

/**
 * Return a string representation of the Class1 HTML code. This
 * method is invoked from the ASP page.
 */
public String generateHTMLRepresentation()
{
    this.initForm();
    return this.generateHTML();
}
}
```

The only differences between the DataServerDynamic and DataServerStatic applications are:

■ Visual J++ 6 has added the *@com.register* directive. (I have replaced an impossibly long globally unique identifier (GUID) with the phrase <GUID> in this listing.)

■ The call to *initForm()* has been removed from the *Class1()* constructor.

■ The method *generateHTMLRepresentation()* has been added.

The *generateHTMLRepresentation()* method first calls *initForm()* to create the DHTML internal representation of the table output. The method then calls *generate-HTML()*, which generates the HTML representation of the internal structures created by *initForm()* that is to be sent to the browser.

The ASP page

Choose Add Item from the Project menu to add an ASP page to the project. Since ASP isn't one of the options listed in the Add Item dialog box, choose Other, and enter the name *Web.asp*. (The name of the page is unimportant, as long as it carries the .asp extension.) Notice that in Project Explorer, the Web.asp file has an icon unique to .asp files.

In Source mode, add the following code to Web.asp:

```
<HTML>
<HEAD>
<META NAME="GENERATOR" Content="Microsoft Visual Studio 6.0">
<TITLE></TITLE>
</HEAD>
<BODY>

<%@ LANGUAGE=VBScript %>

<%

dim svr
set svr = Server.CreateObject("DataServerDynamic.Class1")

Response.Write "" & svr.generateHTMLRepresentation()

%>

</BODY>
</HTML>
```

The *CreateObject()* method creates an object from the *Class1* class of the Data-ServerDynamic.CAB file. The *Response.Write* command instructs the server to write the output of the *generateHTMLRepresentation()* method of *Class1* to the HTML file containing the ASP commands. This is the page being sent to the client browser.

The result

Build the DataServerDynamic project. Notice the creation of a .tlb type library similar to that generated by the ActiveX projects in Chapter 13. This type library is bundled into DataServerDynamic.CAB and registered as a COM object.

For the next step, you'll need access to an IIS or PWS Web server. (You can install the PWS server from the Microsoft Windows 95 or Microsoft Windows 98 installation disk.) Copy the Web.asp and DataServerStatic.tlb files to a folder accessible from the server. (For the PWS server, this folder is probably C:\Inetpub\wwwroot.) Start the Web server. Now bring up Internet Explorer or another browser and enter *http://<local path>/Web.asp* as your URL, where *<local path>* is the root directory for your PWS or IIS installation. (Remember that the COM object must be registered on the same computer that is acting as the Web server.)

The resulting display appears identical to that created by both the DataClientSide and DataServerStatic applications.

CONCLUSION

In this chapter, you've seen how the Visual J++ 6 *wfc.html* package provides access to the features of DHTML. This access results in client-side applications that can react dynamically to user input or to client-side data. However, the real power of the *html* package classes lies in their support of both dynamic and static server-side applications. While these server-side applications can't react directly to user input, they can be used to easily create generic HTML pages based on constantly changing server-side conditions.

Appendix

Java Syntax

This book starts with simple examples and then proceeds to increasingly complicated and more powerful topics that demonstrate the capabilities of Microsoft Visual J++ 6. Even with this graduated approach, you might find some material difficult to follow if you aren't familiar with Java syntax. This appendix contains a quick overview of the syntax of Java.

If you are a C++ programmer, you'll be able to pick up Java with minimal effort. The syntax and the object-oriented features of Java are similar to those found in the C++ language. In those cases where Java syntax differs from C++ syntax, the Java syntax is usually simpler. Nevertheless, you should review the more advanced syntax features of Java, because they tend to differ from those found in C++.

If you are a programmer of another language—for example, Microsoft Visual Basic—you'll have a much higher learning curve to master Java than C++ programmers do. The syntax of Java differs from the syntax of languages other than C and C++. The object-oriented philosophy of Java will be equally unfamiliar to you if you program nonobjected languages, including Visual Basic and C.

The purpose of this appendix is to make Visual J++ 6 available to all members of the programming community.

NOTE The Java overview contained in this appendix will make the reference material contained in the Help system more approachable.

JAVA EXPRESSIONS

A Java statement can be a comment, a block, a declaration, or an expression. Most statements in Java end in a semicolon—blocks and comments are about the only holdouts.

Java considers spaces, tabs, and newline characters to be "white space" and ignores them except when they appear in the middle of an operator or an identifier.

Comments

There are three types of comments defined in Java. The most common type of comment is one line long and begins with a double slash (//). This type of comment continues from the // until the end of the line.

The second comment style is the block comment, which begins with a slash and an asterisk (/*) and ends with an asterisk and a slash (*/). Newline characters are ignored in this type of comment.

The third type of comment, the Javadoc-type comment, begins with a slash and a double asterisk (/**) and ends with an asterisk and a slash (*/). This type of comment is the same as the block comment, except Visual J++ 6 assumes that the statement immediately following the comment is the name of a method (function):

```
/**
 * The following function is an example.
 * @param input is an integer that is ignored
 */
void example(int input)
{
    ⋮
}
```

In this example, as soon as the program finishes the definition of the *example()* method, Visual J++ 6 extracts the documentation contained within the Javadoc comment and adds it to the statement completion feature. This feature helps the programmer complete expressions.

Declaring Variables

You must declare a local variable before using it. A variable declaration consists of the type, followed by the name of the variable, optionally followed by the assignment operator (=) and an expression representing the initial value of the variable.

```
int nAnInt;             // declare a variable
int nASecondInt = 10;   // declare another variable and
                        // give it an initial value
```

Intrinsic Data Types

Table A-1 shows the variable types that are intrinsic to Java. To enhance portability, Java sets the specific size of each type. In addition, a variable is initialized when you declare it. If you don't initialize a variable explicitly, Java gives it the corresponding value as shown in the table. All of the numeric types shown are signed. Java doesn't support unsigned data types.

Data Type	Size [bits]	Default value
boolean	8	false
byte	8	0
char	16	'x0'
short	16	0
int	32	0
long	64	0
float	32	0.0F
double	64	0.0D

Table A-1. *Size of each Visual J++ intrinsic type.*

The *boolean* type isn't a numeric type—it can have only the value *true* or *false*. All other types are numeric and can be mixed within a single computation. The *char* type is a full 16 bits, and is assumed to be Unicode. (Unicode is a superset of ASCII. The first 128 characters are the same as ASCII. After that, Unicode associates other values with special characters like accented characters, umlauts, and ideographic characters.)

Identifiers

A variable name can be any valid Java identifier. Identifiers must start with a letter of the alphabet, an underscore (_), or a dollar sign ($). Subsequent letters can also be the numeric digits 0 through 9.

Constants

There are four types of constants: *boolean*, numeric, character, and string.

Boolean constants

There are two *boolean* literals, *true* and *false*.

Numeric constants

Java assumes that any identifier beginning with a digit is a numeric constant. Constants that begin with 0 are octal, while those that begin with 0x or 0X are hexadecimal. All other constants are decimal.

The digits A through F in a hexadecimal number can be in either uppercase or lowercase. Thus, the following numbers all have the same value:

```
255, 0377, 0xff, 0xFF
```

Java assumes that a numeric literal containing either an exponent or a decimal point is a floating-point number. By default, a floating-point number is assumed to be of type *double*. A floating-point number that ends with the character F is of type *float.* Thus, in the following line the first three constants are *double* while the fourth constant is a *float*:

```
3.14159, 0.1, 1.602E-19, 3.14159F
```

Character constants

Character constants are enclosed in single quotes; for example, ' ' is a space. In addition, a character literal can be defined using '\xNN', where NN is the Unicode value of the character. Thus, '\x20' is also a space. Java defines special symbols for certain common nonprintable characters. For example, '\n' is the newline character. The literal '\\' represents a single backslash character.

String constants

String constants (also known as string literals) are any number of characters contained within double quotes. For example, "Hello, world" is a string constant.

> **NOTE** A Java string constant isn't implemented as a null-terminated array of characters (often called an ASCIIZ string), as it is in C and C++.

Smooth Operators

Table A-2 shows the Java operators. The numbers in the left column indicate the precedence, with 1 being the highest precedence and 15 being the lowest precedence.

Precedence	Operators
1	. [] ()
2	++ -- ! ~ instanceof
3	* / %
4	+ -
5	<< >> >>>
6	< > <= >=
7	== !=
8	&
9	^
10	|
11	&&
12	||
13	?:
14	= op=
15	,

Table A-2. *Operator precedence in Java.*

Precedence refers to the order in which operations are carried out. For example, multiplication (*) is performed before addition (+) when they appear in the same expression. Operators with the same precedence are executed from left to right.

> **C++ NOTE** The Java operators work the same as their C equivalents, except for the addition of two new operators (>>> and ^) and the way the logical operators work when applied to *booleans*. Even the precedence is the same.

The most important of all operators is the assignment operator (=). (The assignment operator is not to be confused with the equality operator [==].) The assignment operator takes the value on its right, and stores it in the object on its left.

To make an assignment successfully, the return type of the expression on the right must be the same as the type of the object on the left. If they're not already of the same type, Java will try to cast the expression for you, but only if it can perform that cast without losing information. The value and type of the assignment operator expression is the resulting value and type of the left object.

Unary operators

Operations on integers fall into two categories: unary and binary. A unary operator involves a single argument. Java doesn't like to deal with arguments smaller than an *int*. Therefore, if the argument to a unary operator is a *byte, char,* or *short* type, the result is an *int*. Otherwise, the result is the same type as the argument. (That is, *int* begets *int, long* begets *long.*)

The unary operators are − (negation), ~ (bitwise complement), ++ (increment), and −− (decrement).

The increment operator increments its argument by one, and the decrement operator decrements its argument by one. The increment and decrement operators both come in two flavors: pre- and post-. The preincrement operator (++x) increments the argument and then evaluates it. The postincrement operator (x++) evaluates the argument and then increments it.

Binary operators

The binary operators involve two arguments, one on either side of the operator. Binary operators include + (addition), − (subtraction), != (inequality), and so on. If both arguments are *int*, the operation is performed in *int* precision. If either argument is *long*, the other argument is converted to *long* and the result is *long*. If the resulting value of an expression is greater than what can be contained in the current precision, the upper bits are lopped off. No overflow indication is generated.

Operations on floats

The same operators that work on integers can also be applied to floating-point values.

Java follows the rules of the Institute of Electrical and Electronic Engineers (IEEE) Standard 754 for floating-point calculations.

Operations on *booleans*

There are two *boolean* operators: **&&** AND and **| |** OR. Java performs short-circuit evaluation of *boolean* operators; for example, in the expression *a* **&&** *b*, *b* isn't evaluated if *a* is false. Likewise, in the expression *a* **| |** *b*, *b* isn't evaluated if *a* is true.

 The *boolean* operators work the same in Java as in C/C++.

Operations on strings

The only operator (other than the assignment operator) that Java defines for strings is addition. If either argument to the plus operator is of class *String*, Java converts the other argument into a *String* and concatenates the two strings.

Special operators

Java supports several sets of unusual operators. The first is a set of operators that combine a binary operator and the assignment operator into one. If *op* were a conventional binary operator, the following *op=* would exist:

```
a op= b;        // is equivalent to a = a op b
```

This works for all binary operators.

Casting about

Java converts expressions implicitly from smaller types to larger types (so-called promoting) unless the cast might lose significant digits.

You can explicitly cast a value to convert it from its current type to another type. The cast appears as the desired type enclosed in parentheses before the value to be converted, as in the following:

```
// convert the float into an integer
int nIntValue = (int)fFloatValue;
```

FLOW CONTROL

Java provides a full set of flow control statements. These flow controls are statements, not expressions—meaning that they don't have a value or a type.

The *if* Statement

The simplest flow control statement is the *if* statement:

```
if (boolexpr)
{
    // any number of statements
}
else
{
    // any number of statements
}
```

First Java evaluates the *boolean* expression. If it's true, the statements contained in the first block are executed. If not, the statements contained in the *else* block are executed. Of course, the *else* clause is optional.

The *while* Loop

The easiest of the Java loop structures is the *while* loop. The *while* loop comes in two variations.

The first variation:

```
while (boolexpr)
{
    // statements
}
```

The second variation:

```
do
{
    // statements
} while (boolexpr);
```

In the first variation, the *boolean* expression *boolexpr* is evaluated. If it's *true*, the Java statements within the block are executed. Once all of the statements within the braces have been executed, control loops back up to the top of the *while* loop and the *boolean* expression is reevaluated, thereby starting the whole process over again. If *boolexpr* isn't *true*, control jumps to the first statement after the closed brace.

The second variation is similar to the first, except that the *boolean* expression isn't evaluated until after the Java statements within the block have executed, so the statements within the block will be executed at least once. If the expression is *true*, control passes up to the top of the block; if the expression is *false*, control passes to the statement immediately following the *while*.

The *for* Loop

The most common of the loops is the *for* loop. A *for* loop is defined as follows:

```
for (int a = 0; a < 10; a++)
{
    // statements
}
```

This is equivalent to the following:

```
{
    int a = 0;
    while(a < 10)
    {
        ⋮
        a++;
    }
}
```

The *break* and *continue* Statements

The keywords *break* and *continue* allow the program to abort execution of the statements from within a loop. The unlabeled *break* statement passes control outside of the loop immediately. In contrast, the *break* statement can be labeled to allow control to pass out of multiple loops at one time.

> **NOTE**   The labeled break addresses the primary reason that programmers say they need a *goto* statement. This controlled exit is about as close as Java comes to a *goto* statement.

The *continue* statement passes control to the closed brace of a loop, causing control to pass directly to the conditional expression. The *continue* statement can also carry a label, in which case control passes to the closing brace of the labeled loop.

The *switch* Statement

The *switch* statement is useful when you are selecting from a number of alternatives:

```
switch(expr)
{
  case cexpr1:
    // Java statements
    break;
  case cexpr2:
    // more Java statements
    break;
  default:
    // even more Java statements
}
```

Java evaluates the expression *expr*. Its value is then compared to each of the constant integer expressions (*cexprn*) listed after the *case* statements. (A constant expression is an expression whose value can be computed at compile time.) Control passes to the *case* statement whose expression value matches. If none of the *case* statements match, control passes to the optional *default* case. If no *default* case is provided, then no case is selected and control passes to the first statement after the closed brace.

The *break* at the end of each case isn't required; however, without it control passes straight through to the next case.

CLASS INFORMATION

Defining a Class

You can define your own types by using the keyword *class*.

> **C++ NOTE** The keyword *class* is the only way Java provides for you to create a new type. Java has no equivalent to *typedef*, *struct*, or *enum* (enumerated types).

A user type definition takes the following form:

```
class CMyClass
{
    // the members of the class go here
}
```

The *class* keyword is followed by the class name. The class name must be a valid Java identifier. (The same naming rules apply for classes as for variable names, as described in the section "Identifiers," on page 573). The members of the class can appear in any order within the class body.

There are two types of members of a class: data members and member functions.

Defining data members

Data members are used to describe the data properties of the class. Data members are declared using the same rules as local variables.

Defining member functions

Members of a Java class can also be functions. Member functions in Java are commonly known as methods of the class, or simply as methods.

> **NOTE** All functions in Java are methods.

A method definition consists of the following:

■ The type of the object that the method returns. If the method returns no object, then the return type is *void*.

■ The name of the method. A method name can be any valid Java identifier.

■ Parentheses containing the parameter list. The parameter list is a comma-separated list of declarations of the arguments to the method. If the method takes no arguments, the argument list is empty.

■ Braces following the argument list that contain the body of the method.

C++
NOTE A separate definition and declaration of a method isn't supported as it is in C++. In addition, defining a method within the class doesn't imply that the method is an inline function, and the *inline* keyword isn't supported in Java. The decision to expand a method inline is left to the compiler.

When a method is called, control passes to the open brace of the method. You can have the code exit from any point by using the keyword *return*. In the absence of encountering a *return* statement, the method exits upon reaching the closed brace. If the method returns something other than *void*, then a *return* statement, followed by an expression indicating the value to return, is required.

The following example declares a class *TV* containing a data member *channel*, and a method *tune()* that changes the channel:

```java
/**
 * Represents a color television.
 */
class TV
{
    int channel;

    /**
     * Change the channel of the television.
     */
    void tune(int newChannel)
    {
        channel = newChannel;
    }
}
```

The Javadoc comments add the documentation for the *TV* class and the *tune()* method to the statement completion. (The Javadoc comments are not included in subsequent examples, to save space.)

Scope

By default, members of a class are not accessible from classes that are outside of the class's own domain. Attaching the keyword *public* makes members available from all classes.

Overloading methods

Java differentiates methods from each other by more than just their name. A method's fully qualified name includes its name, its class, and its arguments. Two methods can have the same name, as long as their fully qualified names are different. This is called function overloading (not to be confused with method overriding, which we'll discuss later).

Even though you have a method *tune()* in the class *TV*, you can still have a separate method *tune()* in the class *Radio*.

Within a class, two methods can have the same name as long as they can be discriminated between on the basis of their arguments. In a given class *Bank*, you could have a method *int tune()* that returns the current channel, and a method *tune(int)* that retunes the TV.

Objects

People sometimes get fast and loose with the terms "class" and "object." A class describes a type of thing. The class *TV* might be used to represent TVs. (Sometimes people use the terms "class" and "type" interchangeably—that's okay.) On the other hand, *myTV* refers to the TV object sitting in my living room. In this case, you can also say that *myTV* is an instance of *TV*.

References to objects

Java programs access objects by means of a reference. The following example declares two references:

```
TV myTV = new TV();
TV yourTV;
yourTV = myTV;
```

The first declaration creates a reference *myTV* to an object of class *TV*. The memory for that object comes from a pool of available memory known as the heap. The second declaration creates a reference *yourTV*, which points to nothing (technically, it points to the *null* object). After the assignment, *yourTV* and *myTV* point to the same *TV* object.

Members of the class *TV* are accessed through reference. The following demonstrates the principle:

```
class TV
{
    int channel;
    void tune(int newChannel)
    {
        channel = newChannel;
    }
}
class LivingRoom
{
    TV tv = new TV();
    void tuneTV(int channel)
    {
        tv.channel = channel;
        tv.tune(channel);
    }
}
```

The two references to the members of *tv* in the *tuneTV()* method have the same effect—one accesses the data member *channel* directly, while the other uses the access method *tune()* to change the channel. Since numerous internal steps can be required to tune a TV other than simply changing the *channel* variable, it's preferable to use the access method.

What is *this*?

Notice that the reference to *channel* within the *TV* method *tune()* isn't qualified to any particular object. The *tune()* methods set the *channel* variable of whichever object it's called with.

```
TV myTV = new TV();
TV sonsTV = new TV();
myTV.tune(HISTORY_CHANNEL);
sonsTV.tune(MTV);
```

The first call tunes *myTV* to *HISTORY_CHANNEL,* while the second call tunes my *sonsTV* to *MTV.* (*HISTORY_CHANNEL* and *MTV* are both constants defined somewhere else.)

A reference to a class member from within a method in the same class refers to the current object. A reference to the current object is called *this.*

Garbage collection

Objects to which there is no longer a reference can't be accessed. The memory for such lost objects is recovered by a background task known as the garbage collector. For example:

```
TV myTV = new TV();
TV sonsTV = new TV();
myTV = sonsTV;
```

By assigning *sonsTV* to *myTV,* the object originally referenced by *myTV* is lost. It will eventually be returned to the heap.

Static members of a class

Members of a class can be declared independently.

```
class TV
{
    static int numberOfTVs
}
```

The static data member *numberOfTVs* is shared by all objects of the class *TV.* Static members can be accessed by means of the class name *TV.numberOfTVs* or an object name *myTV.numberOfTVs.*

Since static members belong to the class *TV* and not to any particular *TV* object, static methods have no *this* reference.

The constructor

A special method that is invoked automatically whenever a class object is created is called a constructor. Its job is to initialize the object to a valid starting state. The constructor method carries the name of the class and has no return type.

```
class TV
{
    int channel;

    TV(int initialChannel)
    {
        channel = initialChannel;
    }
}

class LivingRoom
{
    TV myTV = new TV(HISTORY_CHANNEL);
}
```

The declaration within *LivingRoom* creates a *TV* object initially tuned to *HISTORY_CHANNEL.*

Class Inheritance

One class can inherit the properties of another class. For example, a *ColorTV* class might inherit many of the properties of a generic *TV* class—each of these classes could have a *channel* property as well as a *tune()* method. The *ColorTV* class could have extra properties as well, such as *hue* and *colorIntensity.*

Inheritance in Java

One class inherits from another class using the *extends* keyword. In practice, this appears as follows:

```
class ColorTV extends TV
{
    int color;

    /**
     * Set the color property.
     * @param r - the red component of the color (0-255)
     * @param g - the green component of the color (0-255)
     * @param b - the blue component of the color (0-255)
     */
    void setColor(r, g, b)
    {
        color = new Color(r, g, b);
    }
}
```

In this example, the class *ColorTV* extends the base class *TV* by adding the *color* property and the *setColor()* method. The *ColorTV* class inherits the *channel* property and the *tune()* method.

Note that even though *ColorTV* extends the *TV* class, a *ColorTV* object is a *TV* object. A *ColorTV* object can be used anywhere a *TV* object is called for.

NOTE The *@param* directive defines the meaning of the method arguments to the statement completion feature.

Overriding base class methods

A subclass can override a method in the base class. For example, the class *TV* can define a method *selfAdjust()*, which adjusts the TV according to default values. Since this method doesn't include color, the class *ColorTV* would define its own class *selfAdjust()*. The *ColorTV.selfAdjust()* method overrides the *TV.selfAdjust()* method.

Consider the following method:

```
void someFunction(TV tv)
{
    tv.selfAdjust();
}
```

The call to *selfAdjust()* is dependent upon the exact type of *tv*. If *tv* is an object of class *TV*, the method *TV.selfAdjust()* is invoked, but if *tv* is actually of class *ColorTV*, *ColorTV.selfAdjust()* is invoked instead.

Invoking methods in the base class

Notice in the previous example that *ColorTV.selfAdjust()* might not completely replace the functions in *TV.selfAdjust()*; it might merely add extra properties related to color. It's possible for the method *ColorTV.selfAdjust()* to invoke the *TV.selfAdjust()* method as follows:

```
class ColorTV extends TV
{
    /**
     * Set properties to their default values.
     */
    void selfAdjust()
    {
        // invoke selfAdjust() in the base class
        super.selfAdjust();

            ⋮
    }
}
```

The keyword *super* is the same as *this*, but *super* is of the same class as the base class.

Abstract classes

An abstract class is a class that can't be instantiated with an object. For example, there is no *tv* object that is actually of type *TV*. Perhaps all *TV* objects must be members of the class *BWTV, ColorTV,* or *HDTV.* In this case, the *TV* class is abstract and can't be instantiated with an object.

In the same sense, an abstract method is one that you can't define except in one of the base classes. For example, *tune()* would be an abstract method if the *BWTV, ColorTV,* and *HDTV* objects were all tuned differently. An abstract method is declared abstract and has no method body.

A class that contains an abstract method must be abstract.

Final classes and methods

A method marked *final* in a base class can't be overridden in any class that extends the base class. A data member declared *final* can't be modified once it has been initialized. A data member that is *public, final,* and *static* is treated the same as a constant in other languages:

```
class TV
{
    public final static int HISTORY_CHANNEL = 20;
    ⋮
}
```

Arrays

Arrays of intrinsic types

The following code declares a reference to an array of integers:

```
int array[];
```

The brackets following *array* indicate that this is a reference to an array; however, no number within the brackets is required (or allowed), because the declaration itself doesn't allocate the space for the array. You can place the bracket before or after the reference name. Thus, the following code is also allowed (and is more common):

```
int[] array;
```

The memory for the array is allocated off of the heap:

```
int[] array = new int[5];    // allocate room for five integers
```

You can use an initialization list when declaring an array as follows:

```
int[]array = new int[]{0, 1, 2, 3, 4};
```

This statement allocates an array of five integers off of the heap, and assigns them the values 0 through 4.

Elements within an array are accessed using the brackets as well:

```
// initialize the array to zeros
for (int i = 0; i < 5; i++)
{
    array[i] = 0;
}
```

Java checks the range of every subscript. Thus, if *i* were not in the range of 0 through 5, the statement a*rray[i]* would generate an *ArrayIndexOutOfBounds-Exception* error.

Arrays of objects

The declaration of an array creates room for the array, but it doesn't initialize the elements of the array. The following does NOT create an array of five *TV* objects:

```
TV[] tvArray = new TV[5];
```

Instead, this creates an array of five references to *TV* objects, all of which point to the null object.

You can use a loop to allocate each of the *TV* objects individually, as follows:

```
TV[] tvArray = new TV[5];
for (int i = 0; i < 5; i++)
{
    tvArray[i] = new TV();
}
```

The objects in an array can also be initialized when you allocate them, as follows:

```
TV[] tvArray = new TV[]  {new BWTV(),
                new ColorTV(128, 128, 128),
                new HDTV(),
                null, null};
```

The first three objects declared are different subtypes of *TV.* The final two entries refer to the *null* object, which is of all class types.

The *Array* class

An array is an object of class *Array.* All arrays have the public data property *length,* which contains the number of elements defined in the array.

Inner Classes

Class definitions can be nested as shown in the following example:

```
class ColorTV extends TV
{
    class Tuner extends Receiver
```

```
    {
        float frequency;
        void tune(float frequency)
        {
        }
    }
}
```

The class *Tuner* is an inner class to the class *ColorTV*. The members of *ColorTV* (including *this*) are accessible to the members of *Tuner*. The reverse isn't true, however. Notice that inner classes can extend other classes.

Interfaces

A Java class can't extend more than one class. Java does offer a related concept called interfaces, which relieves much of the necessity for multiple inheritance.

Except for the appearance of the keyword *interface* instead of the keyword *class*, the declaration of an interface is similar to that of a class in which all of the methods are abstract. An interface allows you to describe a set of capabilities that a class must implement. For example, consider the following interface definition:

```
interface ITunable
{
    void tune(int);
    String receive();
}
```

This interface definition represents a promise to implement the method *tune()*. (Beginning the name of an interface with a capital 'I' is a coding convention.)

The *ITunable* interface could be used in a method as follows:

```
class ReceiveNews extends News
{
    void display(ITunable rcvr)
    {
        // first tune the receiver
        rcvr.tune(NEWS_CHANNEL);

        // receive the news currently available
        String s;
        while((s = rcvr.receive).length != 0)
        {
            ⋮
        }
    }
}
```

Here, the class *ReceiveNews* is prepared to receive as an argument to its *display()* method any class that implements the *tune()* and *receive()* methods to receive and display the news. The class *TV* could be used if it were prepared to implement those two methods:

```
class TV extends HouseholdDevice implements ITunable
{
    void tune(int channel)
    {
        ⋮
    }

    String receive()
    {
        ⋮
    }
}

class NewsRoom
{
    ReceiveNews rcvr = new ReceiveNews();
    TV tv = new TV();

    void work()
    {
        // use the TV to receive the news
        rcvr.display(tv);
    }
}
```

Here, the class *TV* extends the class *HouseholdDevice* in order to inherit the properties necessary to work within the house. At the same time, *TV* implements the *ITunable* interface by implementing the *tune()* and *receive()* methods.

The class *NewsRoom* contains a data member *rcvr* of class *ReceiveNews*, which it uses to display the news. The method *NewsRoom.work()* calls *ReceiveNews.display()*, passing it a *TV* object. This is allowed because *ReceiveNews.display()* knows that *TV* implements both the *tune()* and *receive()* methods, since *TV* implements the *ITunable* interface.

A class that implements an interface, but which doesn't override all of the methods of the interface, must be abstract.

OTHER CLASS-RELATED CONCEPTS

Packages

A package is a loose affiliation of classes. Classes that are in the same package can access other classes and members in the package, whether you declare them public or not.

Defining a package

The first line of a Java source code file can include the keyword *package,* followed by the package name. Classes contained within a source file that don't include the keyword *package* are put into the default package.

Accessing the members of a package

Classes that are members of the same package as the current class are automatically accessible to the current class.

The current class can access classes contained in other packages. To do so, the current class specifies the entire class name, including the package name, as in the following example:

```
class TV
{
    com.ms.wfc.ui.Button button = new com.ms.wfc.ui.Button();
}
```

A class in another package can be made directly accessible by importing it using the *import* keyword:

```
import com.ms.wfc.ui.Button;
class TV
{
    Button button = new Button();
}
```

All of the classes of a given package can be imported at the same time using a wildcard character, as follows:

```
import com.ms.wfc.ui.*;
class TV
{
    Button button = new Button();
}
```

It's not possible to import all of the subpackages of a package using the wildcard character. Thus, *import com.ms.wfc.** doesn't import the *com.ms.wfc.ui* package. In addition, no other wildcard character than * is allowed.

Default packages

Since the packages *java.lang* and *java.util* are critical to the operation of any Java program, Java automatically imports these packages.

The *Object* Class

Object is the base class of all classes. If you don't specify a base class, your class extends *Object* directly. Thus, the following two class definitions are completely equivalent:

```
class MyClass1              // extends Object by default
{
}

class MyClass2 extends Object
{
}
```

A method can pass any object to a method that accepts an instance of class *Object* as its argument.

The *String* Class

The class *String* represents Unicode character strings. The *String* class offers a series of useful methods, such as *concat()* to concatenate two strings, *compareTo()* to compare two strings, *toUpperCase()* to convert the string to all uppercase characters, and *toLowerCase()* to convert the string to all lowercase characters. The following two properties—double quotes and +—are reserved to the class *String*.

You can create an object of class *String* by encompassing a string of characters within double quotes. Thus, the two following declarations are equivalent:

```
String s1 = "This is a string";
String s2 = new String("This is a string");
```

In addition, the + operator is extended to the *String* class to perform conversion (if necessary) and concatenation:

```
int count = 1;
String s = "This is the number " + count + " string in the list";
```

EXCEPTIONS

Java uses the exception mechanism to report and process errors that occur while a program is running.

Throwing an Exception

You can generate an exception with the keyword *throw*, followed by an object that implements the interface *Throwable*. User exceptions should extend the class *Exception*, which implements *Throwable*.

A method that throws an exception must include the *throws* keyword, followed by a list of the exceptions thrown in the method declaration, as follows:

```
class TV
{
    void tune(int channel)
        throws IllegalChannel
    {
        if (channel >= MINIMUM_CHANNEL &&
            channel <= MAXIMUM_CHANNEL)
        {
            throw new IllegalChannel(channel);
        }
        :
    }
}
```

Here, *IllegalChannel* is a user-defined class that extends the class *Exception*.

It's not necessary to include a *throws* keyword before throwing run-time exceptions. This is because Java itself generates these exceptions.

Catching an Exception

The keyword *catch* is used to introduce a block of code designed to process an exception. You must follow the *catch* keyword with a class that implements the *Throwable* interface.

A *catch* block must immediately follow a block of code flagged with the *try* keyword, as shown in the following example. The *catch* block is only valid for exceptions thrown from within the *try* block or from within methods called from the *try* block.

```
void myMethod()
{
    try
    {
        :
    }
    catch(Exception e)
    {
        // ...process the exception e...
    }
}
```

The class name next to the *catch* keyword acts as a filter, catching only objects that inherit from *Exception.*

It's not required that a method handle an exception thrown by a method it calls; however, if it doesn't, it must use the *throws* keyword to declare that an exception can be passed out of the method.

Multiple Exceptions

It's possible for a method to handle different types of exceptions independently, as shown here:

```
void myMethod()
{
    try
    {
        ⋮
    }
    // catch IllegalChannel exceptions
    catch(IllegaleChannel ic)
    {
    }
    // catch any type of exception other than
    // the IllegalChannel exception
    catch(Exception e)
    {
    }
}
```

Java processes exceptions in order. Thus, placing a more general *catch* in front of a less general *catch* generates a compile-time error since the second *catch* would be unreachable.

Final

Control exits a *try* block as soon as the program executes a return or an exception is thrown. However, the keyword *final* introduces a block of code that runs no matter how control exits a method.

EVENT PROCESSING

There are several mechanisms for handling external events such as user input.

Event Listeners

The most generic means of handling external events is through the event listener mechanism. To associate an event handler with a user interface object such as a button, you pass an object of a class that implements the proper listener interface (such as *ActionListener*) to a method *addXListener()*, where *X* is the type of event (such as *Action*).

For example, the following code handles a button click:

```
import java.awt.*
import java.awt.event.*;
class TV
{
    Button button = new Button();

    TV()
    {
        // add a MyActionListener to the button defined above
        button.addActionListener(new MyActionListener());
    }

    /**
     * Handle the button press event.
     */
    class MyActionListener implements ActionListener
    {
        public void actionPerformed(ActionEvent ae)
        {
            // ...handle the button pressed...
        }
    }
}
```

The inner class *MyActionListener* implements the *ActionListener* interface with the method *actionPerformed()*. The method *addActionListener()* adds the newly created *MyActionListener* object to the list of objects to receive the action event. The meaning of "action event" is specific to the user interface object, but for a button an action event equates to a user click.

Delegates

WFC objects use an approach to event processing that doesn't require the creation of separate classes.

NOTE The delegate mechanism is based on the *delegate* keyword, which is a Microsoft Visual J++ 6 extension to the Java language.

The delegate approach to event processing is based on classes created by the *delegate* keyword. In the following example, the class *KeyPressEventHandler* is a delegate class designed to handle *keyPress* events.

```
import com.ms.wfc.core.*;
import com.ms.wfc.ui.*;

class TV
{
    Text text = new Text();
    TV()
    {
        text.addOnKeyPress(
                        new KeyPressEventHandler(this.text_keyPress)
                        );
    }

    private void text_keyPress(Object source, KeyPressEvent e)
    {
        // ...process the keypress event...
    }
}
```

The *KeyPressEventHandler()* class is created with a reference to the method *text_keyPress()* and to the current object.

Index

About the Author

Stephen R. "Randy" Davis is a programmer and writer who special-izes in object-oriented languages such as C++ and Java. He counts nine books—which have been translated into numerous languages—and many technical articles to his credit. Randy works as a software process specialist for E-Systems in Greenville, Texas, where he lives with his wife, Jenny; one son, Kinsey; four dogs; and two cats. He can be contacted at *www.stephendavis.com*.

The manuscript for this book was prepared using Microsoft Word 97. Pages were composed by Microsoft Press using Adobe PageMaker 6.52 for Windows, with text in Garamond and display type in Helvetica Black. Composed pages were delivered to the printer as electronic prepress files.

Cover Graphic Designer

Tim Girvin Design, Inc.

Cover Illustrator

Glenn Mitsui

Principal Compositor

Margaret Jane Herman

Principal Proofreader/Copy Editor

Roger LeBlanc

Indexer

Maro Riofrancos

Unlock *the* *power* *of* Microsoft Visual Studio.

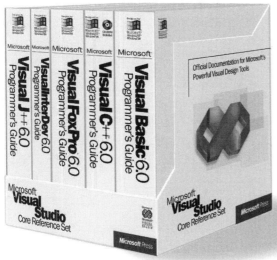

U.S.A. **$129.99**
U.K.   £121.99 [V.A.T. included]
Canada $188.99
ISBN 1-57231-884-8

The MICROSOFT® VISUAL STUDIO® CORE REFERENCE SET contains the programmer's guide for each product in Microsoft Visual Studio 6.0:

- Microsoft Visual Basic® 6.0 Programmer's Guide

- Microsoft Visual C++® 6.0 Programmer's Guide

- Microsoft Visual FoxPro® 6.0 Programmer's Guide

- Microsoft Visual InterDev™ 6.0 Programmer's Guide

- Microsoft Visual J++™ 6.0 Programmer's Guide

The answers that professionals need are close at hand in easy-to-use book form. And because they're from Microsoft's own Developer User Education groups, these volumes provide authoritative and complete information straight from the source. As a bonus, the *Microsoft Visual C++ 6.0 Programmer's Guide* contains a CD-ROM with helpful tools and samples for Visual C++ 6.0 programmers. Get this valuable set working for you today.

Microsoft Press

Expand the reach— and performance— of your server-side applications.

Microsoft Programming Series

FOR ENTERPRISE DEVELOPERS

Network Programming with Microsoft Visual J++ 6.0

Build Web-ready applications faster with Visual J++

Andy Wilson

Microsoft Press

This comprehensive guide delves into the realm of network programming for the Internet, revealing the specific ways Microsoft® Visual J++® can employ and extend the Java network package. You'll examine a wide range of sample network applications—including chat, broadcast, and ping—along with demonstrations that show the advantages of alternative techniques. From learning how to manage device communications to building a custom socket implementation, you'll get the inside track on every essential area of network application development.

U.S.A. **$49.99**
U.K.   £45.99 [V.A.T. included]
Canada $71.99
ISBN 1-57231-855-4

Microsoft Press